Contact and Multilingualism

Editors: Isabelle Léglise (CNRS SeDyL), Stefano Manfredi (CNRS SeDyL)

In this series:

1. Lucas, Christopher & Stefano Manfredi (eds.). Arabic and contact-induced change.

2. Pinto, Jorge & Nélia Alexandre (eds.). Multilingualism and third language acquisition: Learning and teaching trends.

3. Hakimov, Nikolay. Explaining Russian-German code-mixing: A usage-based approach.

4. Sánchez Moreano, Santiago & Élodie Blestel. Prácticas lingüísticas heterogéneas: Nuevas perspectivas para el estudio del español en contacto con lenguas amerindias.

5. Migge, Bettina & Shelome Gooden (eds.). Social and structural aspects of language contact and change

ISSN (print): 2700-8541
ISSN (electronic): 2700-855X

Social and structural aspects of language contact and change

Edited by

Bettina Migge

Shelome Gooden

language
science
press

Bettina Migge & Shelome Gooden (eds.). 2022. *Social and structural aspects of language contact and change* (Contact and Multilingualism 5). Berlin: Language Science Press.

This title can be downloaded at:
http://langsci-press.org/catalog/book/302
© 2022, the authors
Published under the Creative Commons Attribution 4.0 Licence (CC BY 4.0):
http://creativecommons.org/licenses/by/4.0/
ISBN: 978-3-96110-347-8 (Digital)
    978-3-98554-044-0 (Hardcover)

ISSN (print): 2700-8541
ISSN (electronic): 2700-855X
DOI: 10.5281/zenodo.6602539
Source code available from www.github.com/langsci/302
Errata: paperhive.org/documents/remote?type=langsci&id=302

Cover and concept of design: Ulrike Harbort
Typesetting: Shelome Gooden, Sebastian Nordhoff
Proofreading: Alexandra Fosså, Amir Ghorbanpour, Andreas Hölzl, Cesar Perez Guarda, Janina Rado, Jeroen van de Weijer, Jorina Fenner, Laura Arnold, Ludger Paschen, Jean Nitzke, Sandra Auderset, Tihomir Rangelov
Fonts: Libertinus, Arimo, DejaVu Sans Mono
Typesetting software: XƎLATEX

Language Science Press
xHain
Grünberger Str. 16
10243 Berlin, Germany
http://langsci-press.org

Storage and cataloguing done by FU Berlin

Freie Universität Berlin

Contents

Contents

Chapter 1

Social and structural aspects of language contact and change

Bettina Migge
University of Dublin

Shelome Gooden
University of Pittsburgh

Research on language contact, sociolinguistics and language description (of less widely studied languages) are often treated as independent lines of investigation that at best intersect peripherally. One of the people who have excelled in showing that there is a close link between these lines of research and that studying linguistic phenomena always involves paying attention to all of them is Donald Winford. His tireless and proactive research, both individual and collaborative, and mentoring of a broad range of scholars, have significantly contributed to current understandings about analytical frameworks, notions and types of data required in these areas and beyond. Being very humble about his work, the significance of Don's contribution and the breadth and depth of his knowledge is often at least in part underestimated and requires far more attention than it currently has. Don's work charts important research agendas and avenues that remain to be further explored in more detail. The first part of this introduction provides a broad overview of Don's career and his contribution to research. The second part briefly summarizes the research papers in this volume that were written in his honor by his colleagues and students, offer insights into Don's work applied to new contexts. Part three is a reflection on his life, work, teaching and mentorship from colleagues and students. The final part contains a bibliography of his work.

Bettina Migge & Shelome Gooden. 2022. Social and structural aspects of language contact and change. In Bettina Migge & Shelome Gooden (eds.), *Social and structural aspects of language contact and change*, 1–37. Berlin: Language Science Press. DOI: 10.5281/zenodo.6979303

Bettina Migge & Shelome Gooden

1 Bio and research intertwined

Donald Winford or Don, as people generally call him, grew up in Trinidad in the town of San Fernando. While he has not shared much detail about his early life in Trinidad the fact that language in the Caribbean and English-lexified Creoles in particular have been a life-long research interest even after he came to live away from Trinidad suggests that the social context of language use in his home country must have left an important impression on him. Between 1956 and 1962, Don attended *Presentation College* in San Fernando. Based on his excellent performance, he received the prestigious Island scholarship which brought him to London to study English at King's College, *University of London* from 1965 to 1968. Following completion of his BA, he moved to *York University* (UK) where he worked as a graduate assistant and completed a PhD in Linguistics under the supervision of Robert Le Page, one of the trailblazers of research of language in the Caribbean. It is at York that he honed his research interests in Caribbean Linguistics with a focus on sociolinguistics. During his four years at York University he carried out one of the first sociolinguistic studies within the Labovian quantitative sociolinguistic paradigm which charted the patterns of phonetic variation and change within two sociolinguistically distinct communities in Trinidad (Winford 1972). This work was a remarkable achievement and in a real sense is one of the first sociolinguistic analyses of vowel variation in the Caribbean. After completing his PhD, he took up a post as Lecturer at the *University of the West Indies*, St Augustine campus, in Trinidad where he worked for sixteen years, becoming a Senior Lecturer in 1984. While in St. Augustine, he served on many university committees ranging from being the Chair of the Unit for Language and Linguistics, Chair of the inter-Faculty and inter-Campus committee, to being the Elected Faculty Representative on the Assessment and Promotions Committee and Chair of the Advisory Committee on Sports.

During this time, his research and teaching focused on Caribbean language and sociolinguistics. For example, he contributed to discussions on the notion of the community in sociolinguistic research. He examined the social and linguistic makeup of English official Caribbean communities with a view to evaluating the then current models such as diglossia, the post-Creole continuum and the notion of community underlying quantitative sociolinguistic research (e.g. Winford 1974a, 1978a, 1983, 1985a, 1980a;b, 1985a, 1988b, 1994a). Although he also carried out research on language attitudes among teachers in Trinidad (Winford 1976) and has written on Creole culture (Winford 1980a), from early on, his main interests have always been the linguistic aspects of variation. Focusing in particular on morphosyntactic variation, he contributed in large part to establishing research on morphsyntactic variation within the quantitative sociolinguistic paradigm (e.g. Winford 1983, 1984, 1990a, 1994b, 1996a) which until then, and even today, largely focuses on sound variation. This research also contributed to shedding light on various areas of grammar in Creole communities such as negation (Winford 1983), complementation (Winford 1985b) and passives (Winford 1988b). His life-long passion for TMA systems was also already coming to the fore in this early work as was his interest in the development of post-colonial Englishes (Winford 1978b).

At St. Augustine he also supervised two PhD students, Lise Winer and Valerie Youssef whose work focused on the development of Trinidadian Creole from a sociohistorical perspective and the acquisition of the verb phrase among Trinidadian children, respectively. Both went on to play an important role in the development of sociolinguistically-oriented research in the Caribbean. While working as a lecturer in the Caribbean, he also spent two semesters in Texas, at the *University of Austin* and the *University at El Paso*, respectively, where he taught linguistics and a course on English as a world language.

In 1988, Don left Trinidad for Columbus, Ohio where he has been teaching and researching at the Department of Linguistics of the Ohio State University (OSU) ever since, teaching courses on sociolinguistics and language contact. He has been returning to Trinidad on a regular basis for holidays, family visits and sabbaticals and, during his stays, has generously given his time to support the activities of the Linguistics Department in St. Augustine and help to train new generations of Caribbean linguistics scholars. Despite the cold winters in Columbus, his research expanded exponentially and within only 10 years at OSU he advanced from Assistant Professor to Professor of Linguistics! At OSU, he wrote two ground-breaking go-to monographs, his 1993 book *Predication in Caribbean English Creoles* and his meticulously researched *Introduction to Contact Linguistics* (Winford 2003a), edited volumes and authored a large number of important papers across a broad range of topics. The two monographs critically assess and systematize existing research and bring novel data from his own field research to bear on debates in the field; this is an important trademark of all of Don's publications.

While his early work is not only strongly rooted in the quantitative sociolinguistic paradigm but also aims to critically assess the issues that arise in relation to morphosyntactic research within this paradigm (Winford 1990a;b, 1994a;b, 1996a, 1997f), we start to see an incremental shift towards a focus on language contact phenomena and language description, with a focus on the verb phrase (Winford 1993b; Edwards & Winford 1991). At the same time, Don's work came to increasingly focus on language phenomena outside of Trinidad for which he carried out extensive field research in Belize, Guyana and Suriname. As students in OSU linguistics we greatly benefited from these databases in that we used them to learn how to do transcription work and for our first attempts at research on language use in the Caribbean within the quantitative paradigm. Work on these data helped many of us to define our research interests, navigate the nuances of good fieldwork practices and ultimately find the focus of our PhD projects.

In line with developments in the field, Don's research saw a shift from sociolinguistics to matters of Creole genesis and Creole typology and from a focus on Caribbean Creoles proper to the Creoles of Suriname. Again, his astute evaluation of Bickerton's Creole prototype (TMA), which was based on a large database of recordings of Sranan Tongo (Winford 1996a;d, 2000a;d, 2001a) contributed significantly to then current understandings of the structure of the contemporary Creoles of Suriname which had by then received very little concerted attention. His work was also instrumental in demystifying Creole TMA systems and brought terminology and research methods in line with those used for non-Creole languages. Since their publication, subsequent research on Creole TMA systems, and not just those in the Caribbean and Suriname, have largely adopted the framework charted in these publications, improving comparability across Creoles and with other languages. While his initial work focused on critically assessing Bickerton's claims and bringing empirical evidence to bear on it (e.g. Winford 1990a), Don has also generously contributed data to larger databases (Winford 2013f, Winford &Plag 2013a) and wrote comprehensive overview articles that consider TMA phenomena in Creoles from different regions and lexical affiliations (Winford 2018). Although Don's work on TMA is most widely known, he has also made a significant contribution to a better understanding of other areas of creole grammar, namely complementation (e.g. Winford 1985b, Migge & Winford 2013) and the copula domain, particularly property items (e.g. Winford 1990a, 1997e).

Don's interest in Creole genesis directly emerged from his interest in the careful description of Creole grammars, since explanations were required for the many divergences that were found between Creole and lexifier grammars. The research on origins largely focused on African American English (AAE) in the 1990s and was mostly concerned with understanding the connections between AAE and Caribbean Creoles. Don again made crucial contributions to that research by comparing Caribbean copula data with AAE data (Winford 1992a;b, 1998) and by carefully assessing the sociohistorical context of the formation of African American English (Winford 1997d, 2020a). Although Don never discounted universal influences (e.g Winford 2009b) and invested much time in conceptualizing their properties and in understanding the types and nature of their impact, he never doubted that language contact and the influence of the languages of the creators of Creoles played an important role in their formation (Winford 1997a, 2003a). Together with Bettina Migge, he obtained National Science Foundation funding to research the impact of the Gbe languages on the formation of TMA systems (Winford & Migge 2007, 2009) and *fact-type* complements (Migge & Winford 2013) in the Creoles of Suriname. This work (Winford 1972) on language contact and his careful descriptive work have led him to further advance existing theories and approaches to language contact (Winford 2003a;b;c, 2005, 2007b, 2009a;b, 2010a) and shed new light on the relationship between language contact and the emergence of Creoles (e.g. Winford 2008b). This research revealed close similarities between wider language contact phenomena and the emergence of Creoles, thus contributing to the view that creole genesis is not different in kind from other processes of contact-induced change. For over a decade now, Don has also been actively contributing to World Englishes research from a language contact perspective, comparing the mechanisms and processes of change involved in the creation of World Englishes with those that played a role in the formation of Creoles (e.g. Winford 1999a, 2008b, 2009b, 2013g, 2017b).

Arguably his most important service to research on Creoles has been his long term editorship of the *Journal of Pidgin and Creole Languages* (JPCL), which he took over from Glenn Gilbert in 1999. In that role, he has worked tirelessly to bring diverse and innovative research to the wider linguistic community. As editor, he has played an instrumental role in fostering high quality research on Creoles and in supporting early career scholars. In recent years, in line with his own beliefs about the place of Creoles within processes of language contact, he has successively broadened the journal's scope beyond English-based Creoles and topics on creole genesis to include other contact languages and Creoles from a wide range of lexical affiliations and contexts. During his tenure as editor, he has also not shied away from making the journal the home for controversial and at times heated discussions among scholars. With his engagement JPCL has become a highly regarded journal within the linguistics landscape.

Last but not least, Don has provided intellectual guidance and support for a wide range of PhD and MA theses either as main or secondary supervisor or as member of dissertation panels and examination committees at OSU, across the Caribbean and beyond. The topics cover quite a broad range and in a sense mirror the breadth of his own scholarship. These include but are not limited to projects on vowel variation in Korean, Columbus OH English varieties and Chabacano; phonology, phonetics and prosodic aspects of reduplication in Jamaica Creole; language contact and dialect contact effects in rhotic variation in

Loraine OH Spanish; sociolinguistic and grammatical variation in AAVE and Gullah, to language use among Mennonite communities and Afro-Spanish varieties; an in-depth analysis of substrate influence in the formation of the Surinamese plantation Creoles. Almost all of these projects, in true Winford fashion, employed rigorously the qualitative and quantitative approaches of data analysis to address issues on under-researched language varieties or tackle long-standing issues from a new perspective. They also very often combined several methodological or theoretical approaches. Finally, some of these dissertation projects also challenged existing knowledge in the field, such as, the role of substrate influence in creole formation and contemporary prosodic systems, the importance of sociological consciousness in variationist analysis or the role of social factors and speakers' ideological stances in observed phonetic differences. The range of languages covered is equally impressive and highlights the fact that Don's work has a far reaching impact beyond Creoles to a wider range of contact phenomenon, i.e. AAVE, Bahamian Creole, Cantonese, Cavite Chabacano, German, Gbe, Modern Greek, Gullah, Jamaican Creole, Korean, Kotis, Mandarin, Navajo, Pennsylvania German, Spanish (Afro-Bolivian, Puerto Rico), Trinidadian Creole, Maya-Mam, Ndyuka.

2 Papers in the current volume

The planning for this volume started in 2017 when Don first announced that he was soon going to retire. Several of Don's former PhD advisees felt that it would be timely to consider his intellectual legacy. The project had a bumpy start due to everyone's many obligations and when things seemed to move well, Covid-19 struck making it increasingly difficult for everyone to pursue research due to the added pressures. Given restrictions of space and people's availability, it was not possible to accommodate large numbers of papers that would be required to cover all of Don's interests. The papers included here thus focus on Don's core interests, the social and structural aspects of language contact and language variation and change. The papers investigate these broad themes from a variety of disciplinary and empirical perspectives, covering a range of linguistic contexts.

One set of papers looks at the relevance of historical documents for determining the linguistic nature of early contact varieties. Peter Bakker's chapter makes a much needed contribution to furthering current understandings about the nature of pidgins and the processes of their emergence. Drawing on novel historical language data from the French Caribbean context, he provides further evidence for his thesis that Pidgins are structurally and socially distinct from Creoles. Discussing instances of structural differences between them, he argues that socially-induced structural changes that affect Pidgins offer a good "explanation for the genesis of creoles from pidgins, even in the absence of a documented pidgin stage."

Singler's analysis of the transcripts from the Minute and Trial Books of the Philadelphia Mother Bethel A.M. E. Church aims to unearth evidence about the pre-Great Migration and resettlement period varieties spoken by African Americans during the 18th century. After setting out the context and assessing their linguistic value, he demonstrates that the recorded speech contains widely-used non-standard features which are closely identified with African American English. The investigation suggests that northern African American English while distinct nevertheless shared many features with other varieties of English.

Lise Winer's chapter discusses the linguistic insights and issues that are posed by folk presentations of Creole speech in newspaper columns and related Creole writings found in the Caribbean region. Focusing on dialect columns from Trinidad & Tobago, she shows that with careful analysis these give a relatively substantial picture of the nature of Trinidadian Creole from the early part of the 20th century and should be given much more attention in theorizing about the emergence and development of Creoles.

A second set of contributions explores specific processes of contact-induced change that were involved in the emergence and development of these languages. Marivic Lesho investigates processes of contact-induced language change in the context of the emergence and development of varieties of Chabacano. Comparing Zamboanga and Cavite Chabacano with three of the languages that played a role in their emergence and still coexist with them – Hiligaynon, Tagalog and Spanish – she provides a first careful description and analysis of the under-researched grammatical category of *possibility*. The paper demonstrates that some forms that express modality closely parallel substrate/adstrate forms. However, both Chabacano and substrate/adstrate varieties "combine Philippine and Spanish ways of expressing possibility" and possibility markers are based on the same typology which has been much influenced by Spanish.

The process of paradigmatic restructuring and its relationship to jargonization is explored in Clancy Clements' chapter within the framework of Klein & Perdue (1992, 1997) on naturalistic second language acquisition. He first recasts Good's (2012) concept of "jargonization bottleneck" as the stage where speakers start creating grammar using the material they have at their disposal in contexts of non-overlapping language backgrounds. These materials are usually easily detectable and frequent linguistic forms. Clements then applies this to the specific case of verbal paradigms in Indo-Portuguese (IP) Creoles. Clements shows that the model allows to systematically account for the selection and development of verbal forms and the loss of paradigmatic structure. However, it does not prevent the emergence of new structures. In the case of Korlai, he demonstrates the creation of a new verb class to accommodate Marathi verbs and the emergence of a mini-paradigm. It involves the conjunction for 'when' which is used to encode realis and irrealis mood. This strategy is in a way reminiscent of how Portuguese and Spanish highlight indicative and subjunctive verb forms.

Lastly, Piero Visconte & Sandro Sessarego examine the emergence of Afro-Puerto Rican Spanish on the basis of both sociohistorical and linguistic data in order to address current debates on the emergence of Black communities in Latin America and their language varieties. Their evidence challenges existing assumptions that posit that Afro-Puerto Rican Spanish underwent a process of radical restructuring and that some of its linguistic features hail from a Creole stage. They argue that its features are due to "non-radical processes of grammatical restructuring" that emerged in a context that remained relatively unaffected by standardizing pressures.

The final set of papers examines how new datasets, methodological approaches and greater sensitivity to social issues can help to (re)assess persistent theoretical and empirical questions and help to open up new avenues of research. John Rickford's chapter makes a strong case for the greater use of corpora and online corpora in particular for research on language variation and change and applied linguistics purposes. The chapter discusses six examples where the use of corpora proved instrumental for resolving issues in descriptive, theoretical and applied linguistics. The case studies range from the analysis of variation in Jamaican music and large-scale automatized analysis of vowel variation in Californian English to the detection of bias in automated voice recognition technology created by large multi-national companies. He is urging scholars of Creoles to work together to create such corpora by pooling resources.

Durian, Reynard & Schumacher investigate phonological variation among middle and working class African Americans and European Americans in Columbus Ohio. They explore whether African American language use is diverging from Caucasian language use as suggested by some studies in other US cities. Reviewing previous studies, they argue that accounts showing divergence have generally relied on working class data only. Their study suggests that class, race, and age are all robust factors impacting vowel variation among both groups. There are greater differences between working-class African Americans and European Americans, particularly among younger people than middle-class populations. They suggest that greater levels of regular contact among middle-class populations is an important factor promoting convergence.

Changes in language attitudes are the focus of Susanne Mühleisen's paper. Following up on previous survey-based research on language attitudes in the Caribbean that focused on eliciting views from speakers, Mühleisen argues that such attitudinal data can now be fruitfully combined with data from social media and other discussion spaces such as newspaper editorials. They provide a host of qualitative insights into how speakers and communities conceptualize their language practices.

Michelle Kennedy & Tracey Messam-Johnson explore processes of variation and change in the Tense and Aspect system of Jamaican Creole based on language acquisition data from 3-year-olds in Jamaica and language use data of Jamaicans living in Curaçao. They find interesting similarities across the two data sets. There are patterns of change observable in the production of progressive constructions in Jamaican Creole which are affected by the other languages in the contact setting. Creole strategies in both settings, however, persist and show little variation in the case of the realization of the past tense.

3 Reflections about Don's scholarship & life from colleagues and students

This section presents short squibbs written by Don's colleagues and students, discussing Don's work, teaching, mentorship and interaction with colleagues.

3.1 Ian Robertston (UWI, St. Augustine)

I present a brief examination and evaluation of the influence of Don Winford on the discipline of linguistics at the university, national, regional, and international levels during his tenure at *The University of the West Indies*. It also addresses contributions that had consequential impact in areas critical to the university, the discipline more broadly, and the Caribbean region.

Sociopolitical context. The sociopolitical and academic climate in the early post-independence period in Commonwealth Caribbean countries provides an appropriate context for the evaluation of his work and contributions to the development of proper awareness of the Caribbean self. Between 1962 and 1966 four Caribbean countries, Jamaica, Trinidad & Tobago, Guyana and Barbados were granted political independence from Britain. One of the major challenges facing these newly independent countries with a history of centuries of slavery and indenture, was the need to develop social and economic models that could realize the promise of genuine political and economic independence. Issues of self understanding and self-definition impacted expectations of the population and, within a decade of attaining political independence, led to growing levels of popular frustration. The academic community, especially the only regionally owned university, could reasonably be tasked with leadership roles in examining and evaluating the contexts and in charting the options with the highest potential for success.

The university itself was only one decade away from the umbilical links with London University. It had the responsibility for providing the region with the necessary academic leadership to support political independence. The university community became deeply involved in the popular reaction to the failure. By the end of the decade of the sixties, broad based political tolerance had largely dissipated. The euphoria of political independence was being replaced by impatience and frustration at the failure to provide instant change and success to the broad groups in the societies. Public impatience with the political processes manifested itself in a number of political protests and significant public unrest. The public concern was captured and expressed in popular Jamaican song through the use of the saying,

> "Every day carry bucket a di well
> wan day dii bucket bottom must drop out.
> Everything crash".

The two most consequential expressions for the region were the so called 1968 "Rodney Riots" in Jamaica and the 1970 "Black Power" challenge to the government in Trinidad & Tobago. In the former case, the Jamaican government's decision taken in October of 1968, to declare Dr. Walter Rodney, one of the region's foremost young historians and a lecturer in the History Department at the Mona campus, "persona non grata" and to exclude him from reentering the island, after attending an academic conference overseas, became the catalyst for widespread expressions of disappointment and frustration. Rodney himself, the author of *"How Europe Underdeveloped Africa"*, was accused by the government of a level of political activism which was considered inimical to the nation's political stability.

For many in the university community, this presented a challenge to the perception of academic freedom. Massive protest, started by the university community at the Mona campus, brought protesting students and academics into the streets of the Jamaican capital, Kingston. These protests soon spread to include a large section of the urban population who felt a sense of frustration at the continuation of many of the practices they expected to disappear at independence. The frustrations were vented through burning and general unrest in Kingston. A second manifestation of this popular impatience, fueled in part by the rise of Black Power movement in the northern hemisphere, was the uprising in Trinidad in 1970 (Black Power riots). It is to be noted that here again these significant protest movements originated among members of The University of the West Indies community at the St Augustine campus.

Academic context. As a fledgling institution, The University of the West Indies emerged from its status as a college of the University of London in 1962. It, too, was seeking to define itself and to come to terms with its responsibilities to the several stakeholder countries. It was expected to help chart the course of development. Faculties of Arts and General Studies were focused on the staples of History, Languages (French, Spanish, Latin) and English Literature. Linguistics, as a discipline, had not yet emerged as part of the academic offerings. Ironically, it is Linguistics, and in particular the study of Creole languages, that became central to defining Caribbean self, and to providing one of the major growth points, variation studies, in the study of languages worldwide.

Donald Winford joined the staff at the St. Augustine campus in 1972, at a time when new directions had to be set, values had to be established, and aspirations to self definition had to be addressed. As the university itself was still searching, seeking to determine its academic bona fides, disciplines such as Linguistics were initiated through a Senate sub-committee set up to facilitate work in the discipline across its three campuses, and was centered at the Mona campus.

Don's initial appointment in the English Department placed him in the delivery of the *Use of English* course, but Winford's entry brought a new focus in Linguistics. This course had been designed to introduce young undergraduate students to writing, logic, and argument through the media of English. Winford was the first member of the Faculty of Arts and General Studies at the St. Augustine campus who had completed doctoral studies in Linguistics, and only the second such staff member on the entire campus, the other being in the then Faculty of Education. Prior to his appointment, Linguistics as a discipline on the St Augustine campus was serviced entirely by staff members who had been appointed to the English and Modern Languages Departments and, in one case, to the then Faculty of Education.

Winford's tenure at St Augustine brought significant outcomes. Appointed as lecturer in English language and Linguistics, he managed to maximise the obvious links between the two academic remits as well as to address and raise awareness of the relevance of linguistics for education in general, and for a proper appreciation of the Caribbean linguistic profile. Winford's doctoral study, by presenting a sociolinguistic description of language patterns in two communities in

Trinidad, provided what was probably the first such study to be done. More especially, its focus on non-urban, rural communities brought a different level of awareness of the nature, the scope and the significance of language behaviours in such communities which, until then, were treated as being of little significance on the national or even regional scenes.

His position as lecturer in Linguistics facilitated the expansion of the undergraduate offerings by structuring and teaching a new course, *Introduction of Sociolinguistics*, for levels two and three undergraduate students. His presence also facilitated the expansion of the *Caribbean Dialectology* course and the development of a separate course in Creole Linguistics. These offerings ultimately led to an undergraduate major in Linguistics as well as the emergence of a separate Department of Linguistics. This department was to address some aspects of the more fundamental remit of the institution to help Caribbean students to expand their awareness of, and confidence in, the languages which documented the region's history, helped define the region and at the same time presented the most revealing insights into the history of the region.

At the commencement of the 1972–1973 academic year, his first at the institution, he undertook responsibility for the level one course, Introduction to Language Theory. This course provided the undergraduate students with the first exposure to linguistics and its significance. It was essentially descriptive, relying on the standard fare of Smalley, Pike, Nida and Gleason. Phonetics and Phonology, as was to be expected in the post-Bloomfieldian period, formed the basic point of departure and Winford took responsibility for managing the operations of the less than adequate language laboratory facilities to support the exposure of undergraduate students. Despite the challenges, the exposure increased the flow of students into the courses at the next level. His commitment led to the gradual upgrading of this laboratory facility which was itself replaced by a modern and up to date, Centre for Language Learning at the turn of the century. The course in Sociolinguistics opened up new possibilities for both undergraduate and graduate studies and its impact has continued on this campus to the present time. A further input was made at the undergraduate level through the delivery of the course Caribbean Dialectology. This course was pivotal in the development of awareness of the complex linguistic nature of Caribbean societies especially as it reflected the vast range of variation in language use. These factors presented challenges to the existing awareness of the nature of linguistic variation and encouraged research into the nature of such variation.

Don Winford's academic presence also facilitated some level of exposure to teachers enrolled in the Diploma in Education programme at the then Faculty of Education. His inputs into this programme were intended to develop awareness of the relevance of language studies and linguistics to their classroom functioning. This education link provided a significant entrée into one of Winford's research foci, the educational application of sociolinguistics research in Creole-speaking communities. His 1976 *International Journal of the Sociology of Language* article on teacher attitudes toward language variation in Creole communities had implications to explore the critical need for language awareness among teachers in the national and regional communities. This need has become more pronounced today with the facilitation of, and exposure to schooling, to the broad bases of Caribbean populations who are often assumed to have or are expected to have sufficient competence in the official language on which schooling is premised.

A second area of research which Winford pioneered on the campus and one that became one of the most significant dimensions of his entire academic profile, is the study of linguistic variation. Here again, research interest in Creole languages of the Caribbean put a different focus on the ways in which variation in language was to be treated. His work on variation published during the period at St. Augustine included *Phonological Variation and Change in Trinidadian English,* (Society for Caribbean Linguistics, 1979), *The linguistic variable and syntactic variation in Creole continua* (Lingua, 1984). Of even greater significance for linguistics was his exploration of the concept of diglossia and its appropriateness as a descriptor of Caribbean linguistic contexts. (Language in Society, 1985). Beyond these articles, Winford addressed issues of phonetics, phonology and language in Caribbean society, and grammatical characteristics of Caribbean Creole languages. All these provide very significant pathways to the development of the study of language in the Caribbean as well as to language studies in general. At the post-graduate level, Winford had significant inputs into the doctoral programmes having been supervisor for at least two doctoral candidates. His presence at St Augustine was properly rewarded by appointment on indefinite tenure and his promotion to Senior Lecturer well within the normal time for such promotion and before he left the institution.

Don Winford also served as Secretary/Treasurer of the Society for Caribbean Linguistics (SCL), then located at St. Augustine. This post was at the centre of the society's functioning. It required the holder to establish and maintain links with members scattered across Europe, North America, The Caribbean and Latin America. All this in the pre-computer age when the pace of correspondence was both tedious and time-consuming. His contributions in this post helped to ensure the longevity of one Caribbean institution in a historical context of failure of many such regional initiatives. SCL is now into its fiftieth year and continues to be the seed and growth box for the development of the discipline in the region. There was a special collegial relationship with colleagues in the faculty and the campus community during the period he worked with the institution. Those of us who interacted with him learnt to appreciate his frank and generous support and valued his work ethic.

Don Winford's contribution to academia, Caribbean and national understanding of self and the study of linguistics during his tenure at The University of the West Indies provides a significant model for emulation by emerging scholars.

3.2 Reflections from current colleagues and advisees (The Ohio State University)

Mary Beckman, Cynthia Clopper, Hope Dawson, Elizabeth (Beth) Hume, Brian Joseph, Robert (Bob) Levine, Nandi Sims, Luana Lamberti, Justin Pinta

3.2.1 Overview

Don Winford joined the Department of Linguistics at Ohio State University in 1988. Thus, for some of us, he has been a trusted friend, a valued colleague, and an inspiration for more than three decades. And for others of us, the time has been less but the impact of his presence has been no less strong. We offer here some personal reminiscences and other observations.

3.2.2 Beth Hume

Don was an established figure in the department when I joined in 1991 as an assistant professor fresh out of graduate school. I felt an immediate connection to Don for a number of reasons including our shared interests in sociolinguistics and his West Indian roots, having spent time myself in Trinidad as a teenager.

While I could comment on his many academic accomplishments, I prefer to focus on his commitment to mentoring young men. I discovered this initially while playing a game with my young son at the old Larkins gym on campus. To my surprise, Don walked into the gym with a young boy, his "little brother." Over the years I came to know a few of the "little brothers" that Don mentored, supported and loved. In fact, more than one came to live with him, even after they were no longer "little" brothers. And while Don didn't have immediate family in Columbus, his house was always filled with family: the young men he'd mentored, including their partners and children. I wouldn't be surprised if there were also some grandchildren running around now!

I share this to underscore the kindness and generosity that is at the very core of who Don Winford is. Thank you, Don, for all your contributions to linguistics and to society.

3.2.3 Bob Levine

I first met Don in 1988, along with Craige Roberts, when the three of us were new hires in the Department. Linguistics was housed at that time in Cunz Hall – a confusing vertical labyrinth none of whose floors were laid out in exactly the same way, with what I remember as somewhat bizarre layouts that included apparent dead-ends and blocked access between parts of the same floor – and, due to a shortage of office space, Don, Craige and I were housed in a single large room with movable dividers separating our desks. Despite (or maybe in part as a result of) the less-than-optimal conditions, we early on developed a strong camaraderie that, as it turned out, served us well, especially during the first few years, which were often not particularly easy ones for us. I very much appreciated Don's ironic (and often sardonic) humor and his refreshingly straightforward way of talking about both our everyday life at the University and the larger world of linguistics – as well as our frequent exchange of complementary gripes about the Columbus weather (with him hating the winters and me the summers).

And I was quite happy to discover that certain aspects of Don's research on Caribbean English Creoles had a direct bearing on some of my own research on unbounded dependency constructions. In particular, his watershed monograph, *Predication in Caribbean English Creoles (CEC)* (Winford 1993a), shed crucial light on a long-standing argument in syntactic theory about the status of, e.g., *for us* in *John is easy for us to please*, providing unequivocal evidence for treating the Guyanese Creole cognate of *for* here as a complementizer rather than a preposition, with *John* being the subject of an infinitival clause rather than part of a PP. These and other conclusions in Don's work – almost certainly the most formally explicit and empirically robust investigations of CEC to date – informed much of my thinking about the syntax of English.

I'm going to miss Don a lot, as a long-time friend in the Department and as a very distinguished colleague whose international reputation has burnished the Department's own over many decades.

3.2.4 Brian Joseph

I was department chair when the opportunity to hire Don came up. I knew of his work and knew that he would be a valuable addition to the department, given the breadth of his knowledge of sociolinguistics in general and the specialist knowledge he could contribute on language contact.

I had never met him, and this was before the days of Google and the Worldwide Web, so I didn't even know what he looked like. Don arrived at the Columbus airport in early March for his on-campus interview and this came just as we were having a serious cold spell and were in the midst of a snowstorm. Realizing that he was coming from the Caribbean and figuring that he did not have a lot of recent experience with real wintry weather (his time at York University in England having been some 15 years before and his time in the US being in Texas), I brought him a full-length winter coat when I picked him up at the airport. However, I am only about 5'6" and I did not know that Don was over 6' tall! So the coat I brought him was anything but full-length for him, and barely covered him to the waist.

Somehow, Don managed to stay warm during his visit here, and somehow – fortunately – the Columbus wintry slap in the face did not dissuade him from accepting the offer to join that department that came his way a few weeks later.

On a more serious note, I have greatly valued the contribution Don made to the department in general, offering an important socially and empirically informed counterweight to the somewhat more formal and theoretical orientation of the department overall. Moreover, his integrity as a researcher and his high standards of scholarship – what he expects both from his students and from his faculty colleagues – have upped our individual and collective game considerably. On a personal level, Don has added enormously to my own understanding of language contact and of the importance of social factors in language change and I thank him for that. We will definitely miss him; his scholarly rigor and his keen insights will be difficult to replace.

3.2.5 Cynthia Clopper

I joined the department in 2006 and immediately began working alongside Don on a faculty search committee for a sociolinguist and on a number of student qualifying paper and dissertation committees. From those first experiences to the present, I have been struck by Don's approach to our collective work in the department to achieve excellence in research, teaching, and service. Don is incredibly thoughtful and deliberative when it comes to all aspects of his contributions to the department, including governance decisions, student feedback, and faculty promotions. He doesn't always speak up in department meetings, but when he does, his comments cut straight to heart of the topic and serve to advance the conversation. Our collective decisions are better as a result of Don's incisive contributions. In his feedback to our students on their research, Don identifies the critical missing connections between data and theory, encouraging them to push themselves to produce the best scholarship that they can. Our students' work is better as a result of his advice and guidance. In the faculty annual review and promotion processes, Don is always the most prepared member of the faculty, having clearly reviewed all of the materials and taken detailed notes in advance of the discussion. On a more personal note, Don was the Procedural Oversight Designee (POD) for both of my faculty promotions and provided exceptionally detailed suggestions for improving my dossier materials. Our faculty are stronger as a result of Don's commitment to his colleagues' success and career advancement. Don's contributions to encouraging, supporting, and advancing the careers of all members of the department will be greatly missed.

3.2.6 Hope Dawson

I had the great privilege of taking several courses with Don as a PhD student at Ohio State, beginning with Introduction to Sociolinguistics in Spring term of 1998. With my intellectual appetite whetted, I proceeded to take every other course on sociolinguistics and contact linguistics that he offered during my years as a graduate student. He is an excellent instructor, supportive and challenging, and two of my earliest conference presentations were of research done for his courses. Since then I have had the pleasure of working with Don as a colleague at Ohio State, and I greatly value his insights and collegiality.

3.2.7 Mary Beckman

Don joined the department three years after I did, but he had been a linguist and an academic far longer than I had been at the time, so in all ways other than our affiliation with Ohio State, he has been my *sempai* rather than the other way around.

Over the decades since then, the department has gone through two external reviews, the faculty has more than doubled in size, the graduate program has been revised to shorten the time to degree and triple the graduation rate, and the undergraduate major has developed from a minor appendage to the graduate curriculum into a full-fledged curriculum in its own right. Throughout the course of these changes, Don has consistently and thoughtfully contributed his time and his wisdom. I have learned so much from him at department meetings, on search committees, in dissertation defenses, etc.

And I am not the only one to have learned from him. Over the years, I have watched as our graduates, who were his advisees, be the same kind of thoughtful, committed mentor to their advisees (Don's grandstudents). I have watched them contribute in similar ways to the growth and transformation of the departments and programs that hired them.

Finally, more recently, as events in the world around us have forced me to reevaluate my role in society outside of linguistics, I have come to appreciate anew Don's quiet but steadfast commitment to social justice. Living where I do now in the southern half of the Gullah Geechee Cultural Heritage Corridor, I am blessed to be able to also apply insights from his and his students' research as I strive to follow his example of involvement in my community.

3.2.8 Nandi Sims, Luana Lamberti, Justin Pinta

Like many of Don's past advisees, his influence on us, both as scholars and as people, is indelible. We have each experienced his teaching within our first two years of school at Ohio State, which prompted us to subsequently take each class he has offered. While we each work in different regions, his passion for teaching promoted in each of us a love of contact, an appreciation for the subtle differences between transfer and imposition, and an attention to detail that has helped each of us succeed in graduate school and feel prepared for careers in academia.

As an advisor and a committee member, Don's rigorous expectations and meticulous attention to detail have caused each of us to pull out our hair from time to time. In the end, however, these high expectations have translated into each of us having a critical eye in reading, research and writing. His close readings of our papers and grant proposals, careful and detailed feedback, willingness to meet whenever we needed him, and countless letters of recommendation have played a tremendous role in each of our successes in our careers thus far.

Don is the type of professor that has the ability to make one think about language from a different perspective. His courses have inspired each of us to expand our fields. Future students of linguistics at The Ohio State University will surely be missing out without Don's expertise in New World Black Englishes and other contact varieties.

3.3 Reflections on Donald Winford and the Creolist Hypothesis (Tracey L. Weldon, The University of South Carolina)

In the fall of 1991, I moved from Columbia, South Carolina to Columbus, Ohio to begin my graduate studies at The Ohio State University. I had just completed my BA and was interested in learning more about the ways in which what was then called "Black English" was studied by linguists. I had gotten a glimpse into this line of research in my undergraduate classes on "The History of English" and "Modern English Grammar". What perhaps intrigued me most about this planned area of study, however, was a conversation that I'd had with my then future advisor, Professor Donald Winford, during a visit to the Ohio State campus earlier that summer. When I shared with him my plans to study Black English, I distinctly recall him saying, "But it's not English, right? It's a separate language". What's this you say? Black English as a separate language? How can this be? What does this mean? I would later come to understand that Don was endorsing an early version of the Creolist Hypothesis, which posited a separate and autonomous system for Black English resulting from a Creole origin that distinguished it from other varieties of American English. I also later learned that Gullah, an English-based Creole spoken along the coasts of South Carolina and Georgia, was believed to be a critical component to understanding this possible Creole past. And, thus, began my foray into variationist sociolinguistics and the study of Gullah and AAVE under the tutelage of Professor Donald Winford.

My doctoral dissertation, written under Don's direction, ultimately focused on the Gullah-AAVE connection, with a focus on variability of the copula. This line of research dovetailed nicely with Don's expertise in the areas of Creole linguistics and African American language varieties. My decision to focus on Gullah, a more "intermediate" Creole variety, as a point of comparison with AAVE, was particularly inspired by Don's 1992 papers, "Back to the Past: The BEV/Creole Connection Revisited," and "Another look at the copula in Black English and Caribbean Creoles" which demonstrated the utility of comparing AAVE to more intermediate varieties, such as Trinidadian Creole (TC), which as he argues...

> ... provide the soundest basis for comparison between BEV and CEC. Both BEV and TC are vernaculars which have long been in contact with more standard varieties of English, in quite similar social circumstances. Such contact has led to similar patterns of restructuring in both varieties in areas such as the copula system (Winford 1992a: 24)

My research was also significantly informed by Don's comprehensive two-part overview "On the origins of African American Vernacular English – A creolist perspective," in which he presented an alternative view of the Creolist Hypothesis, which positioned AAVE not as a separate and autonomous system resulting from decreolization of an earlier plantation Creole, but rather as an English variety that was shaped by language contact and language shift between speakers of early AAVE and Creole varieties.

According to Winford (1997h), Gullah likely emerged in South Carolina during the period from 1720 to 1775, which was marked by institutionalized segregation and the massive importation of enslaved Africans to meet the growing needs of the plantation economy. Prior to this time, roughly 1670 to 1720, conditions in South Carolina would have favored Africans learning an approximation to the settler dialects. With the introduction of the Creole, the linguistic situation among Africans in South Carolina would have come to resemble a continuum.

> ... Africans in closer contact with whites must have continued to learn closer approximations to their dialects. By the mid-18th century, the linguistic situation on the South Carolina coast would have been similar to that in other Caribbean colonies – a creole continuum within the African population, complicated by continuing input from white dialects on the one hand, and the African languages of newly-arrived slaves on the other (Winford 1997d: 315).

Within this framework, the period from 1780–1860 would have been one of consolidation and leveling across both Creole and dialectal English varieties. And the processes of language contact and language shift between Africans speaking a Creole and those speaking approximations to the settler dialects would have resulted in a significant amount of Creole substratum influence in AAVE.

We can assume that there was a sizeable body of Africans throughout the southern states in this period whose primary vernacular was a creole English, and many of whom shifted over the years to AAVE as their primary vernacular, 'transferring' or preserving in the process certain elements of the creole grammar. I also assume that there was a sizeable body of Africans whose primary vernacular was an earlier form of AAVE which was fashioned after the settler dialects, and which provided the target of the shift. Contact between these groups of Africans on the plantations is likely to have contributed to the development of AAVE (Winford 1997d: 317).

Along these lines, Don argued that a shift scenario would better account for patterns of copula variability in AAVE than decreolization.

My present position is that the copula pattern of AAVE is best explained as the result of imperfect second language learning with transfer from creolized or restructured varieties playing a significant role. On the one hand, many Africans must have acquired a close approximation to the superstrate copula system from the earliest stages of contact. Other groups of Africans speaking African languages, and later, creole or other forms of restructured English in which copula

absence was common, shifted toward these established forms of AAVE, introducing fu[r]ther changes due to imperfect learning (Winford 1998: 111).

From this perspective, copula absence in early forms of AAVE would have
been reinforced by Creole varieties introduced from Barbados and other areas of
the Caribbean, where the copula was most likely also absent in all but nominal
environments. And the early copula system of Gullah would have had a significant impact on the development of the emerging AAVE system. Accordingly,
the decreolization model proposed in Winford (1992a) was "reinterpreted as a
model of shift, with the shift from a 'mesolectal' to an 'acrolectal' copula system
most relevant to the developments in AAVE" (1998: 112). Furthermore, the similarities that he observed between AAVE and TC were attributed to the fact that
both varieties emerged out of situations involving shift between a system with
zero copula (except before nominals in the case of TC) and one with forms of *be*
(1998: 112). And the fact that modern-day TC and other CECs require a copula
in nominal environments while AAVE allows for copula absence was attributed
to differences in substratum input, "with early AAVE affected by restructured
varieties containing no copula in nominal environments ..." (Winford 1998: 112).

This perspective on the Creolist Hypothesis is one that I ultimately endorsed in
my own dissertation research (Weldon 1998) and subsequent publications on the
AAVE-Gullah connection (see e.g., Weldon 2003a; Weldon 2003b) and one that
other scholars have endorsed in various forms as well (see e.g., Mufwene 1997;
Rickford 1997; Rickford 1998). While the field owes much to Donald Winford for
his meticulous contributions to Creole linguistics and the study of African American Vernacular English, I am indebted to him for taking a budding linguist from
South Carolina under his wing and offering her an opportunity to interrogate
the Creolist Hypothesis through an exploration of the AAVE-Gullah connection
in its sociohistorical and linguistic contexts.

3.4 Don's contribution to Sociolinguistics (Robin Dodsworth, North Carolina State University)

Don Winford is probably best known as a leading scholar of Creoles and of contact linguistics, but many of us have known him first as a foundational sociolinguist. Don's initial contribution to sociolinguistics, his 1972 dissertation, was not
only the first sociolinguistic account of Trinidadian English, but also one of the
earliest systematic analyses of sociolinguistic variation. His subsequent publications about Trinidadian English both expanded empirical knowledge and advanced sociolinguistic theory. For example, his 1978b article in the *Journal of*

Linguistics first shows that the variable (th) in Trinidadian English has the now-familiar 'crossover' pattern, in which a central social class uses an overall lower rate of the stigmatized variant, relative to higher social classes, in a word list reading task designed to call attention to the variable. The article next takes issue with Labov (1966), arguing that crossover differs from true hypercorrection, insofar as crossover involves no "irregular" placement of a phonetic variant as in [θin] for 'tin'. True hypercorrection, the article goes on to say, "provides evidence that two distinct systems, each with its own norms of usage, are in contact", which is especially valuable in cases of decreolization (284).

The insights about crossover and hypercorrection foreshadow a consistent theme in Don's subsequent work: the critical appraisal of the relationship between social patterns and linguistic structure. This is especially clear in Don's wide-ranging work in the area of contact linguistics. I think Stephanie Hackert (2005) says it best in her review of Don's (2003a) book *An Introduction to Contact Linguistics*:

> "In its emphasis on uniting linguistic and sociolinguistic approaches to language contact and treating all language-contact phenomena within a single theoretical and methodological framework, Winford's Introduction ... will surely contribute to drawing the various foci of contact linguistics closer together, thus further consolidating the field." (page 115)

I would add that Don's close and systematic attention to social context in relation to linguistic structure helps to consolidate not just the various areas of contact linguistics, but of sociolinguistics more broadly. For example, his (1985b) article in *Language in Society* observes that creole-speaking communities are diglossic in Ferguson's sense. Winford (1997d) argues on the basis of extremely detailed socio-historical and linguistic data that mesolectal Caribbean creoles result mainly from contact with Europeans, language shift, and shift-induced restructuring, and not from a continuous 'decreolization' process. Both of these claims (about diglossia and about 'decreolization') function not only to affirm the importance of social context in understanding linguistic structure, but also to bring together creole studies and variationist sociolinguistics; Creoles result from, among other things, the linguistic effects of social forces that sociolinguists have observed in non-creole settings. The themes of uniting linguistic and social data, and of uniting Creole studies with other kinds of sociolinguistic studies, are also central to his work in discerning the structure and origins of AAE. Winford (1992a) argues that AAE resembles a mesolectal Creole with respect to both structure and history, and that its copula bears structural similarities to the copula in

Trinidad English creole (see also Winford 1997d, 1998). In both varieties, the copula has been restructured over time in response to pressure from a superstrate. Winford (2000c) focuses on the importance of social context in determining the origin(s) of AAE, a notoriously difficult question that he approaches as both a creolist and sociolinguist:

> [I]t is clear that we are dealing with multiple sources whose effects varied according to differences in the nature of the contact settings, their demographics, and the types of social interaction among the groups involved. It should also be clear that for many AAVE features, we are dealing with the effects of multiple causation, involving externally and internally motivated change, leveling, and processes of simplification and restructuring. An understanding of these can come only from a thorough investigation of the sociohistorical contexts of the emergence and development of AAVE. However, this aspect of the genesis of AAVE in all its forms remains relatively unexplored. This is unfortunate because, as every student of language history knows, the sociolinguistic history of a community, and not linguistic factors, is the primary influence on how languages originate, change, and develop. (409–410)

He goes on to lament the absence of several kinds of information about the social contexts in which AAE is used, offering that we do not yet understand how linguistic choices within Black communities convey group identities, group values, and communicative goals, nor do we have the data we need about AAVE in "situated language use, conversational norms, communicative strategies, genres of talk, and the like" (2000: 411). The dual concern with, first, the linguistic processes of variation and change such as leveling and restructuring, and second, the social forces that give rise to and shape the linguistic processes, thus characterizes Don's perspective on questions normally associated with contact linguistics and questions often considered the territory of variationist sociolinguistics.

The primacy of sociohistorical factors, a striking claim in the extended quote above, reappears unattenuated in later work. For example, a chapter on the social factors in language contact, argues that we need more detailed information about the social settings that produced contact languages in order to understand how they arise and why they have particular structural characteristics, e.g. the syntactic frame from one language and some of the lexicon from another language (Winford 2013e). Drawing upon a remarkable knowledge of distinct contact settings around the world, the chapter goes so far as to say that "[t]he evidence now available to us strongly supports the view that social factors play a significant, and in some cases a more important role than linguistic factors, in shaping the consequences of language contact" (page 365). It is clear from this chapter, as well as (Winford 2003a) and many of his other texts about contact linguistics (which are discussed at greater length elsewhere in this volume), that Don considers the outstanding questions in contact linguistics to be mainly about the interaction of social context with linguistic processes. He has observed, for example, that

> ... [W]e cannot always establish clear and consistent correspondences be-
> tween the social contexts and linguistic processes involved in the creation
> of intertwined or other mixed languages. Different social circumstances can
> lead to similar processes of mixture, while different types of mixture may
> arise in what seem to be similar social settings. We still need to investigate
> the reasons for this ... (2013: 379).

I would say that this observation is equally true of other areas of sociolinguistics. In the area of sociolinguistic variation, we haven't identified a clear correspondence between social contexts and linguistic outcomes. We do know some things about this. We have some evidence, for example, that dense, multiplex community networks are associated with maintenance of local vernaculars; and that, relatedly, ethnic segregation promotes inter-group linguistic difference; and that in class-stratified urban contexts, certain kinds of linguistic variables will also be class-stratified; and that linguistic variables with strong social indexicality can show tremendous intra-speaker variation from one interactional context to the next; and that complex internal constraints are often weakened or revised during language change or inter-community transmission. But our predictive ability doesn't go very far beyond these generalities. The most productive way forward when it comes to this question and others is surely to answer Don's call for more consistent, rich social data about the communities in which we study sociolinguistic variation.

With respect to richer social data, one of Don's wishes for the field, and one that made a strong impression on me when I was his student almost twenty years ago, is for better data about the relationship between social network characteristics and language variation and change. He observed that early sociolinguistic work about speakers' participation in dense, multiplex local networks has not led to widespread, systematic investigation of specific ego network characteristics as possible influences on language production or perception. We also have very little network analysis about real social interaction between people. My own work with social networks evolved from these conversations, and even now Don is both an insightful critic and a great supporter of it, always encouraging and remarkably accepting of new approaches to social context and to network data.

All of Don's PhD students have done research that reflects and affirms his commitment to sociolinguistics through engagement with socially contextualized linguistic variation. The topical breadth of their work, and the many strands of sociolinguistic theory that their work contributes to, are natural consequences of working with an advisor who has been a foundational and forward-thinking sociolinguist, and whose work has united distinct areas of sociolinguistics.

3.5 A tribute and a few recollections (Arthur K. Spears, The City University of New York)

As with many colleagues and friends, I cannot remember when I first met Don; but, it was probably either a few years before or after his move to Ohio state in 1988. I do remember our getting together for lunch or dinner at many, perhaps most, conferences we both attended, especially those of the Society for Pidgin and Creole Linguistics (SPCL). To the extent we talked about linguistics, it was about Creole languages, African American English (AAE), and/or tense-mood-aspect (TMA), the last of which, I could say, has been the thread that has tied most of my work on Creoles and African American English together – not to mention Haitian Creole – and which has often triggered my interest in other areas of grammar. We not infrequently talked about negotiating our academic careers and how to avoid the worst pitfalls on the promotion path to full professor. Considering all of the subfields and sub-subfields of linguistics that I do research in, Don shares more of them than any other linguist. My recent linguistic research has concentrated on AAE grammar and history, with a particular focus on how contemporary grammars of AAE can shed light on what is still the central question on AAE history: to what extent was a Creole language, or languages, involved in it? We could go on to ask how such involvement occurred and what Creole language or languages left traces in AAE.

Don's research has indeed been a significant source of inspiration for my own work; and, I have often started very near the beginning of some writing by rereading something of his, just to get my thinking started or to make sure that there was not anything of significance that I was not taking into consideration. Indeed, I frequently find Don's work overstimulating, due to its richness in detail, superb argumentation, and meticulous analyses. There are few times that I return to a writing of his without getting a few new ideas for articles, some better than the central ideas of articles I am already committed to writing. As a result, the probably more interesting Don-inspired articles end up unwritten most of the time.

Actually, at times tiger-related metaphors pop into my mind when I am reading Don. Often his critique, or destruction, of claims and hypotheses does bear the marks of tigerishness in its diligence. I do not want to say ferocity because I am sure that Don never intends to be ferocious. The manner in which he carries himself is always highly suitable for drawing rooms across the United States and certainly the parlors, "yards," etc. all over the Western Hemisphere. This remark about tigerishness reminds me of a story, which I will leave for another occasion.

But then again, what better occasion than this to reveal something deeper in Don's character than what is usually talked about. No, this story is not about Don's sometimes mordant sense of humor. No, it is not about his sometimes directness of expression. 'How did you like your meal?' asked of Don as we were all leaving a traditional wrap-up 'banquet' at an SPCL conference. 'It was awful and way overpriced!' (speaking of a precious rendering of Nouvelle Moroccan cuisine). No mincing of words here. No chopping or sautéing of them either. I broke out laughing at his reply. It was the shock of recognition – of typically African American directness, which, I have come to learn, is simply one branch of an African Diasporic directness of expression that I have witnessed all over the Americas.

No, this story is about something else. One evening, while attending a conference in Graz, Austria, we went out to dinner and talked about the conference and a range of matters. I was already becoming impressed with the food in Austria, and that impression became more prominent in my mind as we finished the meal and attendant matters, and then headed for the exit, passing beside a very long bar. Something was shouted from somewhere at the bar. I could not hear it clearly. Don did, and as if releasing a tiger within him that sprang into action when required, he loudly hurled back a response to whatever it was that had been shouted from the bowels of the bar. "What was that?" I asked, but Don was unwilling to repeat whatever was said, distracted as he was. Don had stopped and turned toward his interlocutors, who I gathered had thrown insults or slurs – or both – at us. I was aware of news coverage of the then extreme-for-Europe anti-immigrant (read anti-brown and black) sentiment in Austria. Don said something. I said, "Let's go," my upbringing during the U.S. Reign of Terror (Jim Crow) kicking in. I am only two years younger than Emmett Till, whose lynching was a conspicuous factor in the launch of the African American (later joined by other groups) Civil Rights Movement. Don caught up with me as I went through the door to the sidewalk, and he remained mum about what had been said. I could not help but admire his courage, his deep reserve of tigerishness, standing his ground, even reprimanding them. I thought about asking him if he had had such encounters in the U.S., but our talk had already turned to other matters, as I thought how helpful the incident was in reminding me to be on high alert since, after the conference, I was going to visit Vienna, a fascinating, old imperial capital – high alert advisable.

3.6 A Career in Linguistics (Anthony Grant, Edge Hill University)

Don Winford chose well in deciding where to pursue his undergraduate degree and his PhD. Having first studied for his BA at King's College London, he ventured north and studied under R. B. (Bob) Le Page at the University of York, which was long one of the main centres for the study of pidgins and Creoles, a field of study which was much endorsed by Bob, the founding Head of the Department who had spent several years at the University of the West Indies at Mona and who was one of the most renowned creolists of his generation. In addition to Don, York produced creolists such as Mark Sebba, who did his doctorate there, Sir Colville Young, titan of Belizean politics, and the late Philip Baker who pursued his BPhil at York before completing his PhD at SOAS University of London. Don would doubtless have drawn intellectual refreshment from the extensive creolistic library which Bob had gathered at the J B Morrell Library, and which remains essentially intact to this day. (On a personal note, it was Creole research which impelled me to matriculate at York as an undergraduate in 1981).

Coming as he did from an island where an English-lexified Creole had been the major medium of communication for over a century (thus largely supplanting an exogenous French-lexified Creole), it is not surprising that Don's research has focused on English-lexified Creoles, though his studies have not been confined to it. One of his early papers (Winford 1975) discusses, with ample illustration, the nature of 'Creole' culture and language in Trinidad.

His monograph *Predication in English-Based Creoles*, drawing on data regarding verb phrases from a number of Caribbean Creoles and beyond, and presenting views on change in verb phrases which were not solely reliant on previous ideas about decreolisation and the (post-)creole continuum, appeared in Winford (1993b).

He co-edited a book on code-switching (Isurin, Winford & Bot 2009), in which psycholinguistic approaches are to the fore, and in which the languages surveyed go well beyond creole languages. In the year when his book on Creole predication appeared, he also saw the publication of a book which he had edited with Frank Byrne on focus and grammatical relations in Creole languages (Byrne & Winford 1993), which goes well beyond its title as it covers a range of topics from predicate clefting to discourse processes. He also edited a well-received book of essays by diverse hands with Arthur K. Spears (Spears & Winford 1997), and several of these papers have become classics of the field.

Don has also written a series of papers on the evolution of African-American Vernacular English (AAVE) in *Diachronica* and elsewhere, culminating in his article on the topic in the Oxford Online Encyclopedia of Linguistics (Winford 2014) and in a collection of papers honouring the work of Professor John R. Rickford (Winford 2020a). In his work on the subject Winford argues from both linguistic and sociohistorical data that AAVE did not undergo decreolization, as many of his predecessors had stated, but that it emerged from an interaction of English dialects, especially Southern English and Scotch-Irish varieties, which were influenced by West African languages and additionally by Creoles emerging in the West Indies, especially Barbados, whence many settlers in Virginia, Maryland and the Carolinas – which Don sees as the likely birthplace of AAVE – had come in the pre-Revolutionary period. Don covered not only creoles but also pidgins and mixed languages and much else besides in his book *An Introduction to Contact Linguistics* (Winford 2003a). In this and subsequent work he has been a champion of the approach to language contact pursued by Frans van Coetsem, in which the two transfer types in which contact-induced linguistic change is involved are borrowing and imposition, which means that elements are brought from the source language into the recipient language (see especially Van Coetsem (1988)). This is not the traditional way of viewing contact-induced change, but it shakes up the linguistic kaleidoscope and allows us to view contact phenomena from a different but equally enlightening angle. An article by Don on the same topic in *Diachronica* (Winford 2005), applying the van Coetsem approach to new scenarios, continued this approach, while Don subsequently published a chapter in Insurin et al. (2009), and also in Winford (2020c), following these theories.

In addition to editing JPCL for more than half its lifespan so far, Don Winford has been a staunch advocate of work by newer scholars, as a teacher, a researcher and an advocate. He has never been afraid to challenge the prevalent views in creolistics research. We salute him!

Abbreviations

AAVE African American Vernacular English
AAE   African American English
ASR   Automated Speech Recognition
CEC   Caribbean English Creole
TC   Trinidadian Creole

TMA   Tense Mood Aspect
JPCL   Journal of Pidgin and Creole Languages
SPCL   Society for Pidgin and Creole Languages

Acknowledgements

This project has taken quite some time to pull together. We (Bettina & Shelome) first shared it with Tracey Weldon and Steve Hartmann-Kaiser who both had a couple of very good suggestions. Sandro Sessarego, during a visit to Dublin, then helped shape the overall character of the book, which was further refined during our talks at the SPCL conference in Tempere. We are very grateful to the authors of the different papers. Many of them have, by now, had to wait for a very long time to see the publication of this book. We would also like to thank Stefano Man-fredi and Isabelle Léglise for accepting to publish the book in their series and for their help with selecting reviewers. We are very grateful to all the reviewers who generously gave of their time to give us and the authors valuable feedback on the papers. Last but not least, we would like to thank Sebastian Nordhoff and his team for invaluable support with the technical aspects of editing and converting the papers into LaTeX, and Emily Martin and Ariana Arrojado, students at the University of Pittsburgh for their help with the editorial work leading up to the final product.

References

Good, Jeff. 2012. Typologizing grammatical complexities, or why creoles may be paradigmatically simple but syntagmatically average. *Journal of Pidgin and Creole Languages* 27(1). 1–47.

Hackert, Stephanie. 2005. Review of Donald Winford, 2003, "An introduction to contact linguistics". *English World-Wide 26* 1. 113–116.

Klein, Wolfgang & Clive Perdue. 1992. *Utterance structure: Developing grammars again.* Amsterdam: Benjamins.

Klein, Wolfgang & Clive Perdue. 1997. The basic variety (or: Couldn't natural languages be much simpler?) *Second Language Research* 13(4). 301–347.

Labov, William. 1966. Hypercorrection by the lower middle class as a factor in lin-guistic change. In W. Bright (ed.), *Sociolinguistics*, 84–113. De Gruyter Mouton. DOI: 10.1515/9783110856507-008.

Mufwene, Salikoko S. 1997. Gullah's development: Myths and sociohistorical evidence. In Cynthia Bernstein, Thomas Nunnally & Robin Sabino (eds.), *Language variety in the South revisited*, 113–123. Tuscaloosa & London: University of Alabama Press.

Rickford, John R. 1997. Prior creolization of African-American vernacular English? Sociohistorical and textual evidence from the 17th and 18th centuries. *Journal of Sociolinguistics* 1(3). 315–336. DOI: 10.1111/1467-9481.00019.

Rickford, John R. 1998. The creole origins of African-American vernacular English: Evidence from copula absence. In Salikoko S. Mufwene, John R. Rickford, Guy Bailey & John Baugh (eds.), *African-American English: Structure, history, and use*, 154–200. London & New York: Routledge.

Van Coetsem, Frans. 1988. *Loan phonology and the two transfer types in language contact*. Dordrecht: Foris.

Weldon, Tracey. 1998. *Exploring the AAVE-Gullah connection: A comparative study of copula variability*. Columbus, OH: The Ohio State University. (Doctoral dissertation).

Weldon, Tracey. 2003a. Copula variability in Gullah. *Language Variation and Change* 15(1). 37–72.

Weldon, Tracey. 2003b. Revisiting the creolist hypothesis: Copula variability in Gullah and Southern rural AAVE. *American Speech* 78(2). 171–191.

Don Winford's publications: A bibliography

Journal articles

Winford, Donald. 2018. Creole tense-mood-aspect systems. *Annual Review of Linguistics* 4(1). 193–212.

Winford, Donald. 2013c. In search of a unified model of language contact. *Bilingualism: Language and Cognition* 16(4). 734–736.

Migge, Bettina & Donald Winford. 2013. Fact-type complements in Gbe and the Surinamese creoles. *Lingua. (Special issue: Cross-linguistic influence in language creation: Assessing the role of the Gbe languages in the formation of the Creoles of Suriname)* 129. 9–31.

Essegbey, James et al. 2013. Introduction: Cross-linguistic influence in language creation: Assessing the role of the Gbe languages in the Surinamese creoles. *Lingua. (Special issue: Cross-linguistic influence in language creation: Assessing the role of the Gbe languages in the formation of the creoles of Suriname)* 129(7). 1–8. DOI: 10.1016/j.lingua.2013.02.005.

Winford, Donald. 2007a. Language contact in Amazonia, and: Dynamics of language contact: English and immigrant languages. *Language* 83(2). 401–421.

Winford, Donald. 2007b. Some issues in the study of language contact. *Journal of Language Contact. Thema: Language Contact: Framing its Theories and Descriptions* 1(1). 22–40. DOI: 10.1163/000000007792548288.

Winford, Donald. 2008c. Processes of creolization and related contact-induced change. *Journal of Language Contact* 1(1). 124–145.

Winford, Donald & Bettina Migge. 2007. Substrate influence on the emergence of the TMA systems of the Surinamese creoles. *Journal of Pidgin and Creole languages. (Special Issue: Substrate Influence in Creole Formation)* 22(1). 73–99.

Winford, Donald. 2005. Contact-induced changes: Classification and processes. *Diachronica* 22(2). 373–427.

Winford, Donald. 2003b. Contact-induced changes: Classification and processes. *OSU Working Papers* 57. 129–150.

Winford, Donald. 2001c. *On the typology of creole TMA systems* (Occasional Paper. Society for Caribbean Linguistics 29).

Winford, Donald. 2000a. Irrealis in Sranan: Mood and modality in a radical creole. *Journal of Pidgin and Creole Languages* 15(1). 63–125.

Winford, Donald. 2000b. Language contact: Issues of classification and types of process. *Diachronica* 17(1). 139–158.

Winford, Donald. 2000c. Plus ça change: The state of studies in African American English. *American Speech* 75(4). 409–411.

Winford, Donald. 1999a. The other Englishes: A contact linguistics perspective. In Marie-Hélène Laforest & Jocelyne Vincent (eds.), *English and the other. Special issue of Anglistica*, vol. 3, 201–217. Napoli: Dipartimento di Studi Linguistici e Letterari dell'Occidente, Istituto Universitario Orientale.

Winford, Donald. 1999b. Variation theory: A view from creole continua. *Cuadernos de Filología Inglesa* 8. 219–237.

Winford, Donald. 1998. On the origins of African American Vernacular English— A creolist perspective. Part II: Linguistic features. *Diachronica* XV(1). 99–154.

Winford, Donald. 1997a. Creole formation in the context of contact linguistics: Guest column. *Journal of Pidgin and Creole Languages* 12(1). 71–84.

Winford, Donald. 1997b. Creole studies and sociolinguistics: Guest column. *Journal of Pidgin and Creole Languages* 12(2). 303–318.

Winford, Donald. 1997d. On the origins of African American Vernacular English— A creolist perspective. Part I: The sociohistorical background. *Diachronica* XIV(2). 305–44.

Winford, Donald. 1997e. Property items and predication in Sranan. *Journal of Pidgin and Creole Languages* 12(2). 237–301.

Winford, Donald. 1997f. Re-examining Caribbean English Creole Continua. *World Englishes* 16(2). 233–79.

Winford, Donald. 1996a. Common ground and Creole TMA: Guest column. *Journal of Pidgin and Creole Languages* 11(1). 71–84.

Winford, Donald. 1996b. Creole typology and relationships: Guest column. *Journal of Pidgin and Creole Languages* 11(2). 313–328.

Winford, Donald. 1993b. Variability in the use of perfect have in Trinidadian English: A problem of categorial and semantic mismatch. *Language Variation and Change* 5(3). 141–187.

Winford, Donald. 1992a. Another look at the copula in Black English and Caribbean Creoles. *American Speech* 67(1). 21–60.

Winford, Donald. 1992b. Back to the past: The BEV/Creole connection revisited. *Language Variation and Change* 4(3). 311–57.

Winford, Donald. 1990a. Copula variability, accountability, and the concept of 'polylectal' grammars. *Journal of Pidgin and Creole Languages* 5(2). 223–252.

Winford, Donald. 1988a. Stativity and other aspects of the Creole passive. *Lingua* 76. 271–297.

Winford, Donald. 1988b. The Creole continuum and the notion of the community as a locus of language. In vol. 71, 91–106. DOI: 10.1515/ijsl.1988.71.91.

Winford, Donald. 1985a. The concept of 'diglossia' in Caribbean creole situations. *Language in Society* 14. 345–356.

Winford, Donald. 1985b. The syntax of *fi* complements in Caribbean English Creole. *Language* 61(3). 588–624.

Winford, Donald. 1984. The linguistic variable and syntactic variation in Creole continua. *Lingua* 62. 267–288.

Winford, Donald. 1980a. Creole culture and language in Trinidad – a sociohistorical sketch. *Caribbean Studies* 15(3). 31–56.

Winford, Donald. 1979. *Phonological variation and change in Trinidadian English – the evolution of the vowel system* (Occasional Paper. Society for Caribbean Linguistics 12).

Winford, Donald. 1978b. Phonological hypercorrection in the process of decreolisation – the case of Trinidadian English. *Journal of Linguistics* 14(2). 277–291.

Winford, Donald. 1976. Teacher attitudes toward language varieties in a Creole community. *International Journal of the Sociology of Language* 8. 45–75.

Winford, Donald. 1974a. Aspects of the social differentiation of language in Trinidad. *Caribbean Issues* 1(3). 1–16.

Papers in edited collections

Winford, Donald. 2020a. Another look at the creolist hypothesis of AAVE origins. In Renee Blake & Isabelle Buchstaller (eds.), *The Routledge Companion to the Work of John R. Rickford*, 64–78. London: Routledge.

Winford, Donald. 2020b. The new spanishes in the context of contact linguistics: Toward a unified approach. In Luis A. Ortiz López et al. (eds.), *Hispanic Contact Linguistics*, 12–41. Amsterdam: John Benjamins.

Winford, Donald. 2020c. Theories of language contact. In Anthony Grant (ed.), *The Oxford handbook of language contact*, 51–74. Oxford: Oxford University Press.

Winford, Donald. 2017a. Some observations on the sources of AAVE structure: Re-examining the creole connection. In Cecelia Cutler Philipp Angermeyer & Zvjezdana Vric (eds.), *Language contact in Africa and the African diaspora in the Americas (CLL 53)*, 203–224. Amsterdam: John Benjamins.

Winford, Donald. 2017b. The ecology of language and the new Englishes: Toward an integrative framework. In Anna Mauranen Markku Filppula Juhani Klemola & Svetlana Vetchinnikova (eds.), *Changing English: Global and local perspectives*, 25–56. Berlin: De Gruyter Mouton.

Winford, Donald. 2017c. World Englishes and Creoles. In Juhani Klemola Markku Filppula & Devyani Sharma (eds.), *Handbook of world Englishes*, 194–210. Oxford: Oxford University Press.

Winford, Donald. 2015a. Creole formation and second language acquisition: A language processing perspective. In Piotr P. Chruszczewski et al. (eds.), *Languages in contact 2014*, 295–322. Wroclaw, Poland: Wydawnictwo wyzszej szkoły Filologicznej We Wrocławiu.

Winford, Donald. 2015b. The origins of African American Vernacular English. In Sonja Lanehart (ed.), *The Oxford handbook of African American language*, 85–104. Oxford, New York: Oxford University Press.

Winford, Donald. 2014. Toward and integrated model of contact-induced change. In Amei Koll-Stobbe & Sebastian Knospe (eds.), *Language contact around the globe: Proceedings of the LCTG3 Conference*, 3–24. Frankfurt: Peter Lang.

Winford, Donald. 2013d. On the unity of contact phenomena: The case for imposition. In Carole de Fe'ral (ed.), *In and out of Africa: Languages in question: A Festschrift for Robert Nicolai*, 1, 47–74. Louvain: Peeters.

Winford, Donald. 2013a. Afterword. In Isabelle Léglise & Claudine Chamoreau (eds.), *The interplay of variation and change in contact settings*, 253–259. Amsterdam: John Benjamins.

Winford, Donald. 2013b. Challenging the old: Exploring the new. A tribute to Ian

Robertson. In Paula Morgan & Valerie Youssef (eds.), *Reassembling the frag-ments: Voice and identity in Caribbean discourse*, 11–26. Kingston, Jamaica: University of the West Indies Press.

Winford, Donald. 2013e. Social factors in contact languages. In Peter Bakker & Yaron Matras (eds.), *Contact languages: A comprehensive guide*, 363–417. Berlin: Mouton de Gruyter.

Winford, Donald. 2013f. Sranan. In Bernd Kortmann & Kerstin Lunken-heimer (eds.), *The electronic world atlas of variation in English: Grammar.* München/Berlin: Max Planck Digital Library in cooperation with Mouton de Gruyter. https://ewave-atlas.org/languages.

Winford, Donald. 2013g. Substrate influence and universals in the emergence of contact Englishes: Re- evaluating the evidence. In Daniel Schreier & Marianne Hundt (eds.), *English as a contact language*, 222–241. Cambridge: Cambridge University Press.

Winford, Donald & Ingo Plag. 2013b. Sranan structure dataset. In Susanne Maria Michaelis et al. (eds.), *Atlas of pidgin and creole language structures online.* Leipzig: Max Planck Institute for Evolutionary Anthropology. https://apics-online.info/contributions/2.

Winford, Donald & Ingo Plag. 2013a. Sranan. In Susanne Maria Michaelis et al. (eds.), *The survey of pidgin and creole languages. Volume 1: English-based and Dutch-based languages*, 15–26. Oxford: Oxford University Press.

Winford, Donald. 2012a. Creole languages. In Robert Binnick (ed.), *The Oxford handbook of tense and aspect*, 428–457. Oxford: Oxford University Press.

Winford, Donald. 2012b. Pidgins and creoles in the history of English. In Terttu Nevalainen & Elizabeth Closs Traugott (eds.), *The Oxford handbook of the history of English*, 592–601. Oxford: Oxford University Press.

Winford, Donald. 2010a. Contact and borrowing. In Raymond Hickey (ed.), *Handbook of language contact*, 170–187. Chichester: Wiley-Blackwell.

Winford, Donald. 2010b. Revisiting variation between *sa* and *o* in Sranan. In Lars Hinrichs & Joseph Farquharson (eds.), *Variation in the Caribbean: From creole continua to individual agency*, 13–38. Amsterdam: John Benjamins.

Winford, Donald. 2009a. On the unity of contact phenomena: The case of borrow-ing. In Kees de Bot et al. (eds.), *Multidisciplinary perspectives on code-switching*, 279–305. Amsterdam: John Benjamins.

Winford, Donald. 2009b. The interplay of "universals" and contact-induced change in the emergence of new Englishes. In Markku Filppula et al. (eds.), *Vernacular universals and language contacts: Evidence from varieties of English and beyond*, 206–230. London: Routledge.

Winford, Donald & Bettina Migge. 2009. The origin and development of possibility in the Surinamese creoles. In Rachel Selbach et al. (eds.), *Gradual creolization: Studies celebrating Jacques Arends* (CLL 34), 129–153. Amsterdam: John Benjamins.

Winford, Donald. 2008a. Atlantic Creole syntax. In Silvia Kouwenberg & John Singler (eds.), *Handbook of Pidgin and Creole languages*, 17–47. Cambridge: Cambridge University Press.

Winford, Donald. 2008b. English in the Caribbean. In Michael Matto & Haruko Momma (eds.), *A companion to the history of the English language*, 413–423. Oxford: Blackwell.

Winford, Donald & Bettina Migge. 2008. Surinamese Creoles: Morphology and syntax. In Edgar W. Schneider (ed.), *Varieties of English 2: The Americas and the Caribbean*, 693–731. Berlin: Mouton De Gruyter.

Winford, Donald. 2006a. Reduced syntax in prototypical Pidgins. In Ljuljana Progovac et al. (eds.), *The syntax of non-sententials*, 283–307. Amsterdam: John Benjamins.

Winford, Donald. 2006b. Revisiting relexification in creole formation. In Janet Fuller & Lind Thornburg (eds.), *Studies in contact lingusitics: Essays in honor of glenn g. Gilbert*, 231–252. Frankfurt: Peter Lang.

Winford, Donald. 2006c. Tense and aspect in Belize Creole. In Hazel Simmons-McDonald & Ian Robertson (eds.), *Exploring the boundaries of Caribbean Creole languages*, 21–49. Kingston, Jamaica: University of the West Indies Press.

Winford, Donald. 2006d. The restructuring of tense/aspect systems in creole formation. In Ana Deumert & Stephanie Durrleman (eds.), *Structure and variation in language contact (CLL 29)*, 85–110. Amsterdam: John Benjamins.

Winford, Donald. 2003c. Ideologies of language and socially-realistic linguistics. In Sinfree Makoni et al. (eds.), *Black linguistics: Language, society, and politics in Africa and the Americas*, 21–39. London: Routledge.

Winford, Donald. 2002. Creoles in the context of contact linguistics. In Glenn Gilbert (ed.), *Pidgin and Creole linguistics in the twenty-first century*, 287–354. New York: Peter Lang.

Winford, Donald. 2001a. A comparison of tense/ aspect systems in Caribbean English Creoles. In Pauline Christie (ed.), *Due respect: Papers on English and English-related Creoles in the Caribbean in honour of Professor Robert LePage*, 155–83. Kingston, Jamaica: UWI Press.

Winford, Donald. 2001b. Intermediate creoles and degrees of change in creole formation: The case of Bajan. In Ingrid Neumann-Holzschuh & Edgar Schneider (eds.), *Degrees of restructuring in Creole languages*, 215–245. Amsterdam: John Benjamins.

Winford, Donald. 2000d. Tense and aspect in Sranan and the Creole prototype. In John McWhorter (ed.), *Language change and language contact in pidgins and Creoles*, 383–442. Amsterdam: John Benjamins.

Winford, Donald. 1997c. Introduction. In Arthur Spears & Donald Winford (eds.), *The structure and status of pidgins and creoles*, 1–33. Amsterdam: John Benjamins.

Winford, Donald. 1996c. The problem of syntactic variation. In Jennifer Arnold et al. (eds.), *Sociolinguistic variation: Data, theory and analysis: Selected papers from NWAVE XXIII*, 177–192. Stanford: CSLI Publications.

Winford, Donald. 1996d. Verbs, adjectives and categorical shift in Caribbean English Creoles. In Pauline Christie (ed.), *Caribbean language: Issues old and new*, 12–26. Kingston, Jamaica: University of the West Indies Press.

Winford, Donald. 1994a. Sociolinguistic approaches to language use in the anglophone Caribbean. In Marceylina Morgan (ed.), *Language and the social construction of reality in creole situations*, 43–62. Los Angeles: Center for Afro-American Studies, UCLA.

Winford, Donald. 1994b. Towards a model of morphosyntactic variation in a creole continuum. In Katharine Beals et al. (eds.), *Papers from CLS: the parasession on variation and linguistic theory*, 321–334. Chicago, IL: Chicago Linguistic Society.

Winford, Donald. 1991a. Directional serial verb construction in Caribbean English Creoles. In Francis Byrne & John Holm (eds.), *Atlantic meets Pacific: A global view of pidginization and creolization*, 183–203. Amsterdam: John Benjamins.

Winford, Donald. 1991b. The Caribbean. In Jenny Cheshire (ed.), *English around the world: Sociolinguistic perspectives*, 565–584. Cambridge: Cambridge University Press.

Winford, Donald. 1991c. The passive in Caribbean Creole English. In Walter Edwards & Donald Winford (eds.), *Verb phrase patterns in black English and creole*, 256–282. Detroit: Wayne State University Press.

Winford, Donald. 1990b. Serial verb construction and Motion verbs in New World creoles. In Arnold Zwicky & Brian Joseph (eds.), *OSU working papers in linguistics*, vol. 39, 109–148. Columbus, OH: OSU.

Winford, Donald. 1983. A sociolinguistic analysis of negation in Trinidadian English. In Laurence Carrington (ed.), *Studies in Caribbean language*, 203–210. St. Augustine, Trinidad: Society for Caribbean Linguistics, University of the West Indies.

Winford, Donald. 1980b. The Creole situation in the context of sociolinguistic studies. In Richard R. Day (ed.), *Issues in English creole - Proceedings of the 1975*

Hawaii conference, 51–76. Heidelberg: Julius Groot Verlag.

Winford, Donald. 1978a. Grammatical hypercorrection and the notion of "system" in Creole languages. In Edward Baugh (ed.), *Language and literature in the commonwealth Caribbean*, 67–83. Kingston, Jamaica: Carib 1.

Winford, Donald. 1976. Teacher attitudes toward language varieties in a Creole community. *International Journal of the Sociology of Language* 8. 45–75.

Winford, Donald. 1975. "Creole" culture and language in Trinidad: A socio-historical sketch. *Caribbean Studies* 15(3). 31–56.

Monographs

Winford, Donald. 2003a. *An introduction to contact linguistics*. London: Wiley-Blackwell.

Winford, Donald. 1993a. *Predication in Caribbean English Creoles*. Amsterdam: John Benjamins.

Winford, Donald. 1972. *A sociolinguistic description of two communities in Trinidad*. University of York. (Doctoral dissertation).

Edited collections

Essegbey, James et al. 2013. Introduction: Cross-linguistic influence in language creation: Assessing the role of the Gbe languages in the Surinamese creoles. *Lingua. (Special issue: Cross-linguistic influence in language creation: Assessing the role of the Gbe languages in the formation of the creoles of Suriname)* 129(7). 1–8. DOI: 10,1016/j.lingua.2013.02.005.

Isurin, Ludmila et al. 2009. *Multidisciplinary approaches to code switching*, vol. 41. Amsterdam: John Benjamins.

Winford, Donald. 2003b. Contact-induced changes: Classification and processes. *OSU Working Papers* 57. 129–150.

Spears, Arthur K & Donald Winford. 1997. *The structure and status of Pidgins and Creoles*, vol. 19. Amsterdam: John Benjamins.

Byrne, Francis & Donald Winford. 1993. *Focus and grammatical relations in Creole languages*. Amsterdam: John Benjamins.

Edwards, Walter & Donald Winford (eds.). 1991. *Verb phrase patterns in Black English and Creole*. Detroit: Wayne State University Press.

Winford, Donald. 1974b. *Language and society*, vol. 2. Special issue of Caribbean Issues.

Chapter 2

The pith of pidginization: How Francophones facilitated the simplification of French through Foreigner Talk in the Lesser Antilles

Peter Bakker

Aarhus University

In the early 17th century, French speakers simplified their language when communicating with indigenous populations and later Africans in the Lesser Antilles. Through a process of mutual adjustment, a pidgin developed. French missionaries were the only ones to leave linguistic observations in the 17th century. The type of reduction as observed in their Foreigner Talk appears also in the speech of Africans and Amerindians. The documentation leads to the conclusion that the resulting French pidgin was a consequence of interaction and a common creation of the three groups.

1 Introduction

This paper deals with a topic that received attention in creole studies until the mid 1980s, but not much after. Several researchers compared the simplification witnessed in pidgins with foreigner talk. If we compare, for instance, English with English pidgins, it is undisputable that the pidgins display considerably less grammatical complexity than the source language. Likewise, simplification can be observed, at least in some cultures, in the way that people address persons who do not (yet) speak the language, such as the speech to foreigners ("foreigner talk", "alien talk"), or to young children ("baby talk", "motherese" or rather "caretaker talk").

Peter Bakker. 2022. The pith of pidginization: How Francophones facilitated the simplification of French through Foreigner Talk in the Lesser Antilles. In Bettina Migge & Shelome Gooden (eds.), *Social and structural aspects of language contact and change*, 39–65. Berlin: Language Science Press. DOI: 10.5281/zenodo.6979305

Several studies comparing foreigner talk and pidgins were published until the mid-1980s, e.g. (Ferguson 1971; Meisel 1975, 1977; Harding 1984 and Hinnenkamp 1984). After this, the topic received almost no attention, but there seems to be a revival in recent years, e.g. (Fedorova (2006); Versteegh (2014) and Avram (2017)).

Foreigner talk is the term used for speech by native speakers of a language who deliberately adjust their language through simplification when speaking to non-native speakers and language learners. Only one of the parties uses it, and it may be more or less conventionalized. A pidgin is a compromise form of speech used by two or more groups who do not share a fully-fledged language. A pidgin is typically lexically and grammatically reduced.

In this paper I continue this tradition of comparing pidgin and foreigner talk data from the 17th century. I will compare the simplified – foreigner talk – French as spoken by native French speakers in addressing indigenous people and people of African descent, with the simplified – or pidginized – French recorded from the mouth of Amerindians and Blacks. Not only do they appear quite similar, in fact the metalinguistic comments by eyewitnesses at the time suggest that the three varieties were considered identical.These data make it clear that native French speakers adjusted their speech to the learners, and that the learners did not have a desire to acquire the full language, but also that they did not have the opportunity to do so. A pidginized version of French was a compromise between the two groups.

I will list all known simplified French utterances by French speakers written down by contemporary observers of the language ecology of the Lesser Antilles, uttered by French speakers in addressing non-French speakers as they were documented. The structures of these utterances will be compared with those of non-native speakers in the same environment in the same period. This study thus contributes to the theory of the genesis of pidgins, and it sheds light on the contribution of foreigner talk to pidginization. This is a topic taken up by Winford in his textbook on language contact (2003).

2 Background

At the Mona Conference on Pidgin and Creole languages in 1968 in Jamaica, Charles Ferguson presented a paper in which he linked the simplified speech spoken to babies and to foreigners, which was published as Ferguson (1971). Ferguson named the phenomenon of people adjusting and simplifying their own speech to conversation partners who are not speakers, Foreigner Talk. This article started a discussion about the role of what came to be known as Foreigner

Talk and the role it could have played in the development of pidgins. Ferguson continued to play a major role in the discussion in the following decade. In connection with pidginization, Ferguson & DeBose (1977) distinguished between Foreigner Talk (FT), a speech form by native speakers who simplify their own speech in order to be more effective in communication, and *Broken Language* (BL), the non-native's version of another language. As for the latter, it should be made clear that the non-natives did not have the language of the others as a target, only successful communication; see Baker (1990) for an eloquent rebuttal of the idea of a target language in pidgin and creole studies. Whinnom (1971: 105) had already written earlier with regards to pidginization that "the target language is removed from consideration". These two types of reduced languages, FT and BL, being similar in form and content, would converge in the process of pidginization, according to Ferguson and DeBose, and thus result in a pidgin. A pidgin is a more or less stable form of speech, developed by groups who had no language in common. A pidgin is always simplified in comparison with its lexifier or, in rare cases, lexifiers.

This paper sheds light on the influence of FT on pidgins, based on early data covering French FT and approximations of French by Amerindians and Africans, which the observers at the time considered a "jargon" or a "baragouin", two terms synonymous with a pidgin in this context. The quotes presented below confirm the role of French speakers in the pidginization process through their FT and their imitation of the BL of the nonnative speakers.

The idea that a pidgin is not a missed target of language learners, but a common creation by native speakers and their non-native communication partners, through mutual adjustments, is at least as old as Coelho (1881: 67) and Schuchardt (1888: 7ff); see also Schuchardt (1909: 443); or p. 69 in Gilbert's 1981 English translation. This idea was also mentioned by Jespersen (1922: 216) and is often attributed to Bloomfield (1933: 472). These authors referred to a variety of cases: the Mediterranean Lingua Franca, Bislama, Chinese Pidgin English, Portuguese creoles/pidgins in the Portuguese colonial empire, Pidgin and Creole French in Vietnam and Mauritius, etc., attesting to the attractiveness of the idea and its empirical grounding.

In the revival of creole studies from the 1960s, the role of FT in pidginization was picked up again by Naro (1978) and others also adopted the idea in their studies of specific pidgins, or pidgins in general. Clements (1992) discussed the speech adjustments by Portuguese priests to creole Portuguese speakers in Korlai, India, in the framework of the origin of Pidgin Portuguese, solidly embedded in work on FT in second language acquisition in general. After this, there were no publications of significance for almost fifteen years.

The idea of mutual adjustment by native and non-native speakers as a factor in the genesis of pidgins is intuitively appealing, and this theoretical claim was backed up by the empirical study of cases in different continents. Somehow, the idea was hardly discussed by creolists/pidginists after the 1970s, even though it continued to play a significant role in the study of second language acquisition (see Dela Rosa & Arguelles 2016 for an overview). It was in the mid-2010s that the role of Foreigner Talk was taken up again as a factor relevant for pidginization. Versteegh (2014) was the first in his study of past-tense reference in pidgins, in which he took the possible role of what he calls "foreigner-directed speech" into account. Avram (2017) makes an excellent comparison of grammatical features of Gulf Pidgin Arabic, linking them with examples from Foreigner Talk (see below). His data leave no doubt on the influence of FT on Arabic pidgins of the Gulf states, but he also emphasizes that FT is not the only factor in the genesis of pidgins. More details are given in Avram (2018), in which he compares structural and lexical features of four Arabic-lexifier pidgins (Pidgin Madame spoken by Sri Lankan maids in Lebanon, Jordanian Pidgin Arabic, Romanian Pidgin Arabic, and Gulf Pidgin Arabic, all spoken by foreign workers and native Arabic speakers in the Middle East). He indicates that FT played a role in the genesis of these pidgins. These data on foreigner talk and its relevance for pidgin genesis contrast remarkably with the theory of pidginization advocated by Mufwene (2015, 2020), which seems to be virtually uncontested. In his view, pidgins cannot be the precursors of creole languages, because they developed later than creoles, and pidgins and creoles are in complementary distribution. Creole languages, according to him, develop in plantation settings and through a gradual process of adjustments to approximations by successive generations of non-native speakers. Pidgins, in contrast, according to him, develop in trade situations, where the presence of interpreters prevented the development of reduced forms of speech, except in later periods when interpreters approximated earlier attempts. Thus, both pidgins and creoles developed gradually: "creoles and pidgins have evolved in ways similar to the Romance languages, by gradual divergence away from their lexifiers" (Mufwene 2020: 302). One of his claims is:

> Although speakers of pidgins as L2 varieties must have started with interlanguages cum individual transitional varieties toward closer approximations of the target language, there is no historical documentation of communal 'interlanguages' as incipient pidgins (...) nor of 'jargons,' (...) (Mufwene 2020: 301).

All of these statements seem far removed from reality. In this paper, I investigate all the sources of French FT in the Lesser Antilles of the 17th century, and compare them with documented utterances of non-native speakers from a structural perspective. In the conclusions, I will relate them to work on pidgins by Avram (2017) and Parkvall (2017), and contrast that with the claims by Mufwene (2020 and elsewhere). Pidgins and creoles are distinct language types, not only from a social point of view, but also from a structural point of view (pace Mufwene). Pidgins are, roughly, second languages for all, and severely reduced in lexicon and structure compared to their source languages. Most conspicuously, verbal and nominal morphology is almost completely eliminated, and generally even more in creoles, than in pidgins (Bakker 2003). Creoles are first languages, either native tongues or main languages for a community. The fact that there are also pidgincreoles (Bakker 2008) indicates that pidgins can become creoles: pidgincreoles share several social characteristics with pidgins, but most structural properties with creoles. A language like Tok Pisin is an example of a pidgincreole: its name refers to its pidgin past, but it has become a creole. Mufwene (2015: 138) does not consider these expanded pidgins a separate category:

> Confusing expanded pidgins such as Tok Pisin with creoles (Thomason 2001; cf Siegel 2008) depends conceptually on whether one subscribes to the position that creoles are nativized pidgins. Discussions that lump them together are informative in showing the extent to which different evolutionary trajectories can nonetheless produce similar structural outcomes.

In this quote, Mufwene does recognize a structural typological profile for creoles, a position which he otherwise does not subscribe to. The wording "subscribes to" suggest that this is a point of view, whereas it is in reality a historical fact for these expanded pidgins. I will use data from historical sources of the pre-creolization stage from the Lesser Antilles. These predate the structural transition from pidgin to creole. This is visible in the absence of innovated articles, innovated plural markers, innovated TMA systems, all universally present in creoles, including Lesser Antilles Creole. For more detailed data and argumentation, see Bakker (2022). I will study pidgin material and the contribution of French speakers to the structure of the pidgin. The Lesser Antilles constitute, by the way, one of the areas (the Caribbean) where simplification or pidginization according to Mufwene never happened. Again, the facts contradict his point of view. I focus here on an aspect that has not received much attention, that is the use of reduced language by native speakers.

3 French speakers using reduced French

We have gathered pidgin-like data from several dozens of sources from the Lesser Antilles from the 17th century (see Bakker 2022), comprising more than 50 quotes and brief texts from different islands, all preceding creolization, i.e. before conspicuous creole grammatical traits were introduced, such as preverbal TMA, innovated plurals, new definite and indefinite articles (or something resembling them) and the like. Some of these simplified phrases were uttered by native speakers of French, and written down by native speakers of French, from their own mouth or from the mouth of their fellow countrymen. We will analyze them by comparing them with utterances by non-native speakers of French from the same region and period. I do not suggest that the French, by simplifying their native language, were solely responsible for the structures and lexical peculiarities of the creole or pidgin. The reduced structures are much more likely the result of mutual accommodation from all sides: simplified forms were strengthened in the contacts between the groups because of their optimal functionality in this situation. In earlier days, students of creoles have suggested that properties of creoles could be explained by an assumption that Europeans spoke in a simplified way to non-Europeans, and that this simplified speech was learned by the first generation of creole speakers. This theory, sometimes called "baby-talk theory" (Velupillai 2015; Stein 2017: 158–159), is no longer in vogue among creolists. One author invoking this was Bloomfield (1933: 472–473), with English as the exemplified lexifier:

> This 'baby-talk' is the masters' imitation of the subjects' incorrect speech. [...] The basis is the foreigner's desperate attempt at English. Then comes the English-speaker's contemptuous imitation of this, which he tries in the hope of making himself understood. [...] The third layer of alteration is due to the foreigner's imperfect reproduction of the English-speaker's simplified talk, and will differ according to the phonetic and grammatical habit of the foreigner's language.

Even though adjustment by native speakers of their own speech in contact situations is no longer as popular as an explanation for language data in creole studies as in the 1970s, there is no doubt that it did play a role in pidginization. It was certainly the case in the Lesser Antilles. Metalinguistic comments on reduced forms of French as used by Amerindians, Africans and Europeans alike can be found in the sources. For a fuller discussion of these metalinguistic comments, see e.g.(Goodman 1964, Hazaël-Massieux 1996, Jennings 1998, Prudent 1999, Hazaël-Massieux 2008 and Thibault 2018), some of which will be discussed below.

There are not only metalinguistic remarks, there is also a remarkable quantity of linguistic material. There are pidginized French data and French foreigner talk data from 1619 to 1696, where European examples cover the period from 1619 to 1682, Amerindians from 1635 to 1696 and Africans from the 1640s to 1698. These dates indicate the period of documentation of simplified but non-creolized forms of French. A source from 1671 from Martinique is the first that shows traits associated with creoles, such as preverbal TMA, indefinite articles, definite articles from demonstratives that are not found in the pidgin stage, or in pidgin varieties around the world (Baker 1995: 11). I will now present quotes from French speakers who simplify their French in communication with non-French speakers, in other words, French foreigner talk, and compare the linguistic phenomena in these sentences with quotes from non-native speakers from the Lesser Antilles.

3.1 Martinique 1619 (anonymous filibuster)

The first phrase in contact French of the Lesser Antilles can be found in an anonymous manuscript about the travels of captain Fleury to the Caribbean in 1619–1620, preceding the French colonization efforts in the Caribbean by a number of years. Fleury and his men spent a considerable amount of time on the island of Martinique. French colonization in the region first started on the island of Saint Kitts in the mid 1620s. The island of Martinique was settled later, from Saint Kitts in 1635, and shortly after 1658 the indigenous population was killed or deported. Enslaved Africans were imported as a labor force from 1635 in Saint Kitts and in the following decades the French settled the Lesser Antilles islands with slaves. A phrase in simplified French (foreigner talk) is quoted (translation maintained) in the account by the anonymous filibuster who authored the manuscript.

(1) France   bon, France   bon
     France/French good France/French good
     'We are French, we (France/the French) are good' (Anonyme de
     Carpentras; Grunberg et al. 2013)
     (French: *La France est bonne* 'France is good')
     (or *Les français sont bons* 'The French are good')

The phrase is used by French soldiers when approaching Indians who feel threatened. The document is anonymous, and the author describes the experiences of the group of filibusters with ample information about the customs of the local Amerindians on Martinique and elsewhere during 1619–1620. The phrase quoted above is the only one in French. Further communication took place in the language(s) of the Amerindians; around 200 words and phrases are quoted in Island Carib. The name of the country in example (1) probably refers to the inhabitants, i.e. the French. In later sources as well, the term 'France' is used with reference to the people rather than the country in the pidgin. Thus, the speakers hope that their interlocutors understand that they express their peaceful intentions. In this very simple phrase, we can observe the following deviations from French, all of them changes vis-à-vis the original, or intended, French text.

(2) A. Replacement of the population by the name of the country;
    B. The copula, obligatory in French, is omitted;
    C. The adjectival predicate meaning 'good' is not inflected for number or for gender, which is obligatory in French (as 'France' has the feminine gender, one would have expected *bonne* rather than *bon*; or /bɔn/ rather than /bɔ̃/);
    D. An article is lacking, which would have been *la*, *les* or *des*, depending on the intended meaning;
    E. Probably the French speakers also assumed that pronouns would not be understood, and they used a full noun 'France' instead of a pronoun *nous* "we".

We will now survey which of these phenomena are found in contemporary quotes from the 17th century by Amerindians and Blacks. We do find the same phenomena in these three utterances by Amerindians some fifteen years later. I am emphatically not suggesting that there was a historical transmission from one manuscript or printed source to the next. I do suggest that the same strategies were used to obtain the same goals of communication. We find the same phenomena in these and other quotes from Amerindians:

(3) Tronchoy (1709): 162; Amerindian speaker, Guadeloupe 1635
    France non point fache
    France/French NEG NEG angry
    'The French are not angry' (French: 'les Français ne sont pas fâchés')

(4) Bouton (1640: 109); Amerindian speaker, Martinique ca. 1635
    Non ça [ca] bon pour France, bon pour Caraibe...
    NEG that good for France good for Carib
    'This [i.e. walking around naked] is not good for France/the French, good for the Caribs' (French: "C'est n'est pas bon pour la France/les Français, c'est bon pour les Caraïbes")

(5) Tronchoy (1709): 165; Amerindian speake, Guadeloupe 1635

Ô Jaques France mouche fache l'y matte Karaibes
O Jacques French/France very angry 3sɢ kill Carib(s)

'Jacques, the French are very angry, they have killed the Caribs'
(In Tronchoy's French: *Jacque les François sont extrêmement fâchez, ils ont tué les Sauvages*)

We find the following properties of the speech of the Frenchmen also in the speech of Amerindians. Note that I use capitals (here A–E) to refer to the same phenomenon throughout this section.

(6) A. The name of a country (France) is used for a population group (French) in (3), (4) and (5).

B. Lacking copula: Examples (3) (4) and (5) likewise display a lack of copula.

C. Agreement: The spelling of the word for 'angry' in (3) indicates that the missionaries who wrote down the phrases did not consider the adjectival predicates as reflecting a plural ('the French') or feminine meaning 'La France' , otherwise it would have been spelled something like *fachée* (feminine) or *fachés* (masculine plural). The plural *-s* is written in French, but not pronounced.

D. Articles: in all three Amerindian utterances, articles are lacking.

E. Personal pronouns: In example (5) there is probably a third person pronoun *l'y*, representing the emphatic third person pronoun *lui*. There is no evidence for pronoun avoidance in this sentence.

3.2 Saint Kitts, 1650s (Pelleprat)

French and British colonization of the Caribbean started in the mid-1620s on the island of Saint Kitts, then called Saint Christopher/Saint Christophe (Parkvall 1995, Jennings 1995). Therefore the island is very important for the settlement history of the Caribbean (Baker & Bruyn 1999), and of its linguistic landscape. Pidgins and creole languages may have diffused from there, together with populations moving to other islands that were settled later. The native population was killed off or deported after their revolt in 1638.

Pierre Pelleprat was a French Jesuit missionary who worked both in French Guiana and on the Caribbean Islands in the 1650s. His Carib language material appears sometimes pidginized, but not always. In addition, he quotes a few phrases in a reduced form of French, uttered by Blacks. He also indicates that not only the Blacks (perhaps also Amerindians) use this 'baragouin', but the missionaries use it as well in addressing non-Europeans. The following utterances by a native French speaker in "broken French" are examples provided by Pelleprat in order to show how he and other missionaries speak to other populations, notably the enslaved people. Here are his two exemplifying sentences of missionaries addressing Black people on Saint Kitts.

(7) Pelleprat (1655): 53

moy	prier Dieu,	moy	aller à l'Eglise,	moy	point
1SG:EMPH	pray God	1SG:EMPH	go to the-church	1SG:EMPH	NEG

manger
eat

'I have prayed to God, I have gone to the church, I have not eaten'
(French: 'J'ai prié à Dieu, je suis allé à l'Église, je n'ai pas mangé')

(8) Pelleprat 1655: 53

demain	moy	manger,	hier	moy	prier Dieu
tomorrow	1SG:EMPH	eat,	yesterday	1SG:EMPH	pray God

'I will eat tomorrow, yesterday I was praying/prayed to God'
(French: 'Je mangerai demain, hier je priais Dieu')

With regard to these phrases, we can make the following observations that coincide with the ones from Martinique (1619) discussed above (1–4).

D. Articles: Both inherited and newly formed articles are usually absent in pidgins. There may be a separate article in the word for 'church' in (7), but it could be part of the word as well.

E. Personal pronouns: the use of emphatic pronouns rather than the otherwise obligatory clitics of French: *moy* (modern spelling *moi*) rather than *je* 'I' . These emphatic pronouns are used in isolation and in emphatic contexts in French. This can be seen in both (7) and (8). In addition, we can add a number of new observations on deviations from French in these lines.

F. Infinitives: infinitives are used rather than inflected forms of verbs. That is the case in most pidgins. It has to be said that, in most cases in French, the spoken form of the infinitive is identical to the past participle. That the forms are infinitives, can be seen in French irregular forms (e.g. *savoir* 'to know' rather than *su* 'known') and a few generalizations of infinitival endings.

G. Prepositions: inconsistent use of prepositions, which are sometimes given and sometimes omitted. A preposition can be seen in (7), as it would be used in French. It is omitted in (8) where it would be expected with the noun *Dieu.*

H. Negation: negation is indicated in (7) with a preverbal particle *point* (modern French *pas*) rather than with a circumverbal locution *ne.... pas/point.* Thus, it differs in two ways from French at the time: only the emphatic part is preserved, and that part is preverbal in the missionary's utterance rather than postverbal as required in French.

I. There is no indication of tense in the verb; instead, time reference is optionally indicated with an adverb to indicate the future. We can see that in (8) with *demain* 'tomorrow' and *hier* 'yesterday', and (7) where there is no indication of time. This is a recurrent structure in pidgins (Parkvall & Bakker 2013, Parkvall 2017), but not typically found in creoles.

Do we have examples, or counterexamples, of these phenomena in Amerindian and African speech in the same region and period? Here are some sentences where we can observe the same phenomena.

(9) (Amerindian; Guadeloupe, 1650s)
Pere moy non plus pour le Mabohia
Father 1SG NEG more for the Maboya
'I am no longer for [=a believer in] the Maboya [Carib deity]' (French: 'Père, je ne suis plus pour le Maboya')

(10) (Amerindian; Martinique 1694; Labat 1724a: 29)
Bon jour compere, toi tenir taffia
Good day friend 2SG have tafia
'Good day, friend, do you have sugarcane liquor' (French: 'Bonjour, mon ami, avez-vous de la liqueur de canne à sucre')

(11) (Black woman; Chatillon (1984): 104; St. Kitts 1682)
Le Bon Dieu apprendre à moi cela
DET good God teach TO 1SG that
'God has taught me that' (French: 'Dieu m'a appris cela')

(12) (Blacks; Chatillon (1984): 134; St. Kitts 1682)
moi prier Dieu demain
1SGpray God tomorrow
'I want to pray to God tomorrow' (French: 'Je veux prier Dieu demain')

(13)   (Blacks; Chatillon (1984: 134); St. Kitts 1682)
　　　moi manger hier,　　　toi donner manger à moi
　　　1SG eat　　yesterday, 2SG give　　food　　to 1SG
　　　'I ate yesterday, you gave me something to eat' (French: 'J'ai mangé hier,
　　　tu m'as donné à manger')

These sentences lead to the following observations:

  B. Copula: the copula is lacking in (9);

  C. Agreement: agreement, including clitics, is lacking in the verbs in (10), (11),
      (12) and (13);

  D. Articles. We find both articles where they belong, as in (9), and lacking
      articles where they should have been present in French, as in (10);

  E. Personal pronouns: only emphatic pronouns *toi* and *moi* are used in (9)
      through (13).

  F. Infinitives: used in (9) through (13); no inflected verbs;

  G. Prepositions: two different ones (*à, pour*) used consistently in (9), (11) and
      (13);

  H. Negation: is preverbal, and it combines *non* 'no' and *plus* 'more' in (9);

  I. Time: there is no tense on the verb in (12), but time is indicated by *hier*
      'yesterday' and *demain* 'tomorrow' in (13).

Thus, again we find striking similarities between foreigner talk by the French
and non-native speech.

3.3 Guadeloupe, 1650s (Chevillard)

The longest text in French adjusted to non-native speakers by native speakers is
the text below as quoted in Chevillard (1659: 145–146). He praises the openness
and flexibility of the enslaved Black people. He says that this is ordinarily the
way they are taught,[1] and then this text follows:

(14)   a. Toy sçavoir qu'il　　　y　a　　VN DIEV
　　　　　　2SG know　that.there.is one God

---

[1]"On les enseigne pour l'ordinaire selon la matiere, en cette maniere." (Chevillard 1659: 145)

b. luy grand Capitou[2]
   3SG big   Captain

c. luy sçavoir tout faire sans   autre pour l'ayder:
   3SG know   all make without other for   help.him

d. luy donner à   tous patates:
   3SG give   TO all   potatoes (bread)

e. luy mouche   manigat pour tout faire,
   3SG much(SP) skilfull for   all do/make

f. non   point autre comme luy.
   NEG NEG other like   3SG

g. Vouloir faire maison, non point faire comme homme,
   Want   make house, NEG NEG make like   man/human

h. car   toy aller chercher hache pour bois,
   because 2SG go   search   axe   for   wood

i. puis coupper roseaux, prendre mahoc[3] &   lienes,   &   ainsi
   Then cut   reed   take   rope   and creepers and thus
   pequino faire case.
   people make house

j. Or Dieu mouche   manigat, luy dire en son esprit,
   but God much(SP) skilfull   3SG say in his spirit

k. moy vouloir monde luy preste miré monde:
   1SG want   world 3SG ready look world

l. Luy dire en son   esprit,
   3SG say in 3SG.M.POSS. spirit

m. Moy vouloir homme luy preste mire homme.
   1SG want   man   3SG ready look man

n. Enfin   luy enuoye meschant en bas   en enfer,
   Finally 3SG send   bad   IN DOWN IN hell

o. au feu auec Mabohia &   autres Sauuages
   TO fire with Devil   and other savages

p. qui n'   ont   point vouloir viure en bons Chrestiens.
   REL NEG have NEG want   live in good Christian

---

[2] *capitou* is also the word which the Amerindians used for their chiefs.
[3] Mahot is a tree of which the bark can be stripped and used as ropes to attach coverings to the roof.

q. Mais pour bon   Chrestien,
   But   all   good Christian

r. luy bon   pour mettre en son Paradis
   3sG good for   put   IN his paradise

s. où   se   trouve tout contentement,
   WHERE.REL REFL find   all   happiness

t. nul mal, nul trauail, &   nulle seruitude ou esclavage,
   zero pain zero work   and zero serfdom or slavery

u. mais une   entière joye et   parfaite liberté.
   But   INDEF entire glad and perfect freedom

'You know that there is a God. He is the big boss. He knew how to create everything without others to help him. He gives food (potatoes, bread) to everybody. He is very skillful in making everything, there is nobody else like him. If he wants to make a house, he does not make it like people, for you have to go and look for an axe for the wood, then cut reeds, take ropes and creepers and thus make a dwelling. But God is very skillful, he says in his spirit: I want the world, he is ready to look at the world. He said in his spirit. I want people ready to look at people. In the end he sends bad people down into hell, to the fire with the Maboya (Island Carib God/Devil) and the other Indians who have not wanted to live like good Christians. But for a good Christian, he is so good to put him in his paradise where one finds complete happiness. No pain, no work and no serfdom or slavery, but full pleasure and perfect freedom.'

We find the same phenomena as previously observed: the absence of a copula (B), the lack of articles (D), everywhere except in the last sentence, the use of emphatic pronouns (E), the use of infinitives (F) and the lack of tense marking (I). In addition, we find a number of non-French words that are known from other sources of Lesser Antilles baragouin (see Jansen 2012 and Bakker 2022), such as *capitou* (14b), *mouche* (14e,j), *manigat* (14e,j), *pequino* (if it means 'child') (14i), *mire* (14e, k, m), *Mabohia* (14o).

On the other hand, especially towards the end, the text becomes more French-like (14s-14u) and less pidgin-like with, for instance, adjectival agreement in (14u), a reflexive *se*, and the use of words with several derivational suffixes (*-ment, -age, -té*). In addition, we find unexpected preverbal clitics (14c), an indefinite article in (14u), "correctly" used prepositions (14f, 14h, 14j, 14l, 14n-r), and *non... point* negation in (14p), which point to more orientation towards French. Still, the overall impression is of a starkly pidginized text rather than French or Creole French.

3.4 Saint Kitts, 1682 (Mongin)

(15) Jesuit missionary Jean Mongin stayed on the island of Saint Kitts in the 1680s. In his letters that have been preserved, he writes that he spoke to the Blacks "in their own jargon". He gives the same example twice, in slightly different wording.

    a. toi de même que nègres anglais, sans   bapteme, sans   eglise,
       2SG of same as Blacks English without baptism without church
       sans   sepulture
       without burial
       'You are just like the English blacks, without baptism without church without burial'
       (Chatillon 1984: 76; St. Kitts 1682)

    b. toi seras traité de   même que nègre anglais, sans
       2SG be. FUT.2SG treat-PARTIC same as Black English without
       baptême, sans   église, sans   sépulture
       baptism without church without burial
       'You will be treated just like the English blacks, without baptism without church without burial' (Chatillon 1984: 135; St. Kitts 1682)

We can observe the following traits that deviate from French:

  B. Copula: the copula is lacking in (15a) but not in (15b);

  C. Agreement: apparent agreement is present in *seras* and *traité* in (15b) but both verbs are omitted in (15a); a non-infinitive form like *seras* is normally not used in pidgins;

  D. Articles. We find no articles where they would be expected, before *nègres/nègre* in (15).

  E. Personal pronouns: only emphatic pronoun *toi* is used in (15).

  F. Infinitives: not used in (15). There is one exception, in (15b) where two inflected (non-infinitival) verbs are found: *seras* and *traité*, the latter written as a past participle.

  G. Prepositions: *sans* is used consistently in (15), perhaps also *que* in (15a)

I. Tense marking as in pidgins: there is no tense on the verb, but time is indicated by *hier* 'yesterday' and *demain* 'tomorrow'.

The missionary Mongin also reports on a conversation he had with a Black Christian woman who used self-flegallation as an expression of her faith. Mongin spoke to her as follows:

(16)   (Chatillon 1984: 104; St. Kitts 1682)
       Mais qui celui la   apprendre à toi cela?
       But who the.one there teach   TO 2sg that
       'But who is the one who taught you that?' (French: 'Mais qui est celui qui vous a appris cela?')

Here again we can observe the use of infinitives (F) and emphatic pronouns (E), and the presence of a preposition *à* (G).

4 Linguistic observations

When we compare the modified forms of French used by French speakers and the quotes in the form of approximations of French from the mouth of non-French speakers, we can observe close parallels. Eight out of nine of the deviations from standard French are found in the speech of Amerindians and/or Africans as well as Europeans. This is a clear indication that the speech of the three groups in interethnic contacts was quite similar, and that mutual adjustments to each other's speech took place. In the next sections, we will consider metalinguistic observations, and these appear to corroborate the linguistic materials. But first let me present some observations on shared lexicon.

The reductions we have observed (elimination of verbal morphology, elimination of the distinction between clitics and emphatic pronouns, dropping of selected prepositions) as well as the uniform solutions in the form of the use of emphatic personal pronouns and infinitives point to a common form of speech of the two groups. However, if these were "universal" processes of simplification, it would still not prove that a common language had developed in the interaction between Indians, Blacks and Europeans. We would also need unexpected lexical items shared across ethnic boundaries and grammatical idiosyncrasies. These are indeed present in the material.

There are for instance idiosyncrasies like the Spanish word *mucho* 'much' and the Amerindian or dialectal French word *manigat* which are found in simplified French utterances by Indigenous people, Blacks and Europeans alike. Also the

Amerindian word *Maboya* (see Bakker 2022) is used by Blacks and Indians as well as the French. Obviously, these are quoted by Europeans, which suggests that they used them as well, and that they were perhaps part of the stereotype of non-native French. We know that these terms became part of the "French of the Islands" (Jansen 2012). Thus, the presence of shared lexicon corroborates that reduced French was shared by French, Amerindians and Blacks.

5 Metalinguistic observations: reduced French

As we have seen above, native speakers of French used reduced forms of French in their communication with the Indigenous people and people of African descent. Thus, the Europeans played an obvious role in the reduction, and they would have addressed Blacks and Indians in the same way. Two kinds of motivations for these adjustments are given by the missionaries: in that way, they are better understood (especially important when spreading God's word), and on the other hand, the French speakers say that they adjust themselves to the way that the Amerindians and Black people speak. It thus seems to be a case of mutual adjustment. This is confirmed in a number of contemporary metalinguistic comments. Pelleprat made the following metalinguistic remarks on the language, clearly indicating that the missionaries adjust to the speech of accommodating speakers:

> We accommodate ourselves nevertheless to the way they [the Black slaves] speak, which is normally by means of the infinitive of the verb. Like, for example, *me pray God, me go to church, me no eat* if they wish to say 'I have prayed to God', 'I have gone to the church', 'I have not eaten'. And adding a word that indicates the time to come, or the past, they say 'tomorrow me eat', yesterday me pray God', which means I will eat tomorrow, yesterday I prayed to God (Pelleprat 1655: 53; my emphasis and translation).[4]

Mongin remarked almost the same:

> The Blacks have learned within a short time a certain *French jargon that the missionaries know and which they use to instruct*, which is through the

---

[4] "Nous nous accommodons cependant à leur façon [des esclaves noirs] de parler, qui est ordinairement par l'infinitif du verbe; comme par exemple, *moy prier Dieu, moy aller à l'Eglise, moy point manger*, pour dire *i'ay prié Dieu, ie suis allé à l'Eglise, ie n'ay point mangé*; Et y adioustant vn mot qui marque le temps à venir, ou le passé, ils disent *demain moy manger, hier moy prier Dieu*, & cela signifie le mangeray demain, hier ie priay Dieu" (Pelleprat 1655: 53).

infinitive of the verb, without ever conjugating it, by adding a few words which indicate the time and the person about whom we are speaking. For example, if they want to say: "I want to pray to God tomorrow", they will say "me pray God tomorrow", "me eat yesterday", "You give food to me", and like this everywhere. This jargon is very easy to teach to the Blacks and to the missionaries also to instruct them, and thus they give it to get an understanding for all things" (my translation and emphasis; Mongin in Chatillon 1984: 134–135).[5]

The remarks that Pelleprat and Mongin make on the grammar (use of infinitives, no conjugation, no person marking, no tense except through adverbs) fit the data, and these concur with observations on pidgins in general (Parkvall 2017, 2020).

As we saw, the differences between the accommodated speech as used by Europeans, Indigenous people and Blacks were minimal. In the linguistic material, the same modifications recur across the different groups. The fact that they were all written down by French speakers may have contributed to the homogeneity, but these are all the data that are available.

The metalinguistic remarks by the missionaries confirm that they perceived the forms of speech used by all three groups to be the same. Du Tertre (1667: II, 510) confirmed that he considered it the same language, for instance:

(...) most of the young Blacks don't know any language other than the French language, and (...) they understand nothing of the native language of their parents; except for only *the pidgin [baragoüin], which they use on the Islands, and which we also use with the Indians*, which is a jargon composed of French, Spanish, English, and Dutch words.[6] (Du Tertre 1667: II, 510; my emphasis and translation).[7]

---

[5]"Les nègres ont appris en peu de temps un certain jargon français que les missionnaires savent et avec lequel ils les instruisent, qui est par l'infititif [SIC] du verbe, sans jamais le conjuguer, en y ajoutant quelques mots qui font connaître le temps et la personne de qui l'on parle. Par exemple s'ils veulent dire: Je veux prier Dieu demain, ils diront moi prier Dieu demain, moi manger hier, toi donner manger à moi, et ainsi en toutes choses. Ce jargon est fort aisé à apprendre aux nègres et aux missionnaires aussi pour les instruire, et ainsi ils le donnent à entendre pour toutes choses."

[6]"De là vient que la pluspart des petits Négres ne sçavent point d'autre langue que la langue Françoise, & qu'ils n'entendent rien à la langue naturelle de leurs parens; excepté seulement le baragoüin, dont ils usent commuuément [sic] dans les Isles, & don't nous nous servons aussi avec les Sauvages, qui est un jargon composé de mots François, Espagnols, Anglois, & Holandois".

[7]Observations on the nature of such languages by local observers are rarely accurate. Also in this case the representation of the lexical sources of the pidgin should be taken with a grain of salt. There is, however, a high degree of correspondence between the observers.

Here Du Tertre not only observes that the parents of Black children use pidgin, and the missionaries use it with the Amerindians, and that they fall with the range of the same pidginized variety of French, he also adds, just like Pelleprat and Mongin, that the French use it themselves as well in communication with the Indians. He further makes remarks about the lexical composition of the pidgin, and that appears generally correct based on the available documentation (Bakker 2022), except that the material does not contain obvious words from English at all. His words on the pidgin and nativization sound surprisingly Bickertonian. Derek Bickerton (1981, 1984) took the influence of children to be the main factor in the appearance of a set of linguistic features he associated with an innate "bioprogram". Observers mention that young Black people only understand and speak the *baragouin* of the islands, which suggests incipient creolization. Labat (1724a: 98) also observed that the Bozals (slaves born in Africa, and hence second language learners) spoke differently than the locally-born, when he mentions "new Negroes who spoke only a corrupt language, which I hardly understood, but to which, however, one is soon accustomed".[8]

The beginning shift to French pidgin/creole by that time is confirmed by a comment through an earwitness from Québec, who wrote in 1670: "If you go to Martinique, you will have a great advantage that we have not had here [in Québec], in that one has no other language to study than the baragouin of the Blacks that you know as soon as you have heard it spoken" (my translation; de L'Incarnation 1681: 196).[9] Another quote suggests that not only Europeans provided French, or French pidgin, input to the congregation, but also that Black people transmitted it to other Blacks: "if need be, *we use Blacks who understand French to teach* those of their nation the elements of our religion" (Pelleprat 1655: 53; also in Jennings 1995: 71; my translation and emphasis). [10] This is confirmed by another quote, following immediately the quote on simplified French (Pelleprat 1655: 54–55): "We [missionaries] make them [Blacks] understand by this way of speaking what they are taught: And that is the method we keep in the initial stages of their instruction."[11] Thus, the French pidgin seems to have been an important means of instruction. The missionaries were obviously aware that they

---

[8] "des Negres nouveaux qui ne parloient qu'un langage corrompu, que je n'entendois presque point, auquel cependant on est bien-tôt accoûtumé".

[9] "Si vous allez à la Martinique, ce vous sera un grand avantage que nous n'avons pas eu ici, de n'avoir point d'autre langue à étudier que le baragouin des Negres que l'on sçait dés qu'on la entendu parler."

[10] "Dans la nécessité nous nous servons des Nègres qui entendent le Français pour enseigner à ceux de leur nation les points de notre créance."

[11] "On leur fait comprendre par cette maniere de parler ce qu'on leur enseigne: Et c'est la methode que nous gardons au commencement de leurs instructions" (Pelleprat 1655: 54–55).

did not speak French as they would speak it with fellow Frenchmen, as is clear from this observation (Labat 1724b: 87): "They know almost all, especially those of Dominica, enough bad French to make themselves understood, and to understand what they are told."[12] The missionaries were clearly aware of the practical advantages of the pidgin, which they generally had a high opinion of, as witnessed in this remark: "they never learn French well, and have only a pidgin, the most pleasant and natural of the world"[13] (Labat 1724b: 57), referring to older Blacks born in Africa.

It is clear that the speech form that had developed was a common creation of French speakers from Europe and the Africans. The simplified speech was developed with the purpose of making communication easier, i.e. for practical reasons.

6 Conclusions

The observed similarities between the three types of reduced and simplified languages (FT and BL non-native approximations and pidgins), suggest strongly that pidgins emerge through mutual accommodations by native speakers and non-native speakers, as is the case with French in the Lesser Antilles. Both the linguistic and metalinguistic documentation point in that direction. Indirect evidence from other parts of the world, especially contact situations involving Russian (Fedorova 2006), Arabic (Avram 2018), Mediterranean Romance (Schuchardt 1909) and Portuguese (Clements 1992), corroborate the genesis of pidgins involving reciprocal adjustments. Nothing in the documentation appears compatible with Mufwene's claims on interpreters, trade and the assumed late development of pidgins. It also shows that there is documentation of pidgins preceding creoles in the Caribbean, the possibility of which was also excluded by Mufwene's allegedly historical approach (e.g. 2015), even though Baker (2001) and many others showed the links between pidgin and creole properties. In a more historical and data-oriented approach, Avram (2017) observed around a dozen structural similarities between Arabic FT and Gulf Pidgin Arabic. Almost all of these are found in most pidgins in general, and most of them also in the Lesser Antilles materials. Many of them are also common in creoles, as summarized in Tables 1 and 2.

---

[12] Ils sçavent presque tous, particulierement ceux de la Dominique, assez de mauvais François pour se faire entendre, & pour comprendre ce qu'on leur dit. (Labat 1724b: 87)

[13] "Lorsqu'ils viennent un peu âgez dans le Païs, ils n'apprennent jamais bien le François, & n'ont qu'un baragouin le plus plaisant & le plus naturel du monde."

Table 1: Structural comparisons between Arabic pidgins, pidgins in general and creoles in general. In this table, Avram's number refer to paragraph numbers (Avram 2017), Parkvall's numbers to section numbers, the Lesser Antilles letters to feature numbers in this paper and APiCS numbers to feature numbers.

Avram (2017) on Arabic pidgins and FT	Parkvall (2017) on pidgins general	Lesser Antilles data	Creoles in general (APiCS)
Loss of dual, numeral 'two' instead (3.1). Loss of plural markers, use of 'all' instead (3.2)	No plural markers (10), no number marking	No plural markers [C]	Innovated and optional plural marking (22, 25)
Loss of definite article, no alternative (3.3)	No definite or indefinite articles (5)	No articles [D]	Innovated definite articles derived from demonstrative (28)
Loss of gender in adjectives and demonstratives, masculine form instead (3.4)	No gender distinctions at all (6, 7) and reduced set of demonstratives	No gender [C], no sufficient data on demonstratives	No gender anywhere, except rarely in third person pronouns (13, 40)
Loss of pronominal suffixes, use of independent pronouns instead (3.5, 3.6)	Personal pronouns instead of verbal inflection (section 2)	Emphatic pronouns [E]	Personal pronouns derived from emphatic pronouns in lexifier (13, 59)
Loss of verbal inflection, use of invariant verb forms instead (3.7)	Not mentioned, but almost universal in pidgins (Parkvall & Bakker 2013)	Invariant verb forms [F]	Invariant verb forms (49, 50, 51, etc.)

59

Peter Bakker

Table 2: Structural comparisons between Arabic pidgins, pidgins in general and creoles in general, cont. In this table, Avram's number refer to paragraph numbers (Avram 2017), Parkvall's numbers to section numbers, the Lesser Antilles letters to feature numbers in this paper and APiCS numbers to feature numbers.

Avram (2017) on Arabic pidgins and FT	Parkvall (2017) on pidgins general	Lesser Antilles data	Creoles in general (APiCS)
Loss of verbal inflection, use of 'make' light verb instead (3.8)	Light verb 'to make, do' used in some pidgins, but not common (11)	Not attested	Close to nonexistent in creoles. (not in APiCS)
Loss of verbal inflection, use of time adverbs to indicate time (3.9)	Adverbs rather than inflection to indicate time (3)	Adverbs to indicate time (optional) [I]	Preverbal tense marker (43, 49, 50)
Loss of verbal inflection, use of a frequent copula-like form instead (3.10)	Usually no copulas, but regularly a verbal marker (8)	No copula [B]	Not a single form, but a handful, with distinct tense-mood-aspect meanings (49, 50, 51, etc.)
Loss of inflection, use of a multi-purpose verbal marker instead (3.11)	Some pidgins have a multi-purpose verbal marker, but most have not	No multi-purpose verbal marker attested	Not a single form, but a handful, with distinct tense-mood-aspect meanings (49, 50, 51, etc.)
Loss of most preposition, use of one multi-purpose preposition instead (3.12, 3.13)	Only few prepositions, one frequently used with broad meaning (4)	Several prepositions [G]	Small set of prepositions (not included; see 4)
Constituent order partly lost, innovation of orders (3.14)	Word order often not like lexifier	Word order not always as in French (negation) [H]	Word order almost always SVO (1)

The fact that many of the structural properties observed in pidgins recur in creoles should be taken as a strong indication that the same processes have played a role in creolization, via the social and structural expansion of pidgins into pidgincreoles and creoles.

We have seen above that the simplified French as used by native speakers is basically indistinguishable from the simplified French as spoken by non-native speakers. We have to keep in mind that French speakers wrote down all of the quotes. This simplified French has the structural characteristics of a pidgin.

This rare case study corroborates Winford's view on the role of foreigner talk in pidginization and creolization Winford (2003: 279, 287, 290, 298). He remarks that "it is widely claimed that the primary input to pidgins came from foreigner talk versions of the major source or lexifier language. Thus, it might be argued that this deliberately reduced and simplified model was the source of many characteristic pidgin features such as absence of morphology and syntactic complexity" (Winford 2003: 279). As for the two types of speech, he suggested that it "seems reasonable to assume that they are all subject to the same universal principles" (Winford 2003: 287). Winford refers to the same principles of simplification in foreigner talk and pidginization. The empirical material from the French Caribbean indicates that he is right.

Acknowledgements

The comments by the editors and the anonymous referees have contributed to a significant improvement of this paper and I am grateful for that.

Abbreviations

TMA	Tense Mood Aspect	SG	Singular
SVO	Subject Verb Object	DET	Determiner

References

Avram, Andrei A. 2017. Superdiversity in the gulf: Gulf Pidgin Arabic and Arabic foreigner talk. *Philologica Jassyensia* 13.2. 175–190.

Avram, Andrei A. 2018. On the relationship between Arabic foreigner talk and Pidgin Arabic. In Stefano Manfredi & Mauro Tosco (eds.), *Arabic in contact*, 251–274. Amsterdam & Philadelphia: John Benjamins.

Baker, Philip. 1990. Off target? *Journal of Pidgin and Creole Languages* 5(1). 107–119.

Baker, Philip. 1995. Motivation in creole genesis. In Philip Baker (ed.), *From contact to Creole and beyond*, 3–15. London: University of Westminster Press.

Baker, Philip. 2001. No creolisation without prior pidginisation. *Te Reo* 44. 31–50.

Baker, Philip & Adrienne Bruyn (eds.). 1999. *St. Kitts and the Atlantic Creoles: The Texts of Samuel Augustus Matthews in perspective*. London: Battlebridge.

Bakker, Peter. 2003. Pidgin inflectional morphology and its implications for creole morphology. In Geert Booij & Jaap van Marle (eds.), *Yearbook of morphology*, 3–33. Dordrecht: Kluwer.

Bakker, Peter. 2008. Pidgins versus Creoles and pidgincreoles. In Silvia Kouwenberg & John Singler (eds.), *Handbook of Pidgin and Creole studies*, 130–157. Oxford: Wiley-Blackwell.

Bakker, Peter. 2022. The crib of creoles. Evidence for pidgins evolving into creoles in the French Caribbean. Ms.

Bickerton, Derek. 1981. *Roots of language*. Reprinted 2016, Language Science Press. Ann Arbor, MI: Karoma.

Bickerton, Derek. 1984. The language bioprogram hypothesis. *The Behavioral and Brain Sciences* 7(2). 173–188. DOI: 10.1017/S0140525X00044149.

Bloomfield, Leonard. 1933. *Language*. New York: Henry Holt & Co.

Bouton, Jacques. 1640. *Relation de l'establissement des français depuis l'an de 1635 en l'Isle de martinique*. Paris: Cramoisy.

Chatillon, M. 1984. L'évangélisation des esclaves au XVIIe siècle — lettres du R. P Jean Mongin. *Bulletin de la Société d'Histoire de la Guadeloupe* 61–62. 3–136.

Chevillard, R. P. André. 1659. *Les desseins de son eminence de Richelieu pour l'Amérique*. Rennes: Jean Durand.

Clements, J. Clancy. 1992. Foreigner talk and the origins of Pidgin Portuguese. *Journal of Pidgin and Creole Languages* 7(1). 75–92.

Coelho, Adolpho F. 1881. *Os dialectos romanicos ou neo-latinos na África, Ásia e América (Boletim do sociedade de geographia de Lisboa 2 ser. N°. 3)*. Lisbon: Casa da Socieade de Geografia.

de L'Incarnation, Marie. 1681. *Lettre CXXVI, à la superieure des Ursulines de Saint Denys en France*. A la mère de Sainte Catherine. In: Lettres de la Vénérable Mère Marie de l'Incarnation: première supérieure des Ursulines de la Nouvelle France. Paris: Louis Billaine.

Dela Rosa, John Paul O. & Diana C. Arguelles. 2016. Do modification and interaction work? - a critical review of literature on the role of foreigner talk in second language acquisition. *Journal on English Language Teaching* 6(3). 46–60.

Du Tertre, Jean-Baptiste. 1667. *Histoire générale des Antilles habitées par les François. Tome II. Contenant l'histoire naturelle, enrichy de cartes & de figures. Par le R.P. dv Tertre, de l'ordre des FF. Prescheurs, de la congregation de S. Louis, missionnaire apostolique dans les Antilles.* Paris: Thomas Iolly.

Fedorova, Kapitolina. 2006. Russian foreigner talk: Stereotype and reality. In Dieter Stern & Christian Voss (eds.), *Marginal linguistic identities. Studies in Slavic contact and borderland varieties*, 177–189. Wiesbaden: Harrassowitz Verlag.

Ferguson, Charles A. 1971. Absence of copula and the notion of simplicity: A study of normal speech, baby talk, foreigner talk and Pidgins. In Dell Hymes (ed.), *Pidginization and creolization of languages*, 141–150. Cambridge: Cambridge University Press.

Ferguson, Charles A. & Charles E. DeBose. 1977. Simplified registers, broken language, and pidginization. In Albert Valdman (ed.), *Pidgin and Creole Linguistics*, 99–128. Bloomington,IN: Indiana University Press.

Goodman, Morris F. 1964. *A comparative study of Creole French dialects*. The Hague: Mouton.

Harding, Edith. 1984. Foreigner talk: A conversational-analysis approach. In Mark Sebba & Loreto Todd (eds.), *Papers from the York Creole Conference, September 24-27, 1983:York Papers in Linguistics 11*, 141–152. Heslington: University of York.

Hazaël-Massieux, Guy. 1996. *Les créoles. Problèmes de genèse et de description*. Aix-en Provence: Publications de l'Université de Provence.

Hazaël-Massieux, Marie-Christine. 2008. *Textes anciens en créole français de la Caraïbe. Histoire et analyse.* Paris: Éditions Publibook Université.

Hinnenkamp, Volker. 1984. Eye-witnessing pidginization? Structural and sociolinguistic aspects of German and Turkish foreigner talk. In Mark Sebba & Loreto Todd (eds.), *Papers from the York Creole Conference, September 24-27, 1983: York Papers in Linguistics 11*, 153–166. Heslington: University of York.

Jansen, Silke. 2012. Les éléments amérindiens dans le "langage des îles" d'après le dictionnaire Caraïbe-François (1665) de Raymond Breton. In Christine Felbeck, Claudia Hammerschmidt, Andre Klump & Johannes Kramer (eds.), *Americana romana in colloquio Berolinensi: Beiträge zur transversalen sektion II des XXXII. Romanistentages (25.-28.09.2011)*, 77–112. Frankfurt a.M: Peter Lang.

Jennings, William. 1995. Saint-Christophe: Site of the first French Creole. In Philip Baker (ed.), *From Contact to Creole and Beyond*, 63–80. London: Battlebridge.

Jennings, William. 1998. Saint-Christophe: The origin of French Antillean Creoles. In Jan Tent & France Mugler (eds.), *SICOL 2nd International Conference on Oceanic Linguistics : Language Contact*, vol. 1, 59–68. Canberra: Pacific Linguistics, Research School of Pacific & Asian Studies, Australian National University.

Jespersen, Otto. 1922. *Language: Its nature, development and origin.* London: Allen & Unwin. New York: Henry Holt & Co.

Labat, Jean-Baptiste. 1724a. *Nouveau voyage aux isles de l'amérique (...), contenant l'histoire naturelle de ces pays, l'origine, les moeurs, la religion et le gouvernement des habitans anciens et modernes, les guerres et les événemens singuliers qui y sont arrivez... Le commerce et les manufactures qui y sont établies... Ouvrage enrichi de plus de cent cartes, plans et figures en taille-douce.* Ch. J. B. Delespine (ed.), vol. 1. Paris: P. Husson.

Labat, Jean-Baptiste. 1724b. *Nouveau voyage aux isles de l'amérique (...), contenant l'histoire naturelle de ces pays, l'origine, les moeurs, la religion et le gouvernement des habitans anciens et modernes, les guerres et les événemens singuliers qui y sont arrivez... Le commerce et les manufactures qui y sont établies... Ouvrage enrichi de plus de cent cartes, plans et figures en taille-douce.* P. Husson, T. Johnson, P. Gosse, J. Van Duren, R. Alberts & C. Le Vier (eds.), vol. 2. La Haye: P. Husson.

Meisel, Jürgen M. 1975. Ausländerdeutsch und Deutsch ausländischer Arbeiter. *Zur möglichen Entstehung eines Pidgin in der BRD. Zeitschrift für Literaturwissenschaft und Linguistik* 5.18. 9–53.

Meisel, Jürgen M. 1977. Linguistic simplification: A study of immigrant workers' speech and foreigner talk. In S. P. Corder & E. Roulet (eds.), *The notions of simplification interlanguages and pidgins in their relation to second language pedagogy,* 88–113. Geneva: Droz.

Mufwene, Salikoko S. 2015. Pidgin and Creole languages. In James Wright (ed.), *International encyclopedia of social and behavioral sciences,* 2nd edn. Oxford: Elsevier.

Mufwene, Salikoko S. 2020. Creoles and pidgins - why the latter are not the ancestors of the former. In Evangelia Adamou & Yaron Matras (eds.), *The Routledge handbook of language contact,* 300–324. Houndsmill UK/New York: Palgrave.

Naro, Anthony J. 1978. A study on the origins of pidginization. *Language* 54(2). 314–349.

Parkvall, Mikael. 1995. The role of St. Kitts in a new scenario of French Creole genesis. In Philip. Baker (ed.), *From contact to creole and beyond,* 41–62. London: Battlebridge.

Parkvall, Mikael. 2017. Pidgin languages. In *Oxford research encyclopedia of linguistics.* Oxford: Oxford Univeristy Press. DOI: 10 . 1093 / acrefore / 9780199384655.013.58.

Parkvall, Mikael. 2020. Pidgins. In Anthony Grant (ed.), *The Oxford Handbook of Language Contact*, 261–281. Oxford: Oxford University Press.

Parkvall, Mikael & Peter Bakker. 2013. *Pidgins*. Berlin: Mouton de Gruyter. 15–64.

Pelleprat, Pierre. 1655. *Relations des missions des P. P. de la Compagnie de Jésus dans les isles et dans la terme firme de l'Amérique méridionale*. Paris: S. & G. Cramoisy.

Prudent, Lambert Félix. 1999. *(2)*. Des baragouins à la langue antillaise. Analyse historique et sociolinguistique du discours sur le créole. Paris: L'Harmattan.

Schuchardt, Hugo. 1888. *Auf Anlass des Volapüks*. Berlin: Oppenheim.

Schuchardt, Hugo. 1909. Die Lingua Franca. *Zeitschrift für romanische Philologie* 33. English translation by Glenn Gilbert in *Pidgin and Creole Languages. Selected Essays by Hugo Schuchardt*. Cambridge: Cambridge University Press. 65--88, 441–61.

Siegel, Jeff. 2008. *The emergence of pidgin and creole languages*. Oxford: Oxford University Press.

Stein, Peter. 2017. *Kreolisch und französisch*. 2nd edn. Berlin: De Gruyter.

Thibault, André. 2018. Témoignages métalinguistiques et histoire du français et du créole dans les Antilles. In Laurence Arrighi & Karine Gauvin (eds.), *Les cas du Père Labat et de Pierre Dessalles. Regards croisés sur les français d'ici* (Collection Les voies du français (PUL)), 149–171. Québec: Presses de l'Université Laval.

Thomason, Sarah Grey. 2001. *Language contact. An introduction*. Edinburgh: University of Edinburgh Press.

Tronchoy, Gautier du. 1709. *Journal de la campagne des Isles de l'Amérique, qu'à fait Monsieur D***. La prise, possession de l'isle Saint Christophe... (...) par G. D. T (...)*. [published anonymously]. Troyes: Jacques Le Febvre.

Velupillai, Viveka. 2015. *Pidgins, Creoles and mixed languages. An introduction* (Creole Language Library 12). Amsterdam: John Benjamins.

Versteegh, Kees. 2014. Pidgin verbs: Imperatives or infinitives? In Anders Holmberg Isabelle Buchstaller & Mohammad Almoaily (eds.), *Pidgins and creoles beyond Africa-Europe encounters*, 141–169. Amsterdam & Philadelphia: John Benjamins.

Whinnom, Keith. 1971. Linguistic hybridization and the 'special case' of pidgins and creoles. In Dell Hymes (ed.), *Pidginization and creolization of languages*, 91–115. Cambridge: Cambridge University Press.

Winford, Donald. 2003. *An introduction to contact linguistics*. London: Wiley-Blackwell.

Chapter 3

African American language and life in the antebellum North: Philadelphia's Mother Bethel Church

John Victor Singler

New York University

Philadelphia was the most important city for African Americans in the Early Republic. In the decades up to the 1830's, neighborhoods emerged with a concentration of African American churches and other public institutions, yet remained majority-white with everyday interracial interaction. The dominant African American institution in Philadelphia was Bethel Church, the mother church of the African Methodist Episcopal Church. Linguistic data from trials in the years 1822 to 1831 in Bethel's *Minutes and Trial Book* (MTB), while limited in domain and size, suggests – tentatively – that the vernacular of church members was for the most part like the vernacular of other Philadelphians. Bethel Church's leader, Bishop Richard Allen, spearheaded the campaign in 1824–1825 for African American emigration from Philadelphia to Samaná now in the Dominican Republic. The provenance of those who went to Samaná establish a northern basis for Samaná English and hence not directly pertinent to AAVE diachrony.

1 Introduction

Prior to the Great Migration of the twentieth century, the African American population of the US lived overwhelmingly in the South (with the South defined as those states where chattel slavery was legal at the beginning of the American Civil War). In every census from 1790 through 1890, 91–95% of all African Americans lived in (ex-)slave states. Consequently, there is a tendency – among linguists and others – to overlook African Americans in the North in earlier eras of

John Victor Singler. 2022. African American language and life in the antebellum North: Philadelphia's Mother Bethel Church. In Bettina Migge & Shelome Gooden (eds.), *Social and structural aspects of language contact and change*, 67–101. Berlin: Language Science Press. DOI: 10.5281/zenodo.6979331

American history. The reality is that, starting in the seventeenth century, slavery had been part of all the American colonies, particularly those on the Atlantic seaboard. Throughout the colonial era, in addition to southern ports like Charleston, slave ships brought their human cargo to Boston; Newport, Rhode Island; and Perth Amboy, New Jersey.[1] Then, in the decades after the American Revolution, the northern states abolished slavery. "In 1790 the black population in New England and the Middle Atlantic [New York, New Jersey, and Pennsylvania] was largely enslaved, with approximately 40,000 enslaved people versus 27,000 free blacks. By 1830 the black population of these areas had become overwhelmingly free, with 122,000 free blacks versus 3,000 slaves (mostly in New Jersey)" (Newman 2008a: 5).

The language and life of African Americans in the North in the early years of American independence merit examination. The focal point of the present study is Philadelphia's Bethel Church, founded in 1794 and then taking on greater significance in 1816 when it became the mother church of the first independent African American religious denomination. Section 2 presents information regarding free African Americans in the Early Republic, Philadelphia's African American population, and the place of Bethel Church in Philadelphia life. The remainder of the study then explores three aspects of Bethel's history, each with linguistic consequences:

- An early *Minutes and Trial Book* from Bethel survives. Section 3 examines the data to be found therein, principally in the transcripts of 33 trials conducted by elders in the years from 1822 to 1831. Part of the discussion in section 3 concerns the limitations of using written data. Beyond those limitations, the amount of data is admittedly somewhat limited. These restrictions notwithstanding, the transcripts are instructive in what they have to say about the language of African Americans in Philadelphia at that time.

- There is much more information about the social setting of free African American society in the Early Republic than we may have assumed. In fact, the importance of Philadelphia in the history of African American cultural institutions, Bethel Church above all others has given rise to extensive analysis by historians of the Cedar neighborhood, the area containing – and grounded by – Bethel. Section 4 draws on historians' extensive

---

[1]For a forty-year period in the mid-eighteenth century, New York and Pennsylvania imposed a tariff on the delivery of enslaved people from Africa and the West Indies to their ports, and New Jersey did not. Thus, Perth Amboy – 50 km south of New York – became the port of entry for the enslaved for the region.

scholarship to present the neighborhood's social and economic character. While it was home to Philadelphia's African American institutions and routinely identified as an African American neighborhood, its population was majority-white. The level of interaction among different ethnoracial groups "points out the pitfalls inherent in generalizing twentieth-century interpretations to nineteenth century situations" (Lapsansky 1975: 277).

- Bethel Church was the primary launching point for African American immigration to Samaná in what is today the Dominican Republic. The English of Samaná has been studied by DeBose 1983, Hannah 1997, and Shana Poplack and her colleagues, beginning with Poplack & Sankoff 1987. For Poplack and her colleagues, the relative conservatism of the language of Samaná has played a central role in their argument for divergence, i.e. that the African American Vernacular English (AAVE) of the early nineteenth century was much more like white vernacular Englishes than is true of AAVE today. In section 5, I look at the information presented throughout this study as well as recent historical scholarship pertaining to Samaná to assess the applicability of Samaná English to the divergence hypothesis.

2 Background

2.1 Cities as gathering points for free African Americans in the Early Republic

The United States in the late eighteenth and early nineteenth century was overwhelmingly rural. In the 1820 census, only eleven cities had a population of more than 10,000. While the country as a whole was rural, free African Americans tended to live in cities, as Table 1 shows. The three largest American cities – New York, Philadelphia, and Baltimore – all had free African American populations of 10,000 or more.

2.2 The provenance of Philadelphia's African American population in the early nineteenth century

While the members of Bethel Church are the central focus of the present study, there is very little information about individual members of the church.[2] Consequently, I turn to what is known of the provenance of African Americans in

---

[2]Exceptionally, there is a considerable amount of information about the Reverend Richard Allen, the founder of Bethel Church, and some information about Joseph Cox, the secretary of the church's board. Both of these men are discussed below.

Table 1: US cities with the largest free African American population, 1820 census. Source: For Philadelphia, Nash (1988: 137); for Baltimore and New York, Curry (1986: 247); for states, *Census of 1820*. Comments: "New York" combines the cities of New York and Brooklyn. For Philadelphia Nash includes the "adjacent urbanized areas of Northern Liberties, Southwark, Moyamensing, and ... Spring Garden and Kensington," (137) all of which were later absorbed into Philadelphia by the 1854 Act of Consolidation.

	Afr. Am. (city)			
	Free	Total	City total	Free (city) as pct. of state
Philadelphia	**12,110**	12,110	c. 108,809	40%
New York	**11,065**	11,773	134,893	38%
Baltimore	**10,326**	14,683	62,738	26%

Philadelphia more generally. Even here, the data is limited. Nash (1988) draws on two sources pertaining to Black mariners that required them to state their place of birth. He then uses the tabulation to get a rough idea of where Philadelphia's African American men as a whole had been born. Nash's chart has appeared in previous work (Singler 1998, Poplack & Tagliamonte 2001: 13, Singler 2007b: 315) and is presented below in the adapted form in which it occurred in those works.[3]

As Nash observes:

> If those who pursued a maritime calling were roughly representative of Philadelphia's free black male population in this period, only about one-twelfth of the city's black residents had been born there. Philadelphia, then, was a city of refuge, not the place of birth of most of its free black populace. Roughly two-thirds of them came from within one hundred miles of Philadelphia (136–137, quoted in Singler 1998, 2007b: 314).

The hundred-mile radius includes New York City, all of New Jersey and Delaware, and Baltimore. Delaware was a slave state, but Nash observes:

> In Delaware, ... the declining viability of slavery, especially in corn-growing New Castle and Kent counties [the two more northerly of Delaware's three counties, hence closer to Philadelphia], together with strong Quaker and Methodist lobbying against slaveholding, reduced the slave population from 8,887 to 4,177 between 1790 and 1810 (137–138).

---

[3]Nash's complete table presents tabulations for 1803, 1811, and 1821. The distribution is comparable in each. The 1821 tabulation has the most relevance to the present discussion.

Table 2: Birthplaces of Black Philadelphia mariners, 1821 (Source: Nash 1988: 136)

	n	%
New England	18	6.3
New York and New Jersey	56	19.7
Philadelphia	24	8.5
The rest of Pennsylvania	55	19.4
Delaware and Maryland	87	30.6
Virginia and North Carolina	26	9.2
Lower South	17	6.0
Africa	1	0.4
	284	

In the 1820 census, African Americans comprised 24% of Delaware's total population. The enslaved population of Delaware was but a quarter of this, thus only 6% of the state's entire population. Further, the number of enslaved people on a given farm tended to be small.

With regard to Maryland and Virginia, Cassidy observes: "In Virginia and Maryland ... slaves were never as separate from the work and general life of their owners as in the South. Plantations or households were much smaller, and the numerical proportion of Blacks to Whites was never as high" (1986, 35, quoted in Singler 2015: 110). Within Maryland, the rural area closest to Philadelphia practiced diversified agriculture, as landholders did not find large plantations with a large enslaved work force to be economically viable. The state did have large tobacco plantations, but they were located in the southern counties, the area furthest from Philadelphia.

People who were formerly enslaved in Delaware, Maryland, or Virginia had still been enslaved; I do not mean to suggest otherwise. Still, if Nash's table is seen as reasonably representative of the provenance of the African American population of Philadelphia, Nash's calculation regarding the 100-mile radius suggests that at the very least two-thirds of those coming from Delaware and Maryland came either from Baltimore or from an area of small-scale agriculture in Delaware and the northeastern part of Maryland (including the northern part of the Eastern Shore).

In sum, the African American population of Philadelphia in the early nineteenth century consisted primarily of people who had moved there from elsewhere, with half of them coming from elsewhere in Pennsylvania or from states to its north and east. Of the other half, most came from nearby areas in Delaware and Maryland, not from large plantations.

2.3 Philadelphia and Mother Bethel Church

The unofficial capital of free African American society at the time of the American Revolution and for decades thereafter was Philadelphia. African Americans in Philadelphia took the lead in establishing what Newman designates the "communal institutions that guided African Americans from slavery to freedom" (2008b: 5).

> Newly freed blacks entered a largely hostile world. Antislavery groups like the Pennsylvania Abolition Society and the New York Manumission Society were important in providing legal support and in establishing schools, but blacks realized they needed their own organizations to promote their own issues in their own language and fashion. Benevolent organizations, fraternal groups, schools and literary societies and churches emerged to provide blacks with their own space, beyond the control or tutelage of whites (Library Company of Philadelphia 2011).

As Gordon observes, "Beginning in the late 1780s and gathering speed during the early 1790s, black religious life became the central expression of African American institution building" (2015:394). The Black church stood as "the one impregnable corner of the world where consolation, solidarity and mutual aid could be found and from which the master and the bossman – at least in the North – could be effectively barred" (Wilmore 1972: 106, quoted in Nash 1988: 114).

In 1787, Absalom Jones and Richard Allen, two leaders of African Americans in Philadelphia, formed the Free African Society, "a mutual aid group composed of free blacks and former slaves dedicated to piety, benevolence and black solidarity" (Newman 2008a: 9) and possibly "the first autonomous organization of free blacks in the United States" (Nash 1989: 332). While not officially a religious organization, the Free African Society came out of African American participation in St. George's Methodist Church, a racially mixed congregation whose African American members were being subjected to growing discrimination by the church's white leadership. The Free African Society gave rise to two Black congregations in 1794. Jones established St. Thomas African Episcopal Church, which was affiliated with the Episcopal Church, and Allen formed the Bethel

African Methodist Episcopal Church. Bethel was originally part of the Methodist Church, but the hostility of whites in the church to African American participation led to Allen's establishing the African Methodist Episcopal (AME) church in 1816 as a separate denomination. It came to be known as Mother Bethel, an acknowledgment of its role as the founding church of the AME denomination, which was in turn the first independent African American denomination.

Below I discuss the Cedar neighborhood where Bethel Church was located. I mention it here because of Lapsansky's (1975) assertion that Mother Bethel was "...a central force in the building of a viable black community ... in the Cedar neighborhood... Bethel, under the leadership of its founder, Richard Allen, had built a membership of several hundred by 1807 and had attracted a number of black residents to settle in the neighborhood..." (180, 182).

The church's meteoric growth continued beyond 1807. Horton & Horton (1998: 139, 142) place its membership at almost 1300 in 1810 and approximately 2000 in 1820 – the latter figure representing one-sixth of Philadelphia's African American population.

Bethel and – to a much lesser extent – smaller African American churches such as St. Thomas African Episcopal Church and First African Presbyterian Church (founded in 1807) served their members in many vital ways. The most important institutions in Black life during this period, "black churches provided opportunities for spiritual worship and guidance, political forums, social and family aid associations, and facilities for community meetings, cultural preservation, entertainment programs, and education and training" (Horton & Horton 1998: 130).

Horton & Horton note that church leaders

> ... often acted as a judicial body. An analysis of church records reveals an institution deeply involved in the daily life of the community, as much concerned with secular relations as with the spiritual well-being of its congregation... It tried to control everything from petty personal disputes between members to more serious criminal acts. The black church attempted to handle internal problems within the community, without recourse to the formal white authority that was seen as unsympathetic, not trusted to render fair judgments or give equitable treatment to African Americans. Trials were held regularly in Philadelphia's Mother Bethel AME Church and judgments were passed on a broad range of offenses, from lying in public, to breach of contract, and assault (1998: 147, 148).

3 The *Minute and Trial Book* of Bethel Church

3.1 Assessing the *Minute and Trial Book*

The trials to which Horton and Horton refer are recorded in Bethel's *Minute and Trial Book* (MTB), which is housed in the Historical Society of Pennsylvania's library in Philadelphia.[4] As the book's title suggests, the MTB contains minutes of the governing board's meetings (often limited to resolutions and actions taken by the board) and the transcripts of trials conducted by elders. The present focus is on 33 trials in the years from 1822 to 1831, and a dramatic account near the beginning of the book of a heated conflict that occurred on a Sunday morning in August, 1822, between Bethel Church and its breakaway neighbor, Wesley Church (cf. Newman 2008b, Chap. 8). In addition to the trials under study, the MTB contains one from 1838 and twelve from the second half of the nineteenth century, but they are not under consideration here.

There are necessarily concerns and caveats in trying to extrapolate the grammar of the spoken language from written data from an earlier era. Schneider (2013: 57) notes that

> ... the written record functions as a filter, as it were: it provides us with a representation of a speech act that we would have liked to have listened to and recorded acoustically and that without the written record would have been lost altogether; but at the same time the rendering of the speech event is only indirect and imperfect, affected by the nature of the recording context in certain ways.

Montgomery (1999: 1) makes a case for the principled use of manuscript documents for reconstructing earlier stages of colloquial English (see also Wolfram & Thomas 2002). In the present case, the most obvious limitations are that the amount of data is limited and the structure of trials is such that the data is constrained in style and range. Under such circumstances, one has to focus on what is present in the documents rather than assigning importance to the absence of individual features. The trials, as formal events, would seem likely to elicit formal speech. Nonetheless, because of the emotion-charged setting, speakers seem likely to have been concentrating more on what they said than on how they said

---

[4]The MTB is part of the microfilmed Bethel AME Church collection at the Historical Society, which is where I saw it. Horton & Horton report that a microfilm copy is "on file at the Afro-American Communities Project at the National Museum of America History of the Smithsonian Institution." (299n).

it. At the same time, the secretary, in writing down testimony, would seem to be much more likely to move it closer to standard English rather than further away.

As a source of information about the spoken English of African Americans in Philadelphia in the early nineteenth century, the MTB has key advantages. Both the speaker and the scribe (the secretary of the board) are African Americans, members of the same Philadelphia community. The written language under study has not been created for its own sake. Rather, recording the testimony "as spoken" has a raison d'être in that the model for the proceedings is the court trial and, as such, there is an underlying quasi-legal motivation in the scribe's attempt to present what a speaker has said verbatim.[5]

3.2 Examples of minutes and trials

The MTB contains minutes as well as trials, and the minutes are – apart from a considerable amount of nonstandard spelling – fairly standard, as illustrated by the minutes of the meeting on 15 June 1824:

(1)   At a special meeting of the Trustees of the corperation of Bethel Ch, at the usual place after prayers we proceeded to Buisness, the buiness of the meeting was stated by Brother Jas Wilson, wich was that the property in Marrets lane belonging to the Corperation was much out of repear, & growing worse, & opon examination the House could not be repard without takeing the chimeny down. we thought it moust advantages to the corperation for the House to undergo a thourreth repear, & also, as there is a vacant space of 8 feet on the West side of the House between our property & our nabours property wich is a recepticle of filth from his slaughter House he being a bucher by trade it was On motion Resolved that the house be moved to the northwes cornor of the lot + undergo a thourreth repear
on motion resolved that we acceed to the propersition of Brother Tho Roberson wich is as followes that he will move the house to the NW cornor as above discribed + do all the carpenters work + glazing for $30. On motion resolved that the foundation wall of the house be stone.

One illustration of the standard character of the minutes in (1) lies in the two occurrences of the subjunctive *be* in the reporting of resolutions that the board passed.

---

[5] "Verbatim" speech is constructed, even when the reporter's goal is to represent exactly what was said.

The trials in the discussion that follows consist of 18 from 1822 through 1825 and 15 from 1829 through 1831. They were conducted by ad-hoc committees of elders, usually five or six men, with certain men (notably Richard Allen and the secretary Joseph Cox) generally a part of the committee. The trials address church members' domestic disputes, financial and other quarrels, and personal impropriety.[6] The range of trial subjects can be seen by the list of topics addressed in the first set of trials, the ones from 1822 through 1825:

Domestic: marital discord, non-support and physical abuse, a man cohabiting with a woman not his wife

Financial: non-payment of a debt, failure to repay a loan, failure to share business earnings with a partner, illegal sale of other people's goods, petty theft

Personal impropriety: imprudent conduct, rumor-mongering, slander, assault, belligerence, flirting with another woman's husband, dispute between a women's church group and an individual woman

The most severe penalty for someone judged guilty was expulsion "from society," i.e. from Bethel Church.

The secretary for Bethel Church – hence the equivalent of a court reporter for the trials during the period under study – was Joseph Cox (1778?–1843).[7] A tanner by trade, Cox became a local preacher and elder. The obituary published by the Philadelphia District Conference of the AME Church said of Cox, "Though not educated, in the popular sense of the term, yet he had greatly enriched his mind by various reading and patient reflection" (quoted in Payne 1968 [1891]:178). Payne estimates Cox's formal schooling as "about as much as a primary school education," adding "but he was well read." He describes Cox as having been "endowed by nature with a powerful intellect as a natural orator and logician" (1968 [1891]:394).

As noted, the MTB also includes an 1822 account of a melee between Bethel Church and its breakaway neighbor Wesley Church. It is not clear who the author is of this account, but its heated style is distinct from Cox's.

The handwriting for the minutes and trials that Cox recorded is not always the same. An October, 1822, resolution stated: "Resolved that we employ a clerk to

---

[6]The trials from the second half of the nineteenth century are different in nature. They are "church trials," where the subject matter is an alleged irregularity in church governance or misconduct on the part of a member of the clergy.

[7]It is not known where Cox was born, but biographers of his much younger sister Patricia Cox Jackson state that she was born in 1795 in Philadelphia to free parents (Schroeder 2007: 60).

record the minutes of Bethel Church in a book to be provided for that purpose." The possibility exists, then, that the clerk introduced errors or "corrected" what he copied. There is no way to identify any changes that would have been introduced in this way. A further point is that the handwriting can present its own problems. One of the clerks places a flourish on word-final <m> that looks like an <e>, thus giving the appearance of <hime> rather than <him>, as in *brother Jonathan Trusty + Shepperd Gibbs is a committe to informe hime of this resolution.* I have assumed that the clerk intended <inform him> and have transcribed it accordingly.

Below I identify individual noteworthy features from the trials. However, the most effective way to convey the character of the trials is by presenting examples of complete trials themselves. Accordingly, I present three trials, selected essentially at random.[8]

(2) Phil. Augt 19th, 1823
[three cases on that date; this was the third]
A charge brought against A[] R[] by D[] T[] of threattning to beat her
____. she ??said?? that D[] was up stairs pretending to be Sick and
Beckoning to her husband out the windows to come to her – up stairs.
AR. ??run?? her fist in D.Ts face and abused her very much
A R[] says that D.T. has from time to time decoyed her husband into DT.
house. I told her of it and that I did not like it. she Borrowed 12 ½ cents
from T. R[] which I did not like, I told her if she parted M[] D[] & wife, or
other men and there wives that she should not part my husband and me.
I also sd. that my husbd had not time to eat his victuals for DT. keeps
sending for him to pray for her 2 or 3 times during one meals victuals.
DT. told me that I was a Devil and that I would go to hell any how. But T.
R[] was a nice man.
We the Committee are of opinion that A[] R[] is guilty of a Breach of the
Discipline and is no more a member of Society

Rev Rich Allen   William Cornish
Jonathan Trusty   James Wilson

---

[8]Two question marks appear on either side of a word or part of a word if I think I can identify the word – or can attest to the presence of a part of the word – but am not certain, e.g. ??run?? and *Break??s??*. When I am not at all sure of a word, I present it with underlining. e.g. *came a running a cross the* ____ *to oppose...* When full names of litigants are used in the MTB, I have reduced them to abbreviations followed by "[ ]." In cases where I present initials without a following "[]," it is because initials were used in the MTB. The date (/dd/mm/yy) after an example refers to the entry in the MTB.

John F. Gibbs   Joseph Cox Secty

(3) October 6th 1823
[two cases on that date; this is the second]
A charge brought against I[] D[] and wife by William Cornish of disputeing [symbol]
J[] D[] states that she went to bed and while she was taking her cloathes off he told her to blow out the candle. I told him that I had just came up to bed

he appeared to just awake out of a dose of sleep and I thought that he did not know that I had just come up.

he told me the second time to blow out the candle. I told him that he was pinched, however I blowed out the candle. Some conversation ensued between us. he asked me what I was a doing there, And why I did not go where I slept for those two nights. I had a great deal of washing to do, and had to work at night to get them ready to take them home in time Some more talk took place, he then put me out of the Bed. I returned to the Bed + took hold of some of the Bed cloathes, and he struck me several times and hurt me very much. I hallowed murder and the watchman came Ann Cleasy states she heard the noise and when the watchman came I ran out the back door and did not return untill the next day
I[] D[] states that his wife came up and awakened him late at night – the candle was shining in my face. I told her to blow it out but she would not. I arose to blow it out then she blew it out. I then asked her where she slept last night. She # that that was her bed and told me to go down stairs to my Bed, Said I suppose you want to have it to ??Say?? of me as C[] T[] Said of his wife that she left his Bed
I told her that we had nothing to do with them
I told her to hush and let me alone or I would put her out of the Bed. She continued to go on in an aggravating way, untill I put her out of the bed. She laid hold of the Bed Cloathes and then took a foul hold of me and she cryed Murder untill the watchman came. Such is her abuse that I cannot speak without there being a noise.
We have taken the above Case into Consideration and we are of opinion that Both of them are guilty of a Breach of the Decipline. They may remain on trial 6 months , But within that time if either of them Break??s?? the decipline they shall be Exspelled from society

(4) Philadelphia April 8th 1829
At a meeting of a committee to here + try the case of H[] H[] + M[] B[].
A charge brought Against H. H[] of Pregency of murdering the child + of
M[] H[] takeing the Chamber pot to the prevey House for her and also
her going into the Room of the said M. H[] in Lumbard St. + the Door
shut after her. + not opend for the space of 10 or 15 minutes althrough
some person knocked at the Door. M. B[] say that she whent to H. H[] to
Borrow a cop as a pattern to cut one out by + She was grinding coffee.
She put Down the coffee + whent into another room Walking half bent +
sent the cop out by a child but did not come out her self, + a pear of
Sissors also by the child but H. H[] did not come out while I stayed at her
house, + M.B. said that she herself had had 4 children + that if ever
herself was with child that she belived H[] H[] was with child at the time
she went to her for the cop. H H[] Defendent, Denyes murdering any
child or being pregnent or with child and as to M. H[] emptying the
chamber pot she had denyed it but he told her that he did do it about
dusk one evening one time the 2 children being sick + she not at home.
Necesaty required it + he done it. and as to her going into her uncles M.
H[] Room in Lumbrd St. at Solamon Clarkson, Choolroom one evening
the Female society meet of Wich she is a member, a Disterbence took
place in the St. the Wachman sprung his Rattels. the members of the
society rund to the Windo to see what was going on. the window bing
croded she whent up one pare of stears into her uncles Room in order to
have a better oppertunity from his Windows to See
he/M.H/ Was sitting at the tabel Writing, as to the Door being Shut or
fasned she could not tell anything. She stayed there but a short time,
before she came Down again.
Bashely Chandler Witness Say that she is aquainted with H.H. that she
lives up stears over her + she never saw any thing in or about her that
looked like her being in a state of Pregency to her Knowledge. She aperd
as to her shop[shape?] always alike She had nothing to say against –
R. Valentine, Witness say that she is aquainted with H. H[]. + knows no
harm of her. She did not viset her House ??perticler?? at the time of this
Report About her because the small pox was in her own family + she did
not think it prudent to visit any of her Nabours at that time, on that
account, she said she never saw any thing about her that look like her
being with child to her Knowledge.
Sybella Oliver Witness say that she knows H. H[] but Knows nothing
Disrespectfull of her, that she always aperd to be an upwright person as

farr as ever she saw. Rosannah Johnson Witness say that she Knows H. H[] but knows nothin, nor never saw anything Disrespectfull of her. Ann Fisher Witness say that she Know H. H[] but that she knows nothing nor never saw anything Disrespectfull of her. Lucy Lewis Witness say that she knows nothing Disrespectfull of H.H.

We the Committee have taken the above case into consideration + are of an oppinion that from the strenght of evedance H[] H[] is not guilty of Breach of the Law of God nor of our Decipline We therefore acquit her.

Names of the Committee

1. Walter Proctor, 3. James Wilson,

2. John Cornish, 4. John?? Tecis??

Joseph Cox Secty

Richard Allen, Preacher in Charge

3.3 Nonstandard features

In the accounts of the trials in the MTB, certain nonstandard features emerge:

3.3.1 Possession

While the possessive morpheme -*s* is usually present, there are some instances where it is not present and where possession is signaled by Possessor-Possessed word order alone.[9]

(5)   her present husband was not the father of Josh Wife 12/12/23

(6)   at the end of 2 weeks Robt wife father told her that she was not marred [married] + obreaded [upbraided] Sarah + all the methodist of leaving... 23/3/30[10]

(7)   A[] T[] say that Anthony Davis never saw anything indeasent or unbecoming by him in Chas B[]s house in his life that he did frequent the house it was true but had no evil desing[design] in it + it was by Chas requst + he did not know that it was disagreabel to Chas 13/10/30

---

[9]An anonymous reviewer questions whether an orthographic convention might exist to signal possession overtly that I was unaware of (e.g. an extra mark at the end of the possessor) and that what I considered zero marking was not in fact the case. I certainly consider this to be a possibility in many instances but not all. For example, it seems clear that this is not the case in the examples that I present in the text.

[10]The absence of overt number marking on *Methodist* is exceptional. In the case of *Methodist*, the singular and plural forms of the noun would be homophonous.

(8)   he saw a half Dollar laying on the carpet + pick et up + put it in his pocket
with the intenson of giveing it to the gentleman at the Brakfast table as
he was not in the room but he saw no more of him untill he met him in
the alderman office at wich time he layed the charge against him 4/7/31

3.3.2 *Be* leveling: the subject type constraint

A phenomenon found in dialects of American English – and English vernaculars more globally – is *be* leveling, whereby *was/were* alternation for past-tense
forms is realized as *was* across the board and likewise, though less frequently,
the *am/is/are* alternation is realized as *is*. This shows up in the MTB but with an
added wrinkle, namely that the leveling occurs only with full NP subjects. This
distinction between *they* and other 3pl subjects is what Montgomery et al. (1993)
designate "Subject Type Constraint". While there are only a limited number of
tokens, the *they*/NP distribution is borne out in the trial testimony. There are
two instances of *they were* (as in 9) and six of plural-NP *was* (as in 10):

(9)   until I hear that they were about parting 18/12/22

(10)   there frocks was open behind 15/4/29

While my focus was on the trial testimony, I also examined the rest of the data
in the MTB for the years from 1822 to 1831, i.e. the report of the Bethel-Wesley
melee as well as the board's minutes. Past-tense *be* variability shows up here as
well, both in the account of the fracas and in the board's minutes. As with the
trial testimony, the leveling can occur when a noun is semantically plural (11) or
the NP consists of co-ordinate singular NP's (12).

(11)   After the objects of the meeting was stated by the chair / Revd Rich^d
Allen / the following resolutions was enterd into ... 22/11/24

(12)   Revd John Boggs + John F. Cisko was apionted judges of the election
11/4/25

The distribution of relevant forms is presented in Table 3.

The only occurrences of 3pl non-past *be* occur in the minutes, not in the trial
testimony nor in the account of the fracas. Here, too, leveling can occur (13) when
the subject is a full NP, but Table 4 shows that this happens much less frequently
in non-past when compared with past.[11]

---

[11]In addition, there is one occurrence of unleveling, i.e. hypercorrection: : we the cmte have
taken the above case into consideration + are of apionion that A[] G[] are guilty of a breach
of decipline by srikin her sister AH + after being parted threatening her again to fight her + is
accordingly disowned. 15/4/29

Table 3: Past-tense forms of *be* by subject type.

Genre	They		NP	
	were	*was*	*were*	*was*
Testimony	2	0	0	6
Fracas	0	0	3	4
Board minutes	2	0	0	4
Total	4	0	3	14

(13)   ... whereby the peopel is detained longer then they otherwise would be
29/11/25

Table 4: Nonpast-tense forms of *be* by subject type.

Genre	They		NP	
	are	*is*	*are*	*is*
Board minutes	3	0	8	4

On the basis of letters written in the 1860's to the Freedmen's Bureau, Montgomery et al. (1993) identify the Subject Type Constraint as a characteristic of mid-nineteenth-century African American English. Further, they identify its source as Northern British English. (Along with the Proximate Subject Constraint, it forms the Northern Subject Rule (Murray 1873).) At the same time, they present data from the McCullough Family Letters, written by Scotch-Irish immigrants to the South Carolina Up County. "The McCullough letters, written by three families of Scotch-Irish immigrants from Ulster and their descendants, show the subject type constraint clearly" (1993: 348). A difference between the MTB and the two data sets in Montgomery et al. is that the Subject Type Constraint in the MTB is limited to forms of *be*.

The Scots Irish – whom Montgomery *et al.* generally designate Ulster Scots, because they were Scots who immigrated first to Ulster and then to America – were a major presence in Philadelphia in the late eighteenth and early nineteenth century. They had a long period of immigration from 1710 to 1776, followed by an intense second period from 1780 to 1820. Ridner (2017) identifies them as 25% of Philadelphia's population in 1790. Whether the members of Bethel Church displayed the Subject Type Constraint as an African American feature of their speech, as a Philadelphia feature owing to Scots Irish influence, or for both reasons is not readily determinable.

3.3.3 Irregular verb forms

While the irregular verb forms that obtain are ordinarily those found in standard English, there are exceptions, of various types:

(14) Past for participle
He said that he had been spoke to about visiting the house so much 13/10/30

(15) Participle for preterit
Necesaty required it + he done it. 8/4/29

(16) Bare root past form
he told me that was his buisiness and give me [no] further satisfaction 18/12/22

(17) Regularized past form
I told him that he was pinched, however I blowed out the candle. 6/10/23

3.3.4 A-prefixing

There are six occurrences of a-prefixing in the MTB. In (18), I present the three that occur in the account of the Bethel Wesley fracas.

(18) he mentioned that he was a going around to the Wesley Church [i.e. was getting ready to go]... As Rev Rich Allen drew near the church. William Perkins, James Bird, Simon Murray & Tobias Sipple came a running a cross the ____ to oppose the people going into the church... While Perkins and his party was a contending at the door, Rev Rich Allen was conveyed in by some of the trustees of the Wesley Church. 18/8/22

In the Yale Grammatical Diversity Project's description of *a*-prefixing in modern American vernaculars (most saliently Appalachian English) (Matyiku 2011), the phenomenon is identified as occurring in narratives, arguably to convey "immediacy or dramatic vividness" (Feagin 1979). While this characterization seems generally to hold for the occurrences in the MTB, the first of the examples given in (18) would not seem to involve either immediacy or dramatic vividness.

In modern vernaculars, there are phonological restrictions in that *a*-prefixing only occurs when the verb is consonant-initial and carries stress on the initial syllable (though Montgomery 2009 presents a limited number of exceptions to the latter constraint). As can be seen, the third example in (18) involves a verb with non-initial stress.

3.3.5 Orthographic variation

As attested by the excerpts from the MTB presented above, there is a fair amount of nonstandard spelling. Much of this can simply be attributed to the scribe's lack of formal education. A noticeable instance where nonstandard spelling suggests a pronunciation pattern involves the sequence of what I assume to be /ɛ/ followed by /r/: *a thourreth repear* (15/6/24), *his shear* (21/5/24), *a pear of Sissors* (8/4/29), *up stears* (8/4/29). Less often, the vowel is spelled <a>, as in *up stars* (n.d.) and *repard* (15/6/24). One frequent site of departure from standard spelling involves unstressed vowels in polysyllabic words, e.g. *propersition* (15/6/24), *simerler* (12/8/29). The Philadelphia dialect at the time, i.e. as spoken by whites, was rhotic. However, the instances introduced above of *propersition* and *simerler* suggest that African American speech in Philadelphia was like African American speech elsewhere in being non-rhotic.

3.4 Summary

A crucial question is whether the trial testimony data in the MTB can be considered vernacular. Given certain formal attributes in the minutes proper, e.g. the use of the subjunctive in the framing of motions, to assert that the trial testimony data displays vernacular features requires that there be distributional differences between the trial testimony data and the minutes. Before considering these, I wish to call attention to unmistakably vernacular features that are all but absent. For example, there are no occurrences anywhere in the MTB of *ain't*. Indeed, there is but a lone instance of a negative contraction. It occurs in a question in the trial testimony data:

(19)   She said, why don't you come and see? 12/12/23

Similarly, there is a lone occurrence of negative concord (20) in the trial testimony data even though there are several instances where it might have been expected, as exemplified in (21–23).[12]

---

[12] In (4) above, there are two examples of the construction "Witness say that she Know H. H[] but that she knows nothing nor never saw anything Disrespectfull of her." I have not considered the use of *never* to constitute negative concord.

(20) He ... acknowlidged that he had acted improper in visiting the house so much + was sorry for it + whould not do so no more except on cases of real necesaty. 13/10/30

(21) She says that A. M[] never offerd anything disrespectfull to her in his life. 8/9/25

(22) She never saw any thing in or about her that looked like her being in a state of Pregency to her Knowledge. 8/4/29

(23) he would come in the morning + go into her bedroom without asking anybody 13/10/30

However, there are other features that show up and only do so in trial testimony data (or, in one case, also in the account of the Bethel-Wesley melee) Thus, the only instances where possession is ever conveyed by word order alone are in the trial testimony. The same is true of nonstandard instances of irregular verbs. Similarly, *a*-prefixing only occurs in the trial testimony plus the account of the Bethel-Wesley fracas. The Subject Type Constraint for 3pl subjects of past-tense copulas is distinct from the other features. It applies to trial testimony data, but it also applies in the other data as well, suggesting that this delineation of the Subject Type Constraint is not just vernacular.

As Montgomery et al.'s examination of the McCullough Family Letters attests, attention to the Subject Type Constraint in nineteenth-century American English is not African American alone. Neither are the nonstandard irregular verb forms illustrated in §3.3.3 nor the use of *a*-prefixing in §3.3.4. On the surface at least, the lone feature that can be identified in the MTB as uniquely African American (among American dialects) is the expression of possession by word order alone.

4 The Cedar neighborhood

Because Philadelphia in the early Republic played a central role in the formation of African American institutions, historians have examined it in depth. One such study is Emma Lapsansky's 1975 dissertation, *South Street Philadelphia, 1764–1854: "A haven for those low in the world."* It is a study of the South Street Corridor, which Lapsansky also terms "the Cedar neighborhood," Cedar Street being the original name for South Street.[13] The neighborhood "developed for urban occupation between about 1760 and 1840" (Lapsansky 1975: xxvi). Lapsansky draws extensively on period directories, maps, and the like. She presents evidence in exhaustive detail, thereby providing a rich and thorough description of the neighborhood's residents and institutions. Above I cited Lapsansky's identification of Mother Bethel Church as a major presence in the neighborhood, one that attracted African Americans to it.

In a work based on her dissertation, Lapsansky comments:

> The black community of Philadelphia was spatially stable... In the 1790s, Bethel African Methodist Episcopal Church had been established at 6th and Lombard Streets. Since then Afro-Americans had increasingly anchored their "turf," setting up a number of institutions – schools, insurance companies, masonic lodges, and several additional churches within a few blocks of Bethel. As early as 1811, a black neighborhood was identifiable at the southern edge of the city, near Bethel church... Though Afro-Americans and their institutions were to be found in all parts of the city and its suburbs, there was, then, an early, clearly defined intellectual, social, and economic focus for the Negro community at the southern edge of the city (1980: 58).

In assessing the Cedar neighborhood in the period under study, Lapsansky cautions:

> The development of the South Street Corridor points out the pitfalls inherent in generalizing twentieth-century interpretations to nineteenth century situations. Not only do the terms "ghetto" and "slum" have no meaning in the context of the 1830s Cedar neighborhood, but our modern view of what constitutes a "black neighborhood" – an area in which no white faces are to be seen – must be adjusted to reflect the nineteenth century realities (277–278).

---

[13]Cedar Street is the original name for South Street. Lapsansky delineates the Cedar neighborhood (or South Street Corridor) as "Lombard Street at the north, Bainbridge Street at the south, the Delaware River at the east and Broad Street at the west" (xxvi). Dorman (2009: 2) reports that, "after the establishment of the Bethel and St. Thomas churches, families flocked to the southern neighborhoods of the city, creating a vital center for black life. By 1820, 75 percent of black households in Philadelphia lived in the city's southern neighborhoods". (It is not clear how much beyond the Cedar neighborhood is included with it in the phrase "southern neighborhoods.") Philadelphia's population was overwhelmingly white, and these neighborhoods were still majority-white.

Lapsansky presents a picture of residential – and, to a lesser extent, occupational – mixing. She identifies Philadelphia in the late eighteenth and early nineteenth century as a "walking city." The absence of public transportation required people, whether management or labor, to live near their workingplace, which meant living near each other. According to Lapsansky:

> There was ... for Philadelphians, a period of about forty years – between 1790 and 1830 – when racial violence was at a minimum, driven underground by acute labor shortages and the absorption of class issues into traditional politics. In this period, ethnic hostility took the more subtle forms of exclusion from churches, clubs, and cemeteries, and of greater numbers of arrests and convictions among the Irish and blacks... Moreover, as racial and economic segregation was impossible in the early Philadelphia walking city – employers and employees simply had to live near their work – and hence near each other – little could be done in the way of using physical distance as a deterrent to either crime or other forms of intergroup antagonism.[14]

It was during this period when racial hostility was latent, that the foundations of the Cedar neighborhood were laid; foundations that as early as 1790 presaged its future directions. The Cedar neighborhood, as evidenced by the 1790 census, consisted of four distinctly identifiable elements: a substantial nativeborn landlord class, and an Irish, Black and white English or other European working class.[15]

Members of the four "distinctly identifiable elements" were mixed together spatially. Describing a block of Gaskill Street in 1811 with attention to each householder, Lapsansky notes, "This block, not highly stratified either occupationally, racially or ethnically, far enough from the river front not to be overly influenced by its demands, is not atypical of the social mix of the early nineteenth century Cedar neighborhood" (131). Moving forward a decade, she writes, "It was as rare in 1820 as in 1811 to find more than three or four families of similar background as near-neighbors" (227).

The mix of ethnicities and race down to the level of the individual city block in the Cedar neighborhood also held – to some extent – for class, Lapsansky

---

[14]Stewart (1999: 692) extends Lapsansky's description of this period in Philadelphia to the North more generally: "[F]rom 1790 until around 1830, society in the North, though suffused with prejudice, nevertheless fostered a surprisingly open premodern struggle over claims of 'respectability' and citizenship put forward by many social groups, and particularly by free African Americans."

[15]Anti-black riots beset Philadelphia in the 1830s and 1840s, subsequent to the current focus.

noting that there was "little social or spatial distance between the upper and lower classes here – few of the resident landlords were more than moderately well-off" (227). (In this, the Cedar neighborhood differed from the city center of Philadelphia, where prosperous whites lived on the major thoroughfares while the working class and the marginalized lived on backstreets.)

> As with the Irish and native-American sectors of the Cedar neighborhood, the occupation of a black resident was a poor predictor of his wealth or location. The frugal black hairdresser or tailor whose comfortable brick house might stand next to the Irish butcher's frame house, the English carpenter's clapboard one, or the poor black laborer's rented shanty, was a frequent occurrence of this neighborhood for many years (124).

Moreover, "one striking aspect of early nineteenth-century Philadelphia was the rarity with which race, ethnicity – or even occupation – was an accurate predictor of wealth" (119–120).

Lapsansky makes the point that, even as the Cedar neighborhood came to be associated with the city's two most stigmatized groups, the Irish and African Americans, many of the white, non-Irish homeowners remained. Others viewed the two groups with "distaste and fear," "yet distaste did not result in the rejection of the Irish or of the blacks" (112, 111).

Lapsansky's work establishes the Cedar neighborhood as "polyethnic" (xxvi), down to the level of individual city blocks. Still, when Lapsansky is interviewed for the 1998 PBS series on "Africans in America," she refrains from describing Philadelphia neighborhoods at the time as integrated. She acknowledges that working-class Germans, Irish, and African Americans in early nineteenth-century Philadelphia "live roughly on the same blocks," but she declined to consider the neighborhoods "integrated" because the different groups

> would have had different institutions, [and] they would not have necessarily spent their leisure time in each other's company. They would have worked together, they would have been mostly polite to each other on the streets, but when it came time to celebrate, when it came time to go to church, to marry, et cetera, people went off to their own ethnic foxholes.

Except, she adds,

> for public gatherings. In the early 19th century, it's clear that public gatherings were what one might call democratic. [For particular holidays,] there's a great deal of action in the public space and that action takes place with

lots of different kinds of people sharing the public space (Lapsansky, quoted in Jones 1998).

Above I presented evidence pertaining to the provenance of Philadelphia's African Americans in the period. The one adjustment to be added in light of Lapsansky's discussion of the Cedar neighborhood is that "by the early nineteenth century, native Pennsylvania blacks, freed by the gradual emancipation law adopted by the legislature in 1780, increased the numbers who called this neighborhood home" (xxvi–xxvii). In other words, the neighborhood that is identified most strongly with African Americans (even though they remained a minority there) had a locally born element, one might even say a locally born foundation.

5 Bethel Church, Samaná, and the divergence hypothesis

5.1 Conflicting assessments of Samaná's history

In 1987 Shana Poplack and David Sankoff published "The Philadelphia story in the Spanish Caribbean," reporting on fieldwork that they had carried out in the African American enclave on the Samaná peninsula of the Dominican Republic. The original settlers had gone there in 1824–1825 as part of the Haitian government's campaign to attract African Americans to Hispaniola. (From 1822 to 1844, the Haitian government controlled Hispaniola in its entirety.) Poplack & Sankoff's designation of the language of the Samaná residents as a "Philadelphia story" reflects the provenance of the original settlers. As Poplack & Tagliamonte (2001) state: "Philadelphia's African Methodist [Episcopal] church was apparently the main driving force in the immigration movement (Nash 1988: 243), and Philadelphia appears to have been the major supplier of immigrants" (12).

Poplack and her colleagues argue that the language of the modern descendants of the original Samaná settlers provides a window into the African American Vernacular English (AAVE) of the time of emigration from the United States. Because the Samaná data is closer to white American vernaculars than is true of AAVE today, Poplack and her colleagues hold that the Samaná data provides evidence that AAVE has diverged from other American vernaculars over time.[16] As such,

---

[16] I am unable to assess the impact of other Englishes on Samaná English (and it takes me too far afield from the Philadelphia focus of this article), but I think it important to acknowledge their presence. Thus, Hoetink's investigation of Samaná church records from the 1870's turns up such frequent intermarriage with Turks Islanders that he speculates that, for the Americans in Samaná "[i]n 1870 Samaná was – together with the United States and the Turks Islands maybe

they see the Samaná data as speaking directly to the divergence/convergence debate that arose in the 1980's (Labov & Harris 1986, Fasold et al. 1987).

The received view regarding AAVE is that it developed on plantations in the South; it seems clear that this is a view Poplack and her colleagues accept (as do I). Thus, the Philadelphia, i.e. northern, tie proves problematic for them.[17] To justify their statement that Samaná English is ancestral to modern AAVE, Poplack & Tagliamonte (2001) set out to establish that "the demographic profile of the remaining input settlers would have been essentially that of the general African American English-speaking population of the time" (p. 37). In contrast, in my own work, I argue that the early Samaná settlers came primarily from the North and consequently that their language cannot be considered antecedent to modern AAVE (cf. Hannah 1997: 341–342).

The works in question (specifically Poplack & Tagliamonte 2001 and Singler 2007b) present two key areas of difference:

- The provenance of the African American population of Philadelphia, hence of those who would have been likely to emigrate from there.

- Immigration to Samaná vis-à-vis immigration to elsewhere on Hispaniola, with special reference to which immigrants remained and which returned to the US.

My assessment of the first of these points is presented in 1.2 above. For a detailed critique of Poplack & Tagliamonte (2001) in this regard, see Singler (2007b). While the general immigration venture sought to bring 6000 African Americans to Hispaniola to form the nucleus of a middle class, there was a pressing strategic need to establish a presence in the contested location of the Samaná peninsula and the bay it commanded. Mann-Hamilton (2013: 224–225) identifies the Bay of

---

– the world" (Hoetink 1962: 21). There were missionaries from England and also Jamaican ones (Hoetink 1962: 14). Vigo (1982) and Davis (2007) report that "the Americans" hired teachers from Jamaica and Turks Islands for their schools. Mann-Hamilton (2013: 224) speaks of a "constant influx of other English-speaking emigrants from neighboring Caribbean islands," and Vigo of "an extensive immigration of laborers from the British West Indies" to work on the building of a railroad and on sugar plantations in the late nineteenth and early twentieth centuries (1987: 6). Corroboration of the West Indian presence comes from Parsons (1928) and Miller & Krieger (1928). In the words of Davis, "Samaná es un microcosmos y une mezcolanza de Afronortamérica, el Anglocaribe, el Francocaribe, y, desde luego, el Hispanocaribe" (Davis 1980: 166).

[17]Poplack & Tagliamonte (2001: 37) make reference to the "misleading title" of Poplack & Sankoff (1987), i.e. "the Philadelphia story."

Samaná as the point of entry for French forces "intent on stifling the events of the Haitian Revolution"; cf. Keim 1870:116–117; Madiou 1988 [1848]:357.

To attract African Americans to Hispaniola and to effect this immigration, President Jean-Pierre Boyer had dispatched the diplomat Jonathas Granville to the American North, equipping him with 50,000 pounds of coffee to be sold to defray the immigrants' travel expenses. Granville's arrival in the American North generated excitement, and organizations formed in northern cities in support of the campaign. He quickly made his way to Philadelphia, where he met with Richard Allen, who took the reins as president of the Haitian Emigration Society there. "Allen led the emigration efforts, convening a meeting of black community leaders at his house in late June 1824 and then calling a mass meeting at Bethel" (Nash 1988: 242). The early immigration activity in Philadelphia seemed poised to send people to Samaná in particular. This is reflected in the MTB. When one of the church's leaders, Thomas Robertson, made plans to immigrate to Samaná, Allen called a special meeting of the "ministers, preachers, exhorters, trustees, and leaders ... [and] ... after meture deliberation on the subject it was on motion Resolved that Brother Thomas Robersen be set apart by holy ??orders?? for Samanah in Hayti" (3/11/24).

Further evidence of Allen's role in immigration to Haiti is Nash's report that "sixty Philadelphia blacks ... gathered their possessions, bade farewell to friends and relatives, and sailed from the Delaware wharves aboard the *Charlotte Corday*.... Hundreds more, encouraged by optimistic reports from the first emigrants and the enthusiasm of Richard Allen, emigrated later in 1824... According to Allen, most of [the emigrants to Haiti from Philadelphia] ... were Methodists" (Nash 1988: 244).

Despite the promising start to the grand immigration scheme, it was, Samaná excepted, by and large a failure. As word of the Haitian venture spread, people wishing to immigrate to Haiti organized in a larger range of cities. With the increase in the range of source cities came a marked deterioration in the selection process. There was a decline in the quality of applicants or – at least – a decline in the scrutiny to which applicants were subjected, and there was a decline in their level of preparedness. According to Jackson, problems arose "in part because Granville had so little control over the recruiters that assisted him. Furthermore, many of them desired only to rid the country of those blacks whom they deemed undesirable" (115). He continues: "Many well-meaning recruiters were not of the caliber of the Reverend Richard Allen ... What had been intended to be selective emigration in reality became en masse emigration which Jonathas Granville was powerless to manage" (Jackson 1976:115, 116).

Thus, there was a distinction between the early Samaná-bound immigrants and those who followed who went elsewhere. As the nineteenth-century Haitian historian Thomas Madiou observes: "Quant aux convois qui furent envoyés à Samana, ils étaient mieux composés que les autres ..." (1988 [1848]:425). The distinction between those sent to Samaná and those sent elsewhere was intensified on Hispaniola itself. While the Haitian government had envisioned that most of the immigrants would engage in farming, apart from those who went to Samaná, most flocked instead to cities, where they competed with the existing labor force and did so at a linguistic disadvantage. They were absorbed into existing Haitian society poorly if at all. A great number of immigrants returned to the US, perhaps as many as a third. In contrast, Samaná was "... una comunidad contenta en la cual hubo muy pocos de sus miembros que ambicionaron retornar a los Estados Unidos" (Penzo Devers 1999: 107; see also Godbout 1987: 230). The distinctive character of the Samaná settlement from the rest of Hispaniola is a point that recent scholarship reinforces, e.g. Mann-Hamilton 2013, 2016, Fanning 2015, Mongey 2019. "As Samana was accessible only by boat from the rest of the island, the Americans were not assimilated, and retained the English language, African American cuisine ..., religious affiliation to Protestantism (the Wesleyans provided a minister when the AME church could not), and their identity as Americans" (Fanning 2015: 111–112). Further, Mann-Hamilton (2013, 2016) lays stress on the role of Bethel church members in the establishment of the Samaná enclave. Certainly, one characteristic of Bethel Christianity that manifested itself in Samaná was the emphasis on education, illustrated by the establishment of church-run English-language schools.

To the extent that the significance of Philadelphia cannot be denied, Poplack & Tagliamonte seek to downplay the degree of interracial interaction to be found there in the years leading up to the immigration to Samaná. They reproduce a map of the "Residential pattern of black households in Philadelphia, 1820" from Nash (1988: 168) (p. 14) and comment, "Residential segregation (and the attendant decrease in language variety contact) had clearly already begun' (13). However, this statement is at direct odds with Nash's own comment regarding the map that "no segregated black community emerged... . Neighborhoods remained mixed by race and occupation" (169). And, with specific reference to a street that was only three blocks long, Nash states: "The twenty-four black families on Gaskill Street in 1816 lived in a neighborhood that formed a nearly perfect cross-section of Philadelphia's industrious middle and lower classes. On a daily basis, black families encountered white neighbors (who still outnumbered them by two to one)" (169–170).[18]

---

[18]Nash's comment directly parallels one by Lapskansky, cited in §3, regarding Gaskill Street.

In terms of linguistic data, that which appears in Poplack & Sankoff (1987) and subsequent works seems qualitatively comparable to the trial data from the MTB. Like the MTB, it displays the Subject Type Constraint regarding verbal –s (Poplack & Tagliamonte 1989). A crucial difference, however, is that the Samaná English data displays variable copula absence (Poplack & Sankoff 1987).

5.2 The divergence hypothesis without Samaná

If the membership of Bethel AME Church was similar to the African American population of Philadelphia at the time more generally and if Nash's (1988) table provides a valid indication of the provenance of the larger population, then at the very least we can see that the population, beyond consisting of free African Americans, is largely northern in orientation, with most African Americans in Philadelphia having been born either elsewhere in the North itself or in the Upper South, specifically in the part of the Upper South where large plantations were not economically sustainable. Within Philadelphia, specifically in the area where Bethel Church stood and where many of the Church's congregants lived, the early-nineteenth-century neighborhood was pervasively mixed in terms of race/ethnicity and social class. It is not surprising, then, that the vernacular elements of the language of the MTB seem more generic than specifically African American. This statement assumes that the features associated with modern AAVE were present in the speech of African Americans elsewhere in this time period, specifically in the South, especially the Lower South. In Singler (2007a, 2015), I brought evidence from Liberian Settler English to bear on the question. In the nineteenth century, 16,000 African Americans immigrated to Liberia under the auspices of the African Colonization Society, primarily in the fifty-year period from 1822 to 1872. There is extensive documentation as to the provenance of the Liberian Settlers (see Singler 1989), and more than 90% came from slave states. Moreover, in the years before the American Civil War brought an end of slavery, a majority of those who went to Liberia were enslaved people for whom immigration to Liberia was a condition for their manumission.

When it comes to the non-use of standard features such as the copula, Samaná English and Liberian Settler English both pattern with AAVE, i.e. in displaying the features' non-use, but so too do other vernacular varieties unconnected to AAVE (Chambers 2004, Szmrecsanyi & Kortmann 2009). Arguably more revealing, Table 5 presents the five **overt** non-quantitative nonstandard features that Myhill (1995) posits as potential innovations in AAVE (cf. Singler 2007b, 2015).

As can be seen, while only one of the features shows up in Poplack & Sankoff's Samaná English corpus and none are present in the MTB, all five are used in Li-

Table 5: Non-standard features: Overt features not found in standard English. Sources of the Samaná English information: Howe & Walker (2000) for the use of *ain't* for *didn't*, and Shana Poplack (p.c.) for the rest.

	MTB (Bethel)	Samaná English	LSE	AAVE
use of *ain't* for *didn't*	✗	✓	✓	✓
be done	✗	✗	✓	✓
semiauxiliary *come*	✗	✗	✓	✓
steady	✗	✗	✓	✓
stressed *been*	✗	✗	✓	✓

berian Settler English. The presence of the features in Liberian Settler English (when taken in tandem with their absence in English-lexifier varieties elsewhere in West Africa) indicates that they are antebellum features of AAVE that the Liberian Settlers took with them when they left the American South. Thus, their absence from the MTB and from Poplack & Sankoff's Samaná English corpus is not evidence of their absence from nineteenth-century AAVE. Further, the presence or absence of particular features is simply more basic, hence more telling, than comparative constraint-ranking in quantitative assessments. This is not to say that the divergence hypothesis for AAVE has been falsified, only that the use of Samaná data has been crucially undermined.

The non-applicability of Samaná data aside, there are still limitations as to how far one can take claims of divergence or convergence. To begin with, as Spears notes in the 1987 panel on divergence vs. convergence,

> It's clear that it [divergence] can be interpreted in several ways.... For one thing, are we talking about global divergence, that is, between language varieties as wholes, or simply divergence with respect to certain features of grammar? Surely, neither Labov nor anyone else is claiming that there is divergence affecting white and black grammars as wholes, that is, with respect to all of their features (Spears in Fasold et al. 1987: 50)[19].

---

[19] Similarly, neither the Neo-Anglicist Origins Hypothesis (Van Herk 2015) nor the Creole Origins Hypothesis (Rickford 2015) has proven to be a tenable account in its "pure," i.e. strong, form as to the origin of AAVE. Rather, a consensus has emerged (including Van Herk and Rickford) that "AAVE ... has been composed of components drawn from standard English, dialectal English, innovative developments, and creole, to varying proportions, and it is best described by carefully weighing moderate assessments that recognize the complexity of its contexts and its linguistic evolution (Winford 1997, 1998, 2015)" (Schneider 2015: 136)

Beyond this, there are reasons for caution. The distribution of the AUX *be done* and stressed *been* in Table 5 provides Liberian evidence attesting to their stature as examples of features of long standing in AAVE. As such, the features stand against divergence. However, while the features may be of long duration, they have expanded their domain of usage in AAVE in ways that they have not in Liberian Settler English. Thus, while (24) is grammatical in Liberian Settler English and AAVE alike, (25) is grammatical in AAVE but not in Liberian Standard English.

(24)   Liberian Settler English
        I BÍN receiving certificates.
        'I have been receiving certificates [for outstanding churchwork] for years now.'

(25)   Speaker A: You gonna quit?
        Speaker B: *I BÍN quit. (Labov 1998: 136)

Strictly speaking, in that other American vernaculars lack *be done* and stressed *been*, the further elaboration of domains where these features obtain cannot be counted as divergence. However, it also shows the limits of invoking convergence as an explanation for the differences between AAVE and other vernaculars.

6 After 1830

Early in the nineteenth century, African Americans in Philadelphia were in daily contact with other Philadelphians. Indeed, the city's "African American" neighborhoods were majority white. The evidence presented here suggests that the African American English of the day was, for the most part, similar to the vernacular of white Philadelphians. If speech of African Americans in Philadelphia was not distinct from that of other Philadelphians in the first three decades of the nineteenth century, the question arises as to when that distinctiveness emerged. Was it not until the Great Migration of the twentieth century? I think that this would be unlikely. To begin with, a succession of riots by whites and increasing employment discrimination against Blacks beginning in the 1830's led to greater segregation, though not all at once. At first, this was because Black and Irish residents alike were targeted. With regard to a succession of riots from 1834 to 1849, Lapsansky observes: "The anti-black riot path and destruction were not randomly spread throughout the neighborhood which the blacks and Irish shared but were concentrated in the areas of greatest black- property-ownership"

(1975:225). However, riots against the two groups gave way fully to conflict between the two groups. Clearly, the period from the 1830's to the onset of the Great Migration in the early twentieth century requires further study.

Acknowledgements

Throughout his distinguished career, Don Winford has continually examined and re-examined key questions in sociolinguistics, creole studies, and African American English studies. Part of his modus operandi in doing this has been by seeking and finding new sources of data. He then brings his findings from these fresh sources to bear on the questions at hand. Winford (2017) is an exemplary case in point. It is in the spirit of reporting on a new source of data and analyzing it that – in frank admiration of Don's ongoing scholarship and the signal contributions that he has made – I present this study.

The late Steve Lynch provided me with a sense of the special character of Philadelphia. I thank the librarians at the Historical Society of Pennsylvania for their assistance. I owe a profound debt to Bethel AME Church for their willingness to make their records available to scholars. One way that non-linguists might look at this article is to say that I am focusing on church members' bad behavior, with special reference to the "bad English" being used to describe it. I don't see it that way at all. It is because Bethel Church made its records available to scholars that we can appreciate the remarkably comprehensive range of services that the church provided for its members, not least being its role as arbiter and adjudicator.

I am grateful to Mercedes Duff and Cara Shousterman for their assistance in transcribing the Mother Bethel Church data and for their observations about it.

Abbreviations

AAVE   African American Vernacular English
AME   African Methodist Episcopal
MTB   Minute and Trial Book

References

Chambers, J. K. 2004. Dynamic typology and vernacular universals. In Bernd Kortmann (ed.), *Dialectology meets typology: Dialect grammar from a cross-linguistic perspective*, 127–145. Berlin: Mouton de Gruyter.

Curry, Leonard P. 1986. *The free black in urban America, 1800-1859: The shadow of the dream.* Chicago: University of Chicago Press.

Davis, Martha Ellen. 1980. That old-time religion: Tradición y cambio en el enclave "americano" de Samaná. *Boletin Museo del Hombre Dominicano* 9. 165–95.

Davis, Martha Ellen. 2007. Asentamiento y vida económica de los inmigrantes afroamericanos de Samaná: Testimonio de la Profesora Martha Willmore (Leticia). *Boletín del Archivo General de la Nación* 32(119). 709–33.

DeBose, Charles L. 1983. Samaná English: A dialect that time forgot. In *Proceedings of the Ninth Annual Meeting of the Berkeley Linguistics Society*, 47–53. Berkeley, CA.

Dorman, Dana. 2009. *Philadelphia's African American heritage: A brief historic context statement for the Preservation Alliance's inventory of African American historic sites.* Philadelphia, PA. http://www.preservationalliance.com/wp-content/uploads/2014/09/HCSAfricanAmericanHeritage.pdf.

Fanning, Sara. 2015. *Caribbean crossing: African Americans and the Haitian emigration movement.* New York: NYU Press.

Fasold, Ralph W, William Labov, Fay Boyd Vaughn-Cooke, Guy Bailey, Walt Wolfram, Arthur K Spears & John Rickford. 1987. Are black and white vernaculars diverging? Papers from the NWAVE XIV panel discussion. *American Speech* 62(1). 3–80.

Feagin, Crawford. 1979. *Variation and change in Alabama English: A sociolinguistic study of the white community.* Washington: Georgetown University Press.

Godbout, Santiago. 1987. *Historia parroquial de Santa Barbara de Samaná.* Santo Domingo: Amigo del Hogar.

Hannah, Dawn. 1997. Copula absence in Samaná English: Implications for research on the linguistic history of African-American vernacular English. *American Speech* 72. 339–72.

Hoetink, Harry. 1962. "Americans" in Samaná. *Caribbean Studies* 2. 3–22.

Horton, James Oliver & Lois E. Horton. 1998. *In hope of liberty: Culture, community and protest among Northern free Blacks, 1700-1860.* New York & Oxford: Oxford University Press.

Howe, Darin M. & James A. Walker. 2000. Negation and the Creole-Origins Hypothesis: Evidence from the early African American English. In Shana Poplack (ed.), *The English history of African American English*, 109–140. Malden, MA, & Oxford: Blackwell.

Jackson, III, James O'Dell. 1976. *The origin of Pan-African nationalism: Afro-American and Haytian relations, 1800-1863.* Northwestern University. (Doctoral dissertation).

Jones, Jacquie. 1998. *Africans in America. Part 3, Brotherly love. Interview with Emma Lapsansky, professor of history, Haverford College. Video.* Boston: WGBH Educational Foundation.

Keim, DeBenneville Randolph. 1870. *San Domingo: Pen pictures and leaves of travel, romance and history.* From the portfolio of a correspondent in the American tropics. Philadelphia: Claxton, Remsen & Haffelfinger.

Labov, William. 1998. Co-existent systems in African-American Vernacular English. In Salikoko S. Mufwene, John R. Rickford, Guy Bailey & John Baugh (eds.), *African-American English: Structure, history and use,* 110–53. London: Routledge.

Labov, William & Wendell A. Harris. 1986. De facto segregation of Black and White vernaculars. In David Sankoff (ed.), *Diversity and diachrony,* 1–24. Amsterdam: John Benjamins.

Lapsansky, Emma Jones. 1975. *South street Philadelphia, 1762-1854: A haven for those low in the world.* University of Pennsylvania. (Doctoral dissertation).

Library Company of Philadelphia. 2011. *Black founders: The free black community in the early republic.* https://librarycompany.%20%7B%7BO%7D%7Drg/blackfounders/section6.%20%7B%7BH%7D%7Dtm.

Madiou, Thomas. 1988. *Histoire d'haïti. Tome VI, de 1819 à 1826. [8 vols.]* [1848]. Port-au-Prince: Editions Henri Deschamps.

Mann-Hamilton, Ryan. 2013. What rises from the ashes: Nation and race in the African American enclave of Samaná. In Philip Kretsedemas, Jorge Capetillo-Ponce & Glenn Jacobs (eds.), *Migrant marginality: A transnational perspective,* 222–238. New York: Routledge.

Mann-Hamilton, Ryan. 2016. *What the tides may bring. Political "tigueraje," dispossession and popular dissent in Samaná, Dominican Republic.* City University of New York. (Doctoral dissertation).

Matyiku, Sabina. 2011. *A-prefixing.* Updated by Tom McCoy (2015) and Katie Martin (2018). http://ygdp.yale.edu/phenomena/a-prefixing.

Miller, Gerris S. Jr. & Herbert W. Krieger. 1928. Expedition to Samaná Province, Dominican Republic. In 43–54. Washington.

Mongey, Vanessa. 2019. Going home: The back-to-Haiti movement in the early nineteenth century. *Atlantic Studies* 16. 184–202.

Montgomery, Michael B. 1999. Eighteenth-century Sierra Leone English: Another exported variety of African American English. *English World-Wide* 20. 1–34.

Montgomery, Michael B. 2009. Historical and comparative perspectives on *a-*prefixing in the English of Appalachia. *American Speech* 84(1). 5–26.

Montgomery, Michael B., Janet M. Fuller & Sharon DeMarse. 1993. "The black men has wives and sweet harts [and third person plural -s] jest like the white men": Evidence for verbal -s from written documents on 19th-century African American speech. *Language Variation and Change* 5. 335–357.

Murray, James A. H. 1873. *The dialect of the southern counties of Scotland: Its pronunciation, grammar, and historical relations.* London: The Philological Society.

Myhill, John. 1995. The use of features of present-day AAVE in the Ex-Slave Recordings. *American Speech* 70. 115–47.

Nash, Gary B. 1988. *Forging freedom: The formation of Philadelphia's Black community, 1720-1840.* Cambridge, MA: Harvard University Press.

Nash, Gary B. 1989. New light on Richard Allen: The early years of freedom. *The William and Mary Quarterly* 46(2). 332–340.

Newman, Richard S. 2008a. *Black founders: The Free Black community in the early Republic.* Philadelphia: The Library Company of Philadelphia.

Newman, Richard S. 2008b. *Freedom's prophet: Bishop Richard Allen, the AME church, and the black founding fathers.* New York & London: NYU Press.

Parsons, Elsie Clews. 1928. Spirituals from the "American" colony of Samana Bay, Santo Domingo. *Journal of American Folk-Lore* 41. 525–8.

Payne, Daniel A. 1968. *[1891]. History of the African Methodist Episcopal Church.* Rev. C. S. Smith (ed.). [Reprinted, 1968. New York. Johnson Reprint Corporation]. Nashville, TN: Publishing House of the A. M. E. Sunday School Union.

Penzo Devers, Gregorio Elías. 1999. *Compendio de la historia de Samaná, 1493-1930.* Santo Domingo: Alfa & Omega.

Poplack, Shana & David Sankoff. 1987. The Philadelphia story in the Spanish Caribbean. *American Speech* 62. 291–314.

Poplack, Shana & Sali Tagliamonte. 1989. There's no tense like the present: Verbal –s inflection in early Black English. *Language Variation and Change* 1. 47–84.

Poplack, Shana & Sali Tagliamonte. 2001. *African American English in the diaspora.* Malden, MA, & Oxford: Blackwell.

Rickford, John R. 2015. The creole origins hypothesis. In Sonja Lanehart (ed.), *The Oxford handbook of African American Language*, 35–57. Oxford, New York: Oxford University Press.

Ridner, Judith A. 2017. *Scots Irish (Scotch Irish).* The encyclopedia of Greater Philadelphia. https://philadelphiaencyclopedia.org/archive/scots-irish/.

Schneider, Edgar W. 2013. Investigating historical variation and change in written documents: New perspectives. In *The handbook of language variation and change*, 2nd edn., 57–81. Oxford, UK: Wiley-Blackwell.

Schneider, Edgar W. 2015. Documenting the history of African American Vernacular English. In Sonja Lanehart (ed.), *The Oxford handbook of African American Language*, 125–139. Oxford & New York: Oxford University Press.

Schroeder, Joy. 2007. Wisdom's voice and women's speech: Hrotswitha of Gandersheim, Hildegarde of Bingen, and Patricia Cox Jackson. *Magistra* 13(1). 41–70.

Singler, John Victor. 1989. Plural marking in Liberian Settler English, 1820–1980. *American Speech* 64. 40–64.

Singler, John Victor. 1998. *Who were the dispersed? Annual meeting, new ways of analyzing variation in English.* The African-American diaspora: University of Georgia.

Singler, John Victor. 2007a. Samaná and Sinoe, Part I: Stalking the vernacular. *Journal of Pidgin and Creole Languages* 22. 123–148.

Singler, John Victor. 2007b. Samaná and Sinoe, Part II: Provenance. *Journal of Pidgin and Creole Languages* 22. 309–346.

Singler, John Victor. 2015. African American English over yonder. The language of the Liberian Settler community. In Sonja Lanehart (ed.), *The Oxford handbook of African American Language*, 105–124. New York: Oxford.

Stewart, James Brewer. 1999. Modernizing "difference": The political meanings of color in the free states 1776-1840. *Journal of the Early Republic. Special issue on racial consciousness and nation-building in the Early Republic* 19(4). 691–712.

Szmrecsanyi, Benedikt & Bernd Kortmann. 2009. Vernacular universals and angloversals in a typological perspective. In Markku Filppula, Juhani Klemola & Heli Paulasto (eds.), *Vernacular universals and language contacts: Evidence from varieties of English and beyond*, 33–53. London/New York: Routledge.

Van Herk, Gerard. 2015. The English Origins Hypothesis. In Sonja Lanehart (ed.), *The Oxford Handbook of African American Language*. Oxford.

Vigo, José A. 1982. Transcript of interview conducted with Dora Vanderhorst, Samaná. Ms. José Vigo Collection, Schomburg Center, New York Public Library.

Vigo, José A. 1987. Language and society in Samaná. Ms., José Vigo Collection, Schomburg Center, New York Public Library. [Expanded version of paper presented at the Mid-Hudson Meeting of the MLA, Marist College, Poughkeepsie, NY, 1986.]

Wilmore, Gayraud. 1972. *Black religion and black radicalism.* Garden City, NY: Doubleday.

Winford, Donald. 1997. On the origins of African American Vernacular English— A creolist perspective. Part I: The sociohistorical background. *Diachronica* XIV(2). 305–44.

Winford, Donald. 1998. On the origins of African American Vernacular English—A creolist perspective. Part II: Linguistic features. *Diachronica* XV(1). 99–154.

Winford, Donald. 2015. The origins of African American Vernacular English. In Sonja Lanehart (ed.), *The Oxford handbook of African American language*, 85–104. Oxford, New York: Oxford University Press.

Winford, Donald. 2017. Some observations on the sources of AAVE structure: Re-examining the creole connection. In Cecilia Cutler, Zvjezdana Vrzić & Philipp Angermeyer (eds.), *Language contact in Africa and the African diaspora in the Americas: In honor of John V. Singler*, 203–224. Amsterdam/ Philadelphia: John Benjamins.

Wolfram, Walt & Erik Thomas. 2002. *The development of African American English*. Oxford: Blackwell.

Chapter 4

"Suzie & Sambo" (1937–1956): What can they tell us today?

Lise Winer
McGill University

The recovery, discovery and "uncovery" of historical texts are particularly relevant to societies which have been traditionally undervalued and stigmatized. In recent decades, more attention has been paid to texts in various Caribbean English/Creoles; the social and linguistic data therefrom have proved invaluable in reconstructing the historical development of these languages (Winford 1997). The "Suzie and Sambo" columns are an excellent, hitherto neglected, source of "dialect" texts from Trinidad & Tobago, published in local pro-labour newspapers between 1937 and 1956. The columns purport to be conversations between "Suzie" and "Sambo", two working-class Tobagonians. They comment on local conditions, politics, events, and scandals, as well as carrying on their own fraught relationship. Winford's approach to Caribbean English Creole language variation (Winford 1997) argues that "continua existed in these situations from the earliest period of contact", and he challenges the claim "that they evolve solely via 'decreolization' of basilects under influence from acrolects." He argues for a co-existent systems approach to the contemporary structure of these continua. The evidence of sociolinguistic studies supports the idea that they result from interaction between relatively stable grammars, conditioned by social and situational factors. The variation produced by this interaction provides insight into the kinds of shift and contact-induced change that have always operated in these situations. The Suzie & Sambo texts help to fill in data for a particular and important time period, and support the contention that "varilingualism" is a long-standing characteristic of this (and other) creole societies.

1 Introduction

Support and investigation of linguistic heritage are important in the study of Caribbean languages. The recovery, discovery and "uncovery" of historical texts

Lise Winer. 2022. "Suzie & Sambo" (1937–1956): What can they tell us today? In Bettina Migge & Shelome Gooden (eds.), *Social and structural aspects of language contact and change*, 103–118. Berlin: Language Science Press. DOI: 10.5281/zenodo.6979313

are particularly relevant to societies which have been traditionally – and to some extent still are – undervalued and stigmatized.[1] Despite creole languages being traditionally generally considered "non-literate" or even "unwritable" due to their supposedly incomplete and inferior nature, there exists quite a larger body of written texts in such languages than might be expected. Considerable attention has been paid to such texts in various Caribbean English creoles (see Baker & Bruyn 1999, Lalla & D'Costa 1990, Migge & Mühleisen 2010, Winer 1991, 1993, 1995, 1997, 2003, Winer & Buzelin 2008, Winer & Gilbert 1987, Winer & Rimmer 1994). These texts, and the social and linguistic – lexical, grammatical and phonological – data therefrom, have proved invaluable in (re-)constructing the historical development of these languages (Winford 1997, discussed below).

For several decades, creolists have been finding and republishing historical texts – newspaper columns, plays, novels (Brereton & Winer 2021). A number of recovered "lost" literary works have been republished by Broadview Press, Macmillan Caribbean Press, and the University of the West Indies Press. In addition to old vinyl records from Cook, Folkways and the Library of Congress, and tape recordings from archived private collections such as J.D. Elder (University of Indiana Archives of Traditional Folk Music), there are reissued collections of recordings, from, for example, Rounder Records and Bear Family Records. Still, few Caribbean newspapers have been microfilmed, and even fewer digitized. Several university and public libraries and archives in the region have been building collections of documents, photographs, and personal papers. Many such valuable linguistic records are neither safe nor accessible, and it is hoped that in this survey of Suzie & Sambo we can see an urgent need to make them both.

The current work seeks to introduce researchers in linguistics and cultural history to the "Suzie and Sambo" columns, an excellent but hitherto neglected source of "dialect"[2] (i.e. creole) texts from Trinidad, published in local newspapers between 1937 and 1956. Although it is not possible at this time to provide a complete linguistic analysis, either qualitative or quantitative, a number of practical applications of such analysis are exemplified and described.

---

[1] An earlier version of a paper on this topic – "'Suzie and Sambo': Linguistic archaism or working class solidarity? Creole columns from *The People*, 1938–1940" – was presented at the joint Society for Caribbean Linguistics/Society for Pidgin and Creole Linguistics Conference, Guyana, August 1994.

[2] The term "dialect" is the most widely used designation in the English Caribbean, replacing "broken English" or "Negro English" and giving way to "vernacular," "local" and "Creole".

2 Context of publication

The known run of all "Suzie & Sambo" columns was published in *The People* and *The Chronicle* newspapers between 1937 and 1956, which are held in the National Archives of Trinidad & Tobago. Retrieved texts comprise 195 columns (a few incomplete) containing over 200,000 words.[3] It appears to have run almost every week from 1937 through the beginning of 1947, and then continued from 1953–1956; appearing also in *The Clarion* in 1955–1956.[4] *The People* was a Trinidad-based newspaper whose views were strongly pro-labour, progressive and anti-colonial; it was taken over after WW II by Tubal Uriah "Buzz" Butler, a well-known political and labour activist, and founder of the Oilfields Workers Trade Union. *The People* was especially popular during the pre-World War II period – a time of important labour unionization, particularly amongst workers in the oilfields and on sugar estates. The newspaper, published by L.F. Walcott in Port of Spain, was especially vigorous in its coverage of and support for both local labour movements and foreign struggles, such as that of Abyssinia (now Ethiopia) against the Italian Fascists. Given the political orientation of the paper, most of the readers (either primary or secondary readers or secondarily read-to),[5] were probably working and lower middle class people of African descent.

The author of almost all of the "Suzie & Sambo" columns was the Afro-Creole Tobagonian L.A. Peters (ca. 1880–ca. 1942) a school-teacher and civil servant known from his initials as "The Lappe" (referring to the *lap* or *lappe*, a prized game animal) (see Craig-James 2008: 83–84).[6] The columns purport to be conver-

---

[3] The original quality of the printing is poor, even compared to contemporary local newspapers. Although the archival staff has skilfully repaired many pages, some issues have illegible areas indicated in transcripts with [...], whether from missing pieces of the paper itself, broken or misplaced type, or faded ink. In some cases, an indicated continuation was not found in the same or subsequent issues. Obvious errors (e.g. an upside-down letter) have been silently corrected; larger inferences are indicated by [ ]. One warning to future researchers: the texts were entered into an MS Word file; unfortunately, the Spell-Check feature was activated, and "corrected" much of the spelling, e.g. *fo* became *for* or *foe*. It is now taking a very long time to recheck and copy-read as many of the pieces as possible.

[4] These texts are being prepared for open-access deposition in the Digital Library of the Caribbean (dLOC), University of Florida-Gainesville. I have deposited there a number of other texts, most from Trinidad & Tobago, including all of *Penny Cuts* (Winer 1995), short stories, newspaper articles, and an 1826 novel set in Dutch Guiana (Suriname). https://dloc.com/results/brief/2/?t$=$lise+winer.

[5] According to the *Trinidad & Tobago Annual Statistical Digest 1991*, the literacy rate of persons over 5 years of age in 1931 was 64%; in 1941 it was 74%.

[6] There are other articles of opinion and reportage in the newspaper signed by LAP or occasionally L.A. Peters. It is not known for certain who took over writing the column after Peters' death, sometime after 1953. Rumour holds that this was an unidentified woman working at *The Chronicle* who had helped in the previous editing of the column when the LAP fell ill.

sations between "Suzie" and "Sambo", two working-class Tobagonians, usually speaking while in Tobago and occasionally in Trinidad. They comment mostly on local conditions, politics, events, and scandals, as well as carry on their own fraught relationship. For example, in the issue of April 23, 1938, Suzie and Sambo discuss a schoolmaster's immoral behaviour and the refusal of the Director of Education to remove the teacher.

3 Implications of the material for creole linguistic models

In its simplest iteration, the question of creole continua has boiled down to whether there are two distinct linguistic systems (basilect and acrolect) "mediated" or scaffolded with approximations of the mesolects, or a whole body of language belonging to one large system with a single grammar and no clear boundaries between varieties (a "seamless whole"). Change was often assumed to be unidimensional and unidirectional, from basilect to acrolect (Winford 1997: 233).

Winford's approach to Caribbean English Creole language variation is that "continua existed in these situations from the earliest period of contact", and he challenges the claim "that they evolve solely via 'decreolization' of basilects under influence from acrolects." He argues for a co-existent systems approach to the contemporary structure of these continua. The evidence of sociolinguistic studies supports the idea that they result from interaction between relatively stable grammars, conditioned by social and situational factors. The variation produced by this interaction provides insight into the kinds of shift and contact-induced change that have always operated in these situations (1997: 233).

Winford positions his view to some extent on both types of explanations, in which:

> a range of variation existed in the early period of settlement... followed later by a period in which the rapidly growing population of field slaves developed a relatively homogeneous creole during the plantation era. It was this creole that was subject to later decreolization under the influence of varieties closer to the superstrate, in the period after emancipation... The character of the intermediate varieties was also shaped by contact with both the basilect and the acrolect, leading to a more complex pattern of variation in the developing continuum. (Winford 1997: 233)

The current paper is not designed to address the validity of various approaches to the structural evolution of linguistic variety in CEC situations. Both the mechanisms and the results of linguistic development in the Caribbean are different according to territory. Examining Jamaica, Guyana, Belize and Trinidad, Winford (1997) notes that concepts such as "decreolization" and "mesolect" can vary greatly between specific territories. However, there are some significant points that should be noted about the particular relevance of the Suzie & Sambo texts for the exploration of these models and hypotheses.

First, the series of linguistic, cultural and social inputs in terms of people that took place in Trinidad was among the most complex in the region (see discussions in Winer (1993, 1995, 2009) and Winford (1997: 249–252)). The most important aspects of this development were: 1) the relative lateness of extensive outside settlement of Europeans and Africans from a wide range of locations; 2) the concomitant extensive variety of English Creoles spoken by incomers; and 3) that French Creole was in fact the lingua franca of many, if not most, Trinidad residents well into the twentieth century.[7]

Newspapers in Trinidad & Tobago have a long tradition of writing in dialect, from one-offs such as "The Sorrows of Kitty" in the *Trinidad Standard* of 1839 (Winer 1993) to long-term regular features such as the "Letters to the Editor" from *Penny Cuts* 1904–06 (Winer & Rimmer 1994), the *Trinidad Guardian*'s 1950s "Macaw" (Macaw 1960) and the uncollected 1970s "Letter from Port of Spain" by "Mamits". All these columns focus on both personal and wider socio-political topics. The authors are anonymous or pseudonymous, although their identity is often an open secret known to contemporary and later audiences. Second, these texts were published between 1937–1956, hence in not only a "post-emancipation phase" (Winford 1997: 238) but, in the case of Trinidad, a significant period of time including the very influential influx of U.S. military personnel during and just after WWII. Change and developments within, as well as between, territories have been an uneven process affected by socio-economic factors (see James & Youssef 2002: 206–210).

Third, these texts support a varilingual model of linguistic competence, in which a child does not learn to produce the language varieties to which s/he is exposed to discretely but rather mixes them systematically (code-switching) according to external factors such as setting and topic. The child does not necessarily acquire *full* competence in the two or three codes of his/her exposure but may rather have full competence in one and partial competence in others, or even partial competence in all three. Full varilingualism suggests full competence in two or more codes where code-mixing is a regular feature of use (James

---

[7]While Winford (1997: 251) correctly points out the great influence of Barbadians on providing models of English and mesolectal CEC forms such as *doz* and *did* for Trinidad, in the *Penny Cuts* texts (Winer 1995) from 1904–1906, "born Trinidadians" aligned themselves even with "small islanders" such as Grenadians in preference to not sounding like Bajans.

& Youssef 2002: 17–18). The Suzie & Sambo texts help to fill in data for a particular and important time period, and support the contention that varilingualism is a long-standing characteristic of this (and other) creole societies.

Fourth, the texts are purported to be uttered by Tobagonians, not Trinidadians. There can be an unwelcome tendency to "romanticize" Tobagonian as an archaic relic, and to exaggerate the current differences to the extent that many Trinidadians, especially, believe that Tobagonian is often unintelligible and more like Jamaican. There have been and are differences between the two overall patterns of usage in which most features overlap, but with general differences in phonology, grammar and lexicon. James & Youssef (2002) describe much of this in detail in Chs. 4 (sound system), 5 (verb phrase), 6 (noun and pronoun system) and 7 (other grammatical differences). However, some of the features now considered Tobagonian and not Trinidadian, such as imperfective pre-verbal marker *a*, e.g. *me a go* 'I am going/I go', and remote (anterior) past marker *bin*, e.g. *me bin go* 'I went [some time ago]' as well as prepositions such as *a* 'to', e.g. *mi a go a market* 'I go/am going to market' were in fact liberally used in earlier texts from the 19th and early 20th centuries set in Trinidad. That is, the language varieties of the two islands land used to overlap a lot *more*.

4 Language of the columns

Linguistically, these columns are a treasure trove, and there are enough of them to enable quantitative as well as qualitative analysis. Typical TT Creole features are plentiful in the texts. They are variable, that is, for example, both *A/Ah* and *me* are used for first person subject pronoun. Grammatical features of interest include those in 1:

(1) a. object marker *am*
         Gime de other $10.00 le me put am up.
         Look de money. No spend am pan dress.
         Dat sarb am right.
     b. future marker *go*
         Wey me go get money fo buy frock[?]
         ... hot water go bun dem.
     c. anterior
         bin Any body bun[?] Joe bin dey?
         He say 'e no bin go tell me t'all.
     d. serial verbs
         come out go meet

e. verb +*say*
   me ya're say

f. initial copula *a*
   O yes gal, a' dat mek me no go lef yo t'all.
   A so me coward.

g. directional preposition
   a ... fo put am a jail.

h. pronouns
   O me gad.
   Me no able tell you.
   Go on play de fool, see if more Horn no grow a' yo head.
   Divide de money between a' yo.

There are many examples of the variation that existed between and within speakers in both Trinidad and Tobago during the 19th and 20th centuries, and continues today. For example, plural is marked by Ø, *dem* and –*s*; more analysis might be able to discover patterns in when each form is favoured. The non-completive marker *a* serves as both habitual and progressive markers; however the habitual is marked by Ø, *a* and *does*, suggesting that the habitual diverged from the non-completive *a* before the progressive did (eventually V + *in*) (see discussion in Winer & Gilbert 1987: 177–178).

Creole lexicon in the columns includes *bush got ayze* 'bush has ears' (i.e., be careful, people may be listening), *make mouth fast* 'talk too much', and *go high, go low* 'no matter what you do'. *Nuh* is both a negator and an emphatic tag soliciting agreement (now usually *na* or *nah*). Vocabulary now associated with (older) Tobagonian Creole rather than Trinidadian includes *la-ka* 'like', *suh tay* (*so till*) 'until', *ya're* 'hear', *yey-water* 'tears', *bless eye on* [someone] 'see (with pleasure)', *ratta* 'rat' and *hi* (expression of surprise or disbelief).[8]

Typical phonological features of interest include consonant cluster reduction *tan* 'stand', *tory* 'story', final post-vocalic v > b, *lib* 'live'. Associated only with Tobago are the h-shifting, i.e. variable /h/ (insertion/absence) as in *hempty* 'empty', *ome* 'home' and *am an hegg* 'ham and eggs', but they do not constitute an overwhelming difference between the two linguistic areas. In many "dialect" columns, the Creole (or nonstandard) features are perhaps "thicker", "deeper" or more frequent than they would be normally (i.e. in authentic speech), either because the

---

[8]Lexical differences between the two islands have not yet been systematically studied, but a quick search of the Dictionary of the English/Creole of Trinidad & Tobago (Winer 2009) reveals fewer than 300 words (out of 12,000+) tagged specifically for Tobago; of which more than half are flora and fauna.

writer wishes to make fun of the speakers, or because the writer wishes to emphasize language solidarity with the readers. It should be pointed out that in these
texts the Creole features are also not as thick as they *could* be. For example, in
many cases in these columns, the author could have used *dem* rather than *-s* for
plural marker. Did he forget to be consistent? Or was he trying to represent a
typically occurring variation, more faithful to actual speech patterns? The same
question may be raised for more recent writing that includes creole language
varieties (see Baker & Winer 1999).

It is not easy to determine *now* to what extent such language may have seemed
exaggeration *then*, particularly in view of the fact that this type of text is a highly
polished rendition of a style of speech admired for its linguistic cleverness. Although no one person may actually have spoken or speak exactly as these texts
are written, they are in fact no more misrepresentative of ordinary speech than
any dramatic play or monologue. That is, while stylistically and statistically they
may be of higher "quality" than ordinary speech, they have counterparts in the
oral domain not only of the practiced formal Creole styles such as *robber talk*,
wedding speech and *speech band*, but the everyday expert use of, for example,
boof, sweet talk and *old talk* (Winer 1993: 57–58). The authors were, in any case,
choosing language deliberately and from within a total repertoire that included
standard formal written English, oral Creole, and some written Creole.

The use of Creole in these writings could indicate, on the one hand, solidarity and sympathy with the group of people thus portrayed, or it could indicate
profound contempt and disrespect. In some cases, the author seems clearly to be
laughing *at* people – because of their stupid actions, characteristics, or foibles,
or the type of language they speak (accented, affected, or stigmatized). How can
one tell if the language in a particular text is an attempt to represent (and perhaps make fun of) linguistic archaisms or to indicate solidarity with the people
(i.e., working class) who speak this way?

One interesting area of investigation is the accompanying illustrations. Each
column has at the top a drawing of Suzie and Sambo. At first and for a long
while, this was as in Figure 1, wherein the two are represented as rather ungainly
peasants; in a number of later cases this was replaced by Figure 2, portraying slim
and fashionably dressed figures.

The representation of Suzie and Sambo's speech is easily understood today
by older Tobagonians.[9] However, many features now considered (rightly or
wrongly) as only Tobagonian, were also found – even common – in Trinidad

---

[9] The question of intelligibility is an interesting one, and potentially subject to empirical testing.
In a non-scientific experiment, presenting this as a "Tobago" text to Trinidadians, even older
ones, seems to have an immediate "squashing" effect on Trinidadians who assume and expect
Tobagonian to be unintelligible.

Suzie And Sambo

A LITTLE NONSENSE NOW AND THEN
IS RELISHED BY THE WISEST MEN

· · · · · · · · · · · ·   · · · · · · · · · · · ·

If you carefully study the ways and wiles of these
two people, you will be wise in time.

Figure 1: Illustration of Suzie and Sambo: Ungainly peasants

at this time. The fact that this column was printed in a newspaper primarily sold to working class readers in Trinidad – presumably not just to Tobagonians living there – is another indication that many of the linguistic features here were still widely understood (if not used) in both islands at this time (see discussion for earlier texts in Winer 1995).

There is plenty of material available in the texts to consider differences between Tobagonian and Trinidadian, although allowances must be made for more rapid loss of older words in many (but not all) Trinidadian contexts. This is complicated by the fact that the demographically much higher population percentage of people of East Indian descent in Trinidad means that opportunity for the use of Bhojpuri-derived lexicon would concomitantly be greater. Despite efforts to emphasize – and perhaps even exaggerate – linguistic differences between Tobago and (some speakers in) Trinidad, the two varieties share more and are more

Figure 2: Later illustration of Suzie and Sambo

similar to each other than to any other CEC variety. In older texts, even well into the twentieth century, the differences are very small; "older" Trinidadian is almost indistinguishable from older Tobagonian. This is a controversial position, and it is important to distinguish contemporary speech patterns from those of the past.

5 Sociolinguistic perspectives

Opinions and attitudes expressed about topics indicate the author's sympathies on social, economic, and political topics. Nonetheless, it can be difficult to decide from the text alone – especially from small or isolated pieces – whether the author is being straightforwardly contemptuous or sarcastic, bitter or rueful, poignant or disgusted. As discussed above, it is likely that virtually all the readers knew – understood and spoke – varieties of Creole similar to those represented in the columns, and were being invited to identify with the social class and opinions – and language – of Suzie and Sambo, while at the same time they could appreciate and laugh/shake their heads at their weaknesses and exaggerations.

Sambo seems to be an inept schemer and generally ineffectual braggart, depending on Suzie but wanting to keep his options free. Suzie also schemes and frequently uses deception, her eventual aim being legal marriage. In the sample column given here (Appendix A), Sambo severely criticizes Suzie (and all women) for only caring about money, and for not providing adequate support (food). Suzie retaliates by reminding him that this is because *he* is not providing adequate support (money). When this problem is temporarily resolved, Suzie professes her love for her Sambo. So, there are plenty of examples of quarrelling and criticism, as well as *sweet talk*. In later columns, Suzie soothes her man not only with food and loving, but with liquor ("Oh-be-joyful", an old American expression). Their relationship is characterized by professions of love, as well as criticism, on her part, and complaints on his.

6 Conclusion

Altogether, these texts provide a coherent corpus that would repay scholarly attention. That such a source has not been explored is almost certainly only the tip of an iceberg; there are many materials in archives and libraries (and private collections) – newspapers and memoirs, song lyrics and recipes – few catalogued, that could shine useful light on the domains of language, gender relations, and socio-cultural history.

Acknowledgements

The author gratefully acknowledges Susan Craig-James for pointing out this source and for her immensely helpful historical work on Tobago (2008); staff at the National Archives of Trinidad & Tobago; and Jo-Anne Ferreira and Lawrence Carrington for thoughtful discussions.

References

Baker, Philip & Adrienne Bruyn (eds.). 1999. *St. Kitts and the Atlantic Creoles: The Texts of Samuel Augustus Matthews in perspective.* London: Battlebridge.

Baker, Philip & Lise Winer. 1999. Separating the wheat from the chaff: How far can we rely on old Pidgin and Creole texts. In *St. Kitts and the Atlantic creoles: The texts of Samuel Augustus Mathews in perspective*, vol. 4 (University of Westminster Studies in Creole Languages). London: University of Westminster.

Brereton, Bridget & Lise Winer. 2021. *Two nineteenth-century plays from Trinidad & Tobago: "Martial law" and "past and present".* Mona, Jamaica: University of the West Indies Press.

Craig-James, Susan. 2008. *The changing society of Tobago, 1838-1938: A fractured whole.* Vol. I: 1838–1900, Vol. II: 1900–1938. Arima, Trinidad & Tobago: Cornerstone Press.

James, Winford & Valerie Youssef. 2002. *The languages of Tobago: Genesis, structure and perspectives.* St. Augustine, Trinidad: Cornerstone Press.

Lalla, Barbara & Jean D'Costa. 1990. *Language in exile: Three hundred years of Jamaican Creole.* Tuscaloosa: University Alabama Press.

Macaw, [Kitty Hannays]. 1960. *Notebook.* Port of Spain: Trinidad Publishing Company.

Migge, Bettina M. & Susanne Mühleisen. 2010. Earlier Caribbean English and Creole in writing. In Raymond Hickey (ed.), *Varieties in writing: The written word as linguistic evidence*, 223–244. Amsterdam: John Benjamins.

Winer, Lise. 1991. New sources for old data. *Carrier Pidgin* 9. 5–6.

Winer, Lise. 1993. *Trinidad and Tobago* (Varieties of English around the World 6). Amsterdam/Philadelphia: John Benjamins.

Winer, Lise. 1995. Penny cuts: Differentiation of creole varieties in Trinidad, 1904-1906. *Journal of Pidgin and Creole Languages* 10(1). [Revised version and complete texts lodged with dLOC, the Digital Library of the Caribbean, University of Gainesville, Florida USA], 127–155.

Winer, Lise. 1997. Six vernacular texts from Trinidad, 1839-1851. *Englishes around the World: Caribbean, Africa, Asia, Australia: Studies in honor of Manfred Gör-lach* 2. 69–83.

Winer, Lise (ed.). 2003. *Adolphus, a tale (anonymous) & The slave son (Mrs. William Noy Wilkins)* (Caribbean Heritage 2). orig. 1853, 1854. Kingston, Jamaica: University of the West Indies Press.

Winer, Lise. 2009. *Dictionary of the English/Creole of Trinidad & Tobago*. Montreal: McGill-Queens Press.

Winer, Lise & Hélène Buzelin. 2008. Literary representations of creole languages: Cross-linguistic perspectives from the Caribbean. In John V. Singler & Silvia Kouwenberg (eds.), *Handbook of pidgin and creole linguistics*, 637–665. Oxford: Blackwell.

Winer, Lise & Glenn Gilbert. 1987. A 19th century report on the English Creole of Tobago: The Uh-Schuchardt correspondence. *English World-Wide* 8(2). 235–262.

Winer, Lise & Mary Rimmer. 1994. Language varieties in early Trinidadian novels, 1838-1907. *English World-Wide* 15(2). 225–248.

Winford, Donald. 1997. Re-examining Caribbean English Creole Continua. *World Englishes* 16(2). 233–79.

Appendix A: Sample "Suzie & Sambo" column

The People, 1 May 1937
A LITTLE NONSENSE NOW AND THEN
Is Relished by the Wisest Men.

Original Version

1. Sambo: O'man, to tell you de truth, ef no bin fo de Law, a' would a' mash you skin an' dreb yo way now, now. Dis a' bittle fo man la'ka me to eat?

2. Suzie: Me ready to go now. No yo one ah man. Yo mus' be mad Nigga Man. Yo wan' me to tief fo feed yo?

3. Sambo: Well a' right. Pack yo grip, an' clare out at once. When man got money any o'man go glad to get am.

4. Suzie: A' dem la'ka yo so a' ha money? Look pan am. Nigga Mans go hide yo' self.

5. Sambo: Oh ho. Yo tink me no ha money. Look. (He pulls out 3 five-dollar bills from his pocket).

6. Suzie: Sambo me honey, a' fun me bin a' mek wid you. Dear Sambo boy, yo tink me go leff you. A' you a' de only man in dis world me lub. Come kiss me an' le me hug yo an' squeeze yo.

7. Sambo: Yo see how ah yo 'omans tan. When man no ha' money, dag better den he.[10]

8. Suzie: No me Sugar, me Honey, me Sambo-Tambo. Gi me de money le me run go ah shop come back. Yo go see how me lub yo me Sambo-Lambo, me own, own, own, own Sambo. Da Nigga man Joe bin a' watch me but –

9. Sambo: Shut up. Yo tink me a' fool no? Me only gi you one gad $5.00.

10. Suzie: A'right, gi me a' me han'. Tell me how yo get so much money dis week.

11. Sambo: Mark yo no tell nobody. Dis a' ded secret. Dem a' bill jetty an' repair market hus dis week. Su when dem see de Boss a' come, them mek stevedo mans liff up one piece a' bode la-ka ef e a' wuk. Mr. Full Stop e' self come down pan de Wafe fo ketch dem but e so no barn yet.

12. Suzie: An how you get su much?

13. Sambo: 'Oman no hax me too much question. Me tell yo, me join Big Fish Club, an' ef dem no run Bo-bul, how dem go mek out.

14. Suzie: A'right me Sweetie. Gi me de other $10.00 le me put am up. (He hands her the money). Tell me wha' 'bout Jumbie Edman case and de Syrian case wha' happen?

15. Sambo: Gal oh... me no know wha fo say. After Jumbie Edmans done bruk the pillice mans 'ed wid stick, de Magistrate say e cant sen' am a' jail be-carse 'e 'ed no good. He want fo sen am whe dem a' sen mad people.

16. Suzie: He right. Jumbie Edman out ob 'e 'ed fo true. An' wha' 'bout de Syrian Case.

17. Sambo: A' gal. Yo bin fo ya're de Inspector talk fo Charles. He only a' say 'Council for de Defence.' He no say 'My Friend' dis time.

18. Suzie: Some body musse tell am. Or 'e does read 'The People.' But how de case pass?

19. Sambo: De two side pay. All de money come up to 'bout $70.00.

20. Suzie: So much. Ah yo Bobul Club get any a' dat?

21. Sambo: 'Oman yo chupit eh? How dem go get dat? Look ya, me wan' fo sleep. Shet yo mout now. When yo see money yo mout a' a fly laka patch-corn.[11]

---

[10] *When man no ha' money, dag better den he.* Perhaps a reference to Growling Tiger's 1935 ca-lypso, "Money is King": "If you haven't money, dog is better than you."

[11] *yo mout' [a] fly laka patch-corn.* i.e. salivates. *Chilibibi* or *samsam*, is a delicacy made of sweet-ened pounded parched corn; when eaten, it can spray out of the mouth.

22. Suzie: A'right Sambo deer, go sleep love, and dream 'bout yo deer Suzie.
    To-marrow marning, me go gi yo Coffee-tea with ham and heggs an' ting
    and ting.[12] Yo know how. The King self no go eat food la-ka yo to-marrow.
    Sleep good dear Sambo boy.

English Version

1. Sambo: Woman, to tell you the truth, if it wasn't for the Law, I would have
   mashed your skin and driven you away right now. This is vittles for a man
   like me to eat?
2. Suzie: I'm ready to go now. Not you alone is man ['You are not the only
   man']. You must be mad, nigger man. You want me to steal to feed you?
3. Sambo: Well all right. Pack your grip, and clear out at once. When a man
   has money any woman will be glad to get him.
4. Suzie: A man like you has money? Look at you. Nigger man, go hide your-
   self.
5. Sambo: Oh ho. You think I have no money. Look. (He pulls out 3 five-dollar
   bills from his pocket).
6. Suzie: Sambo, my honey, I was making fun with you. Dear Sambo boy, you
   think I will leave you? You are the only man in this world I love. Come kiss
   me and let me hug you and squeeze you.
7. Sambo: You see how all of you women are. When a man has no money,
   dog is better than him.
8. Suzie: No, my Sugar, my Honey, my Sambo-Tambo. Give me the money,
   and let me run to the shop and come back. You will see how I love you, my
   Sambo-Lambo, my own, own, own, own Sambo. That nigga man Joe was
   looking at me but –
9. Sambo: Shut up. You think I'm a fool? I'm only giving you one good $5.00.
10. Suzie: All right, give it to me in my hand. Tell me how you got so much
    money this week.
11. Sambo: Mark you, don't tell anybody. This is a dead secret. They were
    building a jetty and repairing the market house this week. So when they
    see the Boss coming, they make the stevedores lift up a piece of board as
    if they are working. Mr. Full Stop himself came down onto the Wharf to
    catch them but the man to catch them isn't born yet.
12. Suzie: And how did you get so much?

---

[12]ham and heggs. This is probably meant to be 'am and heggs.

117

13. Sambo: Woman, don't ask me too many questions. I told you, I joined the Big Fish Club, and if they don't do something crooked, how will they make out?

14. Suzie: All right my Sweetie. Give me the other $10.00 and let me put it aside. (He hands her the money). Tell me what about the Jumbie Edmund case and the Syrian case, what happened?

15. Sambo: Gal oh… I don't know what to say. After Jumbie Edmans broke the police man's head with a stick, the Magistrate said he couldn't sent him to jail because his head is no good. He wanted to send him where they send mad people.

16. Suzie: He's right. Jumbie Edmund is out of his mind in truth. And what about the Syrian Case?

17. Sambo: Ah, gal. You should have heard the Inspector talk for Charles. He only said 'Council for the Defence.' He didn't say 'My Friend' this time.

18. Suzie: Somebody must have told him. Or he reads 'The People.' But how did the case end up?

19. Sambo: The two sides paid. All the money came up to about $70.00.

20. Suzie: So much! Did your Bobol Club get any of that?

21. Sambo: Woman, you're stupid, eh? How would they get that? Look here, I want to sleep. Shut your mouth now. When you see money your mouth flies like parched corn.

22. Suzie: All right, Sambo dear, go to sleep, love, and dream about your dear Suzie. Tomorrow morning, I will give you coffee-tea with ham and eggs and so on. You know how. The King himself won't eat food like you to-morrow. Sleep well, dear Sambo boy.

Chapter 5

The expression of possibility in the Chabacano creoles and their adstrates

Marivic Lesho
Franklin University

This study investigates how possibility is expressed in Zamboanga and Cavite Chabacano and two of their respective adstrates, Hiligaynon and Tagalog. Following Winford's (2000, 2018) call for creolists to use standard typological frameworks to describe creole modality, this study presents questionnaire data elicited for each language and classifies the modals according to categories proposed by van der Auwera & Plungian (1998), Palmer (2001), and Matthewson et al. (2005). The data demonstrate that all four languages have the same typological profile, with mixed Philippine and Spanish elements. *Pwede* 'can' (< Sp. *puede*) expresses deontic, dynamic, and epistemic possibility, as in Spanish, and in the creoles, it also marks nonvolitional circumstances, parallel to Philippine *ma(ka)-*. Epistemic possibility is marked primarily by adverbs in each language, however, with *siguro* 'possibly/probably' (< Sp. *seguro* 'sure') flexibly able to mark necessity. The data support recent proposals (Fernández 2006, 2012a; Sippola & Lesho 2020) that the Chabacano varieties are highly similar not because they descended from a single ancestor but because their adstrates are so closely related. In fact, the adstrate modal systems are nearly identical.

1 Introduction

This paper describes how possibility is expressed in two Philippine-Spanish creoles, Zamboanga and Cavite Chabacano, and two of their respective substrates/adstrates, Hiligaynon and Tagalog. Studies focusing on the modal systems of these languages from a semantic or typological perspective have been scarce. As Winford (2000, 2018) has observed, modality has been a neglected area of creole studies, due in large part to reliance on the coarse-grained categorization

Marivic Lesho. 2022. The expression of possibility in the Chabacano creoles and their adstrates. In Bettina Migge & Shelome Gooden (eds.), *Social and structural aspects of language contact and change*, 119–156. Berlin: Language Science Press. DOI: 10.5281/zenodo.6979315

assumed by Bickerton's (1984) concept of the "prototypical" creole tense–mood–aspect (TMA) system, which he proposed as part of his language bioprogram hypothesis. This approach assumes Irrealis as a grammatical category shared across creoles, with none of the more fine-grained distinctions that are commonly assumed in other TMA literature (e.g., Dahl 1985, Bybee et al. 1994, and Palmer 2001). There are other reasons why creole modality is relatively under explored, such as the fact that some semantic distinctions do not always occur spontaneously during naturalistic field recordings, and thus do not make it into the initial descriptions of a language; however, there is no denying that "Bickerton's rather idiosyncratic terminology and framework left a profound mark on the way research on creole TMA was conducted" for decades (Winford 2018: 1).

Following these tendencies, previous Chabacano research has often discussed the preverbal TMA markers (e.g., Forman 1972, Lipski & Santoro 2007), but only Sippola's (2011) Ternate Chabacano grammar has provided any systematic description of modality. Focusing on two other Chabacano varieties and providing comparison with the adstrates, this paper describes how different subtypes of possibility are marked. It compares the overall modal typology of these languages from a crosslinguistic perspective and discusses how Spanish contact shaped not only the creoles but also their closely related adstrates in this complex contact setting.

2 Background

2.1 Chabacano formation

Chabacano is a collective name for several creoles spoken in the Philippines. In the Manila Bay region in the north, Chabacano is spoken in the towns of Ternate and Cavite City, and it was also once used in Manila and nearby provinces (Fernández 2011). Other Chabacano varieties are spoken in Mindanao in the south, mainly in Zamboanga City and the surrounding region, including nearby islands like Basilan and Jolo. It is also spoken to some extent in Cotabato, and was formerly used in Davao.

Tagalog (Central Philippine) is the substrate/adstrate for the Manila Bay varieties. For the Mindanao varieties, Cebuano and Hiligaynon are generally considered the main substrates/adstrates, though several local languages are spoken there (e.g., Yakan and Tausug). Hiligaynon and Cebuano are in the Visayan branch of Central Philippine but are still closely related to Tagalog. In addition, the country's official languages, English and Filipino (a standardized variety based mainly on Tagalog), are now widely used across all regions. Spanish no longer has any presence in daily life for most Filipinos.

The Chabacano varieties are strikingly similar. They have 95% similarity on the 100-word Swadesh list (Sippola 2011: 27) and share 64% of the value assignments for 107 features in the *Atlas of Pidgin and Creole Studies* (APiCS, Michaelis et al. 2013). Speakers of the different varieties usually say they can understand each other; however, they generally consider their varieties to be distinct, due to the geographical distance between them, lexical influence from the different adstrates, and accent differences (Lesho & Sippola 2014). Historically, these three communities have not had much interaction with each other.

The similarity among the varieties has led to the assumption that they are all directly related. Whinnom (1956) proposed that they all descend from Ternate Chabacano, which he believed originally came from a Portuguese-based contact language transplanted to the Philippines in 1659, when 200 families were transferred from the Moluccas to the Ermita district of Manila, and later resettled in Ternate. This variety would have been relexified with Spanish and emulated by people in Manila and Cavite, and then later spread to Zamboanga after Tagalog soldiers were supposedly transferred there in 1719.

Several aspects of this theory have since been disputed, however, including the supposed Portuguese influence (Lipski 1988); the dates being too early, based on the timing of certain Spanish sound changes that are reflected in Chabacano (Fernández & Sippola 2017); and the historical accuracy of the events Whinnom described (Fernández 2006, 2011, 2012b,a, 2019). For example, Tagalog speakers in Ermita would have already had intensive contact with Spanish before 1659 and thus would not have needed to borrow an outside contact vernacular to communicate (Fernández 2011, 2012b). Historical records also do not support the idea that Tagalog soldiers played any significant role in transmitting a creole to Zamboanga (Fernández 2019).

Many Chabacano scholars now agree that the varieties developed for the most part independently of each other (Lipski 1992, Fernández 2011, 2012b,a, Fernández & Sippola 2017, Sippola & Lesho 2020). Lipski (1992: 12), for example, proposed that rather than being a simple transplant of Manila Bay Chabacano, the Zamboanga variety first formed locally in the mid-1700s "as the natural intersection of Philippine languages which shared cognate grammatical systems, and which had already absorbed a significant quantity of Hispanisms". He suggested that any input from Manila Bay would have been introduced only after this initial formation.

More recent work by Fernández (2006, 2011, 2012b,a, 2019) and Fernández & Sippola (2017), based on meticulous archival research as well as linguistic evidence, has suggested later timelines and even more separate trajectories of formation. Historical accounts or literary texts featuring any mentions or examples of Chabacano were scarce before the late 1800s (see also Lipski 2013). The oldest account that seems to refer to a fully restructured variety comes from 1806, in reference to Cavite, and the earliest Chabacano texts that have been identified so far come from 1859/1860 in Manila (Fernández & Sippola 2017). These facts suggest that Chabacano did not crystallize in Cavite and Manila until the late 18th or early 19th centuries, though Ternate Chabacano formed somewhat earlier (Fernández & Sippola 2017). For Zamboanga, historical accounts indicate that Spanish was widely used by local people there during the early colonial period, and that Chabacano developed much later, only after the population expanded in the late 19th century (Fernández 2006, 2012a).

If the Chabacano varieties do not have a direct genetic relationship, then how is their similarity explained? The answer is that Tagalog and the Visayan languages (and the Philippine family overall) share remarkably similar syntactic structures, morphemes, and semantic features, which led to similar restructuring outcomes in each contact situation (Sippola & Lesho 2020). It is also the case that the Chabacano varieties are not quite as homogenous as they have appeared to be at first glance. If all varieties really descended from one source, we might expect them to be even more similar than they are. Yet it is well known that each variety has its own unique set of pronouns; for example, the 1PL is *mihotro* in Ternate, *niso* in Cavite, and *kame* (exclusive) and *kita* (inclusive) in Zamboanga (Lesho & Sippola 2014: 14, Lipski 2013: 457). By comparing previously published documentation of each variety, Lesho & Sippola (2014: 9–16) identified several other lexical, phonological, and morphosyntactic differences among the varieties that have previously been overlooked.

Sippola & Lesho (2020) compared reciprocal marking, argument marking, and modality in Cavite, Ternate, and Zamboanga Chabacano. They demonstrated that these are areas where the varieties have often followed different grammaticalization paths, suggesting that they do not stem from one source. For example, Zamboanga and Cavite Chabacano use the Philippine circumfix *man-V-han* as well as the Spanish-derived construction *uno'y otro* or *uno a otro* ('one to another') to mark reciprocal actions, whereas Ternate Chabacano grammaticalized *hugá* < (Sp. jugar 'play'), as in *hugá keré* 'love each other' (Sippola & Lesho 2020:115–116). A brief overview of the modals also showed instances where each Chabacano variety functions similarly but grammaticalized different elements from the lexifier. For example, each variety has a necessity verb grammaticalized from different Spanish sources: *ne(se)sita* in Zamboanga (< Sp. *necesita* 'need'), *debi* in Cavite (< Sp. *debe* 'must, owe'), and *dabli* in Ternate (< Sp. *dable* 'possible, feasible') (Sippola & Lesho 2020: 112–113). Taken together with the sociohistorical evidence (e.g., Fernández & Sippola 2017), the differences that have now been documented (Lesho & Sippola 2014, Sippola & Lesho 2020) provide support for the idea that these three Chabacano varieties each developed locally, though the replication of related adstrate features led to similar results in each case. This paper further reinforces these points, following up on Sippola & Lesho (2020) by offering an even more detailed investigation of the Chabacano modal systems and comparing them directly to those of the adstrates.

2.2 Possibility in Chabacano

Previous Chabacano descriptions have mostly glossed over modality, focusing more on the aspect markers: perfective *ya*, imperfective *ta*, and the future *ay* (in Mindanao) or *di* (in Manila Bay). *Ay* and *di* have been described as marking 'future or unreal events' (Lipski & Santoro 2007: 380) or 'both future and modality' (Lorenzino 2000: 58). It is clear, however, that the future markers do not cover all types of irrealis/modal events; in fact, no creole seems to be set up that way (Winford 2018).

Frake (1980: 297–301) listed the possibility verb *puede* 'able' (< Sp. *puede* 'able.3SG') among several other modals in Zamboanga Chabacano. He defined it as expressing 'ability because of physical circumstances such as one's strength or the lack of external strength' (Frake 1980: 298). However, there was no indication of whether it can be extended to permission or epistemic possibility, as Spanish *puede* and Tagalog *puwede* both can be.

Rubino (2008) examined how Zamboanga Chabacano *puede* marks "potentive mode", a category in Cebuano that includes not only ability but also "actions that are brought about accidentally, coincidentally, or without volition or instigation" (Rubino 2008: 279). For example, in (1), the speaker is not discussing their ability or intention to die but rather an eventual death that will occur beyond their control.

(1) Si yo *puede* muri enterra kamo kumigo aki na presioso sitio.
    If 1SG able die bury 2PL 1SG.ACC here LOC precious site
    'If I die, bury me here in this precious site.' (Rubino 2008: 292)

Sippola (2011), following Palmer's (2001) framework of modal description, categorized modal markers in Ternate Chabacano. She described *pwede* 'able' as expressing deontic permission, epistemic possibility, or dynamic ability, and also marking accidental events, as in (2). The verb *mari* 'able' (< Tag. *maaari* 'able') expresses the same range of notions, except for perhaps epistemic possibility (such uses did not occur in Sippola's dataset; if they do exist, they must have very low frequency).

(2) A-*mari/pwedi* miyá yo na mi   panti.
     PFV-able/able pee   1SG LOC 1.SG POSS underwear
     'I (accidentally) peed on my underwear.' (Sippola 2011: 163–164)

In addition, she described two epistemic adverbs, *baka* 'possibly' and *sigúru* 'possibly', listing the latter as marking uncertainty and the former as marking conjecture (Sippola 2011: 209–209).

These few studies show insight into an under-explored area of Chabacano grammar and creoles more generally. In particular, Sippola (2011) offers a point of comparison for work on other Chabacano varieties.

2.3 Possibility in the adstrates

Tagalog has four ability/possibility markers: the "pseudoverbs" *maaari, puwede* (< Sp. *puede*), and *kaya*, and the verbal prefix *ma(ka)-*.[1] The pseudoverbs (labeled as such because they are not inflected for aspect) exhibit some syntactic differences; unlike *puwede* and *maaari, kaya* 'ability, power' functions as a 'modal noun' (Kroeger 1993). How they contrast in meaning, however, is not always clear. For *maaari* and *puwede*, Schachter & Otanes (1972: 261) indicated only that the latter is less formal. They described both as covering ability, permission, and possibility. Asarina & Holt (2005: 14–15) described them as taking deontic/dynamic readings, and *kaya* as being 'strongly preferred' in dynamic contexts.

Ma(ka)- marks ability in some contexts, but it can also mean that the action was not deliberate, as in (3).

(3) *naka*gamit   siya ng manggang hilaw
     PFV.AV.able.use 3SG GEN mango.LNK unripe
     'he was able to use a green mango' or 'he happened to use a green mango' (Schachter & Otanes 1972: 330)

Ma(ka)- has been identified as a marker of "non-volitive mood" (Kroeger 1993) or "ability/involuntary action" (AIA) in Tagalog (Schachter & Otanes 1972), and the "potentive mode" in Cebuano (Rubino 2008). Dell (1983) noted that Tagalog AIA verbs have an actuality entailment in the perfective. For example, the neutral

---

[1]*Maka-* is used in actor voice and *ma-* in other voices (e.g., object or locative voice). *Ma-* can also be used in actor voice for stative verbs. The initial consonant becomes [n] when the action is [+begun] (i.e., in the perfective or imperfective).

form *itinulak* 'pushed' in (4) does not entail that the rock actually moved; in (5), however, the perfective form with *na-* entails that it did.

(4) Itinulak   ni   Ben ang bato.
     PFV.OV.push GEN Ben NOM rock
     'Ben pushed the rock.' (Dell 1983: 179–180)

(5) Naitulak   ni   Ben ang bato.
     PFV.OV.able.push GEN Ben NOM rock
     'Ben managed to push the rock' or 'Ben accidentally pushed the rock.'
     (Dell 1983: 179–180)

AIA forms assert not only that a maneuver has been executed but that a result has also been achieved, whether intentionally or not (hence the two possible readings in example 5).

While *ma(ka)-* marks dynamic/potentive verbs, *ma-* is also part of a separate but overlapping paradigm marking statives (Himmelmann 2006). Stative *ma-* can mark bodily conditions/emotional states (*magutom* 'be hungry', *matakot* 'be scared'), positional predicates (*maupo* 'be seated'), and perception (*makita* 'see'; Himmelmann 2006: 491–494). In addition, the related adjectival *ma-* denotes qualities/properties associated with the root (*maliit* 'small', *mabato* 'stony/having stones').[2] These various functions derive from Proto-Malayo-Polynesian **ma-*, which marked involuntariness and states (Evans & Ross 2001).

There has been less detailed examination of Hiligaynon *ma(ka)-*, but Spitz (2002: 383–384) lists examples showing that it covers a similar range of meanings to those described by Himmelmann (2006). In addition to AIA uses, Spitz observed that *ma-* marks experiences related to cognition/perception, body function, happenstance, or a lack of control over the circumstances (e.g., it occurs with roots like *kita* 'see', *uhaw* 'thirst', *subo* 'sad', *patay* 'die', etc.). Interestingly, Rubino (2008: 292) showed that Chabacano *pwede* occurs with verbs like *murí* 'die'. Thus, *pwede* seems to map onto not only potentive *ma(ka)-* but also at least some of these stative uses of *ma-*.

Asarina & Holt (2005) noted that epistemic modality is not expressed in Tagalog through modal verbs. While this claim is not strictly accurate, since *puwede* and *maaari* can be used epistemically (Schachter & Otanes 1972), it is true that epistemicity is expressed primarily through adverbs. Bader et al. (1994) listed

---

[2] *Ma(ka)-* and adjectival *ma-* also exist somewhat productively in Chabacano with Spanish or even English-origin roots, e.g., Cav. *maka-irrita* 'be irritated' and *ma-quarantine* 'be quarantined' (Escalante 2010: 98–105), or Zam. *mapuersa* 'strong' (i.e., 'having strength').

baka, posible (< Sp. *posible* 'possible'), and *siguro* (< Sp. *seguro* 'sure') as the main epistemic adverbs; however, they glossed all three as 'perhaps', so it is unclear how they might be distinct. This ambiguity is also present in dictionaries for Tagalog, Hiligaynon, and Chabacano. For example, Tagalog *baka, siguro*, and even the verb *maaari* have all been defined as both 'maybe/possibly' and 'probably/probable' (English 2008: 785).

3 Methods

3.1 Data collection

The data come primarily from elicitation using Dahl's (1985: 198–206) TMA questionnaire, modified to include a few additional examples of intentional vs. non-intentional actions. The questionnaire was completed through elicitation sessions with speakers of Zamboanga Chabacano, Cavite Chabacano, Hiligaynon, and Tagalog, as summarized in Table 1.

Table 1: Consultant backgrounds

Language	*n*	Ages	Interview location	Other languages
Zamboanga Chabacano	6	30s–70s	Atlantic City, NJ (5 living there, 1 visiting from Zamboanga)	At least 4 others, some combination of: Filipino, English, Cebuano, Hiligaynon, Yakan, Tausug, Spanish or limited Spanish
Cavite Chabacano	3	50s–60s	San Diego, CA (1), Cavite City (2)	Tagalog/Filipino, English, limited Spanish
Tagalog/Filipino	1	20s	Columbus, OH	English, limited Hiligaynon
Hiligaynon	1	20s	Columbus, OH	Filipino, English, Kinaray-a

Most of these consultants were interviewed in the US at different points during 2009–2010 and had been living there for several years, though all originally came from the Philippines and continued to use their various languages, since they maintained Filipino social networks in both countries. Additional elicitation took place in Cavite City with two Cavite Chabacano consultants in 2016. Since Tagalog and Hiligaynon are already well documented compared to the creoles, there was less focus on finding several speakers; one speaker of each was enough to obtain parallel examples to the Chabacano data.

All of the consultants were multilingual. Zamboanga is a particularly linguistically diverse region, so the Zamboangueños all knew at least four languages. Only one person (from Zamboanga) reported being proficient in Spanish. All the other Chabacano speakers had some exposure to Spanish, either through college classes or from older relatives who used to speak it, but did not use it regularly or list it among the languages they speak.

The consultants all came from socioeconomic backgrounds that could be considered middle class within their respective countries of residence (for example, most had occupations such as nursing or office work). Some of the Zamboangueños originally came from Zamboanga City and some from Basilan, but there were no noticeable differences in the grammatical patterns elicited for this study (although the participants sometimes commented on phonological features that vary by region). Similarly, the Cavite Chabacano speakers were uniform in their modal usage, though they came from neighborhoods with slight accent differences (Lesho 2018). The Hiligaynon and Tagalog consultants' speech was representative of their original hometowns (Iloilo and Manila, respectively).

The elicitation involved presenting the consultants with pragmatic contexts from the questionnaire and asking how they would respond to them. Additional follow-up questions were added spontaneously as needed (e.g., whether they could use another modal in the same context, or if they could think of any other situations where the modal might be used). Negative evidence was also obtained by presenting the consultants with alternative utterances to confirm that using a certain modal in that context would be infelicitous.

The Dahl (1985) questionnaire is useful for systematically eliciting parallel examples for several speakers/languages and obtaining examples that may not happen to arise over the course of a natural conversation. There can be pragmatic gaps, however, and it can be difficult to elicit an intended meaning unless enough context is invented for the speakers. For this reason, a few other speakers in the Philippines were consulted for occasional follow-up questions as needed (usually via email). Occasionally, data from other sources (e.g., blogs, news websites, or grammars) were also used for additional evidence. These few examples from alternative sources are clearly labeled when presented in §4.

3.2 Framework

As Winford (2000, 2018) has observed, until fairly recently, creole TMA systems have often been described in terms of the three 'prototypical creole' categories proposed by Bickerton (1984): Anterior tense, Irrealis mood, and Nonpunctual aspect. As he has shown, however, this classification is too broad to result in accurate grammatical descriptions; it ignores the richness and complexity of individual creole systems, and it obscures variation when comparing creoles. It also makes it difficult to conduct crosslinguistic comparison to the substrates, lexifiers, or other languages in general. Instead, Winford (2000) argued for examining creole TMA systems within standard typological and semantic frameworks (e.g., Bybee et al. 1994, Palmer 2001), demonstrating the value of this approach with his analysis of Sranan. While many creole TMA studies have since moved beyond the 'first phase' of research within Bickerton's paradigm and into a 'second phase' relying on more standard terminology and frameworks of analysis, modality is still an often-neglected area (Winford 2018).

Following Winford's recommendations, this paper examines deontic, dynamic, and epistemic possibility in Chabacano and its adstrates within frameworks more commonly used in crosslinguistic typological studies, primarily those used by Palmer (2001) and van der Auwera & Plungian (1998). These types of possibility are illustrated in (6) for English.

(6) Possibility:

    a. Deontic: *John **can/may** swim* (e.g., his father gave him permission).

    b. Dynamic: *John **can** swim* (i.e., he is able/knows how).

    c. Epistemic: *John **could/might** be swimming* (e.g., you are speculating on his whereabouts).

Possibility contrasts with necessity for each of these modal categories, as shown in the following examples.

(7) Necessity:

    a. Deontic: *John **must/has** to swim* (e.g., his coach told him to).

    b. Dynamic: *John **must** swim back to shore* (e.g., because his boat sank).

    c. Epistemic: *John **must** be swimming* (e.g., you know he usually does so every day at this hour).

According to Palmer (2001), the deontic and dynamic categories comprise the broader category of 'event modality'. Deontic modality involves the imposition of some external authority (see 6a, 7a). In the dynamic examples, in contrast, the situations arise from general circumstances related to John's own ability or the facts of the situation. Epistemic modality differs from event modality because it involves the speaker's assessment of the truth value of a proposition, based on the available knowledge of the situation.

Dynamic modality can include several notions, such as physical or mental ability, learned ability, or possibility arising from circumstances affecting the situation (Palmer 2001). The latter type is distinct from the first two in that, similar to deontic possibility, the possibility arises externally rather than internally to the participant (van der Auwera & Plungian 1998). These different subtypes of dynamic possibility are illustrated for English in (8).

(8) Dynamic possibility:

   a. Participant-internal:

      i. Learned ability: *John* **can** *read* (i.e., he knows how).

      ii. Capability: *John* **can** *run a marathon* (i.e., he has the physical ability and mental drive).

   b. Participant-external:

      i. Circumstantial possibility: *John* **can** *go to the beach whenever he wants* (e.g., he has the time or lives near it).

Rather than dynamic modality, some semanticists (e.g., Kratzer 1991, Matthewson et al. 2005) refer to a category of circumstantial modality, which includes examples like that in (8b). I follow Palmer (2001) in using "dynamic" as the overarching label because it encompasses the diverse range of notions illustrated in (8), and reserve the label "circumstantial" as one of its subtypes. Recognizing the distinctions in (8) is important in describing languages like Tagalog, which encodes each of those notions in a different way (see §4).

In addition, I propose that the various potentive/AIA uses of *pwede* and *ma(ka)-* all fall under the category of participant-external dynamic possibility (which I take to be synonymous with circumstantial possibility). This categorization is inspired by the work of Matthewson et al. (2005) and Davis & Rullmann (2009) on St'át'imcets, a Salishan language that has intriguing similarities to Austronesian AIA marking. Like *ma(ka)-*, St'át'imcets *ka-...-a* encompasses not only 'be able to' meanings but also a range of "out-of-control" or nonvolitional contexts (including accidents, sudden events, 'manage to' readings, etc.). While the semantic parallels to the Philippine and creole languages in this study are not exact (Davis & Rullmann 2009: 219), the similarities to St'át'imcets are close enough to justify grouping all these different semantic notions under the umbrella of participant-external dynamic or circumstantial modality.

I also rely on a framework proposed by Matthewson et al. (2005) to consider the overall typology of the modal systems of the Chabacano varieties and their adstrates. They observed that modals in different languages can be lexically specified along two dimensions: modal base (i.e., circumstantial/dynamic, deontic, or epistemic), and modal force (i.e., weak modals used in possibility contexts vs. strong modals used in necessity contexts). In St'át'imcets, modals are always specified for base but not force. For example, *ka-...-a* is used only in circumstantial contexts and cannot take deontic or epistemic readings, but it has flexible force. The ability reading is the weaker one (e.g., in possibility contexts like 'six people *can* fit in that car'), and the nonvolitional reading is the stronger one (e.g., in necessity contexts like 'Gertie *must/had to* sneeze', because she had a cold; Davis & Rullmann 2009: 228, 231). Similarly, St'át'imcets deontic and epistemic modals take on both strong and weak meanings depending on the discourse context, but they are fixed to one modal base. This type of modal system is the opposite of languages like English or Spanish, which have a tendency to specify modals for force but not base; for example, *can/could* takes either deontic, epistemic, or circumstantial/dynamic readings depending on the discourse context, but it always indicates possibility and not necessity (which is covered by the stronger *must*).

Later research within this framework has found that some languages have 'mixed' modal systems compared to St'át'imcets and English. Gitskan, for example, has circumstantial modals that are specified for modal force (as in English), but the epistemic modals have flexible force (as in St'át'imcets; Matthewson 2013: 350). Paciran Javanese also has a strictly epistemic marker that is used with flexible force (for necessity or possibility), and a necessity modal with fixed force that can be used in various non-epistemic modal contexts (Vander Klok 2013). In this paper, I consider how the Chabacano varieties and their adstrates fit into this typology. I also discuss the overall similarities and differences in the Chabacano modal systems to address questions about the relationships between these varieties and how they developed.

4 Data

This section presents examples of how each language in this study expresses possibility in deontic, dynamic, and epistemic contexts. A few examples of how necessity is expressed are also included to provide overall context and show how the modals contrast in meaning. The examples come from the questionnaire unless otherwise specified.

4.1 Deontic possibility

Each language uses the verb *pwede* to express deontic possibility or permission, as illustrated in (9) and (10). The examples here (and throughout §4) also highlight how structurally similar each language is overall. For example, the default word order is VSO (as in 10) unless a noun is topicalized (as in the Chabacano varieties in 9). The Chabacano tendency to place pronouns between the auxiliary and main verb also comes from both adstrates, as shown in (10).

(9) [Giving permission for a child to stay over at their house.]
    'The child *can* stay/sleep here tonight.'

    a. Zam.
        El   bata *pwede* está akí   esta noche.
        DET child able   stay here DET night

    b. Cav.
        El   kratura *pwede* estar akí   esta noche.
        DET child   able   stay here DET night

    c. Hil.
        Pwede magtener ang bata diri subong nga gab-i.
        able   AV.stay NOM child here now   LNK night

    d. Tag.
        Puwede siyang   matulog dito ngayong gabi.
        able   3SG.NOM.LNK STV.sleep here today.LNK night

(10) [Mother to child: 'If you behave...']
     'You *can* go to the beach/sea with your friends.'

    a. Zam.
        Pwede tu andá na mar hunto   kon tu   amigo.
        able   2SG go LOC sea together with 2SG.POSS friend

    b. Cav.
        Pwede/di pudí tu andá na apláya kompañero mga amigo.
        able/FUT able 2SG go   LOC beach companion PL   friend

    c. Hil.
        Pwede ka   magkadto sa dagat kaupud   imo   mga abyan.
        able   2SG.NOM AV.go   LOC sea   companion 2SG.GEN PL   friend

d. Tag.
Puwede/maaari kang pumunta sa beach kasama ng
able/able 2SG.NOM.LNK AV.go LOC beach companion GEN
mga kaibigan mo.
PL friend 2SG.GEN

While the Tagalog consultant accepted the verb *maaari* in deontic contexts (see 10d), she found it old-fashioned. *Kaya*, however, was not acceptable (see 11). For Hiligaynon and the Chabacano varieties, no cognates to Tagalog *maaari* or Ternate Chabacano *mári* were found.

(11) Tag.
#Kaya niyang matulog dito ngayong gabi.
capability 3SG.GEN.LNK STV.sleep here today.LNK night
'The boy *can* stay here tonight.'

Tagalog and Hiligaynon can use *ma(ka)-* in similar contexts (see 12). In Hiligaynon (12b), it can occur alongside *pwede*.

(12) a. Tag.
'You *can* go to the beach/river with your friends.'
*Maka*kapunta ka sa beach kasama ng mga kaibigan.
able.FUT.go 2SG LOC beach companion GEN PL friend
b. Hil.
Pwede ka *maka*kadto sa suba kaupod imo mga abyan.
able 2SG.NOM able.AV.go LOC river companion 2SG.GEN PL friend

Pwede and *ma(ka)-* are not used to indicate deontic necessity. Instead, necessity is expressed with the pseudoverbs *kinanlan* in Hiligaynon (a reduced form of *kinahanglan*), and *kailangan* in Tagalog (13).

(13) [A mother is speaking to a child.]
'You *must* wash your hands before you eat.'

a. Zam.
Nesesita tu labá tu mano antes de komé.
must 2SG wash 2SG.POSS hand before of eat
b. Cav.
Debi tu labá tu mano bago tu kumí.
must 2SG wash 2SG.POSS hand before 2SG eat
c. Hil.
Kinanlan maghugas ka sang imo kamot bago ka magkaon.
must AV.wash 2SG GEN 2SG.GEN hand before 2SG AV.eat

d. Tag.
Kailangan maghugas ka ng kamay bago ka kumain.
must   AV.wash 2SG GEN hand   before 2SG AV.eat

In the adstrates, *dapat* 'should' could replace *kinanlan* and *kailangan* in (13) to indicate a suggestion or general social obligation (i.e., 'you should wash your hands before you eat'). This is the only sense in which Zamboanga Chabacano can use the modal *debe*, as in (14).

(14) Zam.
Debe era yo está na kasa   pero ya andá yo na party.
should CF 1SG stay LOC house but PFV go   1SG LOC party
'I *should* have stayed home, but I went to a party.'

4.2 Dynamic possibility

There are some differences in how these four languages mark participant-internal dynamic possibility (including learned ability and capability) and participant-external dynamic possibility (i.e., circumstantial possibility, including all contexts that could be covered by the AIA marker in the adstrates). In general, the creoles make fewer lexical distinctions than the adstrates.

4.2.1 Learned ability

Examples of contexts involving learned ability, including either knowledge or physical skill, are shown in (15) and (16). The Zamboanga Chabacano consultants accepted either *sabe* or *pwede* in these contexts, whereas the Cavite Chabacano consultants accepted only *sabe*. Tagalog uses *marunong* 'knowledgeable.'

(15) 'The child *can* read well' (i.e., they know how).

a. Zam.
El   bata *sabe/pwede* le   enbwenamente.
DET child know/able read well
b. Cav.
Akel kratura *sabe/#pwede* le   bweno.
DET child   know/can   read good
c. Tag.
Marunong   siyang   magbasa.
knowledgeable 3SG.LNK AV.read

(16) 'The child *can* swim well.'

    a. Zam.
        El   bata *sabe/pwede* nadá enbwenamente.
        DET child know/able swim well

    b. Cav.
        Akel kratura *sábe*   nadá bweno.
        DET child   know swim good

    c. Tag.
        Marunong   lumangoy ang bata.
        knowledgeable AV.swim   NOM child

Because these examples involve actions that are performed well, the Hiligaynon consultant responded using *maayo* 'good,' as in (17); however, (18) shows that the form for 'can/knows how' is *kahibalo*.

(17) Hil.
     Maayo maglangoy ang bata.
     good AV.swim   NOM child
     'The child is good at swimming.'

(18) Hil.
     Ako man *kahibalo* magluto 'sina'.
     1SG also know   AV.cook that
     'I also *know how* to cook that.' (Wolfenden 1971: 53)

4.2.2 Capability

For capability, the Chabacano varieties use *pwede*, as shown in (19). Hiligaynon can use either *ma(ka)-* or *pwede* (see 19c and 19d). In contrast, Tagalog uses *kaya*.

(19) 'When I was a child, I *could* run (very) fast.'

    a. Zam.
        Kwando bata yo, yo ta   *pwede* korré rápido.
        when   child 1SG 1SG IPFV able   run   fast

    b. Cav.
        Kwando yo chikíto, yo ta   *pwede* kurrí muy rápido
        when   1SG little   1SG IPFV able   run   very fast

    c. Hil.
        Sang bata ako, *maka*dalagan ako dasig.
        when child 1SG AV.able.run   1SG fast

    d. Tag.

      Noong   bata ako, *kaya*   / *#puwede* kong   tumakbo nang

      when.LNK child 1SG capability able   1SG.LNK AV.run   LNK

      mabilis.

      fast

(20)   Hil.

    Pwede siya   maglangoy isa ka milya.

    able   3SG.NOM AV.swim   one NUM mile

    'He can swim a mile.'

Tagalog *kaya* is not limited to contexts like (19) that involve physical ability. It also covers other types of internal determination. For example, only *kaya* works in translating the political slogan *yes, we can* or *sí, se puede*.

(21)   Tag.

      a. # *Pwede* tayo!

           can   1PL.NOM.INCL

           '(Yes,) we can!'

      b. *Kaya*   natin!

           capability 1PL.GEN.INCL

           '(Yes,) we can!'

These examples show that *kaya* is not preferred over *puwede* in dynamic contexts overall (Asarina & Holt 2005: 14); rather, it encodes a distinction between internal and external dynamic possibility not present in Spanish, Chabacano, or even Hiligaynon.

4.2.3 Circumstantial possibility (ability)

For circumstantial possibility contexts related to ability, all four languages use *pwede*. Tagalog and Hiligaynon also use *ma(ka)-*. In (22), no one has granted the speaker permission to attend the party; they can go because circumstances allow it.

(22)   '(I have money now, so) I *can* go to the party.'

      a. Zam.

          Tyene yo sen,   *pwede* yo andá na party.

          have 1SG money able   1SG go   LOC party

b. Cav.
Tyene yo sen,   *pwede* ya   yo andá na party.
have 1SG money able   now 1SG go   LOC party

c. Hil.
Pwede ako   *maka*kadto sa   party.
able   1SG.NOM AV.able.go LOC party

d. Tag.
Puwede/maaari akong   pumunta sa   party.
able/able   1SG.NOM.LNK AV.go   LOC party

These languages often encode circumstantial possibility in contexts where Spanish or English would not, as in (23), which could be replies to 'have you ever been to Manila?' Zamboanga Chabacano does so using *pwede*, and Cavite Chabacano uses *pudí* (< Sp. *poder* 'able.INF'), while the adstrates use the perfective form *na(ka)-*. The creoles also use the perfective marker *ya* in this case, even though *pwede* often goes unmarked for aspect, much like the Tagalog pseudoverb *puwede*. In fact, this aspect marking is likely why Cavite Chabacano tends to use *pudí* in these types of examples, since that form functions like a typical full verb. Perfectivity is overtly marked here because, as with Tagalog *ma(ka)-*, there is an actuality entailment in these types of examples (Dell 1983); perfective *pwede/pudí* indicate that a result has been achieved.

(23) 'I have been to Manila.'

a. Zam.
Ya *pwede* yo andá na Manila.
PFV able   1SG go   LOC Manila

b. Cav.
Ya *pudí* yo andá na Manila.
PFV able 1SG go   LOC Manila

c. Hil.
*Naka*kadto   ako sa   Manila.
PFV.AV.able.go 1SG LOC Manila

d. Tag.
*Naka*punta   ako sa   Manila.
PFV.AV.able.go 1SG LOC Manila

The marking of circumstantial possibility in this type of context is related to the experiential uses of Philippine *ma(ka)-*. Another typical Tagalog example, taken from a news report, is presented in (24).

(24) Tag.
      Natikman   mo   na   ba ang ice cream na   salted egg
      PFV.OV.able.taste 2SG.GEN already Q NOM ice cream LNK salted egg
      flavor?
      flavor
      'Have you ever tasted salted egg flavored ice cream?' (i.e., have you ever
      experienced it/had the opportunity?) (Santos 2018)

Similarly, (25) shows a Caviteña writer using *ya pudi* while recounting her
travel experiences.

(25) Cav.
      Otro dia, *ya pudi* entra nisos na   un   cueva donde hay   como cristal
      other day PFV   enter 1PL   LOC DET cave where EXST like crystal
      colgante.
      hanging
      'On another day, we were able to enter a cave where there were things
      like hanging crystals' (i.e., they had the chance to do so). (del Rosario
      2007)

4.2.4 Circumstantial possibility (nonvolition)

As previously documented in Zamboanga and Ternate Chabacano (Rubino 2008,
Sippola 2011), Cavite Chabacano follows the adstrates in marking nonvolitional
events using an ability verb, again using *pudí* rather than *pwede*. Hiligaynon
and Tagalog use the AIA marker *ma(ka)-*, and although they both use *pwede* for
ability contexts, it is not used for nonvolition.

Examples (26) and (27) show the same proposition, 'I spilled paint on his shirt',
in two contexts. In (26), the spilling was accidental, while in (27), it was deliberate.

(26) [The speaker tripped while carrying a bucket of paint.]
      'I spilled paint on his shirt/clothes.'

   a. Zam.
       Ya   *pwede* yo derramá pintura na   su   kamiseta.
       PFV able   1SG spill   paint   LOC 3SG.POSS shirt
   b. Cav.
       Ya   *pudí* yo butá pintura na   su   kamiseta.
       PFV able 1SG spill paint   LOC 3SG.POSS shirt

c. Hil.
   *N*atuluan   ko   pinta ang iya   bayo.
   PFV.LV.able.spill 1SG.GEN paint NOM 3SG.GEN shirt

d. Tag.
   *N*atapunan   ko   ng pintura ang kanyang   damit.
   PFV.LV.able.spill 1SG.GEN GEN paint   NOM 3SG.GEN.LNK clothes

(27) [The speaker saw someone they have a grudge against and decided to
      spill paint on them.]
      'I spilled paint on his shirt/clothes.'

   a. Zam.
      Ya derramá yo el   pintura na su   kamiseta.
      PFV spill   1SG DET paint   LOC 3SG.POSS shirt

   b. Cav.
      Ya butá yo pintura na su   kamiseta.
      PFV spill 1SG paint   LOC 3SG.POSS shirt

   c. Hil.
      Gintuluan ko   pinta ang iya   bayo.
      PFV.LV.spill 1SG.GEN paint NOM 3SG.GEN shirt

   d. Tag.
      Tinapunan ko   ng pintura ang kanyang   damit.
      PFV.LV.spill 1SG.GEN GEN paint   NOM 3SG.GEN.LNK clothes

Pwede/pudí and *ma(ka)-* also mark other unplanned events, like the sudden
occurrence in (28).

(28) [Do you know what happened to me yesterday when I was walking in
      the forest?]
      'I suddenly stepped on a snake. It bit me on the leg/foot.'

   a. Zam.
      Ya *pwede* yo pisá na kulebra. Ya mordé le konmigo la pierna.
      PFV able   1SG step LOC snake. PFV bite   3SG 1SG.OBJ DET leg

   b. Cav.
      Ya *pwede* yo pisá un kulebra. Ya mordé konmigo na mi
      PFV able   1SG step DET snake. PFV bite   1SG.OBJ LOC 1SG.POSS
      pierna.
      leg

c. Hil.
   *Naka*tapak   ako sang man-og. Ginkagat   niya   ako   sa
   PFV.AV.able.step 1SG GEN snake   PFV.OV.bite 3SG.GEN 1SG.NOM LOC
   siki.
   foot

d. Tag.
   Bigla   akong *naka*tapak   sa isang   ahas. Kinagat
   suddenly 1SG.LNK PFV.AV.able.step LOC DET.LNK snake PFV.OV.bite
   niya   ako   sa paa.
   3SG.GEN 1SG.NOM LOC foot

Note that the verbs for 'bite' in (28) do not use the possibility markers, since only the initial event is surprising.

An example of *pwede/pudí* taking a coincidental reading is shown in (29). In this case, they are also mapped onto a stative verb, with adstrate *ma-* marking perception/experience with the root for 'see'.

(29) [The speaker was shopping and unexpectedly ran into a friend.]
      'I saw her at the market/store.'

a. Zam.
   Ya *pwede* yo mirá kon ele na tyangge.
   PFV able 1SG see OBJ 3SG LOC market

b. Cav.
   Ya *pudí* yo mirá kon eli na plasa.
   PFV able 1SG see OBJ 3SG LOC market

c. Hil.
   *Na*kita   ko   siya   sa tyenda.
   STV.PFV.see 1SG.GEN 3SG.NOM LOC store

d. Tag.
   *Na*kita   ko   siya   sa palengke.
   STV.PFV.see 1SG.GEN 3SG.NOM LOC market

In St'át'imcets, as previously discussed, the circumstantial marker has been analyzed as taking these types of nonvolitional readings in necessity contexts, whereas the ability readings arise from possibility contexts (Davis & Rullmann 2009). This point is one where the Chabacano/Philippine markers differ; circumstantial necessity is expressed not with *pwede, pudí,* or *ma(ka)-* but with Zam. *ne(se)sita,* Cav. *debi,* Hil. *kinahanglan/kinanlan,* and Tag. *kailangan,* as shown in (30). These same markers are used for deontic but not epistemic necessity.

(30) 'We/everyone must eat in order to live.'

    a. Zam.
        Nesita kita   komé para bibí.
        must 1PL.INCL eat   for live

    b. Cav.
        Todo niso *debi* komí para bibí.
        all   1PL must eat for live

    c. Hil.
        Kinanlan magkaon kita   para mabuhi.
        must   AV.eat 1PL.INCL for STV.live

    d. Tag.
        Kailangan nating   kumain para mabuhay.
        must   1PL.INCL.LNK AV.eat for STV.live

4.3 Epistemic possibility

All four languages use *pwede* for epistemic possibility, and Tagalog also uses *maaari*. As previously shown for Tagalog, however, each language marks epistemic modality mainly through adverbs. Spanish *posible* 'possible' is found in all four languages, along with the slightly stronger marker *siguro* 'maybe/possibly/probably' (< Sp. *seguro* 'sure').[3] In addition, Tagalog has *baka* 'possibly' (also used in Cavite Chabacano), and Hiligaynon has *basi* 'possibly'. The Zamboanga Chabacano consultants use all of the markers above as well as *gaha* 'possibly' (< Cebuano *kaha*). Examples of some of these markers are shown in (31).

(31) 'It *might* rain (later) tonight.'

    a. Zam.
        Posible/basi/baka   kay   ulan esta noche.
        possibly/possibly/possibly COMP rain DET night

    b. Zam.
        Man-ulan *gaha*   ara de noche.
        VERB-rain possibly now of night

    c. Cav.
        Baka   di   llubí lwego di noche.
        possibly FUT rain later of night

---

[3] The Chabacano varieties also have *siguraw* and the adstrates have *sigurado* 'surely' (< Sp. *asegurado* 'assured'), but these markers denote complete certainty rather than mere probability.

d. Hil.
   Pwede/basi/posible   mag-ulan subong nga gab-i.
   able/possibly/possibly AV.rain   now   LNK night
e. Tag.
   Baka/posibleng/#puwedeng   umulan mamayang gabi.
   possibly/possibly.LNK/able.LNK AV.rain later.LNK   night

While *pwede* was also acceptable for Hiligaynon in (31), the Tagalog consultant rejected it for this context. However, (32) shows epistemic examples of *puwede* in Tagalog and Chabacano.

(32)   [There was some money on the table, but now it is missing. John is a known thief.]
       'It *could* be John who took the money.'

   a. Zam.
      Pwede le   saká kon el   sen.
      able   3SG take OBJ DET money
   b. Cav.
      Baka   John ya saká el   sen.
      possibly John PFV take DET money
   c. Cav.
      Pwede John saká el   sen.
      able   John take DET money
   d. Hil.
      Siguro si   John ang nagkuha   sang kwarta.
      probably NOM John NOM PFV.AV.take GEN money
   e. Tag.
      Puwedeng/maaaring si   John ang kumuha   ng pera.
      able.LNK/able.LNK   NOM John NOM PFV.AV.take GEN money

In this case, the Hiligaynon consultant used *siguro*, since the background about John's past suggests that he would be likely to steal. Yet the other consultants still used weaker markers.

In addition to producing *puwede* and accepting *maaari* in (32), the Tagalog consultant also offered (33).

(33)   Tag.
       Kaya   ni   John kunin   yung pera.
       capability GEN John ov.take DET   money
       'John could have taken the money.'

Kaya implicates that not only is it possible that John took the money but that, as the consultant explained, 'he has it in him' to do so. This example of *kaya* in an epistemic context was the only one elicited in this study.

The epistemic *pwede* in Tagalog and the Chabacano varieties in (32) contrasts with its dynamic/circumstantial usage in (34).

(34)   [John was seen near where the money was, but he's an honest person.]
       'John could have taken the money, but he didn't (take/do it).'

    a. Zam.
        Ya *pwede* era saká si   John el sen,   pero nuay   le saká.
        PFV able   CF take NOM John DET money but NEG.EXST 3SG take

    b. Cav.
        Pwede saká John el   sen,   pero no eli ya así.
        able   take John DET money but NEG 3SG PFV do

    c. Hil.
        Pwede/posible nga nakuha   ni John ang kwarta, pero indi.
        able/possible LNK PFV.OV.able.take GEN John NOM money but NEG

    d. Tag.
        Puwede/#kaya niyang   kunin, pero hindi niya   kinuha.
        able/capability 3SG.GEN.LNK OV.take but NEG 3SG.GEN PFV.OV.take

In this case, each language uses *pwede*. This context does not involve a judgment of likelihood, as in (33), but rather is concerned with whether the opportunity was even available.

It was often difficult to elicit distinctions among the epistemic markers in regard to possibility vs. necessity/probability. For example, Zamboanga Chabacano consultants used *baka* in contexts intended to elicit weaker and stronger possibility in (35b) and (36), and *siguro* was used for possibility in (35b).

(35)   a. Zam.
        Na kasa ya   *gaha*   si   John.
        LOC house already possibly NOM John
        'John *might* be at home already.'

    b. *Baka/siguro*   talla na kasa ya   si   John.
        possibly/possibly there LOC house already NOM John
        'John *might* be at home already.'

(36)   Zam.
    Baka/posible   talla ya   si   John na kasa.
    possibly/possibly there already NOM John LOC house
    'John must be at home already.'

Admittedly, there was probably not enough context provided to the consultants here, but more detailed follow-up with another Zamboanga Chabacano speaker indicated that he would have similar responses (e.g., in 35, *baka* or *gaha* could be used if there is a possibility John might be somewhere else, like the bank or the store). This speaker found *siguro* acceptable for the sentence in (36) but preferred to use it in response to a more specific context (e.g., to answer a question like 'How did Maria enter the house without a key?').[4]

This difficulty in distinguishing epistemic meanings is partly an artifact of the limited pragmatic contexts of the questionnaire. The considerable overlap among these markers has already been documented in other grammatical descriptions and dictionaries, however, so these markers do in fact seem to be less clearly distinct from each other than English *can* vs. *must*, or *possibly/maybe* vs. *probably*. A similarly blurry distinction between epistemic possibility and necessity has been found in another Austronesian language, Paciran Javanese, which has a possibility marker, *paleng*, that can flexibly take on necessity force in certain contexts (Vander Klok 2013).

With that said, it is safe to say that *siguro* is slightly stronger than the other epistemic markers, and it is possible to elicit consistent differences when there is enough context. As the Hiligaynon example in (37) shows, *siguro* (here reduced to *guro*) is preferred when there is more evidence or there is no reason to think there could be another possibility.

(37) Hil.
    [There are no lights on in John's house.]
    Nagtulog   na   (si)guro si   John.
    PFV.AV.sleep already probably NOM John
    'John must have gone to sleep already.'

According to the consultant, *basi* in this sentence would mean the speaker is just guessing, or maybe John could be doing something else, like attending a party.

There is still the question of whether *siguro* has the default interpretation of necessity or possibility. As Vander Klok (2013: 345) demonstrated, one test is to see whether the epistemic marker can be used in mutually exclusive propositions; for example, a possibility marker makes sense in a context like 'maybe she's taking a nap, maybe she's not taking a nap', but a marker meaning 'must' or 'certainly' cannot appear in both clauses. No such examples were collected in

---

[4]Thanks to Jerome Herrera for providing this example.

the questionnaire, but a search online confirms that Tagalog *siguro* does not get canceled in such constructions, as (38) shows.

(38) Tag.
      Mararamdaman ba natin   kapag may parating   na pagbabago?
      FUT.OV.able.feel Q 1.INCL.GEN when EXST upcoming LNK change
      Siguro. Siguro hindi. *Siguro* minsan.
      maybe maybe NEG   maybe sometimes
      'Can we feel when a change is coming? Maybe. Maybe not. Maybe
      sometimes.' (Yatchi 2012)

This example suggests that, at least in Tagalog, *siguro* is a flexible possibility marker like Paciran Javanese *paleng* rather than a pure necessity marker.

5 Discussion

5.1 Comparison and typological classification

Tables 2 and 3 summarize the modal systems of Zamboanga Chabacano, Cavite Chabacano, Hiligaynon, and Tagalog. In addition, Table 2 includes Ternate Chabacano, although questionnaire data were not obtained for that variety. The categorization of the Ternate Chabacano modals is based on descriptions and examples from Sippola (2011: 156–166, 208–210).

The tables show that all five languages have similar modal systems. Spanish influence is evident in each language through the use of *pwede* and *siguro*. In addition, *posible* is listed for each language except Ternate Chabacano (it did not occur in Sippola's (2011) dataset, though it is listed as a lexical item for all Chabacano varieties in Riego de Dios's (1989) comparative dictionary).

Within the typological framework used by Matthewson et al. (2005) and Vander Klok (2013), each language can be described as having a mixed modal system. *Pwede* has fixed possibility force in all five languages, and the base is left to context, as in many European languages; except for Tagalog *maaari*, it is the only verb in any of the languages that can cover epistemic contexts. The various verbs that express necessity in each language also have fixed modal force and can flexibly express deontic or dynamic (but not epistemic) modality. Finally, most of the epistemic markers cannot be used for other types of modality and have a base fixed to possibility contexts, but *siguro* appears to have somewhat flexible force, and is therefore listed in the tables for now under both possibility and weak necessity.

Table 2: Zamboanga, Cavite, and Ternate Chabacano modality

Modal Type	Zam.	Cav.	Ter.
		Deontic	
Necessity	*ne(se)sita* 'must' (< Sp. *necesita* 'need') *debe* 'should'	*debi* 'must, should' (< Sp. *debe* 'owe, must')	*dabli* 'must' (< Sp. *dable* 'feasible')
Possibility	*pwede* (< Sp. *puede* 'can.3SG')	*pwede*	*pwede* and reduced forms (*pwe, pe, pey*) *mari* (< Tag. *maaari* 'can')
		Dynamic: Participant-internal	
Capability	*pwede*	*pwede*	*pwede* and reduced forms *mari*
Learned ability	*sabe* (< Sp. *sabe* 'know.3SG') *pwede*	*sabe*	*sabe* *sabé* (< Sp. *saber* 'know.INF')
		Dynamic: Participant-external	
Necessity	*ne(se)sita*	*debi*	*dabli*
Possibility (ability)	*pwede*	*pwede* *pudí* (< Sp. *poder* 'can.INF')	*pwede* and reduced forms *mari*
Possibility (nonvolition)	*pwede*	*pwede* *pudí*	*pwede* *mari*
		Epistemic	
Necessity (weak)	*siguro* (< Sp. *seguro* 'sure')	*siguro*	*siguru*
Possibility	*siguro* *baka* (< Tag.) *basi* (< Hil.) *gaha* (< Ceb. *kaha*) *posible* (< Sp. *posible*) *pwede*	*siguro* *baka* *posible* *pwede*	*siguru* *baka* *pwede* and reduced forms

Table 3: Hiligaynon and Tagalog modality

Modal Type	Hil.	Tag.
	Deontic	
Necessity	*kinahanglan/kinanlan* 'must' *dapat* 'should'	*kailangan* 'must' *dapat* 'should'
Possibility	*pwede* *ma(ka)-*	*puwede* *maaari* *ma(ka)-*
	Dynamic: Participant-internal	
Capability	*pwede*	*kaya* 'capability, power'
Learned ability	*kahibalo* 'know'	*marunong* 'knowledgeable'
	Dynamic: Participant-external	
Necessity	*kinahanglan/kinanlan*	*kailangan*
Possibility (ability)	*pwede* *ma(ka)-*	*pwede* *maaari* *ma(ka)-*
Possibility (nonvolition)	*ma(ka)-*	*ma(ka)-*
	Epistemic	
Necessity (weak)	*siguro*	*siguro*
Possibility	*siguro* *basi* *posible* *pwede*	*siguro* *baka* *posible* *pwede* *maaari*

The facts about Chabacano align with Winford's (2018) observation that it is common for creoles to have at least two modal auxiliaries: one corresponding to *must* (necessity) and one to *can* (possibility), with both categories covering a range of deontic, dynamic, and epistemic contexts. This pattern is not surprising, given how common this type of polyfunctionality is in the European lexifiers (van der Auwera et al. 2005, Matthewson et al. 2005). The fact that *pwede* works this way in all Chabacano varieties is a somewhat new finding, since the current descriptions of Zamboanga and Ternate Chabacano in APiCS state that the ability verb is not used to express epistemic possibility (feature 55, Maurer & the APiCS Consortium 2013; but see also Sippola 2011, which shows that *pwede* can be epistemic in Ternate). The extension of the ability verb to epistemic contexts is also found in Palenquero and Papiamentu (Maurer & the APiCS Consortium 2013), so this feature appears to be common to all Spanish-lexified creoles.

The expression of possibility in the Chabacano varieties is significantly influenced by the adstrates in at least two ways. First, Chabacano epistemic modality is expressed primarily through adverbs, which are of both Philippine and Spanish origin. Tagalog *baka* is used in every Chabacano variety, although in Zamboanga, this word is likely a fairly recent borrowing,[5] and the Visayan equivalents *basi* (< Hil.) and *gaha* (< Ceb.) are still used. *Siguro* was semantically weakened as it was grammaticalized from Spanish *seguro* 'surely' in Chabacano as well as the adstrates. It consistently marks a higher degree of necessity or probability than the markers of Philippine origin, under the right contexts. Yet it also seems to mark possibility or general uncertainty, with the native markers left to indicate a more remote possibility.

Second, each Chabacano variety uses *pwede* or a related form to mark not only ability but also nonvolitional circumstances, mapping onto the functions of adstrate *ma(ka)-*. While the nonvolitional function of *pwede* was already documented in Zamboanga and Ternate Chabacano (Rubino 2008, Sippola 2011), these data shows that the same is true in Cavite, but using *pudí*. Furthermore, this study demonstrates just how closely the Chabacano varieties track with the adstrates in overtly marking *pwede/pudí* for perfective aspect in these contexts, in order to mark that a result has been achieved (whether intentionally or not). These circumstantial uses of *pwede* or *pudí* are also related to the experience-marking functions of *ma(ka)-* and some uses of stative *ma-* (e.g., for verbs like 'see' and 'die').

From a broader crosslinguistic perspective, another finding is that while Chabacano *pwede/pudí* and Philippine *ma(ka)-* have remarkably similar functions to the circumstantial marker in St'át'imcets, they differ in some crucial ways. They are not fixed to a dynamic/circumstantial base, and they do not have flexible force (the opposite of how the St'át'imcets marker is specified). Unlike in St'át'imcets, the nonvolitional uses of these markers fall under the realm of possibility and not necessity.

The data also clearly demonstrate that the Hiligaynon and Tagalog systems are nearly identical to each other. They share some Philippine and Spanish forms that are exactly the same (*dapat* 'should', *maka-* 'able', *pwede* 'able', etc.) and others that are also close Philippine cognates (Hil. *kinahanglan/kinanlan* 'must',

---

[5] As Lipski (2013: 461) observed, it is only recent decades that Tagalog/Filipino has become influential enough in Mindanao for people to start borrowing grammatical items from it.

Tag. *kailangan* 'must'). *Pwede* does not cover nonvolitional circumstances in either language. It overlaps with *ma(ka)-* to some extent, but the prefix is not used in epistemic contexts; rather, it is restricted to participant-external event modality (i.e., deontic and circumstantial possibility, including nonvolitional events). The only major differences between the adstrates are that Tagalog marks more distinctions between subtypes of dynamic possibility (using *kaya* for capability instead of *pwede*), and it still sometimes uses *maaari* as a more formal native equivalent to *pwede*.

5.2 Development of the Chabacano modal systems

Given the similarity of the creole modal systems, it might be tempting to assume that came from a common ancestor. Apart from the modals, the examples in §4 are also remarkably similar overall in their syntax and lexicon. I argue, however, that these systems developed separately but congruently because there are few substantial differences in the modal systems and overall structure of the substrates.

The slight lexical differences in the modal systems should not be overlooked, as Sippola & Lesho (2020) have already argued. For example, while it would not have been out of the realm of possibility for one Chabacano variety to have selected either Spanish *necesita* or *debe* as the main necessity verb during the process of creole formation, and then another variety to have later switched to the other through internal change, this does not seem to be what happened. The supposed parent variety in Ternate did not grammaticalize either of these forms but rather uses *dabli* (Sippola & Lesho 2020: 112). The more plausible explanation is that each variety selected different forms because they were separated geographically and socially, and formed during slightly different time periods (as historical evidence also suggests).

The possibility modals also have slight differences in form that are suggestive of development along separate trajectories. *Pwede* is found in all three Chabacano varieties, but in Ternate, it is often reduced to just the first syllable, possibly indicating a higher degree of grammaticalization (Sippola & Lesho 2020). This reduction occasionally happens in Cavite but appears to be much less frequent, and it has not yet been documented for the Zamboanga variety. It is also notable that Cavite Chabacano is the only current variety that uses *pudi* in addition to *pwede*, and Ternate Chabacano is the only variety that uses *mari*.

Ideally, there would be more diachronic data to base this discussion on, but old Chabacano samples are scarce. There are a handful of illuminating examples in the oldest available texts written in the Manila Bay and Mindanao varieties, however. They come from a set of stories from 1859/1860 in Manila Chabacano (reproduced in Fernández & Sippola 2017) and a set of dialogues from 1883 in Cotabato Chabacano (reproduced in Fernández 2012a).

The Manila texts feature six examples each of *puede* (in bare form) and *pode* (usually marked for aspect). The use of *pode* is notable because it is similar in form and function to Cavite Chabacano *pudí*. This similarity makes sense given that Manila and Cavite are so close together and, unlike Cavite and Ternate (let alone Cavite and Zamboanga), have always had a strong social link.

In the Cotabato dialogues, there is one token of *puede* and two of *puedé*, with a final accent mark, which may be evidence of yet another form that does not seem to be found in other Chabacano varieties.[6] Another notable feature of this text, shown in (39), is that *puedé/puede* were used to mark an accident (with *trompesá* 'trip') and an involuntary lack of experience/cognition (with *mirá* 'see').

(39) Cot.

    ...yá *puedé* lang yó trompesá su   pié, ni   no hay gane yó
    PFV able only 1SG trip   3SG.POSS foot NEG.even NEG EXST EMPH 1SG
    puede mirá cay   estaba yó tá apurá el modo de sacá aguja
    able see because was   1SG IPFV hurry DET manner of get needle
    que tá   pidí si ñor Quicon.
    COMP IPFV ask NOM Mr. Quicon
    '...I only accidentally tripped over his foot, I didn't even see (him) because
    I was in a hurry to get a needle that Mr. Quicon was asking for.'
    (Fernández 2012a: 308)

These uses of *puedé/puede* can be attributed to influence from the Visayan languages, since they occur with other specifically Visayan features, like the emphatic *gane* and the use of *no hay* to negate a perfective verb (modeled after how *wala* 'NEG.EXST' is used in Hiligaynon/Cebuano but not in Tagalog). Tagalog influence, of course, could result in constructions like *yá **puedé** lang yó trompesá*, and indeed, modern Ternate and Cavite Chabacano speakers would say it almost exactly the same way, with only slight differences in the form of the possibility verb. The similarity, however, is only because their ancestors grafted the same Spanish lexical items onto identical substrate structures. There is no historical evidence that speakers of any Manila Bay language were involved in the formation of Cotabato Chabacano; in fact, as Fernández (2012a) observed, the existence

---

[6]The accents could be writing errors, of course, but the author clearly knew Spanish and Chabacano and took care in how accents were marked throughout the text.

of this text from this time period even calls into question the common assumption in Chabacano studies that this variety is a direct offshoot of Zamboanga Chabacano.

5.3 Spanish influence on the adstrates

The data in this study also show just how deeply the adstrate modal systems were affected by Spanish contact, which is remarkable, given Stolz's (2002) observation that Spanish grammatical influence on Philippine languages has been mostly superficial. For example, borrowed grammatical features such as gender marking have low productivity, and many borrowed function words are doublets of still existing native equivalents. Stolz suggested, however, that investigating more 'covert' borrowing, including the semantics of borrowed words, might reveal other grammatical areas where a greater degree of hispanization has taken place. Indeed, this study shows that modality is one such area. Functional doublets are still present (e.g., Tagalog *puwede* and *maaari*), but the borrowing of Spanish modals led to changes in the overall structure of the modal system.

The data raise a number of semantic and diachronic issues. Due to the nature of the Philippine contact setting, the directionality and timing of borrowed elements can be unclear. It is often difficult to tell if an item has been borrowed directly from Spanish into a Philippine language, or if it has filtered indirectly into one Philippine language from another. Diachronic analysis is needed to determine the grammaticalization paths of elements of both Spanish and Philippine origin.

One question is whether *siguro* introduced a distinction between epistemic necessity and possibility into Philippine languages, or if it simply replaced some older lexical item(s) related to probability. *Malamang* 'apt, likely' (root: *lamang* 'only') and *marahil* 'possibly, probably' (root: *dahil* 'reason/cause') are two Tagalog candidates for older options. Bader et al. (1994) did not consider these items to have been as grammaticalized as *baka* and *siguro*, however, since unlike those markers, they occur with low frequency and must still take the linking particle *-ng/na*, as modifiers normally do. Dictionaries indicate that these other markers also have some overlap with weaker possibility modals, lending further support to the idea that epistemic markers have rather flexible force in this language (e.g., English 2010: 765 lists *maaari* 'possibly' as a synonym of *malamang* 'likely').

Another question is whether Tagalog *maaari* was used epistemically before *puwede* was borrowed, since the language otherwise maintains a distinction between epistemic and event modality. The root *ari* is related to possession/ownership, suggesting that *maaari* originally had a deontic or dynamic meaning.

Another sign that the original meanings were more strictly deontic/dynamic is that the form used in Ternate Chabacano, *mari*, does not seem to occur in epistemic contexts. Hiligaynon does not have modal counterparts to *maaari* or *kaya*, suggesting that, unlike the older *ma(ka)-*, these items grammaticalized independently in Tagalog.

Finally, it seems likely that *siguro* and *puwede* entered Philippine languages from Spanish and/or Chabacano late into the colonial period, given the way they are still used alongside native counterparts, and the fact that Spanish influence was strongest in the late 19th century.[7] Stolz (2002: 151–152) made a similar argument for the large number of function words borrowed into Philippine languages (e.g., *pero* 'but', *maskin* 'even though', *para* 'for', etc.), pointing out that Filipinos of that era would have used such words as a way to mark their education level and participate in colonial power structures and discourse styles. A look into Philippine texts from different points of the colonial period could help to illuminate some of this speculation about the timing of the borrowings.

6 Conclusion

In an attempt to follow Winford's (2000, 2018) footsteps, this paper has provided a detailed look into how possibility is expressed in the Zamboanga and Cavite Chabacano varieties and their adstrates. By using crosslinguistic frameworks of analysis (van der Auwera & Plungian 1998, Palmer 2001, Matthewson et al. 2005), this paper was able to provide parallel descriptions of these four languages, describe their overall typology, and identify the similarities and subtle differences in how they mark fine-grained subcategories of possibility. The creoles were shown to have rich systems beyond what focusing on only the three "prototypical" creole TMA categories would suggest.

The data demonstrate that the Chabacano creoles, Hiligaynon, and Tagalog each exhibit "mixed" modal systems in two different senses. First, they combine Philippine and Spanish ways of expressing possibility. The data from these languages show more generally how modal systems can be shaped by both language contact and internal change. Second, these languages all have the same typology in how possibility markers are specified according to base and force, with *pwede* being lexically unspecified for modal base but having fixed possibility force, and several markers having a fixed epistemic base and mostly fixed possibility force

---

[7]Spanish was not widely accessible to most Filipinos until the mid/late 1800s, when it became more widespread due to changes to the education system and social class structure (Lesho 2018: 5).

(except for *siguro*, which can also express necessity). These languages still pre-serve a division between event modality and epistemic modality in most ways, but language contact somewhat blurred these lines through the introduction of *pwede*. In the creoles, the use of *pwede* was extended even further, as it came to be used to cover all the functions of Philippine *ma(ka)-*.

Finally, the findings also help to illuminate the grammatical and historical rela-tionships among these languages. This detailed comparison between the creoles and their respective adstrates lends support to theories of Chabacano formation that posit separate but parallel development in each of the Chabacano-speaking communities during different time periods. While the varieties may appear to be homogenous, subtle differences in modality as well as in other aspects of the grammar and lexicon suggest that they do not actually stem from a single source (Lesho & Sippola 2014, Sippola & Lesho 2020). Chabacano is now in at least the "second phase" of creole TMA research (Winford 2018), and these findings pro-vide a foundation for further research into the usage of these modals and how these systems developed.

Acknowledgements

First and foremost, thanks go to Don Winford not only for inspiring this work and guiding me through its earliest stages, but for his mentorship as my advisor and his friendship ever since. There are few who have modeled such a gener-ous and kind approach to scholarship. In addition, I also thank Judith Tonhauser, Scott Schwenter, and Michelle Dionisio for their feedback on earlier versions of this work. I am also grateful to the language consultants and other correspon-dents in New Jersey, California, Ohio, Zamboanga, and Cavite for their hospital-ity and patience in answering my endless questions.

Abbreviations

ACC	accusative	EXST	existential
AV	actor voice	FUT	future/contemplative
CF	counterfactual	GEN	genitive
COMP	complementizer	INCL	inclusive
DET	determiner	INF	infinitive
EMPH	emphatic	IPFV	imperfective

LNK	linker		PFV	perfective
LOC	locative		PL	plural
LV	locative voice		POSS	possessive
NEG	negative		Q	question marker
NOM	nominative		SG	singular
NUM	numeral		STV	stative
OBJ	object		VERB	verb marker
OV	object voice			

References

Asarina, Alya & Anna Holt. 2005. Syntax and semantics of Tagalog modals. In Jeffrey Heinz & Dimitris Ntelitheos (eds.), *UCLA Working Papers in Linguistics, no. 12, Proceedings of AFLA XII*, 1–17. Los Angeles: University of California, Los Angeles.

Bader, Thomas, Iwar Werlen & Adrian Wymann. 1994. *Towards a typology of modality: The encoding of modal attitudes in Korean, Japanese, and Tagalog.* Bern: Universität Bern Institut für Sprachwissenschaft.

Bickerton, Derek. 1984. The language bioprogram hypothesis. *The Behavioral and Brain Sciences* 7(2). 173–188. DOI: 10.1017/S0140525X00044149.

Bybee, Joan L., Revere D. Perkins & William Pagliuca. 1994. *The evolution of grammar: Tense, aspect, and modality in the languages of the world.* Chicago: University of Chicago Press.

Dahl, Östen. 1985. *Tense and aspect systems.* Oxford: Basil Blackwell.

Davis, Lisa Matthewson, Henry & Hotze Rullmann. 2009. 'Out of control' marking as circumstantial modality in st'át'imcets. In Lotte Hogeweg, Helen de Hoop & A. L. Malchukov (eds.), *Cross-linguistic semantics of tense, aspect and modality*, 205–244. Amsterdam: John Benjamins.

del Rosario, Flora. 2007. *Aviso: Newsletter of Cavite City library and museum*, vol. 5. Cavite City: Memorable viaje.

Dell, François. 1983. An aspectual distinction in Tagalog. *Oceanic Linguistics* 22/23(1/2). 175–206.

English, Leo James. 2008. *English-Tagalog dictionary.* Mandaluyong City: Cacho Hermanos, Inc.

English, Leo James. 2010. *Tagalog-English dictionary.* Mandaluyong City: Cacho Hermanos, Inc.

Escalante, Enrique R. 2010. *Learning Chabacano: A handbook.* Manila: Baby Dragon Printing.

Evans, Bethwyn & Malcolm Ross. 2001. The history of proto-Oceanic *ma-. *Oceanic Linguistics* 40(2). 269–290.

Fernández, Mauro. 2006. Las lenguas de Zamboanga según los jesuitas y otros observadores occidentales. *Revista Internacional de Lingüística Iberoamericana* 7. 9–26.

Fernández, Mauro. 2011. Chabacano en Tayabas: Implicaciones para la historia de los criollos hispano-filipinos. *Revista internacional de lingüística iberoamericana* 17. 189–218.

Fernández, Mauro. 2012a. El Chabacano de Cotabato: El documento que Schuchardt no pudo utilizar. In Victoria Vázquez Rozas Tomás Eduardo Jiménez Juliá Belén López Meirama & Alexandre Veiga (eds.), *Cum corde et in nova grammatica: Estudios ofrecidos a Guillermo Rojo*, 295–313. Santiago de Compostela: Servicio de Publicaciones e Intercambio Científico.

Fernández, Mauro. 2012b. Leyenda e historia del Chabacano de Ermita (Manila). *UniverSOS: revista de lenguas indígenas y universos culturales* 9. 9–46.

Fernández, Mauro. 2019. El escenario lingüístico de zamboanga (filipinas) a mediados del siglo XVIII. In Antonio Briz, M.a José Martínez Alcalde, Nieves Mendizábal, Mara Fuertes Gutiérrez, José Luis Blas & Margarita Porcar (eds.), *Estudios lingüísticos en homenaje a emilio ridruejo*, 439–451. Valencia: Universitat de València.

Fernández, Mauro & Eeva Sippola. 2017. A new window into the history of Chabacano. *Journal of Pidgin and Creole Languages* 32(2). 304–338.

Forman, Michael Lawrence. 1972. *Zamboangueño texts with grammatical analysis: A study of Philippine Creole Spanish.* Ithaca: Cornell University. (Doctoral dissertation).

Frake, Charles O. 1980. Zamboangueño verb expressions. In Anwar S. Dil (ed.), *Language and cultural description: Essays by Charles O. Frake*, 277–310. Stanford: Stanford University Press.

Himmelmann, Nikolaus P. 2006. How to miss a paradigm or two: Multifunctional *ma-* in Tagalog. In Alan Dench Felix K. Ameka & Nicholas Evans (eds.), *Catching language: The standing challenge of grammar writing*, 487–526. Berlin: Mouton de Gruyter.

Kratzer, Angelika. 1991. Modality. In Dieter Wunderlich & Arnim von Stechow (eds.), *Semantics: An international handbook of contemporary research*, 639–650. Berlin: de Gruyter.

Kroeger, Paul. 1993. *Phrase structure and grammatical relations in Tagalog.* Stanford: Center for the Study of Language & Information.

Lesho, Marivic. 2018. Folk perception of variation in Cavite Chabacano. *Journal of Pidgin and Creole Languages* 33(1). 1–47.

Lesho, Marivic & Eeva Sippola. 2014. Folk perceptions of variation among the Chabacano creoles. *Revista de crioulos de base lexical portuguesa e espanhola* 5. 1–46.

Lipski, John M. 1988. Philippine Creole Spanish: Assessing the Portuguese element. *Zeitschrift für Romanische Philologie* 104. 25–45.

Lipski, John M. 1992. New thoughts on the origins of Zamboangueño (Philippine Creole Spanish). *Language Sciences* 14(3). 197–231.

Lipski, John M. 2013. Remixing a mixed language: The emergence of a new pronominal system in Chabacano (Philippine Creole Spanish). *International Journal of Bilingualism* 17(4). 448–478.

Lipski, John M. & Maurizio Santoro. 2007. Zamboangueño Creole Spanish. In John Holm & Peter L. Patrick (eds.), *Comparative creole syntax*, 373–398. London: Battlebridge Press.

Lorenzino, Gerardo. 2000. *The morphosyntax of Spanish-lexified creoles.* München: LINCOM.

Matthewson, Lisa. 2013. Gitksan modals. *International Journal of American Linguistics* 79(3). 349–394.

Matthewson, Lisa, Hotze Rullmann & Henry Davis. 2005. Modality in St'át'imcets. In J. C. Brown, M. Kiyota & T. Peterson (eds.), *Papers for the 40th international conference on Salish and neighbouring languages*, 166–183. Vancouver: University of British Columbia Working Papers in Linguistics.

Maurer, Philippe & the APiCS Consortium. 2013. Ability verb and epistemic possibility. In Susanne Maria Michaelis, Philippe Maurer, Martin Haspelmath & Magnus Huber (eds.), *Atlas of pidgin and creole language structures.* Leipzig: Max Planck Institute for Evolutionary Anthropology. https://apics-online.info/parameters/55#2/16.5/10.0 (20 February, 2019).

Michaelis, Susanne Maria, Philippe Maurer, Martin Haspelmath & Magnus Huber (eds.). 2013. *Atlas of pidgin and creole language structures.* Leipzig: Max Planck Institute for Evolutionary Anthropology. http://apics-online.info (20 February, 2019).

Palmer, Frank R. 2001. *Mood and modality.* Cambridge: Cambridge University Press.

Riego de Dios, Maria Isabelita O. 1989. *A composite dictionary of Philippine Creole Spanish (PCS)* (Studies in Philippine Linguistics 2). Manila: Linguistic Society of the Philippines & Summer Institute of Linguistics.

Rubino, Carl. 2008. Zamboangueño Chavacano and the potentive mode. In Susanne Michaelis (ed.), *Roots of creole structures: Weighing the contribution of substrates and superstrates*, 279–300. Amsterdam: John Benjamins.

Santos, Jamil. 2018. *Natikman mo na ba ang ice cream na salted egg flavor? GMA news.* (12 September, 2020). https://www.gmanetwork.com/news/balitambayan/talakayan/674621/natikman-mo-na-ba-ang-ice-cream-na-salted-egg-flavor/story/.

Schachter, Paul & Fe T. Otanes. 1972. *Tagalog reference grammar.* Berkeley: University of California Press.

Sippola, Eeva. 2011. *Una gramática descriptiva del chabacano de Ternate.* Helsinki: University of Helsinki. (Doctoral dissertation).

Sippola, Eeva & Marivic Lesho. 2020. Contact-induced grammatical change and independent development in the Chabacano creoles. *Bulletin of Hispanic Studies* 97(1). 105–123.

Spitz, Walter. 2002. Voice and role in two Philippine languages. In Malcolm Ross & Fay Wouk (eds.), *The history and typology of western Austronesian voice systems*, 379–404. Canberra: Pacific Linguistics.

Stolz, Thomas. 2002. General linguistic aspects of Spanish-indigenous language contacts with special focus on Austronesia. *Bulletin of Hispanic Studies* 79(2). 133–158.

van der Auwera, Johan & Vladimir A. Plungian. 1998. Modality's semantic map. *Linguistic Typology* 2(1). 79–124.

van der Auwera, Johan, Andreas Ammann & Saskia Kindt. 2005. Polyfunctionality and Standard Average European. In Alex Klinge & Henrik Høeg Müller (eds.), *Modality: Studies in form and function*, 247–272. London: Equinox Publishing.

Vander Klok, Jozina. 2013. Pure possibility and pure necessity modals in Paciran Javanese. *Oceanic Linguistics* 52(2). 341–374.

Whinnom, Keith. 1956. *Spanish contact vernaculars in the Philippine islands.* Hong Kong: Hong Kong University.

Winford, Donald. 2000. Irrealis in Sranan: Mood and modality in a radical creole. *Journal of Pidgin and Creole Languages* 15(1). 63–125.

Winford, Donald. 2018. Creole tense-mood-aspect systems. *Annual Review of Linguistics* 4(1). 193–212.

Wolfenden, Elmer P. 1971. *Hiligaynon reference grammar.* Honolulu: University of Hawaii Press.

Yatchi. 2012. *Change: Definitely Filipino.* https://definitelyfilipino.com/blog/change-2/ (20 February, 2019).

Chapter 6

Paradigmatic restructuring: The case of Northern Indo-Portuguese Creoles

Clancy Clements

Indiana University

Good (2012) discusses the claim that '[t]he world's most paradigmatically simplified grammars are jargonized grammars.' In this contribution, I consider the process of paradigmatic restructuring resulting from jargonization from the perspective of Klein and Perdue's (2002, 1997) notion of 'basic variety'. Good's concept of 'jargonization bottleneck' is recast as an instance of form selection constrained by frequency, lexical connections, and detectability in the process of naturalistic subsequent language acquisition. In this context, the case of verbal paradigm reduction in the northern Indo-Portuguese creoles is presented. Two recent developments in Korlai are also discussed: the addition of a fourth verb class and the creation of a new paradigm with 'when' conjunctions. This evidence shows that paradigmatic structure can and does again take form.

1 Introduction

Good (2012) advances the claim that creole languages, as a group, are paradigmatically simple but syntactically average. Given that the nature of his paper was, as he expressed it, "largely programmatic", it did not establish a verifiable claim about all contact languages, but did offer a more narrowly focused claim that "[t]he world's most paradigmatically simplified grammars are jargonized grammars" (2012: 37). In other words, his claim is that languages that have historically undergone jargonization will show a reduction in paradigmatic structure that would be detectable typologically. This paper has two goals: first, I will examine what the processes of "jargonization" and concept of "bottleneck" might involve,

Clancy Clements. 2022. Paradigmatic restructuring: The case of Northern Indo-Portuguese Creoles. In Bettina Migge & Shelome Gooden (eds.), *Social and structural aspects of language contact and change*, 157–182. Berlin: Language Science Press. DOI: 10.5281/zenodo.6979317

and second, I will highlight more recent developments that suggest complexification has already begun in the Indo-Portuguese (IP) creoles examined. For the first goal, I recast the two notions in question within the model developed by (Klein & Perdue 1992, 1997), based on their study of naturalistic second language acquisition and their notion of the "basic variety". I then consider this approach as it applies to the process of abrupt creolization, which I assume to have taken place in the formation of the IP creoles. For the second, I discuss the addition of a fourth verb class in the IP creoles spoken in Korlai and Daman and the development of a new paradigmatic structure in Korlai IP, which are sensitive to the realis-irrealis distinction.

2 The "basic variety", jargonization, and the bottleneck

2.1 The "basic variety" and the formation of jargons, pidgins, and creoles

Before the discussion on Klein and Perdue's notion of the "basic variety"(see discussion below), I will briefly define, as a point of departure, the other terms. A jargon is a rudimentary communication system preceding the development of a pidgin. It may have limited vocabulary, messages such as 'give me this', 'what do you want', 'a little bit' etc. (Bakker 1994: 29), and may also reflect successful attempts at communication in people's experimentation with forms and structure before systematic conventionalization takes place (Bakker 2003).

The notion of "bottleneck" refers to the result of a kind of language transmission "that is qualitatively distinct not only from 'canonical' transmission of language between generations but also from the transmission involved in successful second language acquisition which, while not resulting in full grammatical transmission, does have an end stage wherein the transmitted grammar can be viewed as a variant of the original language" (Good 2012: 4). That is, lexical items may be transmitted but no, or only some, grammatical marking. Good (2012: 6) uses the notion of transmission in a broad sense, "to refer to transmission from any of the languages in a contact situation into an emerging jargon", without presupposing the speakers fully replicate linguistic material from the source language, into the jargon. I would like to recast these two notions (jargon and bottleneck) within Klein and Perdue's "basic variety",to be outlined below, in an attempt to frame the discussion of jargonization within the process of naturalistic language acquisition/creation. It is reasonable to assume that the formation of jargons, pidgins, and creoles involves, very broadly, language acquisition, language processing, and language production, as well as innovation and propagation of linguistic forms. In the process that leads to the formation of a jargon, and subsequently of a pidgin or a creole, the principle of uniformity (see, for example, McColl Millar 2007: 360–361) allows us to expect that the same laws governing language acquisition in general, including language processing/production, also apply in the conventionalization process that yields a new language variety. With regard to language acquisition proper, the principle would mean that in the formation of a new language variety, the co-creators would process input as second language learners process input: they would acquire content words such as nouns, verbs, and adjectives before function words such as prepositions or verb auxiliaries. They would acquire content words first because these denote entities, activities, events, and states in the world, which tend to be phonetically more substantial than function words and thus more detectable in the speech chain. As a corollary, such learners would also acquire more frequently used forms first before less frequently used forms assuming both are equally detectable. I will return to this below.

Perdue (1993a,b) and Klein and Perdue (1992, 1997) report on findings carried out as part of a project named "Second Language Acquisition by Adult Immigrants" that took place between 1981 and 1988 in five European countries (France, Germany, Great Britain, The Netherlands, and Sweden). In the study, the speech of 40 adult learners representing six native and five target languages was analyzed over a two and one-half year period: native Punjabi and Italian speakers learning English, native Italian and Turkish speakers learning German, native Turkish and Arabic speakers learning Dutch, native Arabic and Spanish speakers learning French, and native Spanish and Finnish speakers learning Swedish. In their data analysis, three developmental stages were identified:

1. Stage 1: Nominal utterance organization (NUO), during which speakers' utterances contain nominal elements;

2. Stage 2: Infinite utterance organization (IUO), during which speakers' utterances also contain verbs that are not marked for tense or aspectual distinctions;

3. Stage 3: Finite utterance organization (FUO), during which speakers' utterances contain nominal and verbal elements and there is evidence of tense/aspect marking.

The Klein and Perdue note that, of the 40 learners whose speech they studied, about two-thirds (27/40) reached the FUO stage, all reached the IUO stage, and that up to the IUO stage the development of all participants was found to be similar in that they all developed a relatively stable system to express themselves. This system, which was primarily determined by the interaction of a small number of organizational principles, was largely (though not totally) independent of the specifics of source and target language organization. Moreover, it was simple, versatile, and highly efficient for most communicative purposes.

For about one-third of the participants (13/40) in the study, they note that "acquisition ended on this structural level; some minor variation aside, they only increased their lexical repertoire and learnt to make more fluent use of the BV [basic variety]" (Klein & Perdue 1997: 303). Specifically, the learners developed a versatile, functional basic learner variety governed generally by three constraints: the focus of the utterance appears last (pragmatic), the controller of the utterance appears first (semantic), and the most common syntactic orderings in utterances are: NP1 V NP2, NP1 Cop NP2/AdjP/PP, V NP2 (in presentational utterances only).

Assuming the notion of "basic variety" is on the right track, its relation to jargonization and relevance for pidgin/creole formation can be formulated as follows:

- The notion of jargonization discussed in Good (2012) – with subsequent though variable conventionalization of structural patterns in communicative discourse – fits within the NUO-IUO stages, from stage 1 to stage 2 of language development;

- In the NUO and IUO stages, the three general constraints influence the formation of linguistic structures.

Thus, one would expect that, given certain conditions, speakers would not strive to learn target-language systems in order to communicate, but rather would build their own linguistic systems using the material they had at their disposal. This developmental process would be largely governed by the aforementioned basic principles, as well as by (I claim) cognitive processes interacting with frequency of occurrence, including lexical connections, and detectability of elements in the speech chain. If jargons, pidgins, and creoles share comparable acquisitional histories whereby speakers developing them were guided by basic constraints in situations of continuous communicative interaction, material that is superfluous for communication, the verbal paradigms encoding tense, mood, aspect, person, and number, for example, would not be acquired. Rather, speakers would create other means using the lexical items they have acquired to express what they need. The question about what lexical items speakers acquire in such situations involves the notion of "bottleneck", which will now be discussed in further detail.

2.2 The "bottleneck" and the formation of jargons, pidgins, and creoles

As stated above, the notion "bottleneck" refers to the result of a kind of language transmission in the language acquisition process. It does not necessarily result in full grammar transmission of a target language, but can result in a system where a speaker's target language grammar is a variant of that of the target language. Within a contact situation, Good (2012: 6) states that transmission can happen from any of the languages in contact into an emerging jargon. As a working hypothesis, I assume that the conventionalization process would likely follow the organization principles identified by Klein & Perdue (1992, 1997) and discussed above.

2.2.1 Frequency

In the acquisition process, the frequency with which a lexical form appears in discourse impacts when in the acquisition process it may be acquired. To capture this, (Andersen & Shirai 1996) proposed the Distribution Bias Hypothesis (DBH) to account for which forms of a lexical item are acquired first in the acquisition process. In essence, the DBH states that in L2 acquisition the frequency with which, say, a verb form appears in language use affects the order in which it is first acquired.[1]

To give an illustrative example, in the data I have on Chinese Immigrant Spanish, one of the speakers talked about a number of events related to their background. The verb form used in the narrative is overwhelmingly the 3SG present-tense form, independently of person, number, or temporal/aspectual reference. This is the case, as will be discussed in more detail below, because of the conjugated forms of any given verb the 3SG present-tense form is the most frequently

---

[1] Related to the DBH is the Primacy of Aspect Hypothesis (POA) (Andersen 1993, Andersen & Shirai 1996). The POA states that the lexical aspect of a verb is important in determining in which verb forms a given verb more commonly appears. For example, stative verbs (such as Spanish *saber* 'know') and atelic dynamic verbs (such as *andar* 'walk') which appear more commonly in imperfective forms, than do telic punctual verbs (such as *nascer, nacer* 'be born' or *chegar, llegar* 'arrive'), which appear more commonly in perfective forms than do atelic dynamic and stative verbs.

occurring in written and spoken Portuguese and Spanish, as shown by the to-ken counts of verb forms from the Davies (2002) language corpora data. There is an exception to this strong pattern though. When relating differences about their parents' backgrounds (place of birth), the speaker in question used the 3SG preterit form *nació* 'was born' (a telic punctual verb). The immediate ques-tion arises: why wasn't the 3SG present-tense form selected? Again, the Davies' Spanish-language corpus provides a reasonable answer if we assume the DBH, as well as the POA. Of all the present-tense. preterit, imperfect, and infinitive forms of *nacer* found in the corpus, the 3SG preterit form is the most frequent one, with 15% more tokens than the next most frequent form (See Table 1).

Table 1: Present-tense, preterit, imperfect, and infinitival forms of *nacer* 'to be born' in Davies' Corpus del Español (2002), listed by token fre-quency.

P/N	T/A	Form	Token	%
3SG	PRET	nació	1,643	35
3SG	PRS	nace	975	20
	INF	nacer	802	17
3PL	PRS	nacen	568	12
3PL	PRET	nacieron	300	6
1SG, 3SG	IMPFT	nacía	154	3
3PL	IMPFT	nacían	84	2
2SG	PRET	naciste	80	2
1PL	PRS	nacemos	44	1
1PL	PRET	nacimos	42	1
2SG	PRS	naces	14	0.3
2PL	PRET	nacisteis	8	0.2
1SG	PRS	nazco	6	0.2
2PL	PRS	nacéis	1	0.1
2SG	IMPFT	nacías	1	0.1
1PL	IMPFT	nacíamos	1	0.1
2PL	IMPFT	nacíais	0	0
Total			4,723	100

Although the use of a corpus in this manner is admittedly an imperfect tool and only an approximate manner of gauging frequency of use of verb forms of a paradigm in discourse, it nevertheless makes the correct prediction in the case of the forms of *nacer*, as well as in the large majority of cases, as we will see below.

Returning to how to recast the process of jargonization, then, the relative frequency of a form in discourse, and I will argue its detectability and lexical connections as well, are important in how speakers build their grammars.

If we assume that in the formation of an immigrant variety (as in the discussion of the "basic variety"), a jargon, a pidgin, or a creole, speakers are negotiating a system of communication in which lexical meaning is most important and grammatical meaning is deduced through the situation and the context (i.e. pragmatically, as suggested by Mühlhäusler 1997), speakers will acquire word forms that are most frequently used in discourse, most lexically connected, and most easily detectable. We can define frequency as the number of times in a given corpus that a certain item or form appears. Following the aforementioned principle of uniformity, we assume as a working hypothesis that the most frequently used word forms in corpora are, roughly speaking, also the most frequently used forms in discourse in a contact situation and the ones that would be the most likely candidates for selection in the formation of a jargon, pidgin, or creole.

The data I consider in this section suggests that, in the process of jargonization, the selection of one form over others can be accounted for by appealing to frequency of occurrence, already touched upon; lexical connectedness of forms that are likely candidates for selection in the conventionalization process; and the detectability of forms that are likely candidates for selection in the conventionalization process.

To give an example, in the Portuguese-language corpus of Davies & Ferreira (2006), the most frequently occurring present-tense form of the atelic dynamic verb *beber* 'drink' is the 3SG form *bebe*, while the most frequently occurring nonfinite form by far is the infinitive form *beber* (see Table 2).

Thus, in a situation in which an immigrant variety, pidgin, or creole is taking shape, if frequency of occurrence plays a role in the form selection process, and if learners were to select from among the candidate forms listed in Table 2, they would select *beber*, the overall most frequently occurring form, and after that *bebe*, the second-most frequently occurring form. As we will see below, the base form in the contact varieties studied in this paper derive either from the infinitival form, or from the 3SG present-tense form, the two most frequently occurring forms in the Davies & Ferreira (2006) data base.[2]

Bybee (1985: 123–27) discusses another factor linked to frequency, which she calls lexical connections; that is, shared phonetic material among different forms.

---

[2] For purposes of exposition, the non-present forms are not included, as they are numerically weakly represented relative to the present-tense and infinitival forms.

Table 2: Lexical frequency (strength) of present-tense and some non-finite forms of *beber* 'drink' from two periods (Davies and Ferreira 2006).

P/N	Form	1500–1799		1900s	
		n	%	*n*	%
INF	beber	682	73	580	68
1SG	bebo	9	0.8	42	5.5
2SG	bebes	6	0.5	28	3
3SG	bebe	155	17	128	15
1PL	bebemos	8	0.7	21	3
2PL	bebeis	0	0	0	0
3PL	bebem	73	8	46	5.5
Total		933	100	845	100

In a paradigm, such as the forms in Table 2, there are two key sets of lexical connections, shown in Figure 1. These are distinguished by stress assignment: In the left hand column, the connection common to all forms is ′bebe, indicated by the vertical lines.

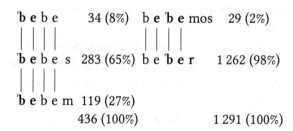

Figure 1: Lexical connections of present-tense and the infinitive forms of *beber* 'drink' (both periods combined).

In the righthand column, the connection common to all forms is be′be, also indicated by the vertical lines. If lexical connections are important for form selection in naturalistic second (or subsequent) language acquisition in a language contact situation, the most strongly represented candidate, in terms of frequency and lexical connections, would be be′be and it would also be the preferred candidate over ′bebe, the second most-preferred candidate. The same is applicable to Spanish. Assuming, then, that the relative distribution of forms of *beber* is comparable for other atelic dynamic verbs, such as *cantar* 'sing' or *andar* 'walk', it is possible to extrapolate, and advance the claim that, in the conventionalization process of a language contact variety such as an immigrant variety, a pidgin, or a creole, there are two main candidates for selection in the present-tense Portuguese and Spanish paradigms, $'\sigma\sigma$ and $\sigma'\sigma$, and the latter will be selected. As indicated, these predictions are largely borne out in the data sample used in Clements (2014, 2018). The results are given in Table 3. We see, then, that the infinitival form of the lexifier language is most often preferred, and if there is a secondary form, it is the 3sg form. Thus, taking lexical strength and lexical connections into account allows us to formulate a falsifiable hypothesis about form selection in the conventionalization process of contact language such as an immigrant variety, a pidgin, or a creole.

Table 3: Default form and verb form source

Language	Verb form source from Portuguese/Spanish
a. Angolar	INF
b. Papiamentu	INF and 3SG
c. Palenquero	INF
d. Bozal Spanish	INF and 3SG
e. Chinese Coolie Spanish	variable but 3SG (62%) and INF (17.5%) preferred
f. Macau Portuguese	INF
g. Chinese Immigrant Spanish	variable but 3SG (48%) and INF (19%) preferred
h. Korlai Indo-Portuguese	INF
i. Daman Indo-Portuguese	INF

2.2.2 Detectability

The notion of detectability (see 1 below), is based on two uncontroversial distinctions and one descriptive observation. The observation is the ubiquity of CV structure in the world's spoken languages. As for the distinctions, those between stress-bearing vs. non-stress-bearing syllables between free vs. bound morphemes are relevant here. Thus, for the purposes at hand detectability is defined in relative terms: syllables containing or consisting of a CV structure are more easily detected in the speech chain than those without a CV structure (e.g.

V or VC structure), and that stressed syllables and free-standing morphemes are more easily detected in the speech chain than unstressed syllables and clitics/affixes, respectively. This can be stated as in (1).

(1) Definition of Detectability
  a. CV is more detectable than VC, V
  b. stressed syllables are more detectable than unstressed syllables
  c. free-standing morphemes are more detectable than clitics and affixes

Based on the foregoing, then, I assume that in the conventionalization process of a language-contact variety, the nature and extent of restructuring, and thus the relative importance of frequency, lexical connections, and detectability in shaping a newly-emerging language variety, depend on the individual makeup of a given contact situation. At the same time, it must be acknowledged that the adult agents of the acquisition/creation process already know one or more languages and that in creating a language contact variety, speakers may introduce into the new language elements from their own language(s). In the literature, this is variably called imposition or interference through shift.

Having defined frequency, lexical connections, and detectability, I would like to illustrate now how they operate in the selection process of a form, namely, the copula, in the aforementioned contact varieties. It turns out that frequency and detectability seem to interact in the selection process.

2.2.3 Illustrative example of the "bottleneck": Frequency, lexical connections, and detectability in copula selection

In Portuguese and Spanish, there are two copulas: *ser* and *estar*. Restricting myself to the infinitive and present-tense forms for the present discussion (these are the most relevant), I assume that all forms of both copulas were possible candidates for selection in the formation of the contact varieties in question. Based on frequency counts gleaned from the Davies & Ferreira (2006) Portuguese-language corpus and the Davies (2002) Spanish-language corpus, shown in Tables 4 and 5, and Tables 6 and 7, we see that the 3SG is by far the most frequently occurring form in both languages, for all periods (16th–18th c., 18th–19th c.) and in both genres (written vs. oral). The second most frequently occurring form is different for the two languages. In Portuguese, the infinitival form *ser* is more frequent than *são* 3PL in the written data (16th to 20th century), but in the oral data the two forms are roughly equally frequent. In Spanish, while *ser* is more frequent in the 16th–18th centuries, in the 19th–20th centuries the two forms *ser* and *son* 3PL are roughly equally frequent and in the oral data *son* is more frequent. Thus, it is reasonable to say that, in terms of frequency, these two forms competed with one another in the selection process. Given that the other forms of the respective paradigms are rather weakly represented, based on frequency alone, that is, the frequency distributions in Tables 4 and 5, the following predictions can be made. If frequency alone is favored in copula selection during the conventionalization process of a contact variety such as an immigrant variety, a pidgin, or a creole, the 3SG copula form *é* for Portuguese and *es* for Spanish should be selected, because they are by far the most frequently occurring forms, respectively. As we will see below, the forms *é, es* are seldomly selected. The conclusion is, then, that frequency alone is not a reliable predictor for form selection in the formation of the contact languages being examined here.

Table 4: Distribution of the infinitive and present-tense forms of Portuguese *ser* 'be' in two periods and two genres

Form	16th–18th c.		19th–20th c.		Oral	
3SG é	21,261	(41.5%)	249,188	(52%)	47,681	(78.6%)
INF ser	18,777	(37%)	161,781	(33%)	5,808	(9.6%)
3 PL são	9,294	(18%)	59,285	(12%)	5628	(9.3%)
1SG sou	1,132	(2%)	9,109	(2%)	1,153	(2%)
1PL somos	487	(1%)	2,060	(0.4%)	335	(.45%)
2SG és	207	(0.5%)	2,855	(0.6%)	34	(.05%)
Total	51,158	(100%)	484,278	(100%)	60,639	(100%)

With respect to the other copulas, forms of Portuguese and Spanish *estar* 'to be', the frequency distribution of the same forms (infinitival and present-tense) are shown in Tables 6–7.

The most frequently occurring form by far in both languages, in all centuries and in both genres, is the 3SG form *está*. Thus, in terms of frequency of occurrence, this form would be the main competitor to *é, es*. But there are other factors that we need to take into consideration, namely lexical connections and detectability. As stated above, lexical connections refers to shared phonetic material among different forms. The lexical connections of the copula forms are displayed in Tables 8 and 9.

In terms of detectability, the lexical connections involving Portuguese *é, és* and Spanish *és, eres* in Table 8 are disfavored because the forms either do not

Table 5: Distribution of the infinitive and present-tense forms of Spanish *ser* 'be' in two periods and two genres

Form	16th–18th c.		19th–20th c.		Oral	
3SG es	284,568	(62%)	257,156	(67%)	66,804	(77%)
INF ser	81,376	(18%)	55,240	(14%)	7,351	(8%)
3PL son	67,371	(14%)	54,643	(14%)	10,239	(12%)
1SG soy	17,548	(4%)	10,210	(3.3%)	1,569	(1.5%)
2 SG eres	6,768	(1.5%)	4,019	(1%)	337	(.5%)
1PL somos	2,445	(0.5%)	3,113	(0.7%)	894	(1%)
Total	460,076	(100%)	384,381	(100%)	87,194	(100%)

Table 6: Distribution of the infinitive and present-tense forms of Portuguese *estar* 'be' in two periods and two genres.

Form	16th–18th c.		19th–20th c.		Oral	
3SG está	4,852	(43.5%)	42,105	(53%)	6,666	(54%)
INF estar	3,066	(27.5%)	8,736	(11%)	1,174	(9.5%)
3 PL estão	1,723	(15.5%)	13,795	(17%)	1,888	(15%)
1SG estou	984	(9%)	9,325	(11%)	1,445	(12%)
1PL estamos	412	(3.5%)	3,792	(5%)	1,061	(9%)
2SG estás	114	(1%)	1,950	(3%)	54	(0.5%)
Total	11,151	(100%)	79,703	(100%)	12,288	(100%)

Table 7: Distribution of the infinitive and present-tense forms of Portuguese *estar* 'be' in two periods and two genres.

Form	16th–18th c.		19th–20th c.		Oral	
3SG está	45,483	(49%)	47,014	(49%)	12,251	(47%)
3PL están	16,135	(17.5%)	18,311	(19%)	4,614	(18%)
INF estar	13,481	(15%)	10,581	(11%)	2,257	(9%)
1SG estoy	11,089	(12%)	9,944	(10%)	2,760	(11%)
1PL estamos	2,242	(2.5%)	6,500	(7%)	3,192	(12%)
2SG estás	3,727	(4%)	3,523	(4%)	856	(3%)
Total		(100%)	95,873	(100%)		(100%)

Table 8: Lexical connections of the infinitive and present-tense forms of Portuguese and Spanish *ser*

Portuguese		Spanish	
CV(C)	V(C)	CV(C)	V(C)
s o u	é s	s o y	e r e s
‖			‖		
s o m o s	é	s o m o s	e (s)
‖		‖	
(s o i s)		‖	
‖ \		‖	
s ã o	s o n		
s e r	s e r		

Table 9: Lexical connections of the infinitive and present-tense forms of Portuguese and Spanish *estar*

Portuguese	Spanish
CC-ʹCV(C/G)	CC -ʹCV(C)
e s t o u	e s t o y
‖‖	‖‖
e s t á s	e s t á s
‖‖‖	‖‖‖
e s t á	e s t á
‖‖‖	‖‖‖
e s t a m o s	e s t a m o s
‖‖‖	‖‖‖
e s t ã o	e s t á n
‖‖‖	‖‖‖
e s t a r	e s t a r

contain or consist of a CV structure, or are infrequent (*és, eres*), or both. Thus, it would be predicted that these forms would not be selected. By contrast, the other sets of lexical connections in Tables 8 and 9 do include frequently occurring forms (Portuguese *são, está*; Spanish *son, está*) that contain a CV structure. Based on this observation, two predictions can be advanced. If detectability alone is favored in copula selection, we should find a number of candidates selected that consist of, or contain, a CV structure. These candidates are Portuguese *sou, estou, estás, está, estar, somos, estamos, ser, são, estão* and Spanish *soy, estoy, estás, está, somos, estamos, son, ser, están*. If the combination of detectability and frequency is favored in copula selection, the prediction is that we should find few forms (or reflexes thereof) as copulas, namely, Portuguese *são, ser, está* and Spanish *son, ser, está*. If lexical connections is also taken into consideration, the infinitival form *ser* in both Portuguese and Spanish is disfavored, but *estar* adds its shared phonetic material to the most frequently occurring form *está*. The combination of frequency, detectability, and lexical connections in form selection turns out to be important in the great majority of cases. The copulas of the varieties examined here are shown in Table 10. Note that in almost all cases the predicted forms, that is, reflexes of *são/son, está(n/r)/estão* were selected.

In those cases in which a form was selected outside of the candidate pool shown in Tables 8 and 9, some of the aforementioned predictions would still apply. That is, any form selected as a copula would have to be one of the most frequently occurring forms of its paradigm and contain, or consist of, a CV structure. This prediction is borne out in all relevant cases except one, that of *sendá* in Palenquero (in Table 10c), whose source is most likely the verb form *sentar* [sen-ˈtaɾ] 'sit down'. All other forms are indeed 3SG forms that contain a CV structure: Palenquero *fwe* (in Table 10c) and Indo-Portuguese *te, tɛ* (in Table 10h, Table 10i).[3]

In three cases, the current model advanced above does not make the correct predictions based on a selective process involving frequency, detectability, and lexical connections. Specifically, the model would not predict Portuguese *é* or Spanish *es* to be selected because they lack a CV structure, although they are by far the most frequently occurring copula forms in the corpora, independently of historical period or genre. There may be other reasons that have influenced the selection process. In the case of Palenquero (in Table 10c), its speakers have been bilingual in Spanish and Palenquero for more than a century. In the second

---

[3]Information sources for these contact varieties are Lorenzino 2007 (Angolar), Kouwenberg & Ramos-Michel 2007 and Maurer 1998 (Papiamentu), Schwegler 1998 and Schwegler & Green 2007 (Palenquero), Clements 2009 (Bozal Spanish, Chinese Coolie Spanish, Chinese Immigrant Spanish), Batalha 1974 and Pinharanda 2010 (Macau), Clements 1996 (Korlai), Clements & Koontz-Garboden 2002 (Daman).

Table 10: Contact-language copulas with Portuguese and Spanish source forms. †: infrequent

Language	Copula	Source form
a. Angolar	θa	< Ptg. est-á/-ão/-r
	ta	< Ptg. est-á/-ão/-r)
b. Papiamentu	ta	< Ptg. est-á/-ão/-r)
c. Palenquero	fwe	< Sp. fue 'was'
	sendá	< Sp. sentar 'sit down-INF'
	é	< Ptg. é and/or Sp. e(s)
d. Bozal Spanish (Cuba)	son	< Sp. son
e. Chinese Coolie Span (Cuba)	son	< Sp. son
f. Macau Portuguese	sã	< Ptg. são
g. Chinese Immigrant Spanish	son	< Sp. son
	está	< Sp. est-á/-án/-ar
	es[†]	< Sp. es
h. Korlai Indo-Portuguese	tɛ	< Ptg. tem (3SG), têm (3PL) 'have'
i. Daman Indo-Portuguese	te	< Ptg. tem (3SG), têm (3PL) 'have'
	é	< Ptg. é

case, speakers of Daman Indo-Portuguese have had the presence of European Portuguese from the time of its formation in the late 16th century up until 1961, with a reduced presence from that year till the present day. In the third case, that of Chinese Immigrant Spanish, the form *es* is infrequently used in favor of *está* and *son*. Thus, in all three cases there are circumstances that appear to have overridden the prediction that the selected form is predictable from the combination of frequency, detectability, and lexical connections.

Thus, the "bottleneck" referred to in Good (2012) can be recast as a set of restrictions on processability: the relative lack of frequency, detectability, and lexical connections of any given form used in communicative interaction represents a "bottleneck" in the conventionalization process of a language variety that yields an immigrant variety (Klein and Perdue's "basic variety"), which in turn can give way to a jargon, pidgin, or creole. Stated a different way, the most frequently occurring forms that are most detectable and lexically connected are most likely to be selected as part of the jargonization process. For the nine language varieties being discussed here, the combination of frequency, detectability, and lexical connections gives the correct predictions to a large extent. If frequency alone is considered, that is, the most frequently occurring forms in the corpora consulted, we only have one part of the bottleneck. If detectability and lexical connections are combined with frequency, the reduced pool of copula candidates (Portuguese *está, são* and Spanish *está, son*) are the most likely forms to be selected. This statement also applies to Portuguese 3SG *tem* 'has', by far the most frequently occurring form of the present-tense paradigm in all historical periods, as well as in the written and oral genres, as shown in Table 11.

Table 11: Frequency counts of Portuguese present-tense forms of *ter* 'have' from the 16th to the 20th century, listed in order of frequency, representing written and oral (only 20th c.) genres

Form	16th–18th c.	19th–20th c.	Oral
3SG tem	17,620 (71%)	46,740 (57%)	10,147 (59%)
1SG tenho	3,433 (14%)	13,600 (17%)	3,031 (18%)
3PL têm	1,638 (7%)	11,979 (14%)	2,034 (12%)
1SG temos	1,813 (7%)	6,523 (8%)	1,822 (10.5)2
SG tens	222 (1%)	2,798 (4%)	98 (.5%)
Total	24,726 (100%)	81,640 (100%)	17,132 (100%)

Thus, in the creation of contact varieties such as immigrant language, pidgins, and creoles, the data considered from the nine contact varieties in question strongly suggest that the bottleneck is profitably defined in terms of frequency of the forms in discourse, how much phonetic material is shared by forms in the paradigm (lexical connections) and the syllabic structure of such forms (detectability).

Although the languages being discussed are paradigmatically more streamlined than their respective lexifier languages, they of course have continued to evolve. Interestingly and not unexpectedly, they have developed new paradigmatic structures. I would just like to highlight two such developments in order to suggest that paradigmatic structure in a language may decrease or increase, depending on the nature of the contact situation.

3 Two developments in Korlai IP after its formation

As shown in Appendix A, the northern Indo-Portuguese creoles spoken in Korlai, Daman, and Diu are unique in that they have retained the three verb classes from Portuguese (*-a, -e, -i*) with the corresponding allomorphy. This suggests that these creoles have a shared history that goes back to the 16th century. It is note-worthy that no other Portuguese-lexified creoles have retained the morphology present in these Indo-Portuguese creoles, although it is clear the paradigmatic richness is greatly reduced (see Appendix B for comparison). In independent developments, Korlai IP, and to a lesser extent Daman IP, have added a fourth verb class. Moreover, Korlai IP has developed a paradigm involving conjunctions referring to 'when'. I will briefly describe these two innovations.

3.1 The fourth verb class in Korlai IP

Given that there has not been any systematic investigation of the fourth verb class in Daman IP, my focus here will be on Korlai IP's fourth verb class. In addition to the three conjugation classes surveyed above, Korlai IP has developed a wholly new conjugation class as a result of the contact between Korlai IP and Marathi: the *-u* class. Korlai speakers use this verb class extensively to borrow verbs from Marathi. The Marathi form is the invariable imperative verb form (see Clements & Luís 2014 for details). The form borrowed in Daman IP is still being investigated. Its verbs are conjugated the same way as verbs belonging to the other classes. The full paradigm *-u* verb class member *loṭú* 'push' is shown in Table 12, together with verbs from the other three classes together with verbs from the other three classes (*katá* 'sing', *bebé* 'drink', and *irgí* 'get up').

Table 12: The four verb classes in Korlai IP with illustrative examples.

	Class 1	Class 2	Class 3	Class 4
a. Unmarked	*kat-á*	*beb-é*	*irg-í*	*loṭ-ú*
b. Past	*kat-ó*	*beb-é-w*	*irg-í-w*	*loṭ-ú*
c. Gerund	*kat-á-n*	*beb-é-n*	*irg-í-n*	*loṭ-ú-n*
d. Completive	*kat-á-d*	*beb-í-d*	*irg-í-d*	*loṭ-ú-d*

The verb forms in Table 12 reveal that *loṭ-ú* 'push' takes the same inflectional endings as the verbs in the other three verb classes, with one exception: the past form is syncretic with its unmarked form. All borrowed verbs from Marathi in Korlai IP belong to Class 4 (Clements & Luís 2014).

Semantically, borrowed verbs in general can make different semantic contributions to its lexicon. They may: a) fill in a semantic gap (in which case they constitute an extension to the lexicon), b) be synonymous to already existing verbs, or c) simply replace a word that has become obsolete (Wohlgemuth 2009).

In the case of Korlai, some loan verbs are synonyms of native Korlai verbs while others are not. An example of a loan verb and native-verb pair (i.e., lexical variants) is Korlai *av ḍu* 'like' (< Marathi *av ḍu* 'like-IMPERATIVE') and *gostá* (< Ptg. *gostar* 'like'), also found as *gostí* 'ditto', the form favored by the younger speakers. However, while some loan verbs in Korlai overlap semantically with native Korlai verbs, they do have different contexts of use. Two examples of this are shown in (2).

(2)   Loan   Native
    aṭu   *finhika*   'shrink/become small'
    bənu *kudzinya* 'prepare, cook'

The loan verb *aṭu* 'shrink' is used only for clothes and other fabrics that can shrink, and the loan verb *bənu* 'prepare' is often used in the context of cooking, but is coming to be used in other contexts, as well, whereas the native verb *kudzinya* 'cook' is restricted to food preparation.

3.2 The emergence of a paradigm involving Korlai IP conjunctions 'when'

The full scope of how 'when' is expressed in Korlai IP includes interrogative (direct and indirect) and assertive speech with subordinate clauses headed by conjunctions (finite clauses), as well as postpositions (non-finite clauses). The expression of 'when' in subordinate clauses is sensitive to mood (realis-irrealis). That is, mood is coded in the 'when' conjunctions in Korlai.

To express direct and indirect interrogative 'when' in Korlai, *kɔr* is used, as shown in (3a) and (3b), respectively.

(3)   a.   *Teru   kɔr   lə   vi?*
      Teru   when   FUT   come
      'When will Teru come?'

    b.   *Teru   kɔr   lə   vi,   kẽ   sab.*
      Teru   when   FUT   come   who   know
      'Who knows when will Teru come.'

'When' in subordinate clauses with future reference can be expressed with the postposition *-ni* in non-finite clauses, as in (4a), or with the conjunction *kɔrki* in finite clauses, as in (4b).

(4) a. *Teru* vin-ni,   *nɔ lə   anda Boməy.*
     Teru come-when   FUT come who know
     'When Teru comes, we will go to Mumbai.'

   b. *Teru kɔrki lə*   vi,   *nɔ lə   anda Boməy.*
     Teru when FUT come 1PL FUT go   Mumbai
     'When Teru comes, we will go to Mumbai.'

In subordinate clauses with past-reference 'when', the postpositional structure is not used. Rather, the conjunction *ki* expresses 'when', as shown in (5). Thus, the use of one or another conjunction depends on mood. If the temporal subordinate clause headed by 'when' has past reference, *ki* is used; if it has future reference, *kɔrki* is used.

(5) *Teru ki yav e, nɔ yaho Boməy*
     Teru   when came 1PL went Mumbai
     'When Teru came, we went to Mumbai.'

The conjunction *ki* 'when' never appears as the head of a clause with future reference (irrealis), as shown in (6b). Similarly, *kɔrki* 'when' heading a clause with past reference (realis) is equally unacceptable, as shown in (6a).

(6) a. ** Teru kadz kɔrki jav e   nɔ ti   kumen.*
     Teru house when came 1PL PST eating
     'When Teru came, we were eating.'

   b. ** Teru kadz ki   lə vi   nɔ lə kume.*
     Teru house when FUT come 1PL FUT eat
     'When Teru comes, we will eat.'

Thus, what has developed in Korlai I consider to be a two-member paradigm with the conjunctions expressing 'when' that are sensitive to mood. This is shown schematically in (7).

(7) [CP XP *ki* [IP _(realis)__]] Matrix Cl
     [CP XP *kɔrki* [IP _(irrealis)_]] Matrix Cl

These developments in Korlai have taken place more recently though it is impossible to say when. What the developments suggest is that as languages with paradigmatic structures evolve, speakers are likely to create new paradigms that encode distinctions in novel ways using the means available to them.

In sum, in this section I have briefly highlighted two innovations found in Korlai: the development of an additional verb class that Korlai speakers use productively to borrow verbs from Marathi, and the emergence of two-member paradigm consisting of 'when' conjunctions whose use are sensitive to the realis-irrealis mood distinction. Interestingly, this distinction found in the selection of one or another 'when' conjunction in Korlai encodes part of what Portuguese encodes with different verb forms. In Portuguese, subordinate clauses headed by 'when' with past reference contain a preterit (i.e., a realis) verb form (8a), while subordinate clauses headed by 'when' with future reference contain a future imperfect (i.e., irrealis) verb form, as in (8b).

(8) a. Quando chegou   Teru, nós fomos   para Lisboa.
         when   arrive.PST.3SG Teru 1PL go.PST.1PL for   Lisbon
         'When Teru arrived, we went to Lisbon.'

     b. Quando chegar   a   Teru, nós   vamos para   Lisboa.
         when   arrive.FUT.IPFV Teru 1PL go.PRS.1PL for   Lisbon
         'When Teru arrives, we will go to Lisbon.'

4 Concluding remarks

In this contribution, I offered a recast of the process of jargonization and the concept of the bottleneck discussed in Good (2012) as a cognitive process of form selection, within Klein and Perdue's model of naturalistic L2 acquisition resulting in what they call the "basic variety". In this model, jargonization can be understood as a speaker's developmental utterance organization evolving from a stage of nominal utterance organization to a stage of non-finite utterance organization. At this latter stage, the verbal communication system is (according to Klein & Perdue 1992, 1997) efficient for communicative purposes. It is at this stage 2, I have argued, that speakers begin to build their own grammar from the material they already have available to them if the circumstances prompt them to do so. I have proposed that the notion of bottleneck can be understood to refer to a number of cognitive and social aspects of how humans communicate (form selections in parsing and producing utterances) in situations of regular communicative interaction among speakers who do not share a common language. For communication, humans target and acquire frequently used, detectable forms with robust lexical connections and they build their grammar using these forms, again, if the circumstances favor it.

Applying the notions of the basic variety development and form selection, the forms found in the nine contact varieties examined in this contribution can be accounted for in a principled way. In the same way, loss of paradigmatic structure can also be accounted for. Good's claim that creoles, as well as other contact varieties discussed in this paper, are paradigmatically simple can be more comprehensively understood within the model of the basic variety (with its constraints), frequency, detectability, and lexical connections.

This, of course, in no way precludes the development of new categories and new paradigms in such restructured languages and I have discussed two such cases here: the addition of a new verb class in Korlai that is used to accommodate verbs borrowed from Marathi into Korlai, and the emergence of a two-member paradigm in Korlai that contains two 'when' conjunctions, one that encode realis mood (*ki*) found in subordinate 'when' clauses with past reference, and another that encodes irrealis mood (*kɔrki*) found in subordinate 'when' clauses with future reference. What these developments suggest is that a language variety, even if highly restructured historically, does develop new, more complex, structures and patterns as it evolves, in order to accommodate the needs of its speakers.

Abbreviations

FUT	future	IPFV	imperfective	PRS	present
IMPFT	imperfect	PL	plural	PST	past
INF	infinitive	PRET	preterit	SG	singular

References

Andersen, Roger W. 1993. Four operating principles and input distribution as explanations for under-developed and mature morphological systems. In K Hyltenstam & A Viborg (eds.), *Progression and regression in language*, 309–339. Cambridge University Press.

Andersen, Roger W. & Yasuhiro Shirai. 1996. The primacy of aspect in first and second-language acquisition: The pidgin-creole connection. In William C. Ritchie and Tej K. Bhatia (ed.), *Handbook of second language acquisition*, 527–570. San Diego, CA: Academic Press.

Bakker, Peter. 1994. Pidgins. In Jacques Arends, Pieter Muysken & Norval Smith (eds.), *Pidgins and creoles: An introduction*, 25–39. Amsterdam: Benjamins.

Bakker, Peter. 2003. Pidgin inflectional morphology and its implications for creole morphology. In Geert Booij & Jaap van Marle (eds.), *Yearbook of morphology*, 3–33. Dordrecht: Kluwer.

Batalha, Graciete Nogueira. 1974. *Língua de Macau*. Macau: Imprensa Nacional de Macau.

Bybee, Joan. 1985. *Morphology*. Amsterdam & Philadelphia: John Benjamins.

Cardoso, Hugo C. 2009. *The Indo-Portuguese language of Diu*. Amsterdam: Landelijke Onderzoekschool Taalwetenschap.

Clements, J. Clancy. 1996. *The genesis of a language: The formation and development of Korlai Portuguese*. Amsterdam: Benjamins.

Clements, J. Clancy. 2009. *The legacy of Spanish and Portuguese: Colonial expansion and language change*. Cambridge: Cambridge University Press.

Clements, J. Clancy. 2014. Form selection in contact languages: Evidence from some Portuguese- and Spanish-lexified contact varieties. In Patrícia Amaral & Ana Maria Caravalho (eds.), *Portuguese-Spanish interfaces: Diachrony, synchrony, and contact*, 377–401. Amsterdam & Philadelphia: John Benjamins.

Clements, J. Clancy. 2018. The Iberian challenge: Creole languages beyond the plantation setting. *Journal of Pidgin and Creole Languages* 33(2). 447–452. DOI: 10.1075/jpcl.00025.cle.

Clements, J. Clancy & Andrew Koontz-Garboden. 2002. Two Indo-Portuguese creoles in contrast. *Journal of Pidgin and Creole Languages* 17(2). 191–236.

Clements, J. Clancy & Ana R. Luís. 2014. Contact intensity and the borrowing of bound morphology in Korlai Indo-Portuguese. In Francesco Gardani, Peter Arkadiev & Nino Amiridze (eds.), *Borrowed morphology*, 217–237. Boston & Berlin: De Gruyter Mouton.

Davies, Mark. 2002. *Corpus del Español:100 million words, 1200s-1900s*. http://www.corpusdelespanol.org.

Davies, Mark & Michael Ferreira. 2006. *Corpus do Português:45 million words, 1300s-1900s*. http://www.corpusdoportugues.org.

Good, Jeff. 2012. Typologizing grammatical complexities, or why creoles may be paradigmatically simple but syntagmatically average. *Journal of Pidgin and Creole Languages* 27(1). 1–47.

Klein, Wolfgang & Clive Perdue. 1992. *Utterance structure: Developing grammars again*. Amsterdam: Benjamins.

Klein, Wolfgang & Clive Perdue. 1997. The basic variety (or: Couldn't natural languages be much simpler?) *Second Language Research* 13(4). 301–347.

Kouwenberg, Silvia & Abigail Ramos-Michel. 2007. *Papiamentu (Creole Spanish/-Portuguese)*. John Holm & Peter L. Patrick (eds.) (Westminster Creolistics Series 7). London: Battlebridge. 307–332.

Lorenzino, Gerardo A. 2007. *Angolar (CreolePortuguese) or Lunga Ngola*. John Holm & Peter L. Patrick (eds.) (Westminster Creolistics Series 7). London: Battlebridge. 1–23.

Maurer, Philippe. 1998. El papiamentu de Curazao. In Matthias Perl & Armin Schwegler (eds.), *América negra: Panorámica actual de los estudios lingüísticos sobre variedades hispanas, portuguesas y criollas*, 139–217. Frankfurt & Madrid: Vervuert.

McColl Millar, Robert. 2007. *Trask's historical linguistics*. 2nd edn. London: Arnold.

Mühlhäusler, Peter. 1997. *Pidgin & Creole linguistics*. 2nd edn. Colombo: Battlebridge Publications.

Perdue, Clive. 1993a. *Adult language acquisition: Cross-linguistic perspectives. Field methods*, vol. 1. Cambridge: Cambridge University Press.

Perdue, Clive. 1993b. *Adult language acquisition: Cross-linguistic perspectives. The results*, vol. 2. Cambridge: Cambridge University Press.

Pinharanda, Mário. 2010. *Estudo da expressão morfo-sintática das categorias de tempo, modo e aspecto em Maquista*. University of Macau. (Doctoral dissertation).

Schwegler, Armin. 1998. El Palenquero. In Matthias Perl & Armin Schwegler (eds.), *América negra: Panoramic actual de los estudios lingüísticos sobre variedades hispanas, portuguesas y criollas*, 218–291. Frankfurt: Vervuert.

Schwegler, Armin & Kate Green. 2007. *Palenquero (Creole Spanish)* (Westminster Creolistics Series 7). London: Battlebridge. 273–306.

Wohlgemuth, Jan. 2009. *A typology of verbal borrowings*, vol. 211. Berlin: Walter de Gruyter.

Appendix A Verbal paradigms in three Northern Indo-Portuguese Creoles (Clements & Koontz-Garboden 2002 and Cardoso 2009)

	Korlai	Daman	Diu
Pres. -a	—	—	fal say
Pres./Inf. -a	halá say	fəlá say	falá say
Pres. -e	—	—	beb drink
Pres./Inf. -e	bebé drink	bebé drink	bebé drink
Pres. -i	—	—	durm sleep
Pres./Inf. -i	drumí sleep	durmí sleep	durmí sleep
Pres./Inf. -u	tapú heat	babrú mutter	—
	pres./past progressive		adverbial gerund
Pres. Ptcpl. -a	(tɛ/ti) halán	te/tiŋ fəlán	falán
	(AUX) saying	AUX saying	saying
-e	(tɛ/ti) bebén	te/tiŋ bebén	bebén
	(AUX) drinking	AUX drinking	drinking
-i	(tɛ/ti) drumín	te/tiŋ durmín	durmín
	(AUX) sleeping	AUX sleeping	sleeping
-u	(tɛ/ti) tapún	te/tiŋ babrún	—
	(AUX) heating	AUX grumbling	
	past	past	past
Past -a	haló said	fəló said	faló said
-e	bebéw drank	bebéw drank	bebéw drank
-i	drumíw slept	durmiw slept	durmíw slept
-u	tapú heated	babrú grumbled	—
	pres./past pfct		participial adj.
Past Ptcpl. -a	(tɛ/ti) halád	te/tiŋ fəlád	falád
	(AUX) said	AUX said	said
-e	(tɛ/ti) bebíd	te/tiŋ bebíd	bebíd
	(AUX) drunk	AUX drunk	drunk
-i	(tɛ/ti) drumíd	te/tiŋ durmíd	durmíd
	(AUX) slept	AUX slept	slept
-u	(tɛ/ti) tapúd	te/tiŋ babrúd	—
	(AUX) heated	AUX grumble	

Appendix B The paradigms (partial) of the Portuguese verb system

Table 13: Portuguese verbal paradigms simple forms

PRET	IMPFT	PRS	FUT	COND
cantei	cantava	canto	cantarei	cantaria
cantaste	cantavas	cantas	cantarás	cantarias
cantou	cantava	canta	cantará	cantaria
cantámos	cantávamos	cantamos	cantaremos	cantaríamos
cantastes	cantáveis	cantais	cantareis	cantaríeis
cantaram	cantavam	cantam	cantarão	cantariam

PLUPERFECT	IMPFT SBJV	PRS SBJV/IMP	PERSONAL INF	
cantara	cantasse	cante	cantar	
cantaras	cantasses	cantes/canta	cantares	
cantara	cantasse	cante/cante	cantar	
cantáramos	cantássemos	cantemos	cantarmos	
cantáreis	cantásseis	canteis/cantai	cantardes	
cantaram	cantassem	cantem	cantarem	

PRET	IMPFT	PRS	FUT	COND
bebi	cantava	bebia	beberei	beberia
bebeste	cantavas	bebias	beberás	beberias
bebeu	cantava	bebia	beberá	beberia
bebemos	cantávamos	bebíamos	beberemos	beberíamos
bebesteis	cantáveis	bebíeis	bebereis	beberíeis
beberam	cantavam	bebiam	beberão	beberiam

PLUPERFECT	IMPFT SBJV	PRS SBJV/IMP	PERSONAL INF	
bebera	bebesse	beba	beber	
beberas	bebesses	bebas/bebe	beberes	
bebera	bebesse	beba/beba	beber	
bebêramos	bebêssemos	bebamos	bebermos	
bebêreis	bebêsseis	bebais/bebei	beberdes	
beberam	bebessem	bebam	beberem	

Table 14: Portuguese verbal paradigms compound perfect forms

IMPFT	PRS	FUT	COND
tinha cantado	tenho cantado	terei cantado	teria cantado
tinhas cantado	tens cantado	terás cantado	terias cantado
tinha cantado	tem cantado	terá cantado	teria cantado
tínhamos cantado	temos cantado	teremos cantado	teríamos cantado
tínheis cantado	tendes cantado	tereis cantado	teríeis cantado
tinham cantado	têm cantado	terão cantado	teriam cantado

IMPFT SBJV	PRS SUBJ	PERSONAL INF	
tivesse cantado	tenha cantado	ter cantado	
tivesses cantado	tenhas cantado	teres cantado	
tivesse cantado	tenha cantado	ter cantado	
tivéssemos cantado	tenhamos cantado	termos cantado	
tivésseis cantado	tenhais cantado	terdes cantado	
tivessem cantado	tenham cantado	terem cantado	

IMPFT	PRS	FUT	COND
tinha bebido	tenho bebido	terei bebido	teria bebido
tinhas bebido	tens bebido	terás bebido	terias bebido
tinha bebido	tem bebido	terá bebido	teria bebido
tínhamos bebido	temos bebido	teremos bebido	teríamos bebido
tínheis bebido	tendes bebido	tereis bebido	teríeis bebido
tinham bebido	têm bebido	terão bebido	teriam bebido

IMPFT SBJV	PRS SBJV	PERSONAL INF	
tivesse bebido	tenha bebido	ter bebido	
tivesses bebido	tenhas bebido	teres bebido	
tivesse bebido	tenha bebido	ter bebido	
tivéssemos bebido	tenhamos bebido	termos bebido	
tivésseis bebido	tenhais bebido	terdes bebido	
tivessem bebido	tenham bebido	terem bebido	

Chapter 7

Loíza Spanish and the Spanish Creole debate: A linguistic and sociohistorical account

Piero Visconte
University of Texas, Austin

Sandro Sessarego
University of Texas, Austin

This study combines sociohistorical and linguistic insights to cast light on the nature and origin of Loíza Spanish (LS), an Afro-Hispanic vernacular spoken in Loíza, Puerto Rico by the descendants of the Africans brought to this region to work as slaves during the colonial period. The present work assesses the evolution of this variety and its implications for creole studies. In so doing, it challenges the posture that would picture certain contemporary features of LS and other Afro-Hispanic dialects as the traces of a previous creole stage (de Granda 1968 et seq.). Thus, this article contributes to the long-lasting Spanish Creole Debate (Lipski 2005) by providing new information on a so-far little-studied Afro-Puerto Rican vernacular.

1 Introduction

For the past five decades, the field of Spanish contact linguistics has been characterized by a heated debate on the nature and origins of the vernaculars that formed in the Americas from the contact of African languages and Spanish in colonial times (de Granda 1968 et seq). A central aspect of this academic discussion, which Lipski (2005: Ch. 9) has labeled the "Spanish Creole Debate", has to do with the paucity of attested Spanish-based creoles in this part of the world.

Piero Visconte & Sandro Sessarego. 2022. Loíza Spanish and the Spanish Creole debate: A linguistic and sociohistorical account. In Bettina Migge & Shelome Gooden (eds.), *Social and structural aspects of language contact and change*, 183–212. Berlin: Language Science Press. DOI: 10.5281/zenodo.6979319

Indeed, it is well known that there are only two contact varieties in the Americas that have traditionally been classified as Spanish creoles – Papiamentu (spoken in the Netherlands Antilles) and Palenquero (used in a former maroon community, the village of Palenque, Colombia) – a situation in sharp contrast with the relative abundance of their English- and French-based counterparts (Holm & Patrick 2007). In addition, some linguists would even question the status of Papiamentu and Palenquero as "Spanish-based". In fact, they would claim that these languages may be classified as Spanish creoles only in a synchronic sense, since diachronically they would have developed out of Portuguese-based contact varieties, which only in a second phase of their evolution were relexified with Spanish words (Schwegler 1996, Martinus 1996, McWhorter 2000, Jacobs 2012). This proposal would, then, imply that Spanish never really creolized in the Americas.

A number of authors have tried to account for the paucity (or lack) of Spanish-based creoles by providing a variety of diverging hypotheses on pretty much every single Afro-Hispanic dialect spoken in the Americas (see Sessarego 2021: Ch.1 for an overview). One of these hypotheses came to be known as the Decreolization Hypothesis (de Granda 1978), which suggests that a Spanish creole once existed in Latin America, and that, after the abolition of slavery by the end of the 19th century, it quickly decreolized, and thus came to resemble the standard norm, leaving behind only a few grammatical traces of its former creole stage (e.g., "creole-like" features). Several scholars have embraced the Decreolization Hypothesis (Perl & Schwegler 1998, Schwegler 1999, Otheguy 1973, Megenney 1993, Guy 2017), while others have questioned its validity by providing linguistic, sociohistorical, and even legal data to offer alternative explanations to the scarcity of attested Spanish creoles in the Americas (Mintz 1971, Laurence 1974, Lipski 1993, McWhorter 2000, Sessarego 2017).

To describe the heterogeneity of opinions on this topic and the lack of common agreement among the scholars involved in this animated discussion, Lipski (2005: 304) stressed that "the last word [...] has yet to be written" on the Spanish Creole Debate. Lipski's statement is sixteen years old now, but given the current range of diverging views on this issue (see, for example, the contrastive perspectives collected in Sessarego 2018a), it is certainly still valid today. Far from providing the "last word" on this topic, this paper will add more fuel to the debate by casting light on the nature and origin of a so-far little-studied Afro-Hispanic dialect from the Caribbean, Loíza Spanish (LS), a black vernacular spoken in Loíza, Puerto Rico by the descendants of the Africans taken to this region to work as slaves on the sugarcane plantations that developed on the island during the sugar boom in the 19th century. In particular, besides providing a linguistic account of the features encountered in this dialect that have traditionally been identified as indicators of a potential creole past for other Spanish Caribbean varieties (de Granda 1968, Otheguy 1973), this article adds a sociohistorical dimension to the analysis of slavery in the region, which will offer a more well-rounded perspective on the evolution of this Afro-Hispanic vernacular, and thus contribute in a broader sense to the Spanish Creole Debate.

Figure 1: Loíza, Puerto Rico. (Map data ©2021 OpenStreetMap contributors)

This paper is organized as follows: §2 offers a brief analysis of the Spanish Creole Debate. §3 provides an outline of some grammatical traits belonging to LS, which have commonly been classified in the literature as "creole-like" features, and that were detected in this dialect during linguistic fieldwork carried out in summer 2020. §4 offers a sociohistorical account of black slavery in Puerto Rico, with a particular focus on Loíza, to understand whether a process of (de)creolization could be at the root of the attested grammatical configurations. Finally, §4.1 summarizes the main findings, elaborates on the origin and nature of LS, and provides the concluding remarks.

2 The Spanish Creole Debate

De Granda (1968, 1970, 1978) was the first Hispanist who formulated a hypothesis to account for the scarcity of Spanish-based creoles in the Americas. He suggested that, since slavery in the Spanish colonies was presumably not that different from the forced-labor systems implemented by other European powers, Spanish creoles must have also existed in Spanish America, and that the contemporary lack of such contact varieties in these territories could only be explained as the result of a decreolization process (or approximation to the standard norm), which would have been driven by contact with the standard variety after the abolition of slavery. Such a decreolization process, in de Granda's view, would not yet be completely over. Indeed, it would still be possible to detect some grammatical traces of this previous creole phase in the speech of a number of black communities across the Americas. According to de Granda, therefore, the presence of "creole-like" features in these varieties should be taken as linguistic evidence corroborating his model, which came to be known in the literature as the "Decreolization Hypothesis".

A number of proposals have embraced the Decreolization Hypothesis, which was originally adopted to account for a set of grammatical features common to Caribbean Spanish varieties (Otheguy 1973, Schwegler 1991, 1996, Megenney 1993). In this regard, Otheguy (1973: 334–335) could not be more explicit when, after analyzing several grammatical traits encountered across these dialects (i.e., reduced number agreement across the Determiner Phrase, high rates of overt subject pronouns, presence of non-inverted questions, etc.), he stated:

> In summary, the data presented here strongly suggest that the *habla bozal*[1] spoken in the Spanish Antilles (and possibly throughout the Caribbean) during colonial times was a Creole... Given this, the sample points of coincidence presented here between features which are shared by most Creoles but which are peculiar to Caribbean Spanish cannot be discarded as coincidence and must be taken into account in any explanation of the historical genesis of this major dialect type.

A group of scholars, on the other hand, began to question such claims, and pointed out that the living and working conditions on the Spanish haciendas in Cuba and Santo Domingo were not as harsh as those found in other European plantations – especially before the sugar boom of the 19th century – and thus a creole origin for the Cuban and Dominican varieties would be quite doubtful (Mintz 1971, Laurence 1974, Chaudenson 1992, Lipski 1993, Ortiz-López 1998, Clements 2009). Some linguists came to suggest that, even though Cuba and Santo Domingo might not have been the ideal places for Spanish creolization, other Spanish mainland territories, such as coastal Venezuela, Chota Valley (Ecuador), coastal Peru, Veracruz (Mexico), Los Yungas (Bolivia) and Chocó (Colombia), may have presented the proper sociodemographic conditions for creole formation (Schwegler 1999, 2018, Lipski 2008, Perez 2015; Álvarez & Obediente 1998,

---

[1]The expression *habla bozal* indicates the speech of *bozal* slaves, African-born captives, who acquired a limited version of Spanish in the Americas.

McWhorter 2000). In contrast to these claims, a set of specific case studies on the aforementioned Afro-Hispanic communities have provided sociohistorical and linguistic data that reject a potential (de)creolization model for such vernaculars (Díaz-Campos & Clements 2008, Sessarego 2013a,b, 2014, 2019, in press). In addition, some proposals have added a legal dimension to the Spanish Creole Debate, by claiming that one of the main factors preventing the creolization of Spanish in the Americas had to do with the peculiarities of the Spanish legal system in matters of slavery, which would have facilitated the integration of slaves into free society and thus their acquisition of the colonial language (Sessarego 2015, 2017, 2018b).

In recent years, a revival of the Decreolization Hypothesis has been proposed by well-known sociolinguists, who have indicated that Caribbean Spanish, as well as a few other Mainland Afro-Hispanic and Afro-Lusophone varieties, may indeed have creole roots (Guy 2017, Schwegler 2014, 2018). A clear example of this more recent trend is Guy (2017: 72), who highlighted how Afro-Bolivian Spanish (ABS) could be taken as an example of a variety that would have gone half-way through this supposed (de)creolization process, which, in his view, affected many other Afro-Latino vernaculars, including Popular Brazilian Portuguese and Caribbean Spanish (Guy 1981). He stated:

> Its history of linguistic isolation implies that ABS must be more basilectal, closer to the speech of the earliest generations of Africans in the Americas, than Brazilian Portuguese and Caribbean Spanish. This in turn implies a historical trajectory by which all of these varieties started out as creoles, or at least restructured varieties tending toward the creole end ..., and then acquired their present form through differing degrees of standardization.

While most of the studies on the supposed (de)creolization of Caribbean Spanish have been primarily concerned with the Afro-Hispanic dialects of Cuba and the Dominican Republic, with the exception of a few works, such as those by Álvarez-Nazario (1959, 1974) and Mauleón de Benítez (1974), not much attention has ever been paid to Afro-Puerto Rican Spanish. This article aims at filling this gap by focusing on LS. In so doing, it will not only document a so-far little-studied Afro-Puerto Rican variety; it will also add a new piece to the Spanish Creole Debate puzzle and thus contribute to explaining the paucity of Spanish creoles in the Americas.

3 An account of Loíza Spanish "creole-like" features

Linguistic data were collected during summer 2020 in Loíza, the municipality of Puerto Rico with the highest percentage of inhabitants who self-identify as "black" – more than 64% of the total local population (Moya 2003; US Census 2010). Sociolinguistic interviews and grammaticality judgments were carried out with 53 informants of different ages (ranging from 19 to 92) and levels of education (ranging from illiterate people to speakers holding a college degree). Findings indicate – as expected – that the older and lesser-educated informants tend to present the highest rates of vernacular feature use, while the language use of younger and more educated members of the community more closely resembles the standard variety, even though the use of non-standard forms is still quite noticeable in their speech.

Even if full light has yet to be cast on the genesis and evolution of LS, from the analysis of the speech of this heterogeneous sample of *loiceños*, it is evident that, as it is currently spoken, this variety does not show the radical grammatical restructuring that characterizes Spanish creoles such as Papiamentu (Jacobs 2012) or Palenquero (Schwegler 1996). Present-day LS displays several phonological and morphological reductions, some African lexical borrowings, and other minor traces of contact-induced language change, but it definitively lacks the more intense traits of grammatical restructuring that are typically encountered in creole languages (Winford 2003). For this reason, LS is – for the most part – easily understandable to any speaker of standard Spanish and, in broad terms, it could be said that it classifies more as a "Spanish dialect" than a "Spanish creole" (McWhorter 2000: 10).

Even though LS is not that divergent from standard Spanish, it, nevertheless, presents some grammatical phenomena that have repeatedly been reported in the literature as potential indicators of a previous creole stage (de Granda 1968, Otheguy 1973, Álvarez & Obediente 1998): (1a) high use of overt subject pronouns; (1b) instances of lack of subject-verb agreement; (1c) variable gender agreement in the Determiner Phrase (DP); (1d) reduced number agreement across the DP; (1e) sporadic presence of bare nouns; (1f) cases of agglutination of the article with the following noun; (1g) copula reduction by aspiration or apheresis; (1h) lack of subject-verb inversion in questions; (1i) /ɾ/ reduction on infinitive verb forms.

(1)   a. Si *tú* tiene[s] el pecho apreta[d]o, *tú* te toma[s] un guarapillo [d]e curía.

          'If you feel that your chest is tight, you should take a *curía guarapillo* (infusion).'

b. La lluvia y el viento *estaba[n]* fuerte fuerte en la playa [d]e Villa Pesquera.

'The rain and the wind were very strong at Villa Pesquera beach.'

c. Teníamo[s] *todo [toda]* la tierra pa[ra] nojotros[s].

'All the land was for us.'

d. Había *tres gato[s] negro[s]* en la calle.

'There were three black cats in the street.'

e. [El huracán] María se llevó *[el]* techo.

'Hurricane Maria tore off the roof.'

f. Vamo[s] [a] comprá[r]*lalmueso* [el almuerzo].

'Let's buy lunch.'

g. *[Es]tá* tó[do] bien.

'Everything is fine.'

h. ¿Qué *tú hace[s]*?

'What are you doing?'

i. Oye lo que te va [a] *decí[r]* tu mai.

'Listen to what your mother is going to tell you.'

It is relevant to point out that the features reported in (1) parallel those found in a number of Puerto Rican literary texts representing colonial *habla bozal* (2), such as *La juega de gallos o el negro bozal* (Caballero 1852), *Décimas de 1898* (Mason 1918), *Tío Fele* (Derkes 1883) – all of which have been recompiled by Álvarez-Nazario (1974) – as well as *Flor de una noche* by Escalona (1883) and *Dinga y Mandinga* by Vizcarrondo (1983).

(2) a. *Yo tiene* uno becero en casa [se]ño[r] Juan de Dio, *yo tiene* dinero juntado y niña Federica ba a da a mí pa comprá uno llegua.

'I have a calf in the house of Mr. Juan de Dios, I have money saved and the girl Federica is going to give me to buy a mare.' (Caballero 1852, in Álvarez-Nazario 1974: 384)

b. ¡[La] niña Fererica *son [es]* buen amo!

'The girl Federica is a good master.' (Caballero 1852, in Álvarez-Nazario 1974: 384)

c. Tú siempre tá jablando a mí con *grandísima [grandísimo]* rigó[r].

'You always speak to me with great rigor.' (Caballero 1852, in Álvarez-Nazario 1974: 384)

    d. Un día en e[l] trabajo co[n]tándole *las pata[s]* a un gusano.

       'One day at work counting the legs of a worm.' (Escalona 1883: 77)

    e. Llava llevá *[la]* señora.

       'The lady is going to bring it.' (Derkes 1883, in Álvarez-Nazario 1974: 390)

    f. *Lamo [el amo]* Pantaleón ta bravo.

       'Master Pantaleon is angry.' (Caballero 1852, in Álvarez-Nazario 1974: 385)

    g. Nanquí *toy* ma Mákinley.

       'Here I am, my Mákinley.' (Mason 1918, in Álvarez-Nazario 1974: 396)

    h. ¿Po qué *tú no ta queré* a mí?

       'Why don't you like me?' (Caballero 1852, in Álvarez-Nazario 1974: 384)

    i. Ayé[r] me diji[s]te negro y hoy te boy a *contejtá[r]*.

       'Yesterday you called me black and today I am going to answer you.' (Vizcarrondo 1983: 77)

    The examples given in (1) and (2) confirm that LS is an Afro-Hispanic vernacular presenting a set of features that diverge quite significantly from standard Spanish and that are rooted in the traditional colonial speech of black *bozales*. All these grammatical elements have been commonly attested across a number of Spanish contact varieties (Klee & Lynch 2009) and vernacular dialects (Zamora-Vicente 1989, Lipski 1994). They are not only commonly found in creole languages; rather, some of these features also systematically occur in advanced L2 varieties of Spanish, as well as attritional L1 and heritage varieties (e.g., instances of lack of subject-verb agreement, variable gender agreement in the DP, sporadic presence of bare nouns, high use of overt subject pronouns) (Montrul 2008, 2016, Geeslin 2013, Romero & Sessarego 2018). In addition, a subgroup of these grammatical traits – such as reduced number agreement across the DP, cases of agglutination of the article with the following noun, copula reduction by aspiration or apheresis, /ɾ/ reduction on infinitive verb forms – appear to be quite widespread across several rural dialects of Spanish (e.g., rural varieties of Canary Island Spanish, Andalusian Spanish, and Murcian Spanish, to mention a few) (Alvar 1996), for which a (de)creolization trajectory is certainly not plausible. Thus, as explained elsewhere in greater detail (Sessarego 2019), all of these phenomena may be understood as either quite common vernacular features (e.g., various

types of phonological agglutination and reduction as well as morphological sim-
plifications; see Sessarego 2011), or as byproducts of processing constraints applying at the interface between different linguistic modules (i.e., pronominal use
→ syntax/pragmatic interface; agreement reductions → morphology/semantics
interface, bare nouns → syntax/semantics interface; see Sessarego 2021), which
are naturally found in all cases of contact-driven restructuring, and thus should
not necessarily be taken as indicators of a previous creole stage.

The linguistic data collected for LS, therefore, should not be taken as tangible
evidence in support of the Decreolization Hypothesis for this Afro-Caribbean
vernacular, as some authors seem to suggest (de Granda 1970, Otheguy 1973,
Guy 2017). Rather, the attested grammatical configurations may be understood
as the result of advanced L2 processes and vernacular rural traits, which were na-
tivized and conventionalized at the community level in this Afro-Puerto Rican
community, a scenario that has similarly been reported for a number of other
Afro-Hispanic varieties in the Americas (Lipski 2005, Sessarego 2013a). This being said, in order to get a more precise picture of the origin and evolution of this
vernacular, a sociohistorical account of the nature of slavery in the region will
be provided in the following section.

4 A socio-historical account of black slavery in Puerto Rico

Black slavery lasted in Puerto Rico for almost four centuries, from the early
phases of the Spanish colonization of the island by the end of the 15th century
to its abolition in 1873. Nevertheless, as in the rest of Latin America, the formal elimination of slavery, in practice, did not automatically imply for the Afro-
descendant population of Puerto Rico the same degree of freedom and wealth
enjoyed by the white and mestizo citizens living on the island (Bas-García 2009).

Indeed, the post-abolitionist system in place was designed in a way that would
force former slaves to pay for their own freedom. Essentially, they were turned
into debtors, who had to repay their value to their former masters. Thus, they
became *peones* 'peons', who fundamentally had to work for free for their former
owners (Bas-García 2009). Even after the end of *peonaje* in the 20th century, the
living and working conditions of most Afro-Puerto Ricans was far from being
optimal, and the effects of such a situation can still be observed in the present.
Indeed, the municipalities of Puerto Rico with the highest concentrations of black
inhabitants tend to be characterized by poor infrastructure and few higher educational centers. More than two thirds of the inhabitants of Loíza, for example,

are currently living below the poverty line (US Census 2010), while government studies have repeatedly highlighted how a significant number of the citizens of this community feel marginalized and experience some degree of social exclusion (Rivera-Quintero 2014).

Since the black presence in Puerto Rico spans a period of almost four hundred years of slavery followed by more than a century of freedom, it is impossible to approach this phenomenon in a homogeneous way. For this reason, in order to better appreciate the position of Afro-descendants in the Puerto Rican society over time and the parallel evolution of their language, three main historical phases will be analyzed. This will help us understand whether, at any point in the history of Puerto Rico, Spanish could (de)creolize on the island.

The first phase (1510–1791) goes from the first documented introduction of black slaves into the island in 1510 to the Haitian Revolution of 1791, which triggered the sugar boom in the Spanish Caribbean. This period consists of a relatively reduced percentage of African-descendants in Puerto Rico, who worked on small-scale farms and in mines. The second phase (1791–1873) includes the sugar boom, which led to a more significant introduction of an African workforce and the development of bigger sugarcane haciendas. This phase ends with the decline of the sugar industry and the abolition of slavery. The third and last phase (1873-present) concerns the post-abolition period, characterized by a progressive acquisition of civil rights by Afro-Puerto Ricans up to the present day.

Before getting into the details of these phases, we wish to provide some demographic data, which serve the purpose of understanding the dimensions of the slave trade to Spanish America in general, and to Puerto Rico in particular, in comparison with the volumes of African captives that were introduced in the rest of the European colonies overseas.

Indeed, as Lucena (2000: 115) indicates (see Table 1, from Curtin 1969: 88), the African slaves taken to Spanish America over four centuries represent only a small fraction (less than 15%) of the total number of black captives introduced into the Americas. The reason for this, as explained by a number of historians (Andrés-Gallego 2005, Cushner 1980, Brockington 2006), has to do with the fact that Spanish colonies, at least until the sugar boom of the 19th century, had never relied on a black workforce on a massive scale. Indeed, to adopt Berlin's (1998) famous dichotomy, Spanish colonies were not "slave societies", but rather "societies with slaves", in which black captives were certainly present and performed a variety of jobs, though the institution of slavery was not the main drive of local economies.

In relation to this point, it is worth looking at the breakdown of imports across Spanish colonies as estimated by Curtin (1969: 89) and reported here in Table 2.

Table 1: African slave importations to European colonies in the Americas

Colonies	16th c.	17th c.	18th c.	19th c.	Total
Spanish	75,000	292,500	578,600	606,000	1,552,100
Portuguese	50,000	500,000	1,891,400	1,145,400	3,586,800
English		527,400	2,802,600		3,330,000
French		311,600	2,696,800	155,000	3,163,400
Dutch		44,000	484,000		528,000
Total	125,000	1,675,500	8,453,400	1,906,400	12,160,300

As the table shows, Curtin's calculations indicate that almost 50% of all slaves taken to Spanish America arrived via Cuba. As (Clements 2009: 70) correctly highlights, it makes sense to expect that it would be there where we would "find the necessary conditions for the formation of a Spanish-lexified creole language", which, among other sociodemographic factors, would imply significant disproportions between African-born slaves and Europeans on the island. Nevertheless, historical data indicate that, except for a short period around 1532, blacks never outnumbered whites until 1811, when more Africans were introduced in the island as a result of the sugarcane boom, at which point Afro-descendants came to represent 54.5% of the population (cf. Masó 1976: 115; Clements 2009: 77).

Clements (2009: 78–79) also compares the Cuban figures with the demographic data for colonial Haiti to highlight how even Cuba, the most sugar-oriented economy of the Spanish Caribbean, was far from presenting the demographic disproportions between Africans and Europeans that led to language creolization in other Antillean regions. He states:

> Comparing the population distributions of different Caribbean islands, we see that the distribution of Cuba's population was more balanced than that of the other islands. For example, at the end of the eighteenth century (1792), Cuba had 54,152 (20 per cent) free colored, 84,590 (31 per cent) slaves, and 133,559 (49 per cent) whites. By contrast, around that time Haiti had 452,000 (98 per cent) slaves and 11,000 (2 per cent) whites.

When we turn our attention to Puerto Rico, which received almost ten times fewer African slaves than Cuba (estimated to be 77,000; see Table 2), it stands to reason to think that the chances of a Spanish creole forming on this island

Table 2: Distribution of the estimated slaves in Spanish America

Country	Number
Cuba	702,000
Ecuador, Panama, Colombia	200,000
Mexico	200,000
Venezuela	121,000
Argentina, Uruguay, Paraguay, Bolivia	100,000
Peru	95,000
Puerto Rico	77,000
Dominican Republic	30,000
Central America	21,000
Chile	6,000
Total	1,552,000

appear to be quite slim. Álvarez-Nazario (1974: 72) provides a rough breakdown of the importation of African slaves to Puerto Rico from the 15th to the 19th century. His numbers align – to a good extent – with Curtin's, since he estimates anywhere between 54,000 and 75,000 captives (Table 3). His records also indicate a significant increase during the 18th and 19th centuries, which parallel the years of the sugar boom in the rest of the Spanish Caribbean.

Table 3: African slave importations to Puerto Rico (15th–19th centuries)

16th c.	from 6,000 to 8,000
17th c.	from 8,000 to 12,000
18th c.	from 20,000 to 30,000
19th c.	from 20,000 to 25,000
Total	from 54,000 to 75,000

Given these numbers, it is already possible to observe how a (de)creolization model to account for LS and the rest of the Spanish Caribbean varieties appears quite unlikely. Nevertheless, to better understand the potential dynamics of contact and Afro-Hispanic language evolution, in the following sections a more detailed sociohistorical analysis will be provided for the three aforementioned historical phases.

4.1 First phase (1510–1791)

Upon the arrival of the first Spanish colonizers in Puerto Rico by the end of the 15th century, the local indigenous population, the *taíno* people, rapidly began to decline, as a result of warfare, European diseases, and the harsh working conditions imposed by the Spaniards (Rouse 1994, Brinton 1997, Bernárdez 2009). As a way of supplying the island with more laborers to work in the mines, in the local mint, and on farms, black slaves were gradually introduced. The first documented arrival of blacks to the island dates from 1510; it concerns two captives who were sent from Spain to help in the minting of gold coins. Díaz-Soler (1974: 30) describes the event with the following words:

> A la isla de Puerto Rico arriban los primeros esclavos africanos en el año de 1510 cuando su Majestad autorizó a Jerónimo de Bruselas para traer a dos esclavos negros que habrían de ayudarle en el desempeño de su oficio de fundidor real.
> ('The first African slaves arrived on the island of Puerto Rico in the year 1510 when his Majesty authorized Jerónimo de Bruselas to bring two Black slaves who were to help him in the performance of his office as royal foundryman').

During the 16th and 17th centuries, as the numbers reported in Tables 4–5 suggest, the local economy did not rely much on an enslaved workforce. In fact, contrary to the policies implemented by other European powers in the Americas, Spain, for a concomitance of reasons, did not support a massive introduction of enslaved Africans into its overseas colonies. Among other factors that compressed the importation of black slaves into Spanish America was the Crown's monopoly on slave trading. The Crown, in fact, assigned a limited number of import licenses to individual traders, who would be responsible for supplying Spanish America with black captives. Being a monopoly, the market was much constrained and the Crown would charge import taxes (*alcabalas*) and sales taxes (*almojarifazgos*) on each slave introduced into the colonies (Palmer 1976).

As for Puerto Rico, besides the aforementioned taxes, in 1513 it was established that for each slave entering the island, an additional fee of two ducats would have to be paid to the local authorities (Álvarez-Nazario 1974: 29). The effects of these policies generated complaints and frustration among the Spanish settlers, who often saw these restrictions as barriers to the agricultural exploitation of the island and its economic development. Even the first Governor of Puerto Rico to be born on the island, Juan Ponce de León y Troche, in the second half of the 16th century commented on the wish for a more significant enslaved workforce to exploit the natural resources of the colony. Tió (1961: 487) quotes the Governor's words stating:

> ...no hay otro remedio tan ymportante para la conservación desta tierra y no haziéndose creo durar[á] su población no más de cuanto duren los pocos esclavos que hay en ella ay.
>
> 'there is no other equally important solution for the conservation of this land [than by exploiting the labor of enslaved people], and I believe that, without doing it in that way, the survival of its population will last no longer than that of the few captives who currently live there.'

The local economy, at that time, consisted of small farms, where blacks and whites worked side by side. Demographic data from the end of the 16th century show that the white population was 55%, blacks were 28%, while mixed race people represented 17% (see Table 4, Álvarez-Nazario 1974: 74). Race mixing, in fact, was common practice in Spanish colonies, and children born from the union of white masters with their black slaves tended to be freed at birth, thus generating a rapidly growing free group of mixed-race people (Mintz 1971, Laurence 1974).

Table 4: Population of Puerto Rico by the end of the 16th century

White	2,000 (55%)
Black	1,000 (28%)
Mixed race	600 (17%)

It must also be pointed out that not all black people at this time were brought directly from Africa and thus only spoke African languages. On the contrary, as has been shown on a number of occasions (Palmer 1976, Restall 2000, Brockington 2006), during the early phases of the Spanish colonization of the Americas, a good number of slaves were not shipped directly from Africa to the Americas. On the contrary, on many occasions, these were people who had lived in Spain with their masters for a long time before crossing the Atlantic. For this reason, they spoke Spanish (either natively or as an L2), were Christians, and knew the Spanish way of life. The word used in Spanish to describe these black servants was *ladinos*, which distinguished them from those directly proceeding from Africa, *bozales*. Given the aforementioned data, it is likely that the *bozal* population, which was intuitively less than the total percentage of blacks (28%, see Table 4), managed to acquire Spanish from the whites, the *ladinos* and the members of the mixed-race group, and thus did not develop a creole variety during the 16th century.

As for the 17th century, Álvarez-Nazario (1974: 74) states that there is no abundance of data that would allow us to closely follow the numerical evolution of the Afro-descendant population in Puerto Rico. Nevertheless, given the economic stagnation and diffused poverty that characterized the island, especially after gold mining was exhausted and the conquest of some Mainland territories transferred the colonizing enthusiasm of the Spaniards outside the Antillean region, not many incentives were found in Puerto Rico to import expensive black slaves. Álvarez-Nazario (1974: 36) describes with the following words the reduced participation of this region in the transatlantic slave trade:

> ...el país [Puerto Rico] y, por lo que parece, los puertos antillanos en general, no participaron de los embarques de bozales que se trajeron al Nuevo Mundo.
> 'the country [Puerto Rico] and, apparently, the Antillean ports in general, did not participate in the shipments of *bozales* that were brought to the New World'.

Over time, especially since the second half of the 17th century, the local economy began to slowly grow thanks to the gradual development of the sugar industry. In an attempt to supply local sugarcane planters with a cheap labor force, in 1664 the then Governor of Puerto Rico, Miguel de La Torre, offered freedom to marooned slaves escaping from English, French and Dutch colonies, if they decided to settle on the island, convert to Catholicism and work in the agricultural sector. De La Torre's policies resulted in a significant increase in the black population on the island, which is partially reflected in the San Juan 1673 census (Table 5), in which captives and free *pardos* (mulattos) constitute more than 54% of the total population (Álvarez-Nazario 1974: 75).

In the following decades, throughout the 18th century, the population of Puerto Rico showed a constant growth, mainly due to the numerous arrivals of Spaniards from the Canary Islands and the more significant introduction of African slaves to be employed in different economic sectors (see Table 6, Álvarez-Nazario 1974: 75). During this phase, the Puerto Rican sugarcane industry was still composed, for the most part, of small and middle-sized haciendas. Thus, despite the exploitation of a more consistent black workforce, census data indicate that black captives represented a minority (12%), significantly less than the white population (36%) on the island (see Table 6, Álvarez-Nazario 1974: 76).

Table 5: San Juan population by 1673

Whites	820	(45.78%)
Slaves	667	(37.24%)
Free *pardos*[a]	304	(16.98%)
Total	1,791	(100.00%)

[a] *Pardos:* mulattoes.

Table 6: Puerto Rican population by 1765

Whites, *pardos* and free *morenos*[a]	39,846 (88%)
[Whites]	[14,344 (36%)]
[*Pardos* and free *morenos*]	[20,719 (52%)]
Slaves	5,037 (12%)
Total	44,883 (100%)

[a] *Morenos:* blacks.

It is of interest to see that the majority group at this point consists of *pardos* and free *morenos* (52% of the population), a factor that highlights two important aspects of Puerto Rican society: 1) racial mixing was highly common; 2) most Afro-descendants were free people. If we contrast this situation with the one reported by Clements (2009: 78–79) when comparing the Cuban and Haitian demographics by the time of the Haitian revolution, we can immediately realize that the Puerto Rican economy, which relied on only 12% of slaves, was even less slave-dependent than the Cuban one, which had 31% of them, and was significantly different from Haiti's, which had 98% of enslaved people. All these considerations strongly suggest that 18th-century Puerto Rico was nothing like the ideal place for the creolization of Spanish. Rather, it was, in all likelihood, a colony in which black slaves – even those proceeding directly from Africa (*bozales*) – would be able to acquire the colonial language over time.

4.2 Second phase (1791–1873)

The crisis caused by the Haitian Revolution (1791–1803) created the economic environment for the demand in sugar on the international market, to be supplied by the colonies of the Spanish Caribbean (Villagómez 2005), especially by Cuba and Puerto Rico. The same did not happen in Santo Domingo (now the Dominican Republic), since Spanish planters feared that introducing more Africans into the region to develop the sugarcane industry could cause the Haitian uprisings to spread to the Spanish-controlled side of Hispaniola (Ott 1973, Gibson-Peterhouse 2010).

Puerto Rico, on the other hand, tried to develop this agricultural sector to supply the international market with sugarcane products. Incentives were provided for planters to move to the island so that in less than 30 years its population almost tripled (Dietz 2018). In this period, the highest number of captives in the entire history of Puerto Rico is recorded (see Table 7, Álvarez-Nazario 1974: 76). Nevertheless, as indicated by several historians (Morales Carrión 1978, Martínez-Fernández 1993, Stark 2009), its percentage never achieved the dimensions observed elsewhere in the Caribbean.

Table 7: Population of Puerto Rico by 1794

Number of captives	Total population
17,500 (13,76%)	127,133 (100,00%)

In relation to this, Blanco (1948: 74) highlights how the Afro-descendant population in Puerto Rico was significantly more reduced than that of other Caribbean colonies. On this point, he states:

> No obstante el gran crecimiento que experimenta la población de color en Puerto Rico para fines de XVIII, su número sigue siendo insignificante visto sobre el conjunto general de los habitantes de otras islas del Caribe por la misma época.
>
> 'Despite the great growth experienced by the people of color in Puerto Rico at the end of the 18th century, their number continues to be insignificant compared to the overall population in other Caribbean islands at the same time'.

In an effort to further attract planters to Puerto Rico, in 1815 Spain decreed the *Cédula de Gracias*, which established favorable conditions for the production and sale of sugar. In particular, it eliminated some taxes – including those on the importation of slaves – and encouraged the immigration of white settlers willing to develop the agricultural business by providing them with six acres of land per family member plus three acres per slave they could bring (Baralt 1981, Dorsey 2003).

As Álvarez-Nazario (1974: 77) pointed out (see Table 8), despite the significant increase in the Black population due to the development of the sugar industry, it must be kept in mind that slavery in Puerto Rico never achieved the dimensions observed in the English and French Antilles, not even during the 19th-century sugar boom.

Table 8: Population of Puerto Rico in the first third of the 19th century

Year	Whites		Free Mulattos		Free Blacks		Captives[a]		Total
	n	%	*n*	%	*n*	%	*n*	%	
1802	78,281	(48.0)	55,164	(33.8)	16,414	(10.1)	13,333	(8.1)	163,192
1812	85,662	(46.8)	63,983	(35.0)	15,833	(8.6)	17,536	(9.6)	183,014
1820	102,432	(44.4)	86,269	(37.4)	20,191	(8.8)	21,730	(9.4)	230,622
1827	150,311	(49.7)	95,430	(31.5)	25,057	(8.3)	31,874	(10.5)	302,672
1830	162,311	(50.4)	100,430	(31.2)	26,857	(8.4)	32,240	(10.0)	321,838
1836	188,869	(52.9)	101,275	(28.4)	25,124	(7.0)	41,818	(11.7)	357,086

[a]Blacks and Mulattos

In the first decades of the 19th century, mulattos and blacks taken together tend to slightly outnumber the whites on the island, a pattern that is reversed after 1830, due to the more intense arrival of Spaniards from both the Iberian Peninsula and the Canary Islands, as well as whites proceeding from Latin America and other European colonies (from Venezuela, the French Antilles, Santo Domingo, Louisiana, and Florida) (Álvarez-Nazario 1974: 77–78). Overall, whites, free mulattos, and free blacks, who were probably Spanish speakers, make up more than 88% of the population at any point in time. Captives, who were made up by blacks and mixed-race people, are never more than 12%. Thus, also in this case, even in the middle of the sugar boom, demographic data do not appear to support a potential creolization process for Afro-Puerto Rican Spanish, at least at the national level.

Similar demographic figures are reported by Moya (2003: 329), who indicates that despite the significant increase in the black labor force in the period that spans from 1750 to 1850, Puerto Rico continued to be a "society with slaves" rather than a "slave society". According to his account, in fact, during this period the percentage of black slaves ranged between 7% and 11% of the population, precisely the reverse of the Caribbean slave societies, where only 3% to 10% of the population was free.

Even though Puerto Rico never achieved the demographic composition of a prototypical "slave society", the sugar boom caused a shift from small haciendas to middle-sized and large plantations. The more significant employment of an enslaved workforce required a new regulation, the *Reglamento sobre la educación, trato y ocupaciones que deben dar a sus esclavos los dueños y mayordomos en esta Isla* (Regulation on the education, treatment and employment that the owners and overseers on this island must give their slaves), which was approved by Governor De La Torre in 1826 (Zavala-Trías 2003).

The *Reglamento* outlined a series of rights and obligations for both the enslaved Africans and their masters. It consisted of sixteen chapters that touched on topics of a varied nature: Catholic education, captives' entertainment, food and clothing, tools of labor, marriage and family rights, manumission, correctional punishment, fines for the masters who did not follow the rules, etc. A close analysis of this legal text reveals that, in line with what observed in a number of works on comparative colonial slave law (Tannenbaum 1946, Watson 1989; de la Fuente 2004), and more recently also in some linguistic studies (Sessarego 2015, 2017, 2019), Spanish slaves, in sharp contrast with any other European slave, had legal personality, and thus benefited from a variety of rights that derived from their status of legal persons: the right to own property, family preservation, (Christian) education, manumission, etc. (Sessarego 2018c). All of these legal peculiarities, which differentiated the Spanish slave from any other black captive in the Americas, can certainly help us cast additional light on the paucity of Spanish-based creoles in this region (Sessarego 2018b, Visconte & Sessarego forthcoming).

As for the Puerto Rican case, it appears of interest to highlight the importance given by the government to the religious education of black captives, which, as has been stressed elsewhere (Sessarego 2013b, 2015, 2019), certainly contributed to language transmission. Indeed, an entire chapter was dedicated to slaves' education (*De la educación cristiana y civil que deben dar los amos a sus esclavos* 'On the Christian and civil education that masters must give their slaves'). According to this chapter (see Zavala-Trías 2003), masters had to instruct slaves in the principles of the Catholic religion and baptize them within a year of residence (article 1). Christian education had to be provided on a regular basis. Article 2, in fact, states as follows:

> Esta instrucción será todas las noches después del toque de oraciones, haciendo se rece en seguida del rosario de María Santísima con la mayor compostura y devoción, la cual está generalizada en toda la Isla.

'This instruction will take place "every evening after the call to prayer", by "having them pray," once the Holy Mary's rosary is recited, with the greatest composure and devotion, which is the common practice throughout the Island'.

In addition, article 3 established that:

...en los domingos y fiestas [...] deberán los dueños de hacienda hacer que los esclavos ya bautizados oigan misa y la explicación de la doctrina cristiana. 'On Sundays and holidays [...], the hacienda owners must make the baptized slaves hear mass and the explanation of Christian doctrine'.

This piece of information on "the systematic Christian education of captives (which implicitly implies Spanish language transmission), in addition to the data so far provided in relation to racial mixing", manumission and overall demographic composition of the Puerto Rican population, strongly suggests that a Spanish creole was not likely to form in 19th-century Puerto Rico.

4.3 Third phase (1873–present)

The years preceding and following the abolition of slavery in Puerto Rico (on March 22nd of 1873) record a constant growth of whites, parallel to a decrease in blacks, which further reduced the possibilities of the creolization of Spanish (Álvarez-Nazario 1974: 78–79).

Table 9: Population of Puerto Rico before and after the abolition of slavery in 1873

Year	Whites		Blacks		Mulattos	
	n	%	*n*	%	*n*	%
1872	328,806	(53.19)	31,635	(5.12)	257,709	(41.69)
1877	411,712	(59.48)	39,781	(5.75)	240,701	(34.77)
1887	471,933	(62.46)	36,985	(4.9)	246,647	(32.64)
1897	573,187	(63.77)	35,824	(3.99)	289,808	(32.24)
1899	589,426	(61.84)	59,390	(6.23)	304,352	(31.93)

The post-abolition phase in Puerto Rico coincides with the US intervention on the island. Indeed, in 1898 Puerto Rico ceased to be a Spanish colony and came under the control of the United States with the signing of the Treaty of Paris, at the end of the Spanish-American War (Orama-López 2012).

The constant growth in the number of whites registered in the last three decades of the 19th century continued through the 20th century. Álvarez-Nazario (1974: 79) emphasized how the racial categories used in the United States Census diverge from those adopted during the Spanish colonial period, so that mulatto people would now be classified as blacks (see Table 10, Álvarez-Nazario 1974: 79).

Table 10: US Census 1910–1950 in Puerto Rico

Year	Total	Whites		Blacks	
		n	%	n	%
1910	1,118,012	732,555	(65.52)	385,437	(34.48)
1920	1,299,809	948,709	(72.99)	351,062	(27.01)
1930	1,543,913	1,146,719	(74.28)	397,156	(25.72)
1940	1,869,255	1,430,744	(76.54)	438,458	(23.46)
1950	2,210,703	1,762,411	(79.76)	446,948	(20.24)

The US invasion of the island had significant effects on the lives of its inhabitants and the local economy (Shekitka 2017). As for the agricultural sector, in the first decades of the 20th century the Puerto Rican sugar industry, despite experiencing a great boom thanks to modern American machinery (its production increased by 331%), did not provide much employment to manual workers, and thus accelerated the Puerto Rican migration to the United States (Ayala & Bernabe 2007). On the other hand, the second postwar period (1945–1970) registered waves of bilateral migration, with many Puerto Ricans returning to the island, tempted by the modernization and industrialization in progress at the time, but also due to the difficulties of adaptation to living in the US (Thomas 2010). This constant travel to the United States, still very much in vogue today, has given life to the notion of "Puerto Rican Nation on the move" (Duany et al. 2000), which highlights the migratory patterns of the Puerto Rican diaspora to and from the United States.

Nowadays Puerto Ricans who self-identify as "blacks" for US census purposes correspond to 12,39% of the total population (US Census 2010). They primarily reside in the municipalities of Loíza, Arroyo and Maunabo, where Afro-descendants make up 64,25%, 32,46% and 30,43% of the population, respectively. Loíza is, therefore, the region with the highest concentration of black people on the island

Piero Visconte & Sandro Sessarego

and, for this reason, the following section will be focused on this community and its development in relation to the sugarcane industry.

5 Focus on Loíza

During the Spanish colonial period, the perceived need for employing captives of African origin in the sugar industry concentrated the highest percentages of blacks and mulattos in regions like Loíza, located on the coastal plains, that were particularly well-suited for sugarcane production (Mayo-Santana & Negrón-Portillo 2007). The first sugar mills appeared in the region by the end of the 16th century (Ungerleider 2000). At that time, people of both European and African ancestry worked side-by-side in small haciendas dedicated to the production of sugarcane products (Mauleón de Benítez 1974).

Over the 17th and 18th centuries the sugar industry in Loíza gradually expanded. The region began to develop, to the point that in 1690 the Governor of Puerto Rico, Gaspar Arrendondo, requested permission from the Spanish King to establish the *Villa de Loíza*, officially declaring it in 1719 as one of the six existing municipalities on the island (Mauleón de Benítez 1974, Ungerleider 2000).

Upon the Haitian sugar crisis caused by the Haitian revolution and the consequent sugar boom in the Spanish Caribbean, the region of Loíza experienced an additional period of economic expansion, which implied the introduction of a significant black labor force. Nevertheless, even in the middle of the growth of the sugarcane business, the demographic figures reported for this region are nothing similar to what could be observed in the English and French Caribbean. Indeed, by 1828, the population of Loíza numbered a total of 4,198 inhabitants, the vast majority of which were free (82%); only 18% were slaves (Ungerleider 2000: 39–40).

While the sugar boom provided economic development for the region during a good part of the 19th century, by the 1860s the sugar industry began to lose traction (Picó 1986). The abolition of slavery in 1873 certainly did not help to reinvigorate the sector. Most black slaves living in the region became peons. Thus, the new *libertos* (freedmen) remained living in the haciendas as *agregados*, economically dependent individuals who sold their labor in exchange for lodging and food (Meriño Fuentes & Perera Díaz 2009). Over the 20th century, thanks to the Land Reform of the 1940s, some of these peons received small parcels of land and thus became landowners (Stahl 1966). Nevertheless, the living and working conditions of most *afroloiceños* remained quite precarious, and even today are far from being optimal.

Table 11: Population of Loíza between 1779 and 1828

	Free Afro-descendants				
Whites	Mulattos	Blacks	Otras castas[a]	Slaves	Total
556 (13%)	1,133 (27%)	714 (17%)	1,053 (25%)	724 (18%)	4,198

[a]*Otras castas*: other mixed racial categories. It was common custom in Spanish colonies to classify mixed-race individuals according to their racial background: *mulato* was the result of white and black mixing, *morisco* was the result of black and *mulato* mixing, *chino* was the result of *morisco* and white mixing, and so on.

Loíza is, nowadays, an economically and socially depressed region. US census data indicate that some 67% of the population lives below the poverty line, 8% is still illiterate, and the region has one of the highest unemployment rates in the island (Ungerleider 2000: 47–49). Some locals see military service as an opportunity to migrate to the United States (Aramburu 2012). Those who decide to stay in the community tend to work in the production or sale of coconut, shellfish, fish, cassava, *pitorro* (a black-market rum), and street food (Ungerleider 2000: 44–45). Loíza's economic and social isolation is, in part, exacerbated by its geographic location, surrounded by rivers, canals and the ocean, and connected to the nearby capital city of San Juan only by the *ancón*, a transporter boat, which crosses the *Río Grande de Loíza* (Ungerleider 2000: 44).

Given the particular socioeconomic segregation that has been affecting Loíza over the past century and half, after the abolition of slavery in 1873, it is difficult to imagine that, if a Spanish creole ever existed in the region, it would have disappeared so completely due to processes of standardization, schooling and normative pressure.

6 Conclusions

This study has combined linguistic and sociohistorical data to cast light on the nature and origin of LS, an Afro-Hispanic dialect spoken in Loíza, Puerto Rico. In so doing, it has also added new fuel to the Spanish Creole Debate (Lipski 2005). In particular, this study has evaluated the feasibility of the Decreolization Hypothesis (de Granda 1968 et seq.) for the Puerto Rican context.

Linguistic data indicate that LS presents a set of morphological and phonological reductions, as well as a number of other vernacular features, which should not necessarily be linked to a creole origin, since they tend to appear in most Spanish contact varieties and in some rural dialects (Klee & Lynch 2009, Zamora-Vicente 1989, Lipski 1994). As for the sociohistorical analysis, our findings suggest that at no point in the history of Puerto Rico were the conditions in place for a creole language to develop. A concomitance of sociohistorical factors (demographic, religious, economic, legal, etc.) favored the non-creolization of Spanish and the acquisition of the colonial language by the enslaved population. In particular, contrary to what could be observed across the English and French Caribbean (Mintz 1971, Laurence 1974, Clements 2009), in Puerto Rico the black population was never the majority group, racial mixing was highly common, and free Afro-descendants outnumbered enslaved blacks.

In conclusion, both linguistic and sociohistorical findings strongly indicate that the Decreolization Hypothesis is not a feasible option to account for the nature and origin of LS. On the other hand, in line with recent studies on other Afro-Hispanic vernaculars (Díaz-Campos & Clements 2008, Sessarego 2014, 2019), LS appears to be a dialect presenting the linguistic traces of moderate grammatical restructuring, which do not imply any previous (de)creolization stage.

Abbreviations

LS Loíza Spanish
L2 Second language

References

Alvar, Manuel. 1996. *Manual de dialectología hispánica*. Barcelona: Ariel.

Álvarez, Alexandra & Enrique Obediente. 1998. El español caribeño: Antecedentes sociohistóricos y lingüísticos. In Matthias Perl & Armin Schwegler (eds.), *El español caribeño: Antecedentes sociohistóricos y lingüísticos*, 40–61. Madrid: Iberoamericana.

Álvarez-Nazario, Manuel. 1959. Notas sobre el habla del negro en Puerto Rico durante el siglo XIX. *Revista del Instituto de Cultura Puertorriqueña* 2. 43–48.

Álvarez-Nazario, Manuel. 1974. *El elemento afronegroide en el español de Puerto Rico*. San Juan: Instituto de Cultura Puertorriqueña.

Andrés-Gallego, José. 2005. *La esclavitud en la América española*. Madrid: Ediciones Encuentro.

Aramburu, Diana. 2012. The migrant nation in "La guagua aérea" by Luis Rafael. *Cuaderno internacional de estudios humanísticos* 18. 46–54.

Ayala, Cesar J. & Rafael Bernabe. 2007. *Puerto Rico in the American century.* Chapel Hill, NC: University of North Carolina.

Baralt, Guillermo. 1981. *Esclavos rebeldes: Conspiraciones y sublevaciones de esclavos en Puerto Rico, 1795-1873.* Río Piedras: Ediciones Huracán.

Bas-García, José R. 2009. *La abolición de la esclavitud de 1873 en Puerto Rico.* San Juan: Centro de Estudios Avanzados de Puerto Rico y El Caribe.

Berlin, Ira. 1998. *Many thousands gone.* Cambridge, MA: Harvard University Press.

Bernárdez, Enrique. 2009. Spanish Caribbean Literature. *Journal of Caribbean Literatures* 6(2). 1–16.

Blanco, Tomás. 1948. *El prejuicio racial en Puerto Rico.* New York: Arno Press.

Brinton, Daniel G. 1997. The depopulation of Hispanic America after the conquest. *The Public Historian* 19(2). 154–180.

Brockington, Lolita. 2006. *Blacks, Indians, and Spaniards in the Eastern Andes.* Lincoln: University of Nebraska Press.

Caballero, Ramón. 1852. *La juega de gallos o el negro bozal.* Reprinted[2015]. San Juan, PR: Instituto de Literatura Puertorriqueña.

Chaudenson, Robert. 1992. *Des iles, des homes, des langues.* Paris: L'Harmattan.

Clements, J. Clancy. 2009. *The legacy of Spanish and Portuguese: Colonial expansion and language change.* Cambridge: Cambridge University Press.

Curtin, Phillip. 1969. *The Atlantic Slave trade: A Census.* Madison: University of Wisconsin Press.

Cushner, Nicholas. 1980. *Lords of the land: Sugar, wine, and the Jesuit estates of coastal Peru.* Albany: University of New York Press.

de la Fuente, Alejandro. 2004. Slave law and claims-making in Cuba: The Tannenbaum debate revisited. *Law and History Review* 22(2). 339–369.

de Granda, Germán. 1968. La tipología criolla de dos hablas del área lingüística hispanica. *Thesaurus* 23. 193–205.

de Granda, Germán. 1970. Un temprano testimonio sobre las hablas 'criollas' en África y América. *Thesaurus* 25. Reprinted 1988, 1–11.

de Granda, Germán. 1978. *Estudios lingüísticos afrohispánicos y criollos.* Madrid: Gredos.

Derkes, Eleuterio. 1883. *Tío Fele: Comedia en un acto.* Ponce, PR: Imprenta de Morel.

Díaz-Campos, Manuel & J. Clancy Clements. 2008. A Creole origin for Barlovento Spanish? *Language in Society* 37. 351–383.

Díaz-Soler, Luis M. 1974. *Historia de la esclavitud negra en Puerto Rico.* San Juan: Editorial Universitaria, Universidad de Puerto Rico.

Dietz, James L. 2018. *Economic History of Puerto Rico.* Princeton, NJ: Princeton University Press.

Dorsey, James C. 2003. *Slave traffic in the age of abolition: Puerto Rico, West Africa, and the non-Hispanic Caribbean, 1815-1859.* Gainesville: University Press of Florida.

Duany, Andres, Elizabeth Plater-Zyberk & Jeff Speck. 2000. *Suburban nation.* New York City, NY: North Point Press.

Escalona, Rafael E. 1883. *Flor de una noche.* San Juan: Imprenta de Carlos González Font.

Geeslin, Kimberly. 2013. *The Handbook of Spanish Second Language Acquisition.* Hoboken, NJ: Wiley-Blackwell.

Gibson-Peterhouse, Carrie E. 2010. *The Impact of the Haitian Revolution on the Hispanic Caribbean, c. 1791-1830.* Cambridge: University of Cambridge. (Doctoral dissertation).

Guy, Gregory. 1981. *Linguistic Variation in Brazilian Portuguese.* Philadelphia, PA: University of Pennsylvania. (Doctoral dissertation).

Guy, Gregory. 2017. The African diaspora in Latin America. In C. Cutler, Z. Vrzic & P. Angermeyer (eds.), *Language contact in Africa and the African diaspora in the Americas,* 49–78. Amsterdam: John Benjamins. DOI: 10.1075/cll.53.03guy.

Holm, John & Peter L. Patrick (eds.). 2007. *Comparative creole syntax.* London: Battlebridge Press.

Jacobs, Bart. 2012. *Origins of a Creole.* Berlín: De Gruyter.

Klee, Carol A. & Andrew Lynch. 2009. *El español en contacto con otras lenguas.* Washington DC: Georgetown University Press.

Laurence, Kemlin. 1974. Is Caribbean Spanish a Case of Decreolization? *Orbis* 23. 484–499.

Lipski, John M. 1993. *On the non-Creole basis for Afro-Caribbean Spanish.* Albuquerque NM: University of New Mexico Press. http:/www.personal.psu.edu/jml34/noncreol.pdf.

Lipski, John M. 1994. *Latin American Spanish.* New York: Longman Group Limited.

Lipski, John M. 2005. *A history of Afro-Hispanic language:Five centuries and five continents.* Cambridge: Cambridge University Press.

Lipski, John M. 2008. *Afro-Bolivian Spanish.* Madrid: Iberoamericana.

Lucena, Salmoral Manuel. 2000. *Los códigos negros de la América Española.* Madrid: Ediciones UNESCO.

Martínez-Fernández, Luis. 1993. The sweet and the bitter. *New West Indian Guide* 67. 47–63.

Martinus, Efraim Frank. 1996. *The Kiss of a Slave: Papiamentu's West African Connections*. Amsterdam: Universiteit van Amsterdam. (Doctoral dissertation).

Masó, Calixto. 1976. *Historia de Cuba*. Miami: Ediciones Universal.

Mason, John Alden. 1918. *Décimas de 1898*. San Juan: Instituto de Cultura Puertorriqueña.

Mauleón de Benítez, Carmen Cecilia. 1974. *El español de Loíza Aldea*. Madrid: Gráficas ARABI.

Mayo-Santana, Raúl & Mariano Negrón-Portillo. 2007. *La esclavitud menor*. Río Piedras, PR: Centro de Investigaciones Sociales.

McWhorter, John. 2000. *The Missing Spanish Creoles*. Berkeley, CA: University of California Press.

Megenney, William. 1993. Elementos criollo-portugueses en el español dominicano. *Montalbán* 15. 3–56.

Meriño Fuentes, Maria & Aisnara Perera Díaz. 2009. Familias, agregados y esclavos. Los padrones de vecinos de Santiago de Cuba (1778-1861). *História: Questões & Debates,* 51. 151–177.

Mintz, Sidney. 1971. The Sociohistorical Background to Pidginization and Creolization. In Dell Hymes (ed.), *Pidginization and creolization of languages*, 481–498. Cambridge: Cambridge University Press.

Montrul, Silvina. 2008. *Incomplete acquisition in bilingualism*. Cambridge: Cambridge University Press.

Montrul, Silvina. 2016. *The acquisition of heritage languages*. Cambridge: Cambridge University Press.

Morales Carrión, Arturo. 1978. *Auge y decadencia de la trata negrera en Puerto Rico (1820-1860)*. San Juan: Instituto de Cultura Puertorriqueña.

Moya, José C. 2003. Migración africana y formación social en las Américas, 1500-2000. *Revista de Indias* 72(255). 321–348.

Orama-López, Carmen I. 2012. Puerto Rico y sus pugnas político-lingüísticas. *Lenguas en contacto y bilingüismo* 4. 1–23.

Ortiz-López, Luis. 1998. *Huellas etno-sociolingüísticas bozales y afrocubanas*. Madrid: Iberoamericana.

Otheguy, Ricardo. 1973. The Spanish Caribbean: A Creole Perspective. In C-J. Bailey & R. Shuy (eds.), *New Ways of Analyzing Variation in English*, 323–339. Washington: Georgetown University Press.

Ott, Thomas. 1973. *The Haitian revolution: 1789-1804*. Knoxville: University of Tennessee Press.

Palmer, Colin A. 1976. *Slaves of the White God: Blacks in Mexico, 1570-1650*. Cambridge, MA: Harvard University Press.

Perez, Danae. 2015. Traces of Portuguese in Afro-Yungueño Spanish? *Journal of Pidgin and Creole Languages* 30(2). 307–343.

Perl, Matthias & Armin Schwegler. 1998. *América negra.* Madrid: Iberoamericana.

Picó, Fernando. 1986. *Historia general de Puerto Rico.* Río Piedras, PR: Ediciones Huracán.

Restall, Matthew. 2000. Black Conquistadors: Armed Africans in Early Spanish America. *The Americas* 57(2). 171–205.

Rivera-Quintero, Marcia. 2014. *El vuelo de la esperanza: Proyecto de las comunidades especiales Puerto Rico, 1997-2004.* San Juan, PR: Fundación Sila M. Calderón.

Romero, Rey & Sandro Sessarego. 2018. Hard Come, Easy Go. In Jeremy King & Sandro Sessarego (eds.), *Language Variation and Contact-Induced Change,* 83–110. Amsterdam: Benjamins.

Rouse, Irving. 1994. *The tainos: Rise and decline of the people who greeted Columbus.* Princeton NJ: Princeton University Press.

Schwegler, Armin. 1991. La doble negación dominicana y la génesis del español caribeño. *Lingüística* 3. 31–87.

Schwegler, Armin. 1996. *Chi ma nkongo: Lengua y rito ancestrales en El Palenque de San Basilio (Colombia).* Madrid: Iberoamericana.

Schwegler, Armin. 1999. Monogenesis Revisited. In J. Rickford & S. Romaine (eds.), *Creole Genesis, Attitudes and Discourse,* 235–262. Amsterdam: Benjamins.

Schwegler, Armin. 2014. Portuguese Remnants in the Afro-Hispanic Diaspora. In Patrícia Amaral & Ana Maria Carvalho (eds.), *Portuguese-Spanish interfaces: Diachrony, synchrony, and contact,* 403–441. Amsterdam: Benjamins.

Schwegler, Armin. 2018. On the Controversial Origins of Non-Canonical Spanish and Portuguese Negation: Case closed? *Current Trends in Afro-Hispanic Linguistics, Lingua* 202. 24–43.

Sessarego, Sandro. 2011. On the Status of Afro-Bolivian Spanish Features: Decreolization or Vernacular Universals? In Michnowicz J. (ed.), *Proceedings of The 5th International Workshop on Spanish Sociolinguistics (WSS5),* 125–141. Somerville, MA: Cascadilla.

Sessarego, Sandro. 2013a. Afro-Hispanic contact varieties as advanced second languages. *Iberia* 1. 96–122.

Sessarego, Sandro. 2013b. *Chota Valley Spanish.* Madrid: Iberoamericana.

Sessarego, Sandro. 2014. *The Afro-Bolivian Spanish Determiner Phrase.* Columbus, OH: The Ohio State University Press.

Sessarego, Sandro. 2015. *Afro-Peruvian Spanish.* Amsterdam: Benjamins.

Sessarego, Sandro. 2017. The legal hypothesis of Creole genesis. *Journal of Pidgin and Creole Languages* 32. 1–47.

Sessarego, Sandro (ed.). 2018a. *Current Trends in Afro-Hispanic Linguistics. [Lingua Special Issue]*. Amsterdam: Elsevier.

Sessarego, Sandro. 2018b. Enhancing dialogue in the field: Some remarks on the status of the Spanish creole debate. *Journal of Pidgin and Creole Languages* 33(2). 197–203.

Sessarego, Sandro. 2018c. *La schiavitù nera nell'America spagnola*. Genoa: Marietti Editore.

Sessarego, Sandro. 2019. *Language Contact and the Making of an Afro-Hispanic Vernacular: Variation and Change in the Colombian Chocó*. Cambridge: Cambridge University Press.

Sessarego, Sandro. 2021. *Interfaces and Domains of Contact-Driven Restructuring*. Cambridge: Cambridge University Press.

Sessarego, Sandro. In press. Another Piece of the Puzzle: Afro-Veracruz Spanish and the Spanish Creole Debate. In Salikoko S. Mufwene & Enoch Aboh (eds.), *Uniformitarianism in Genetic Creolistics*. Cambridge: Cambridge University Press.

Shekitka, John. 2017. *On Arrival: Puerto Ricans in Post-World War II New York*. Ney York City, NY: Columbia University Teachers' College Center on History & Education.

Stahl, John. 1966. *Economic development through land reform in Puerto Rico*. Ames, IA: Iowa State University. (PhD Dissertation).

Stark, David. 2009. A new look at the African Slave Trade in Puerto Rico through the use of Parish Registers: 1660–1815. *Slavery & Abolition* 30(4). 491–520.

Tannenbaum, Frank. 1946. *Slave and Citizen*. New York: Vintage Books.

Thomas, Lorrin. 2010. *Puerto Rican Citizen*. Chicago: University of Chicago Press.

Tió, Aurelio. 1961. *Nuevas fuentes para la historia de Puerto Rico*. San Juan, PR: San Germán.

U. S. Census Bureau. 2010. *2010 census of population and housing*. Tech. rep. https://www.census.gov/prod/cen2010/cph-1-53.pdf.

Ungerleider, Kepler D. 2000. *Las fiestas de Santiago Apóstol en Loíza: La cultura afro-puertorriqueña ante los procesos de hibridación y globalización*. San Juan, Puerto Rico: Isla Negra.

Villagómez, Rosita E. 2005. *El Silenciamiento del sujeto de origen Africano en las Letras Puertorriqueñas del Siglo XIX*. Tallahassee, FL: Florida State University. (Doctoral dissertation).

Visconte, Piero & Sandro Sessarego. Forthcoming. *How law shapes language: Puerto Rican Slave laws and the (de)creolization hypothesis.* Austin: The University of Texas at Austin.

Vizcarrondo, Fortunato. 1983. *Dinga y mandinga: Poemas.* San Juan de Puerto Rico: Instituto de Cultura Puertorriqueña.

Watson, Alan. 1989. *Slave law in the Americas.* Athens: The University of Georgia Press.

Winford, Donald. 2003. *An introduction to contact linguistics.* London: Wiley-Blackwell.

Zamora-Vicente, Alonso. 1989. *Dialectología española.* Madrid: Gredos.

Zavala-Trías, Sylvia. 2003. *Reglamento de Esclavos de 1826.* Last upgrade on July 2nd, 2003. rootsweb.com/%7B%5Ctextasciitilde%7Dponcepr/reglamento.html.

Chapter 8

The value of online corpora for the analysis of variation and change in the Caribbean

John R. Rickford

Stanford University

In recent years, corpora have proven to be very powerful tools, impacting not only the field of linguistics, but other fields like Oral Literature, Folklore, History, Anthropology, Sociology, Education, Speech Recognition and Criminal Justice. However, there are still very few large-scale corpora available for research on Caribbean and other Creole settings. This paper reviews six examples that illustrate the multiple contexts in which corpora have proven to be a meaningful instrument for understanding language variation and change. The examples come from theoretical and descriptive areas and from applied areas. Particular focus will be paid to how online corpora can benefit criminal justice. Together the examples discussed here suggest many future ways in which online corpora can serve as an invaluable for furthering research on language variation in on Caribbean communities.

1 Introduction

It's an honor and a pleasure to contribute to this volume in honor of Donald Winford, because he has been at the forefront not only of developments in creole and language contact studies (see his books and articles and his long editorship of the *Journal of Pidgin and Creole Languages*), but also of the study of language variation and change in Anglophone Caribbean varieties and African American Vernacular English (AAVE). His 1972 University of York dissertation, *A sociolinguistic description of two communities in Trinidad*, was a masterpiece, demonstrating the value of quantitative analysis of social stratification and stylistic differentiation

John R. Rickford. 2022. The value of online corpora for the analysis of variation and change in the Caribbean. In Bettina Migge & Shelome Gooden (eds.), *Social and structural aspects of language contact and change*, 213–232. Berlin: Language Science Press. DOI: 10.5281/zenodo.6979333

in St. James and Mayo. And virtually everything he has written since exemplifies the value of excellent fieldwork and careful and insightful analysis. He is also a good friend, and this paper is intended as a tribute and a gift to him.

One of the best ways of honoring Winford and the other pioneers in the study of the Caribbean is not only by looking back, but also by looking forward, creating and making available online corpora of Anglophone Caribbean language varieties (and of course Francophone and other varieties too). In recent years, corpora have proven to be very powerful tools, impacting not only the field of linguistics, but other fields like Oral Literature, Folklore, History, Anthropology, Sociology, Education, Speech Recognition and Criminal Justice. As a result, it would be incredibly important to equip future researchers with this important resource. Six examples in particular (four from theoretical and descriptive areas, two from applied areas) illustrate the multiple contexts in which corpora have proven to be a meaningful instrument for understanding language variation and change, and in turn suggest future ways in which online corpora of Caribbean language could be invaluable. The sixth case I will discuss at some length, because it shows how online corpora can benefit criminal justice and it has not been presented in any other publication to date.

2 Variation in the use of Creole variants in Jamaican popular music, 1962–2011

A corpus was an essential tool in Byron Jones' (2019) examination of the use of Creole variants in Jamaican popular music for his PhD thesis. Jones compiled data for the Corpus of Popular Jamaican Music (COPJAM) and quantitatively analyzed it.[1] Through this corpus, he was able to explore a variety of factors including linguistic variable, gender, genre, decade, theme, and others, which he discusses with very sophisticated quantitative tools in his thesis, *Beyond de riddim: Language use in Jamaican popular music*, University of the West Indies, St. Augustine, Trinidad.[2] The availability of such a corpus allowed him to track Creole variant usage over time, in the language of the top 20 Jamaican songs each decade from 1962–2012, which showed a dramatic *increase* in the frequency of Creole forms across this period from 3.7% in 1962–1971 to 63.4% in 2002–2011. (See Table 1.) This research was especially important for expanding the conversation surrounding language use and attitudes into the domain of music. It dramatically

---

[1]As far as I know, COPJAM is not available for general or public use.

[2]I was privileged to serve as external examiner on Jones' excellent thesis.

shows how the existence of a corpus can greatly extend the possibilities for the study of linguistic variation and change.

Table 1: Relative frequency of Creole variants in Jamaican songs from 1962–2011. (From table 9, p. 155, Jones 2019)

Decade	% Creole in song lyrics	# of Creole variants out of total
1st: 1962–1971	3.7	111/2,987
2nd: 1972–1981	19.8	692/3,501
3rd: 1982–1991	47.1	2,849/6,045
4th: 1992–2011	56.9	4,181/7,353
5th: 2002–2011	63.4	4,687/7,388

3 Variation and change in the verbal coda of "as far as" noun phrases

Stanford's online "Searcher" corpus of English literature from 1800 to 1959 was similarly helpful in our study of the variable absence and loss of *is/are concerned* or *go(es)* in *as far as* phrases in English (Rickford et al. 1995). For years, as part of interest in relatively understudied syntactic variation, I had been collecting examples like:

(1)   *As far as* filling out the details Ø, that isn't a problem.

(2)   People think I'm constantly in motion, *as far as* making films Ø.

I was curious about what influenced whether the sentence coda (*goes* or *is concerned*) was omitted and if the omission after the NP was increasing. I asked Tom Wasow about the syntax of the NP after *as far as*, and his interest piqued, he joined the project as well. We added two students to the team – Norma Mendoza-Denton and Julie Espinoza. Our data were from the "Searcher" online corpus and we also elicited intuitions, made new recordings, collected overheard examples, and perused usage manuals, collecting over 1200 *as far as* tokens. We coded 1065 of these tokens for various factors, looking at the NP following "as far as", the mode of communication, and the speakers themselves. The factors that had a statistically significant effect on the observed variation are shown below along with their likelihood of affecting verb absence.

Table 2: VARBRUL (variable rule) weights for significant factors in *as far as* verb absence. Sample size per factor is indicated in parentheses. Originally Table 3 in Rickford et al. (1995), reprinted with the permission of the Linguistic Society of America.

SYNTACTIC COMPLEXITY OF THE NP		
Noun, with or without modifiers	0.31	(679)
Conjoined NPs and NPs with PPs	0.46	(163)
Sentential NPs	0.86	(314)
MODE		
Speech	0.62	(732)
Electronic mail, or written exams	0.33	(322)
Writing (newspaper, articles, books)	0.21	(95)
AGE OF SPEAKER/WRITER		
≤ 19	0.69	(17)
20–39	0.56	(306)
40–59	0.44	(180)
≥ 60	0.24	(31)
PROSODIC STRUCTURE OF THE NP		
Branching	0.57	(682)
Nonbranching	0.40	(483)
SEX OF SPEAKER/WRITER		
Male	0.47	(670)
Female	0.56	(295)
POSITION OF *as far as* PHRASE IN SENTENCE		
Initial	0.54	(550)
Noninitial	0.46	(605)

Relative time 0 (18th c.):   0

Relative time i (19th c.):   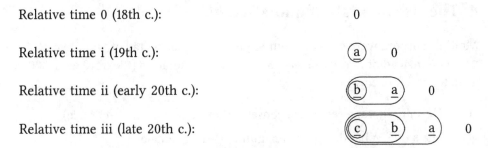   0

Relative time ii (early 20th c.):

Relative time iii (late 20th c.):   0

Figure 1: Spread of the rule deleting the verbal coda in topic-restricting *as far as* constructions, depicted in terms of the Baileyan wave model. (Adapted from Fig. 2 [Bailey 1973: 68], in which, as Bailey's caption notes, 'The letters represent successively later, or lighter-weighted, environments in which the rule operates.'). In our case, a, the earliest environment affected by the rule, refers to sentential NPs, as in ex. (3) above; b, the next environment affected by the rule, is prepositional or conjoined NPs, as in ex. (4) above, and c, the most recent environment affected by the rule, includes simple NPs, as in ex. (5) above. Source: Fig. 5 in (Rickford et al. 1995), reprinted with the permission of the Linguistic Society of America.

The "Searcher" corpus also gave us access to data that allowed us to examine the historical development of the *as far as* NP *be concerned* construction and allowed us to see the historical evidence for wavelike spread of verb absence in *as far as* phrases. According to our corpus data, the verb absence first appeared in *as/so far as* phrases with a sentential NP, as shown in (3) below. This later spread to *as/so far as* phrases with prepositional or conjoined NPs as in (4). And it finally spread to *as far as* phrases with simple NPs, as in (5).

(3)   And I will own to you, (I am sure it will be safe), that *so far as* our living with Mr. Churchill at Enscombe Ø, it is settled. [1816, Jane Austen, *Emma*, p. 460]

(4)   The cabin ... was in perfect condition *so far as* frame and covering Ø until 1868. [1939, Henry Seidel Canby, *Thoreau*]

(5)   *As far as* the white servants Ø, it isn't clear. [Renee Blake, 22, 1987, (p.c.)]

This spread to new environments with increasing frequency is depicted in terms of the Baileyan wave model in Figure 1.

The "Searcher" corpus was an invaluable tool in understanding these factors in the variability and change of verb absence in *as far as* phrases, greatly extending the number of tokens and the span of time we were able to analyze.

4 The rise and fall of quotative *all*

Multiple corpora were critical to our study of the rise and fall of quotative *all*, i.e. using *all* instead of *like, go,* or *say* to introduce a quotation (Rickford et al. 2007), as in (6) and (7) below:

(6) He's *all*, "Let me see your license; is that your car?" (Latino Male)

(7) She's *all*, "What do you mean, gum?" (White female)

For this study, we used data from multiple sources and corpora:

- 1990/1994 recordings of native California adolescents & young adults collected by Ann Wimmer (Stanford undergrad senior thesis) & Carmen Fought (Pitzer College, LA area)

- New 2005 recordings of high school & college students from Palo Alto, Stanford, & San Francisco

- A multi-source corpus: examples from conversation, but also from publications (Waksler, *American Speech* 2001), web pages, TV series (*Buffy the Vampire Slayer*) & movies (*Clueless*). Lots of *all* tokens (253 quotatives), but not accountable like recorded corpora (cf. Labov 1972:72), since we did not have corresponding examples of where other variants besides *all* were used.

- **The Google News groups Corpus, 1981–2005**: Billions of words including at least 354 examples of quotative *all*.

This search of corpora yielded some interesting observations. For example, the first time this usage appeared was in 1982. In fact, the first Switchboard Corpus, collected in 1988–1992, and the Santa Barbara Corpus of Spoken American English, part I, collected in 1988, each has only 1 example of quotative *all*. Clearly, the use of quotative *all* was new. In addition, our data from the Google News groups corpus, 1981–2005, suggested that quotative *all* peaked in 1999 and then declined steeply, as shown in Figure 2 (originally figure 4 in Rickford et al. 2007).

This peak and decline was supported by evidence from our other corpora. For example, in the 1990/94 corpus, *all* was the primary quotative introducer (*all* used 46% of the time, *like* 17%, unframed 16%, *say* 11%, Other 8%, and *go* 2%). In contrast, in our new 2005 corpus, *all* was much less frequent as the quotative introducer (4%), overtaken by *like* (69%), and the quotative *all like* had emerged.

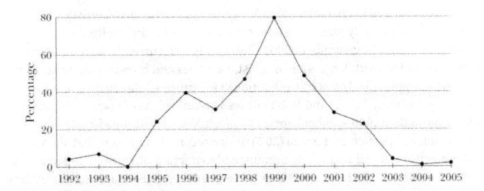

Figure 2: Frequency of quotative *all* over time, normalized for number of posts per year over a composite of very frequent words (*word, other, make, look, write, see, number, way, people, first, the,* and *is*)

Through our corpora, we were also able to look at what factors favored the use of quotative *all* at different points in time. VARBRUL (variable rule) analysis showed that in the 1990/94 corpus, the primary favoring factor is present tense, then Quoted Speech (vs. Thought), then Perseverance (quotative *all* in 5 preceding lines). In the 2005 corpus, tense was not significant, and while Quoted Speech (vs. Thought), still favored quotative *all*, Perseverance *dis*favored it. Once again, the availability of corpora gave us the opportunity to see the feature across time and in a variety of environments, allowing for a more robust understanding of this usage's variation and *change*.

5 FAVE alignment, DARLA, and the *Voices of California* project

These possibilities for linguistic study have expanded even further with the advent of new automatic processing and analysis technologies which make rapid analysis of large corpora achievable. Tools such as FAVE align/extract[3] and DARLA[4] are aligners that allow for audio samples and transcripts to be paired and aligned. With the help of lexicons like the Carnegie Mellon University (CMU) Pronouncing Dictionary,[5] these aligners facilitate the rapid measurement of

---

[3]https://github.com/JoFrhwld/FAVE/wiki/FAVE-align
[4]https://linguistics.dartmouth.edu/research/darla-dartmouth-linguistic-automation
[5]http://www.speech.cs.cmu.edu/cgi-bin/cmudict

vowels for acoustic characteristics. Measuring acoustic characteristics of vowels which historically was more time consuming and individualized can now be completed on a large-scale, quickly. Put simply, we currently have technology that allows for swift, large-scale linguistic analysis and broader generalizations.

For example, the *Voices of California* (VOC) project,[6] directed by my faculty colleagues Penny Eckert and Rob Podesva at Stanford, has drawn on recordings with more than 1000 speakers across California to look at broad-scale language variation and change. Mengesha (2020) is one recent VOC project that showcases the speed and detail that FAVE aligning and extracting offer for large scale analysis. Looking at FEEL-FILL mergers in Bakersfield and Sacramento, the author analyzed a total of 48 vowel tokens from African Americans, and 330 tokens from whites, force-aligning word list data into word and sound segments using FAVE, and creating PRAAT scripts to take 11 measurements across the rhyme (EEL or ILL). Among other things, Mengesha found that FEEL is lowering over time and becoming more monophthongal among African Americans, particularly among those with college and graduate degrees. FILL is also lowering and becoming more monophthongal among African Americans, also with education and gender effects; African American women maintain a monophthongal FILL while African American men maintain a diphthongal FILL.

There are many similar projects around the world, for instance the Linguistic Data Consortium at the University of Pennsylvania[7] and the Origins of New Zealand Corpus Project (ONZE).[8]

Unfortunately, the study of Caribbean language is way behind this curve, in part because the CMU pronouncing dictionary, which FAVE and DARLA use, is based on Standard Mainstream American English (MUSE). We will need aligners that are more specifically geared to Caribbean English words and pronunciations, whether at basilectal, mesolectal or acrolectal levels. The good news is that University of Pittsburgh Professor Shelome Gooden (2019) and others are trying to solve these problems. Some progress in the area of digital corpora of Caribbean English has been made, for example Dagmar Deuber (Münster) has "made a forced aligner that orients toward either 'neutral' or Trinidadian English" (Lars Hinrichs email 6.16.19). See also the papers by Phillip Meer (2019, 2020), who works with Deuber, on some of the specific challenges of using state of the art aligners with Trinidadian English. However, more work must be done in order to harness this useful technology for the study of Caribbean languages.

---

[6] http://web.stanford.edu/dept/linguistics/VoCal/index.html
[7] https://www.ldc.upenn.edu
[8] https://www.canterbury.ac.nz/nzilbb/research/onze/

With these new automated tools, analysis of large-scale corpora, provided they exist, will be within reach.

6 Automatic speech recognition by race in US high tech companies

Corpora have also been important in the application of linguistics research to the field of technology. One such example is the impact of research focusing on automated speech recognition by race in U.S. high tech companies. Using digital corpora from online corpora, a team of sound engineers and linguists at Stanford and Georgetown universities (Koenecke et al. 2020) assessed the relative accuracy of automated speech recognizers and transcribers used by Google, Amazon, Apple, and other companies for Black and White speech samples. In order to do this research, we used CORAAL (Corpus of Regional African American Language)[9] for Black speakers and VOC (Voices of California) for White speakers. With these corpora, we were able to analyze 2,141 Black snippets and 2,141 White snippets, with an average length of 17 seconds. Our results indicated that the speech recognition error rate was statistically higher for Black speakers than for white speakers in the speech recognizers for all 5 major tech companies examined, as shown in Figures 3 and 4 (corresponding to figures 1 and 2 in the original). Figure 4 in particular supports the point that we make in the paper: "if one considers a WER of 0.5 to be the bar for a useful transcription, more than 10 times as many snippets of black speakers fail to meet that standard. In this sense, the racial disparities we find are even larger than indicated by the average differences in WER alone."

Additionally, we found that the greater inaccuracy for Black speakers was related to their use of AAVE features. Using a combined phonological and grammatical Dialect Density measure, we found that Black speakers who used more AAVE features were significantly more likely to be mis-transcribed than Black speaker who used fewer such features. This use of corpora illuminates an important next step for tech companies: to train systems more on AAVE and other ethnic dialects so that they are indeed accessible to all.

Similar results have been found by Alicia Beckford Wassink (Wassink 2020) and her colleagues and students at the University of Washington. She reported that an automated transcription service known as CLOx, developed at her university, showed very different error rates for four ethnic dialects of English represented in recordings of sixteen speakers. CLOx is actually an ASR service built on

---

[9]https://oraal.uoregon.edu/coraal

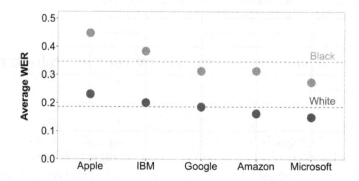

Figure 3: The average Word Error Rate (WER) across Automated Speech Recognition (ASR) services is 0.35 for audio snippets of Black speakers, as opposed to 0.19 for snippets of White speakers. The maximum Standard Error (SE) among the 10 WER values displayed (across Black and White speakers and across ASR services) is 0.005. For each ASR service, the average WER is calculated across a matched sample of 2,141 Black and 2,141 White audio snippets, totalling 19.1 hours of interviewee audio. Nearest-neighbor matching between speaker race was performed based on the speaker's age, gender, and audio snippet duration.

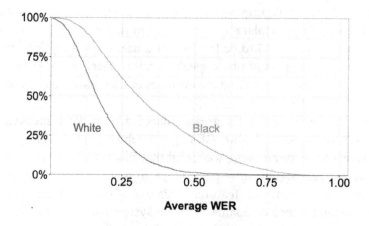

Figure 4: The Complementary Cumulative Distribution Function (CCDF) denotes the share of audio snippets having a WER greater than the value specified along the horizontal axis. The two CCDFs shown for audio snippets by White speakers versus for those by Black speakers use the average WER across the five ASR services tested. If we assume that a WER >0.5 implies a transcript is unusable, then 23% of audio snippets of Black speakers result in unusable transcripts, whereas only 1.6% of audio snippets of White speakers result in unusable transcripts.

the Microsoft Speech development toolkit, so it is using Microsoft's automated speech recognition system. Note that CLOx had 2.7 times more errors when attempting automated transcriptions of speech by African American as it did with speech by Caucasian American speakers, and 5.8 times more errors with ChicanX and Yakama English speakers than with Caucasian American speakers. These results are similar to those shown in Figures 3 and 4, but they show that it's applicable too to other ethnic dialects.

Table 3: Errors in Automated Speech Recognition by CLOx as applied to samples of four ethnic Washington English dialects. nf = number of errors in corpus/total word count in the corpus x 100 words, the base of normalization. (Source: Wassink 2020)

Group	*N*	nf
Caucasian American	6,654	1.5
African American	16,276	4.1
Chicanx	3,986	8.8
Yakama	14,581	8.9

7 Corpora as relevant to criminal justice: *I'm good* 'No (thank you)'

Corpora have also proved to be useful in applied research in another way – the determination of criminal justice. For example, in a criminal case where there was contention over the meaning of *I'm good*, I was asked to provide a deposition as a Linguistics "expert" about its meaning. In this case, a Drug Enforcement Agency (DEA) agent asked two sisters if they would consent to a pat-down. While one of the sisters, Harriet, consented to a body pat-down, Tamika did not, responding *I'm good*. The DEA agent chose to interpret this as a 'yes', and did the body search despite the countervailing evidence – Tamika remained seated, while Harriet had stood up to facilitate the body search – and the prosecution at the trial was actively supporting the DEA agent. To explore the usage of *I'm good* to mean 'No', I assembled several kinds of evidence:

- Crosswords, movies

- Dictionaries (Urban Dictionary, Oxford English Dictionary)

- The Corpus of Contemporary English Usage (COCA), BYU

- Twitter

- Crowd-sourced experiments.

In this paper I'll focus on the online corpora (COCA and a small set of examples from Twitter), since these were essential to establishing compelling evidence that *I'm good* is used unequivocally to mean 'No', and never to mean 'yes' – that is, that Tamika's body search *was done without her consent*. In order to understand how each critically contributed to aiding the defendant, we will consider each individually.

The online Corpus of Contemporary American English [COCA], in 2017 "a more than 450-million-word corpus of American English," provided a window into "more than 560 million words from more than 160,000 texts, including 20 million words from each of the years 1990 through 2017" (*Wikipedia*). The corpus, created and maintained at Brigham Young University in Utah, is an invaluable resource on which scholars studying variation and change in language rely heavily, "used by approximately tens of thousands of people each month, which may make it the most widely used "structured" corpus currently available. For each year, the corpus is evenly divided between the following five genres: spoken, fiction, popular magazines, newspapers, and academic journals."

A search of COCA yielded 330 tokens of *I'm good*. A critical element that a dictionary definition does not specify, but a corpus search was able to clarify, is that the *kind* of question to which *I'm good* is a reply, affects the meaning of *I'm good*. When the question is *How are you?* or *(Are) you good/okay/fine/allright etc.?* or something similar, as in (8–9), an *I'm good* answer assumes its most literal meaning: 'I am in good shape/am feeling fine/doing ok/am content', and so on. Most of the 330 tokens in the IG (*I'm Good*) search were of this type.

(8)   # MIRTHA # Hey, George. You okay? # GEORGE # Yeah. I'm fine. *I'm good.* [from *Blow*, a 2001 work of FICTION]

(9)   AL ROKER (08:22:40): How are you? DANA-EISEN- (08# 22:41): *I'm good,* Al. How are you? [from, *The Today Show*, 2017, 7:00 am, EST, in the SPOKEN genre]

However, when the question is a "Yes/No" question representing an offer or request, as in egs. (10–11), *I'm good* almost always means 'No', achieving its effect by representing the respondent as satisfied with the way things are, declining the food, drink or service offered or the suggestion made, and so on. There were 80 tokens of this type (*I'm good* 'No, thanks') in the IG COCA search; note that we count repeated instances of *I'm good* in the same extract as different examples, since they need not have been repeated, indeed often are not.

(10)   The waitress turned to Charlotte again. "Are you sure I can't get you anything? Maybe an appetizer or a salad?" # "*No, I'm good.* Really." (emphasis added). [from *Love, Honor and Betray*, 2011, in the FICTION genre]

(11)   Guilfoyle: You don't want to comment on this, Eric? Bolling: *I'm good.* (CROSSTALK)
Guilfoyle: Right. Who can say it better? Dana? [from Marco Rubio, *The Five*, 5:00 PM EST, 2015, in the SPOKEN genre]

On the basis of these 80 tokens of *I'm good* 'No', several observations pertinent to the legal case were made. With COCA's scope of time and genre, as well as its availability of contextual information, these tokens were able to provide many unique insights with regard to the usage of *I'm good* over time, the contexts in which it appears, and its cooccurrence with the word *No*.

First, using COCA, we found that *the usage of I'm good to mean 'No' has been rapidly increasing in frequency over the past three decades.* From 1990–2005 (a span of 16 years) there are 12 attestations; from 2006–2011 (6 years), there are 29 attestations, and from 2012 to 2017 (6 years) there are 39 attestations. See figure Figure 4. On the evidence of COCA, it was possible to show that the encounter between the Drug Enforcement Agent and defendant Tamika took place in a six-year span at which this usage of *I'm good* was at its peak.

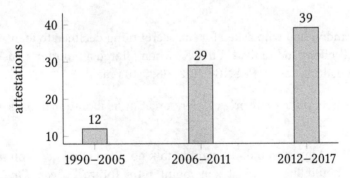

Figure 5: COCA evidence that use of *I'm good* 'No thanks' has increased steadily between 1990 and 2017

Secondly, investigation of the COCA corpus showed that while this usage may have originated in response to offers of food or drink, this is not the only appropriate context for its use. In fact, only 25% (25/80) of the examples of *I'm good* 'No' in the IG COCA search are a response to offers of food or drink. This is important because the prosecution had suggested that the agent's use of *I'm good* was not an appropriate context for signaling 'No' since it was not in a social setting in which food or drink was being offered. However, in light of the COCA evidence, where a great majority of the *I'm good* 'No' examples do *not* involve offers of food or drink, the suggestion that this use of *I'm good* is restricted only to situations involving offers of food or drink is not persuasive.

Thirdly, the COCA corpus helped call into question the Prosecution's claim that Tamika does not choose the familiar and customary phrase of negation, *No, I'm good thanks*, opting significantly to omit the operative word *No* when she says *I'm good.* This statement by the prosecution went against the evidence of the IG COCA corpus that while 54% (43/80) of the attestations of *I'm good* 'No' include a preceding *No* or other explicit negative, as in (10), another 45% (37/80) of them include no explicit negative, as in (11).

Fourthly, while *I'm good* is the primary way of signaling 'No' in the *I'm ___-_* frame, the COCA corpus showed that *I'm okay, I'm fine* and *I'm cool* are other alternatives, sometimes used in conjunction with or in place of *I'm good*:

(12) "Do you want something to eat?" she calls. "*Nah, I'm cool.* I grabbed a burger on the drive." (Jeff P. Jones, Antioch Review, 2015, vol. 73, no. 3, p. 495–512, FICTION genre)

Outside of the COCA corpus, there is an interesting recent TV example in which MSNBC reporter Rachel Maddow reads this segment of the News (exhibit #4):

(13) The individual who asked for the secret filing declined to identify himself or his client and replied "I'm OK" when offered a reporter's business card to remain in touch. (MSNBC 10/25/18, 9:40 pm)

Maddow goes on to perform a mock re-creation/elaboration of the scene, using *I'm OK* 'No':

(14) # "Well, I know you don't want to talk now, but can I give you my card if you should like to talk at some point in the future?" "*Yeah, I'm OK.* I don't need your business card. If I go home with your business card in my pocket, I'll disappear. Ha ha. In fact, I was never even here!" (MSNBC 10/25/18, 9:40 pm)

Note that the presence of *Yeah* in the *I'm good* or *I'm OK*, etc. frame does not, as example (14) shows, necessarily signal assent to the request or offer to which it is a response, especially when an offer or request is repeated, as is frequently the case, and when that request or offer is unpleasant, or potentially threatening the responder's "face," sense of appropriateness, health or freedom. This is certainly the case with the "pat down" that the DEA agent sought permission to do.

Bearing these points in mind, I was able to call into question the observation of the Prosecution in their Amended Prosecution Response that in this exchange, Tamika's response of *I'm cool* to the agent's *Okay?* "gave ultimate completeness to the consent that she gave to his request to search her":

(15)   DEA Agent: You give me permission just pat you down?
       Tamika: I'm good.
       DEA Agent: Okay?
       Tamika: I'm cool, yeah.

This is certainly a possible interpretation, but in light of the following example (16) from the COCA corpus, it is also possible to see Tamika reaffirming the *I'm good* 'No' of her first response. The presence of *Yeah* here is most probably a repudiation of her initial negative *I'm good* as it is in example (16) below. And indeed, in context (a second response to a less than pleasant request) this is the more likely interpretation.

(16)   JOSH-ELLIOTT-1-AB# (Off-camera) I do want to say, Melissa and I shared
       a car afterwards, we're going back to the hotel and she says, do you want
       some Advil? And she'd done it before, and I said, no, you know, I'm tired,
       I have an empty stomach, *I'm good.* I'll get some later. She said, you're
       sure? I said, yeah, *I'm good*, and I forgot to take some. [from Josh and
       Melissa on Wipeout, ABC, SPOKEN genre, 2011]

In addition to the COCA corpus, we also selected 75 Twitter examples from selected dates in 2015, 2016 and 2018 in which *I'm good* was used in the sense of 'No (thanks)', as in this example:

(17)   You think I work my ass off to take you out on a date? Smoke you out?
       Buy you shit? Nah b, I enjoy my own company. *I'm good.* (BamBriaan,
       Nov 6, 2015)

Twitter is a very "oral" medium, which is huge and constantly growing. In this medium, the innovative usage is extremely frequent. It is also interesting that the percentage of examples in which *I'm good* is preceded by *No, Naw* or another negative is about the same as in the COCA corpus, 52% (39/75). About half of the time (48%, 36/75) *I'm good* retains its negative force without an accompanying overt negative form, suggesting, once again, that Defendant Tamika did not need to use an overt *No* for her *I'm good* to mean 'No (thanks)'.

One perhaps relevant observation is that most of the Twitter examples come from African Americans. (Twitter examples often include a photo of the sender.) It is not my contention that *I'm good* 'No' is a distinctly African American usage; the examples in COCA demonstrate clearly that while it a relatively new usage, it is used by a wide cross section of the American public. However, Twitter is extremely popular among African Americans, and the frequency with which the *I'm good* 'No' tokens come from African Americans suggests that this usage would not have been unfamiliar to Tamika. Very likely it is something she encountered and perhaps used frequently in talking with and reading Twitter posts from other African Americans.

Three other observations about the Twitter examples that might be of more interest to linguists than the court are these. Firstly, and this may be related to the 140-character restriction of Twitter, many of the examples do not contain the Yes/No questions or assertions to which they are a response. Sometimes these are evident in the tweets of one or more other persons to which they represent a response. Secondly, a number of idiomatic spinoffs of *I'm good,* have emerged in this medium. One is *I'm good, luv, enjoy* (adding a sarcastic twist) as in:

(18)   You done pissed me off for the LAST time. *I'm good luv, enjoy!* *
       (ayootw33t, Nov 3, 2018)

Another is the use of *I'm good* with a following prepositional phrase, as in:

(19)   Too much fake love at FAMU* **I'm good off all that* * (JoseTheTre Oct 29, 2018)

Thirdly, the use of *I'm good* to reject offers that are less than pleasant and potentially self-incriminating (as was true of the body search invitation Tamika declined) is evident in examples like this one, where the tweeter suggests that the *free tattoo* might result in hepatitis:

(20)   Some guy just messaged me a video on FB of him sitting at a coffee table
       with a tatoo machne, made it buzz and said, "Come and get a free tatt"
       ..."I'm good on hepatitis, my dude" (_frvitbat, Oct 29, 2018)

So how did this evidence pan out for Tamika's case? In consultation with her lawyer, she opted to plea bargain rather than go to trial, as happens in more than 96% of U.S. cases, for complex reasons, including the evidence of her sister's case. However, the lawyer submitted my evidence for the usage of *I'm good* to mean 'No' in a final, extended "Expert Notice" to the court, drawing on the COCA evidence and the evidence from the Twitter examples. This apparently persuaded the prosecution to agree to more favorable terms (maximum 3 years, including the one already served) for the plea bargain of 10 years that would otherwise have been the case. As a result, her final sentence was 2 years, rather than 10, including time served, demonstrating another way in which linguistic analysis based on corpora can be very impactful in applied contexts.

8 Summary and conclusion: Towards online corpora of Caribbean Languages

As the above six examples have shown, online corpora can provide an invaluable, sometimes *essential* resource for the study of linguistic variation and change, in theoretical, descriptive, and applied contexts. They are particularly valuable when they are online and publicly available, allowing our analyses to be replicated and validated.

In the English-speaking Caribbean, we already have multiple sources for these kinds of corpora, although they are at different levels of public availability and accessibility:

- Creole recordings already in the Jamaican Language Unit (*Jumieka Langwij Yuunit*), University of the West Indies, Mona, for a long time under the direction of Hubert Devonish, now directed by Joseph Farquharson.

- ICE (International Corpus of English) Jamaica – by design, mainly acrolectal/standard.

- CCJ (Corpus of Cyber Jamaican) – all levels – Christian Mair, U Freiburg, Mair adds (in an email from 5/16/19) that the best and most comprehensive showcase of these data is a PhD thesis produced by Andrea Moll (see Moll 2015).

- Several hundred Creole recordings and transcripts I have from Guyana, Jamaica and Barbados (many made by me, a native Guyanese, others by local linguists from Guyana and Jamaica). Most of these will be available in digital form via Stanford University Library.

- Don Winford's recordings/transcripts from Sranan Tongo, Belize Creole, Guyanese Creole, and Trinidadian Creole, which he has promised to contribute to online corpora being assembled by Bettina Migge, at the University of Dublin.

- Peter Patrick's Jamaican recordings/transcripts. Of these he notes (email of 5/20/19) that "The Veeton recordings from 1989- 90 include more than 100 hours of interviews with about 75 different individuals, many in repeat recordings, plus a series of family and youth-club recordings". I also made a small series of recordings in rural locations in 1991 - principally St. Thomas and Hanover, when I was trying to revisit as many remote sites where Fred Cassidy and David DeCamp made recordings.

- Veronique Lacoste (email of 5/28/19) notes that she has about ~10GB of Jamaican Creole child language data, mostly recorded in schools.

- Other sources: Pauline Christie, Walter Edwards, Shelome Gooden (see Gooden 2003), Hazel Simmons-McDonald, Velma Pollard, Ian Robertson, and the many others who have done field work on anglophone Caribbean varieties may be willing to contribute recordings from their collection, and should be actively approached about doing so.

There should be similar efforts for the French-speaking Caribbean, the Spanish-speaking Caribbean, and so on. Indeed, there undoubtedly already are. For instance, Nicte Fuller Medina has corpora of Belizean Spanish as well as English/Creole on her Language, Culture and History project website.[10]

Building on and using these resources will not be without challenges. We would need to determine how to collect, catalog, digitize, and safely store recordings and transcripts of Caribbean language varieties, deciding on real names or pseudonyms depending on available permission forms and local IRB (Institutional Review Board) rules. We'd also need to decide about placement: that is what would go where, whether there would be sharing between sites, and so on. Furthermore, we'd need to develop tools for the automatic analysis of digital recordings and transcripts that can handle Caribbean lexicon, phonology, and morphosyntax, along the lines that Shelome Gooden and others have begun to pioneer. And while there are numerous necessary steps to this process, we do have the people who can make it happen.

In order to accomplish this, we could perhaps start with small meetings (facilitated by funding from agencies like the National Science Foundation) of key

---

[10] https://nfullerm.wixsite.com/website/research

players to discuss the issues. We could also get the advice or involvement of experts like Tyler Kendall (University of Oregon, and the developer of two web-based language archives, including CORAAL) and Christian Mair.[11] But we need to begin soon, because one of the best ways we can honor pioneer linguists of the Caribbean, before they pass on, is by equipping their successors with online corpora of Caribbean languages. They are invaluable, indeed essential tools for 21st century Linguistics.

Acknowledgments

I am grateful to the following Stanford students for assistance in the preparation of this paper: Mea Anderson, Jane M. Boettcher, Susan Chang, Julia Gong, and Zion Ariana Mengesha. And as always, for the encouragement and support of Angela Eunice Rickford, my intellectual companion for more than 50 years. I also thank the two anonymous referees for their helpful comments on an earlier draft.

Abbreviations

AAVE	African American Vernacular English
ASR	Automated Speech Recognition
VOC	Voices of California
WER	Word Error Rate
COCA	Corpus of Contemporary American English
CORAAL	Corpus of Regional African American Language
ICE	International Corpus of English
IRB	Institutional Review Board

References

Bailey, Charles-James N. 1973. *Variation and linguistic theory.* Washington DC: Center for Applied Linguistics.

Gooden, Shelome. 2003. *The phonology and phonetics of Jamaican Creole reduplication.* The Ohio State University. (Doctoral dissertation).

Gooden, Shelome. 2019. Afro-American intonation and prosody: An evolving ecology. Plenary presentation at the Mervyn C. Alleyne commemorative conference, University of the West Indies, Mona, Jamaica, June.

---

[11]https://blogs.uoregon.edu/lvclab/people/tyler-kendall/ and https://www.researchgate.net/profile/Christian_Mair

Jones, Byron. 2019. *Beyond di riddim: Language use in Jamaican popular music, 1962-2012.* University of the West Indies, St. Augustine. (Doctoral dissertation).

Koenecke, Allison, Andrew Nam, Emily Lake, Joe Nudell, Minnie Quartey, Zion Mengesha, Connor Toups, John R. Rickford, Dan Jurafsky & Sharad Goel. 2020. Racial disparities in automated speech recognition. In Judith T. Irvine (ed.), *Proceedings of the National Academy of Sciences,* vol. 117, 7684–7689. DOI: 10. 1073/pnas.1915768117.

Labov, William. 1972. *Sociolinguistic patterns.* Philadelphia: University of Pennsylvania Press.

Meer, Phillipp. 2019. Sociolinguistic variation in (Standard) Trinidadian English vowels: A semi-automatic sociophonetic study of selected monophthongs and diphthongs. In *Proceedings of the 50th Congress of the Brazilian Linguistics Association, May 2–9.* Maceió, Alagoas: Brazilian Linguistics Association.

Meer, Phillipp. 2020. Automatic alignment for New Englishes: Applying state-of-the-art aligners to Trinidadian English. *Journal of the Acoustical Society of America* 147.4. 2283–2294.

Mengesha, Zion. 2020. The social meaning of vowel trajectories: FEEL-FILL merger among African Americans in California. Ms., Department of Linguistics, Stanford University.

Moll, Andrea. 2015. *Jamaican Creole goes web: Sociolinguistic styling and authenticity in a digital yaad.* Amsterdam: Benjamins.

Rickford, John R., Isabelle Buchstaller, Thomas Wasow & Arnold Zwicky. 2007. Intensive and quotative ALL: Something old, something new. *American Speech* 82.1. 2–31.

Rickford, John R., Thomas Wasow, Norma Mendoza-Denton & Juli Espinoza. 1995. Syntactic variation and change in progress: Loss of the verbal coda in topic-restricting *as far as* constructions. *Language* 71.1. 102–31.

Wassink, Alicia Beckford. 2020. Automatic speech recognition and ethnicity-related dialects. Uneven success. Paper presented at the meeting of the American Association for the Advancement of Science, February 14, 2020. https: //depts.washington.edu/sociolab/publications/documents/AAAS-2020-Wassink.pdf.

Wikipedia. 2019. *Corpus of contemporary American English.* Wikimedia Foundation, 8 Apr. 2019. %7Bhttps://en.wikipedia.org/wiki/Corpus_of_Contemporary_American_English%7D.

Winford, Donald. 1972. *A sociolinguistic description of two communities in Trinidad.* University of York. (Doctoral dissertation).

Chapter 9

Apart, and yet a part: Social class, convergence, and the vowel systems of Columbus African American English and European American English

David Durian[a], Melissa Reynard[b] & Jennifer Schumacher

[a]Pennsylvania State University [b]North Carolina State University

Thomas (1989) and Durian et al. (2010) found that increased segregation among working-class African Americans and European Americans in Columbus, Ohio in the second half of the 20th century, led to conflicting patterns of divergence and convergence in speaker's vowel systems rather than divergence as in other American cities (Thomas & Yeager-Dror 2010). However, this research did not investigate vowel systems of middle-class residents who had been less impacted by segregation during that time period. This paper attempts to fill this gap by comparing the vowel systems of African and European American Columbusites of both working- and middle-class backgrounds. Results reveal that both sets of African Americans show convergence with European Americans for fronting of /uː/, /ʊ/, and /oʊ/. However, middle-class African Americans display stronger similarities with middle-class European Americans for retraction of /æ/, /ɑ/, /ɛ/, and /ɪ/ suggesting greater levels of integration among middle-class than among working-class Columbusites.

1 Introduction

Despite sociolinguists' detailed knowledge of general patterns of variation in African American English (AAE) morphosyntax and phonology/phonetics, the types and extent of phonetic and phonological variation as distributed by socio-economic class among middle and working class speakers, and their similarities

David Durian, Melissa Reynard & Jennifer Schumacher. 2022. Apart, and yet a part: Social class, convergence, and the vowel systems of Columbus African American English and European American English. In Bettina Migge & Shelome Gooden (eds.), *Social and structural aspects of language contact and change*, 233–262. Berlin: Language Science Press. DOI: 10.5281/zenodo.6979323 and differences to equivalent European American vowel systems in communities throughout the United States, has largely remained understudied (see Britt & Weldon (2015) for more details). In particular, several questions remain underexplored: (1) How are the vowel systems of speakers of AAE from working class and middle class backgrounds living within the same community similar to and different from one another? (2) How do these vowel systems compare and contrast with those of working class and middle class European Americans living in the same community? Are they becoming more alike (convergence) or less alike (divergence) as time goes on? (3) What can a more refined understanding of the impact of social class on patterns of linguistic variation bring to our understanding of language variation in AAE?

As our discussion will illustrate, each of these questions is significant in current studies of AAE, as different communities throughout the US have been found to show different results in previous studies. For instance, at a national level, Labov et al. (2006) found in their regional dialect survey of US English that African Americans generally do not appear to be participating in local patterns of vowel shift found among European American speakers in the areas surveyed throughout their study. Meanwhile, studies at the community level find a more complex set of results. For example, in Philadelphia and Chicago, research has shown that strong patterns of divergence can be found among speakers of AAE and European American English (EAE) (e.g., Labov & Harris 1986, Gordon 2000). In contrast, in cities such as Memphis and Texana, NC, research has revealed that stronger patterns of convergence can be found among speakers (e.g, Fridland 2003, Fridland & Bartlett 2006, Childs et al. 2010). Given this diversity at the community level, researchers have begun to explore this issue in some detail in communities throughout the US in recent years.

Studies on the influence of social class on patterns of language variation among African Americans have been generally lacking, with the exception of two early sociolinguistic studies: Wolfram (1969) in Detroit and Pederson (1965) in Chicago. Both of these studies found social stratification of linguistic features such as the use of more standard variants among middle class speakers and more nonstandard features among working class speakers. In the years since, studies of African American communities have tended to leave out analysis of social class, either leaving out consideration of this social factor altogether, or dealing with it in only a cursory way. Thus, we know little as a field of how social class might influence patterns of vowel variation among African Americans, including how the influence of social class may be similar to, and different from, the influence of social class on other ethnic groups in the US, such as European Americans.

Generally, this has led us to have a body of research on AAE in the US that, although rich in complex and meaningful findings on a variety of linguistic issues, has been incomplete in regard to exploring social class as a key factor influencing language variation.

The present study attempts to answer each of the research questions noted above via the instrumental exploration of conversational data obtained from speakers living in Columbus, Ohio. Columbus provides an informative context for exploring contrasts and similarities between both working class and middle class African American and European American vowel systems for several reasons. Columbus is a metropolis located in the heart of the North American Midland, as it has been defined on the basis of both lexical and phonological features by Carver (1987) and Labov et al. (2006). According to the 2010 US Census, Columbus has a population of 787,000 residents. Among the population, roughly 28% are African American and roughly 61.5% are European American (U.S. Census Bureau 2010). In the urban core, there is frequent contact between working class European Americans and African Americans, resulting from migration patterns among both ethnic groups tracing back to the late 19th century and early-to mid-20th century. Furthermore, there is frequent contact between middle class European Americans and African Americans in areas at the periphery of the core and in surrounding suburban space, as a result of changes to Columbus's socio-geographic landscape beginning in the 1970s.

Taking these attributes into account, we present the results of a pilot study comparing middle class African American and European American speaker vowel systems, as well as looking at how these systems compare to previously documented systems of working class African American and European American speakers, via data collected in Columbus in two studies. In doing so, we focus first on describing and analyzing similarities and differences in the vowel systems of working class and middle class African Americans. This is something which has not been explored in previous studies of Columbus AAE vowel systems (Durian et al. 2010, Thomas 1989). Second, we focus on whether AAE and EAE are showing patterns of growing similarity (convergence) or growing dissimilarity (divergence) as varieties of English over time in Columbus. In addition, we consider the relationship of our findings in Columbus to recent studies of vowel variation in AAE and EAE that have investigated convergence and divergence in other communities through the United States. Finally, we consider the social motivations for the class-based patterns of convergence and divergence between middle class and working class African Americans and European Americans in our data.

Before turning to our analysis of vowel variation in Columbus, however, it will first be useful to understand relevant background on each of the issues we will explore in some detail. In section §2, we discuss the key findings of previous comparative studies of vowel variation in AAE and EAE vowel systems in the US. While doing so, we will also explore what these studies have revealed about the importance of considering the influence of community level segregation and integration on the patterns of vowel system convergence and divergence observed. In section §3, we turn to providing background on Columbus as a speech community, as well as Thomas's (1989) and Durian et al.'s (2010) earlier studies of Columbus vowel systems.

2 Previous comparative studies of AAE and EAE vowel systems in the US

Among studies of phonetic and phonological variation in US English, there has been a long history of variation involving the vowel systems of speakers living in communities throughout the United States. This tradition goes back to the earliest studies of vowel pronunciation conducted in the United States – the regional dialect atlas surveys of Hans Kurath and his colleagues beginning in the 1930s with the *Linguistic Atlas of New England* (Kurath et al. 1939). During the earliest era of study, dialectologists such as Kurath tended to focus on individual vowel pronunciations in individual words, analyzing how these individual pronunciations distinguished one regional dialect of US English from another. At the time, although some of the research conducted did include African Americans, the bulk of the research focused on patterns of variation found primarily among European Americans – in particular, older rural males (e.g., Kurath & McDavid 1961, Wetmore 1959, Atwood 1951).

Beginning with the work of Labov et al. (1972), linguists began to look at the vowel system holistically, rather than on a vowel-by-vowel basis. This led researchers to find patterns of vowel variation involving systematic shifts in the pronunciation of several vowels at one time. These vowel shifts can be either chain shifts or parallel shifts, as shown in Figure 1 and Figure 2. Note that for all vowel classes referenced in this essay, we use Well's (1982) keyword notation.

Figure 1 shows the Northern Cities Shift, a commonly described chain shift found in the vowel systems of many European Americans living in the US Inland North dialect area (as per Labov et al. 2006). The numbers in the diagram indicate the stages in which the vowels typically shift. Figure 2 shows a parallel shift involving the fronting of the nuclei of the back vowels GOAT and GOOSE. This vowel shift is found among many European Americans living in the US Midland dialect area (as per Durian 2012).

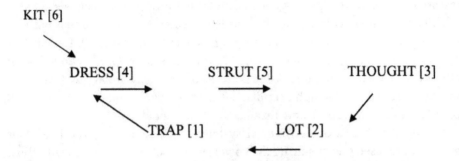

Figure 1: The Northern Cities Shift (NCS) as per Labov et al. (2006)

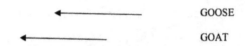

Figure 2: Parallel fronting of the back vowels in GOOSE and GOAT (as per Durian (2012)

Within this body of research, vowel variation among African American speakers was not looked at systematically with any regularity until the late 1980s with the work of Erik Thomas ([1989]/1993) in Columbus, OH. Since that time, a number of studies have been conducted, most prominently since the late 2000s, when Thomas & Yeager-Dror (2010) assembled a paper collection by scholars specifically focused on systematic vowel variation in AAE speech. This recent work typically adopts an instrumental approach to analyzing the patterns of vowel variation, including and analysis using F1 by F2 vowel plots.

Also, during the 1980s, discussion of whether African American and European American speech patterns were becoming more or less alike as time goes on began with the work of Labov & Harris (1986) in Philadelphia. In that study, Labov and Harris looked at several grammatical and consonantal patterns of variation among African Americans and European American Philadelphians. Based on the overall patterns found, Labov and Harris concluded that AAE and EAE in Philadelphia appeared to be showing strong patterns of difference (divergence) between the language varieties as time went on, rather than more similarities (convergence).

This finding has led to some controversy in the field in the years since, as researchers began to explore whether similar patterns of divergence existed in other communities. This exploration has led researchers to find similar patterns of divergence in cities like Cleveland Heights, OH (Thomas 2007), Detroit (Anderson 2002), and the Calumet region of Northwestern IN (Gordon 2000), while others have instead found increasing patterns of similarity among AAE and EAE speakers in cities like Memphis (Fridland & Bartlett 2006, Fridland 2003), Roswell, GA (Andres & Votta 2010), and Texana, NC (Childs et al. 2010).

Among the studies of AAE vowel systems carried out since the late 1980s, most have focused on comparing the vowel systems of AAE speakers with those of EAE speakers living in the same community, with an emphasis on exploring patterns of convergence or divergence in those vowel systems. In addition, these studies have similarly focused on age and sex as important secondary characteristics impacting the patterns of vowel variation; none, however, have explicitly explored the impact of social class. This is an issue we will return to later in this section.

Generally, these studies have tended to find that African and European speakers living in areas that are more Southern or rural tend to have vowel systems showing more similarity to one another as time goes on, while speakers living in areas that are more Northern or urban often show vowel systems that are growing more and more distinct. This is especially true of studies that have been conducted at the community level in these regions. For instance, in studies conducted in both Memphis, a Southern city, and Texana, NC, a more rural (and Southern) community, speakers were found to be showing increased fronting of the back vowels in GOAT and GOOSE, a trend most prevalent in the speech of younger speakers in both communities. Additionally, in Memphis, as well as some other Southern communities, such as Roswell, speakers of both ethnic groups also show growing similarities in showing the reversal of the nucleus of FACE and DRESS, two vowels involved in the US Southern Vowel Shift. This is a pattern that does not often extend to the GOOSE and KIT vowels, however, which are also involved in the general rotation of the long and front short vowels that typifies the Southern Vowel Shift. This pattern of shift is typically found among EAE speakers, but not AAE speakers, in studies of Southern communities.

In contrast to these patterns, in the US North, studies such as Thomas (2007) and Gordon (2000) have found increasing patterns of divergence in vowel systems of speakers, a trend most prevalent in the speech of younger speakers in both communities. In particular, Thomas (2007) found that speakers in Cleveland Heights seem to be engaging in two distinct vowel shifting trends, with the Northern Cities Shift (shown earlier in Figure 1) found in the vowel systems of EAE speakers, and what he called the African American Vernacular English

(AAVE) Shift (shown in Figure 3) found in the vowel systems of AAE speakers. The Northern Cities Shift involves the shifting of 6 vowel classes: TRAP, LOT, THOUGHT, DRESS, STRUT, and KIT. In particular, the shift involves the raising and fronting of the nucleus of the TRAP vowel, the fronting of nucleus of the LOT vowel, the lowering and fronting of the nucleus of the THOUGHT vowel, the backing of the nucleus of the DRESS and STRUT vowels, and the lowering and backing of the nucleus of the KIT vowel.

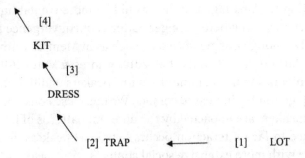

Figure 3: The African American Vernacular English (AAVE) Shift, as per Thomas (2007)

In contrast is the AAVE Shift, which involves the raising and fronting of the nucleus of the TRAP, DRESS, and KIT vowels, and the fronting of the nucleus of LOT. This makes the patterns of vowel variation for TRAP and LOT similar to some extent among EAE and AAE speakers in Cleveland, but different for KIT and DRESS. However, because the vowels are interlocked in two distinct patterns of chain shift for speakers of each ethnic group, Thomas (2007) argues that the shifts ultimately show an overall pattern of divergence from one another. This can be seen by comparing the stages over which the shifts occur. In the Northern Cities shift, TRAP fronting and raising is typically seen as the first stage of the shift, followed by LOT fronting. In the AAVE Shift, LOT fronting appears to be the first stage of the shift, followed by TRAP fronting and raising as the second stage.

Regardless of the differences in vowel variation patterns noted between Southern and Northern cities in the discussion above, a common thread found in many of these previous studies is the influence that patterns of residential segregation appear to have had on the patterns of language use observed. In the North, residential segregation was often stronger historically than in the South, especially during the period of the Great Migration (Lemann 1991, Collins 2020). There, we often see stronger patterns of divergence among speakers, as the stronger degree of residential segregation limited contact opportunities among African Americans with European Americans, as well as other ethnic groups, in many urban settings. This is the case in cities such as Cleveland, Detroit, and Philadelphia, where strong patterns of divergence have been found (Thomas 2007, Anderson 2002, Labov & Harris 1986). In the South, residential segregation was often less robust historically, and speakers typically lived in communities where speakers of different ethnicities resided side by side. This situation would allow more contact between speakers, making for language use that would be more similar among speakers. This is the case in areas where stronger patterns of convergence have been reported, especially among younger speakers, such as in Memphis, Texana, or Roswell (Fridland & Bartlett 2006, Childs et al. 2010, Andres & Votta 2010).

However, increased integration in a community with speakers of different ethnicities does not by itself guarantee increased contact. We must also consider how the social networks of speakers are impacted by the different patterns of integration, and how much face to face interaction occurs between speakers. Studies have revealed that those with more extensive social contacts with speakers from a wide range of social and ethnic backgrounds are more likely to converge with the language use patterns of these other social contacts, either in overall daily speech or the use of more elaborate codeswitching between AAE and EAE, while those with less extensive social networks will be more likely to show less convergence (Labov & Harris 1986, Childs et al. 2010, Britt & Weldon 2015).

3 The social and linguistic context of AAE in Columbus

Having now laid the groundwork for our discussion of the analysis of vocalic variation as it has been studied in previous work on AAE throughout the US, we turn to a discussion of the important issues discussed throughout section §2 specifically in Columbus. As we do so, it is important to understand how several significant aspects of this city as a speech community are useful for exploring variation in the vowel systems of both working class and middle class AAE and how that variation is similar to, and different from, variation in the vowel systems of EAE speakers of similar social class backgrounds living in the community. First, we discuss the social history of African Americans in Columbus, including how historical patterns of segregation have impacted language contact patterns among European Americans and African Americans in the city. We then discuss the results of two earlier studies of vowel variation conducted in the community that provide the necessary background for the present study.

3.1 A brief social history of African Americans in Columbus

To understand the context of contact among European Americans and African Americans in Columbus, it is instructive to look briefly at the community's social history, particularly the years directly following the Civil War. During this time, and again in the post-World War I and World War II periods, a significant number of African Americans moved to the southern and eastern parts of the urban core to pursue industrial jobs in factories. A portion of this population migrated directly from the South and Appalachia, while others moved first to eastern cities such as Philadelphia and Pittsburgh before later resettling in Columbus (Bryant 1983, Murphy 1970). In most cases, African Americans migrated to areas in the urban core where they found themselves in daily contact with recent European American migrants of predominantly Upper Southern, Lower Northern, and Appalachian backgrounds, as well as long time Columbus residents, whose families had begun settling in Columbus since the late 1700s (Lentz 2003).

Until the 1970s, most African Americans in Columbus were working class, as a result of Columbus having a predominately "separate but equal" community structure, which endured since the founding of Columbus in 1803 (Jacobs 1994, James 1972). Following the end of the Civil War, this "separate but equal" structure led to decades of discrimination in hiring practices by local businesses, as well as housing segregation, due to *de facto* segregation resulting from restrictive deed covenants and the displacement of members of the African American community during the 1960s due to the construction of Interstates 70 and 71 (Oriedo 1982, Burgess 1994). This developed into a situation where the majority of African Americans in Columbus now live in an eastward arch surrounding the periphery of the original "central core" area (Jacobs 1994, Reece et al. 2012). As a result, these factors prevented African Americans from obtaining higher skilled labor positions, either physically, due to geographic distance, or socially, due to job accessibility limitations.

During the late 1960s, however, the situation began to change as a result of the Civil Rights Movement and the passage of the Civil Rights Act of 1968, which put an end to enforcement of overt housing and employment discrimination practices in the community (Jacobs 1994). In conjunction with these changes, the Columbus Public Schools underwent changes from a system that was strongly characterized as "separate but equal" to one that was, at first, voluntarily desegregated, as in the late 1960s, but later court ordered to desegregate via the use of busing in 1979 (Foster 1997). Even with these changes in place, present-day Columbus continues to remain strongly socio-geographically stratified by social class, with race playing a significant role as a secondary factory in the process, given the community's history. We can see the effects of these patterns on the Columbus landscape over the period 1970–2010 via Map 1 (Figure 4) and Map 2 (Figure 5). Map 1 shows the areas of Columbus that were predominately African American populated in 1970. The darkest areas are those where African Americans were most heavily concentrated at the time. Map 2 (Figure 5) shows the community in 2010. It uses the same conventions as Map 1 and shows the impact of displacement and housing segregation practices in the community. Based on the 2010 U.S. Census, Columbus has a Taueber Index Score of 61.0 (U.S. Census Bureau 2010).

In present day Columbus, a growing middle class African American population tends to reside in more socio-economically and racially mixed parts of Columbus – either in areas at the periphery of the core to the West and North, to the Northeast of the core in the neighborhood known as North Linden, or in nearby dormitory suburbs. At the same time, a significant portion of the African American population remains working class and living in areas closely surrounding the urban core, due to the lack of economic opportunity to move elsewhere. As a result, contact among many working class European Americans and African Americans continues to occur in areas closest to the core, such as the southeast and east sides, while in areas further from the core, contact between middle class European Americans and African Americans now occurs. We will return to these trends later in our discussion.

3.2 A brief discussion of historical dialect patterns in Columbus speech

The dialect features of Columbus speech that have emerged during this period are a complex mixture of Northern and Southern features and are strongly Midland in character. As Thomas (2001) and Durian (2012) have discussed, Columbus speech of the early 20th century included features typically associated with the Southern Shift, such as the frontward movement of the nuclei of MOUTH, GOAT, FOOT, GOOSE, and SHOES, and historically North Midland features, such as r-fullness, the backing of LOT, and the merger of the NORTH and FORCE classes. This was especially true of working-class European American English, but also true to a lesser extent in middle class speech (Durian 2012). Less diachronic information about Columbus AAE is available. Features traditionally assumed to be most strongly affiliated with more Southern or older supra-regional AAE were a strong element of AAE in Columbus in the early 20th century. Some of these features include r-lessness; glide weakening of PRICE in open syllables and before voiced consonants (a similar pattern to Southern speech); and the tendency

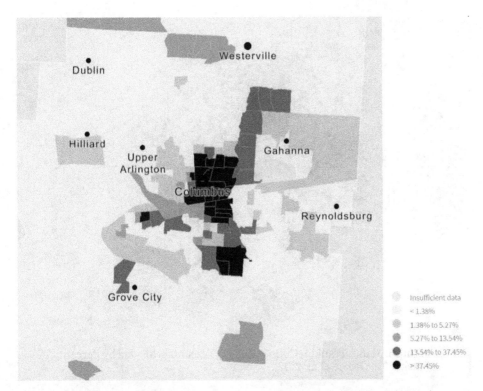

Figure 4: Map 1. Franklin County Census Tract Map, Shaded by Percent Black, 1970 (Reece et al. 2012)

for GOOSE, SHOES, GOAT and MOUTH to remain back (Thomas 1989).

During the second half of the 20th century, these patterns of difference between ethnic groups appear to have diminished. Among working class African Americans and European Americans, this can be seen via the results of two previous studies of vowel systems in Columbus. The first is Thomas'(1989) primary impressionistic study based on data collected during the 1980s from working class African Americans and European Americans born between 1968–1970. The second is Durian et al.'s (2010) primarily instrumental study that analyzed speech among working class African American and European American speakers belonging to two age cohorts. One group was older speakers who were born between 1950–1960, while the other was a younger group of speakers who were born between 1969–1985. Both studies found not only the decreased presence of the historical AAE features we discussed earlier, but also evidence that Columbus African American speakers have begun to realize a partial merger of LOT/THOUGHT before /t/ and the frontward movement of the nuclei of MOUTH,

Figure 5: Map 2. Franklin County Census Tract Map, Shaded by Percent Black, 2010 (Reece et al. 2012)

GOAT, FOOT, GOOSE, and SHOES.

In addition to these results, Durian et al. (2010) also found some evidence of nucleus lowering for GOAT among some older female and younger male African American speakers, which is not found as pervasively among working class European American speakers. Furthermore, tendencies were found among African American speakers towards raised KIT, DRESS, and TRAP articulations, lowered FOOT realizations, and fronter realizations of LOT and THOUGHT. These patterns indicate evidence of divergence from European American patterns for these vowel classes. Working class European Americans, in comparison, showed tendencies toward backer articulations of LOT and THOUGHT, non-lowered FOOT realizations, and either non-raised or mildly lowered KIT and DRESS realizations. As well, the TRAP vowel among many working-class European Americans shows a strong backing and lowering trend over time, increasing as speakers get younger in age. In addition, African Americans tended to show evidence of more robustly raised STRUT-realizations when compared to European Americans. Across speakers, the majority of these patterns of convergence and divergence were found to have stronger tendencies among younger speakers. Table 1 summarizes the differences described here between working class AAE and EAE.

In middle class speech, it is currently not known how the varieties are converging or diverging, since no previous studies of middle class African American vowel systems have been completed. These trends will be investigated in the following sections of this analysis. Before turning to this analysis, it is useful to present a brief recap of what is known about vowel variation trends in middle class European American speech. The most extensive study of this group to date is Durian (2012), which studied the vowel systems of four generations of Columbusites born between 1895 and 1990. Among middle class European Americans, Durian found increasing patterns of fronting of the nuclei of GOAT, STRUT, FOOT, GOOSE, and SHOES. These tendencies each increase as speaker age decreases. Durian also found fronting for the nucleus of MOUTH among many speakers born before the 1970s, but this trend has begun to reverse itself among younger speakers, who now show nucleus retraction. Furthermore, Durian found a strong tendency towards merger or near merger of LOT and THOUGHT, a trend also found extensively in Labov et al (2006's) mostly middle-class Columbus speakers, interviewed for the *Atlas of North American English*.

Table 1: Comparison of results among working-class AAE and EAE speakers

Working class AAE vs. EAE
AAE and EAE show convergence for: - Fronting of the nucleus of SHOES, GOOSE, FOOT, GOAT, and MOUTH
AAE and EAE show divergence for: - The AAVE Shift (Raised articulations of KIT, DRESS, and BAT, and fronter articulation of LOT) - Fronter articulation of THOUGHT and raised articulation of STRUT

In addition, Durian (2012) found strong trends for backing of the nucleus of LOT, and backing/lowering of the nuclei of TRAP, DRESS, and KIT, a characteristic of Columbus speech that resembles significantly the same vowel shifting trends for these vowel classes found previously in Canada (e.g, Clarke et al. 1995, Boberg 2005, Roeder & Jarmasz 2010) and California (e.g, Luthin 1987, Kennedy & Grama 2012, Podesva et al. 2015). Given this similarity, Durian (2012) coined the term "The Third Dialect Shift" to describe the shift in Columbus, since all three dialect areas have essentially the same shift as well as being unified previously as a dialect group by Labov (1991) based on the overlapping occurrence of the LOT/THOUGHT merger as a dialect feature in each area. As with other features, usage of the Third Dialect Shift appears to be increasing in middle class Columbus speech as time goes on. The Third Dialect Shift is shown in Figure 4, with numbers indicating stages of the chain shift.

Compared to working class EAE speakers, middle class EAE speakers show many of the same vowel shifting tendencies. However, the extent to which those features are used within each social class group differs. Among the features of EAE that are shared between both groups, fronting of the nucleus of the back vowels SHOES, GOOSE, FOOT, GOAT, and MOUTH is more robust among working class speakers, and the merger of the LOT and THOUGHT classes is often more complete as a process among working class EAE speakers than middle class EAE speakers. In contrast to this, use of the Third Dialect features (especially backing and lowering of the nucleus of TRAP, DRESS, and KIT) are usually stronger among middle class EAE speakers than working class EAE speakers. Table 2 presents a summary of these trends as they are found in working and middle class EAE, while also showing the contrast in use with the patterns discussed earlier in this section for working class AAE.

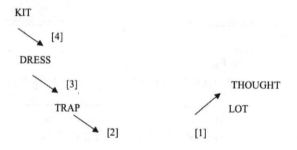

Figure 6: The Third Dialect Shift (as described in Durian 2012)

As a final note in closing, although not labeled as such in their studies, aspects of the Third Dialect Shift, in particular the backing and lowering of the nucleus of TRAP, have been found in several studies of other US Midland cities in recent years. This includes Johnstown, OH (Thomas 1996); Indianapolis, IN (Fogle 2008); and several cities located in Southern, IL (Bigham 2010). It should be noted that although Labov et al. (2006) did not find the Third Dialect Shift in their analysis of the US Midland, the occurrence of the Third Dialect Shift in a variety of these other, individual Midland cities, demonstrates this chain shift is a more general US Midland dialect feature, and it will be discussed as such throughout section §4.

Table 2: Vowel variation features of Columbus AAE and EAE found in previous studies. (Features used most strongly by a given EAE group are shown in bold).

Working class AAE	- Fronting of the nucleus of SHOES, GOOSE, FOOT, GOAT, and MOUTH
	- Fronter Articulation of THOUGHT and raised articulations of STRUT
	- The AAVE Shift (Raised Articulations of KIT, DRESS, and BAT, and Fronter Articulation of LOT)
Working class EAE	- **Fronting of the nucleus of SHOES, GOOSE, FOOT, GOAT, and MOUTH**
	- **(Near) merger of the LOT and THOUGHT vowels**
	- The Third Dialect Shift (Lowering and backing of the nucleus of LOT, TRAP, DRESS, and KIT)
Middle class EAE	- Fronting of the nucleus of SHOES, GOOSE, FOOT, GOAT, and MOUTH
	- (Near) merger of the LOT and THOUGHT vowels
	- **The Third Dialect Shift (lowering and backing of the nucleus of LOT, TRAP, DRESS, and KIT)**

4 A comparative analysis of present-day Columbus AAE and EAE vowel systems

Now that we have established an understanding of previous patterns of vowel variation found in the speech of working class African American and European Americans, as well as middle class Europeans Americans, we move to presenting the results of our comparative analysis of middle class African American vowel variation trends. The analysis follows the model provided in Durian et al. (2010), by presenting a side-by-side analysis of representative speaker vowel plots for African and European American Columbusites, with commentary on the significant trends found with the plots. This approach allows patterns of vowel variation among middle class speakers to be understood within the wider context of the previous studies of Columbus speech discussed above, while also allowing us to showcase the new information on middle class Columbus African American vowel systems available from our data. Following the comparative analysis of middle-class speech trends in section §4.2, we move in section §4.3 to a comparative analysis of our middle-class data set with the working-class data set analyzed by the first and third authors in Durian et al. (2010).

4.1 Methodology

In order to make a meaningful comparison between the Durian et al. (2010) data set and the middle-class data we analyze here, two age cohorts were analyzed and plotted. Older speakers were born from 1955–1963, while younger speakers were born from 1976–1985. Speakers were chosen from a larger sample of speakers interviewed for two sociolinguistic studies of Columbus speakers conducted by Don Winford and his associates in 2007–2008, and by David Durian in 2008–2009. All subjects were speakers who were born and raised in the greater Columbus metropolitan area and all have continued to live in the Columbus metropolitan area as adults.

In both surveys, sociolinguistic interviews were conducted by the field workers involved, and large samples of conversational speech were collected during the interview process. African American field workers elicited data from African American speakers via sociolinguistic interviews, while data for European American speakers were elicited via interviews by a European American field worker. In the case of the African American interviews, all data collected was conversational. In the case of the European American interviews, data was collected from several tasks, including conversational speech, word lists, and dialect term elicitation. Through the analysis presented here, all data analyzed is drawn from conversational speech.

The European American speakers' vowel systems were all originally analyzed in Durian (2012), and the speakers selected here for comparison thus represent only a small sample of the larger available pool of 62 speakers included in that study. As such, the reader is directed to the vowel plots included in Appendix B of Durian (2012) to see the data for all 62 European American speakers. Socioeconomic status for all speakers in both studies was determined using available information from the interview recordings. Not all informants discussed this information to the same degree, and so our assignment of class is limited to occupation level of adult informants, and mean household income of the area in which informants were raised (if known) during the time of their childhood.

The sociolinguistic interviews were recorded at 44.1 KHz to a Sony DAT recorder. These files were then digitized as .wav files for acoustic analysis in PRAAT (Boersma & Weenink 2020), using a variable window of 10–14 LPC coefficients depending on the quality of the token. Initial formant measurements were taken by all three authors, aided by a custom-made formant extraction script in PRAAT, and adjustments were made by hand to correct problematic measurements, when needed. The data were checked for inter-rater reliability across measurements following the initial coding. For all vowel classes analyzed here, no tokens with a preceding or following /r/ or /l/ were used, and tokens with a following nasal were also excluded. In addition, following velars and nasals were excluded for the BAT class. Each of these segment types was avoided as they can lead to irregularities in formant patterns that make instrumental vowel analysis more difficult. No more than three instances of a particular lexeme were extracted for inclusion in our mean measurements. Following formant measurement, the data were normalized using the Lobanov (1971) z-score formula. Data were normalized using measurements extracted across an entire speaker's vowel system from the conversational speech portions of the interviews. F1 and F2 were measured at three points in the vowel's duration – 20%, 50%, and 80%. Measurements of F1 were taken to represent vowel height, while measurements of F2 were taken to represent vowel frontness/backness.

Vowel plots were then created using R (R Core Team 2020), and the data compared across speakers. For all vowel plots used in this analysis, ten tokens per vowel class were measured, with the value of each class plotted representing the mean across those ten tokens. These values are plotted using Wells' 1982 notation system for all vowel classes save two: BAT and SHOES. The SHOES vowel class is a special subclass of /u/ that separates out pre-vocalic coronals, as these segments have been found to condition significant fronting versus non-coronals in previous studies of Columbus vowel systems (e.g., Durian 2012, Durian et al. 2010, Thomas 2001). Meanwhile BAT is a combined vowel class that includes short /ae/ tokens belonging to both Wells's BATH and TRAP classes. Note that the PRICE class has been left out of our vowel plots to allow a clearer picture of how BAT, LOT, THOUGHT, and MOUTH occupy the low vowel space for each speaker.

For analysis and vowel plotting purposes, the traditional monophthongs (KIT, DRESS, BAT, LOT, THOUGHT, STRUT, and FOOT) use a measurement of the steady state taken at the 50% point of the vowel's duration. Vowels that are commonly treated as diphthongs (FLEECE, FACE, MOUTH, GOAT, GOOSE, and SHOES) use measurements taken at 20% and 80% to represent the nucleus and offglide, with arrowheads marking the offglide.

4.2 Middle class comparative analysis

Turning first to the older female speakers, shown in Figure 7, we can see that the older African American woman (S001) has a more conservative vowel system than the older European American woman (S002). This is most clearly seen by the position of GOOSE, GOAT, BAT, and DRESS in S001's vowel system. BAT is fronter and higher, while GOOSE and GOAT are somewhat backer than these same vowel classes in S002's system, as most easily noted by comparing the relative position of these vowel classes to THOUGHT noted in both women's systems. As discussed in more detail in Durian (2012), S002's BAT and DRESS show somewhat backed and lowered realizations, trends indicating the early progression of the Third Dialect Shift. This trend is typical for women born around the same time as S002 in Columbus. In terms of other vowel trends found in previous studies of Columbus, S001 also has a LOT and THOUGHT that are more distinctive than S002, who shows closer means, which, as also discussed in more detail in Durian (2012), are indicative of a partially merged set of classes. Compared to other speakers in Columbus, S001's FLEECE is also more diphthongal, as indicted by the somewhat pronounced offglide. Meanwhile, S001's FACE, KIT, and MOUTH classes are in the "standard position" for a speaker from Columbus.

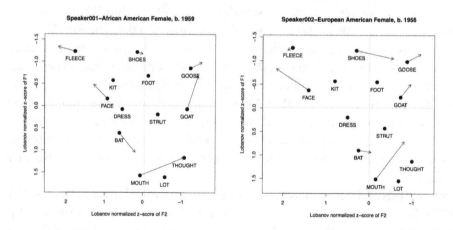

Figure 7: Vowel system of older women

In comparison to S001 and S002, as shown in Figure 8, S003 and S004 show more pronounced patterns of vowel shift for many of the vowel classes indicated to be undergoing notable variation in middle class European American English in Durian's (2012) analysis. These include the fronting of nuclei of SHOES, GOOSE, FOOT, and GOAT, and the backing/lowering of the nucleus of BAT, DRESS, and

KIT. These changes together represent three of the four that Durian (2012) cou-
pled together as the Third Dialect Shift. In addition, both women show some
retraction of the nucleus of MOUTH, and both speakers show at least partial
merger of LOT and THOUGHT. Here the overlap between classes is more pronounced in S004's vowel system, a trend that is more indicative of the larger community, where younger African American women are also beginning to show the
LOT/THOUGHT merger, but less frequently than European American women.

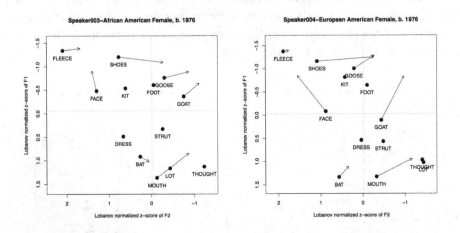

Figure 8: Vowel systems of younger women

As with the older speakers, the European American speaker (S004) shows
each of these vowel change tendencies more robustly than the African American speaker (S003). However, both women show change tendencies in the same
direction, and both have changes in that direction that show an intensification of
these patterns versus the S001 and S002. This leads us to conclude that: a) each
of these vocalic change trends appear to be a change in progress for both middle
class European and African American women in Columbus; b) middle class European American women are leading these changes versus their African American
counterparts; and c) by showing changes in the same direction, European American and African American females show strong patterns of convergence for these
vowel classes.

Turning to our male speakers, we can see that, as with our female speakers,
older male speakers in both groups have more conservative patterns of vowel
variation than younger speakers. This is especially true for the nuclei of the back
vowels GOOSE, SHOES, GOAT, and FOOT, as well as the short front vowels BAT,
DRESS, and KIT. Generally, between groups, European American men show

more robust lowering of the nucleus of BAT and DRESS versus African American men, and less robust, but still notable lowering of the nucleus of KIT. This is shown clearly in the vowel plots for S005 and S006, both shown in Figure 9. For the back vowels, European American men also show somewhat stronger fronting trends for the back vowel classes GOOSE, SHOES, and GOAT, than African American men, as also shown in the plots. For FOOT, the African American male (S005) shows a stronger pattern of fronting than the European American male. This is a trend that shows less consistency among men in this age group than the other trends discussed here. In other words, sometimes African American men show more fronting for this class, as in the plots here, while other times, European American men show more fronting.

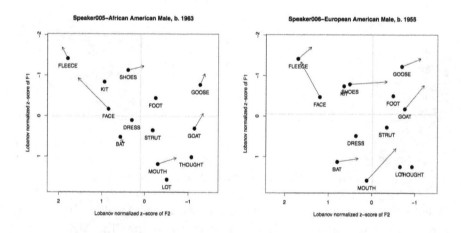

Figure 9: Vowel system of older men

For the LOT and THOUGHT merger, the African American male (S005) does not show signs of extensive merger, whereas the European American male does. In addition, the African American male (S006) shows strong retraction of MOUTH, whereas the European American male does not. Given that similar differences are found between our younger men for these classes, we argue these differences may represent the residual influence of Southern speech on male speech in Columbus, while the retraction of MOUTH may represent a secondary influence of Pittsburgh speech. This is an idea we will return to in the next section.

For the younger men (S007 and S008) and shown in Figure 10, like younger women, we see a continuation of the vowel variation trends found in the vowel systems of the older men, with a stronger increase in each of those trends in the younger men's vowel systems. For SHOES, GOOSE, and GOAT, in particular, the younger men show more fronting than the older men. Between the younger men, the European American male S007 shows stronger fronting for SHOES, GOOSE and GOAT than S008, the African American male. We also see further lowering and backing of BAT and DRESS for the younger men versus the older men, with the European American male showing stronger lowering trends than the African American male. KIT also continues to show backing, although the data here does not suggest a strong generational difference between the older men's groups and the younger men's groups, nor a strong difference between men based on race. As with the back vowels, the vowel lowering/backing trends for BAT, DRESS, and KIT show a continuation and intensification of the vowel variation patterns found in older men's speech.

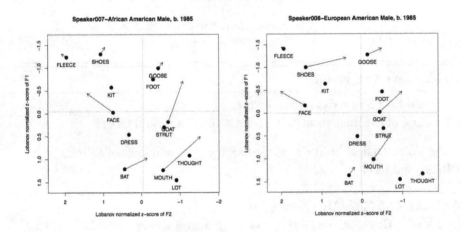

Figure 10: Vowel system of younger men

Overall, the male trends shown here lead us to reach similar conclusions to those we drew for women's speech. Namely: a) each of these vocalic change trends appear to be a change in progress for both middle class European and African American men in Columbus; b) middle class European American men are leading these changes versus their African American counterparts; and c) by showing changes in the same direction, European American and African American males show strong patterns of convergence for these vowel classes. As with women's speech, these findings suggest middle class African American males also appear to be making use of the Third Dialect Shift, albeit to a lesser extent than either European American males or African American females. Related to this trend is also the noticeable difference in LOT and THOUGHT realization for African American men in our study – the lack of LOT/THOUGHT merger. Since LOT is not as back as it would be due to the merger in these men's vowel spaces, this allows less space for BAT to retract, and by analogy, also less space for DRESS to retract.

In sum, the analysis in this section reveals that middle class African Americans and European Americans are showing increasing convergence in their vowel systems. This trend can be seen most clearly in two areas of the vowel system: a) the back vowels SHOES, GOOSE, FOOT, and GOAT; and b) the short front vowels BAT, DRESS, and KIT. More generally, b) suggests that both ethnic groups are converging by showing increasing use of the Third Dialect Shift. At the same time, these groups also show some increasing divergence from one another, with LOT and THOUGHT (near-)merger found more heavily in middle class EAE than in middle class AAE. These realization patterns are summarized in Table 3.

Table 3: Comparison of results among working-class AAE and EAE speakers

Middle class AAE vs. EAE
AAE and EAE Show Convergence for: - Fronting of the nucleus of SHOES, GOOSE, FOOT, and GOAT - The Third Dialect Shift (in particular, lowered and backed articles of BAT, DRESS, and KIT)
AAE and EAE Show Divergence for: - Lack of LOT/THOUGHT merger (among male speakers)

4.3 Summary: A comparison of middle class/working class AAE and EAE vowel systems

Taken together, the trends revealed in section §4.2 suggest a general pattern of convergence is found among middle class African Americans and European Americans not only for the back vowels SHOES, GOOSE, FOOT, and GOAT, but also the short front vowels BAT, DRESS, and KIT. This contrasts with the working-class data analyzed for Columbus in Durian et al. (2010), where we find convergence between African Americans and European Americans for fronting of the nuclei of the non-low back vowels SHOES, BOOT, FOOT, and GOAT, but then divergence for the nuclei of KIT, DRESS, BAT, THOUGHT, and LOT. As mentioned earlier, working class African Americans show the use of the AAE Shift in their speech. That is, KIT, DRESS, and BAT raising, and THOUGHT and LOT fronting, while working class European Americans show backer articulations of THOUGHT and LOT and non-raising or mild lowering of KIT, DRESS, and BAT.

For the working-class speakers, divergence of the KIT, DRESS, and BAT classes appears to be a result of working-class African Americans participating in the AAVE Shift (as per Thomas 2007), while for middle class speakers, the convergence of these classes appears to be the result of middle-class African Americans participating in the Third Dialect Shift (as per Durian 2012).

Table 4: Comparison of results among middle- and working-class AAE and EAE speakers

Working class AAE vs. EAE	Middle class AAE vs. EAE
AAE and EAE show convergence for: - Fronting of the nucleus of SHOES, GOOSE, FOOT, GOAT, and MOUTH	AAE and EAE show convergence for: - Fronting of the nucleus of SHOES, GOOSE, FOOT, and GOAT - The Third Dialect Shift (lowered and backed articulations of LOT, BAT, DRESS, and KIT)
AAE and EAE Show Divergence for: - Fronter articulation of THOUGHT and raised articulation of STRUT - The AAVE Shift (Raised articulations of KIT, DRESS, and BAT, and fronter articulation of LOT)	AAE and EAE Show Divergence for: - Lack of LOT/THOUGHT merger (among male speakers)

More generally, considering not only the number of vowels showing stronger similarities, but also the degree of similarity found between middle class speakers versus working class speakers, our middle-class African Americans show stronger convergence with the vowel systems of the middle-class European Americans than our working-class African Americans show with working class European Americans. The overall differences between these patterns of convergence and divergence are summarized in Table 4. Vowel plots of the working class African Americans showing the patterns referenced here can be found in Durian et al. (2010) for comparison.

As also shown in Table 1, although overall there are stronger patterns of convergence in middle class speech, one important difference remains between the middle class African Americans and European Americans in our data set. African Americans show a notable difference in the use of merged LOT and THOUGHT realizations. This difference is most notable in the speech of men, who do not appear to be engaging in the merger. However, women in our study also show less extensive participation than their European American counterparts. As younger women appear to be beginning to make some use of the merger, however, it remains to be seen whether this may eventually impact men's speech, as well. This question will make for an interesting area of study in future research.

5 The cross-regional and social implications of vocalic variation in Columbus

With regard to the relationship of Columbus African American speech to African American speech elsewhere, it would appear that, over time, the non-low back vowels of both working class and middle-class Columbus African Americans are becoming more like those described recently for certain other communities, namely Hyde County, NC (Wolfram & Thomas 2002), Texana, NC (Childs et al. 2010), and Memphis, TN (Fridland 2003, Fridland & Bartlett 2006). In these communities, similar tendencies towards back vowel fronting among African Americans and European Americans have been found. This is perhaps unsurprising, since historically, these vowels have typically shown evidence of this Southern-Shift-like-tendency in each of these areas, although the influence in Columbus may actually be from western Pennsylvania instead of the South proper.

The trends found among working class African American speakers for the raising of BAT, DRESS, and KIT, and the fronting of LOT, also resemble those found in Memphis by Fridland & Bartlett (2006), as well as Brooklyn, NY, and Cleveland Heights, OH by Thomas (2007). This suggests that working class African American speech in Columbus may be showing stronger alignment with more recent supra-regional African American English norms than middle class speech for these vowel classes. In particular, the supra-regional norm in play here appears to be participation in the AAVE Shift. On the other hand, the tendency towards lowering and backing of KIT, DRESS and BAT (the Third Dialect Shift) among middle class African Americans suggests middle class African American English shows stronger alignment with local Columbus norms, given their occurrence among at least some middle class European Americans, as well.

Turning to an exploration of potential social motivations for the patterns of convergence and divergence by social class in our study, it is important to consider the context in which contact between African Americans and European Americans in Columbus occurs. This situation may be leading to a complex situation of "home" vs. "school" language influence impacting the patterns shown in our study. For instance, the pattern of back diphthong convergence, especially among our young speakers, may be best explained by considering the impact of Columbus's school desegregation policies in the late 1960s to mid 1990s. Our older speakers went to school either before desegregation occurred or during the period when desegregation was purely voluntary. This led to a situation where only small groups of students began to attend more desegregated schools. On the other hand, following the implementation of busing in 1979, schools typically became strongly desegregated, such that schools that may have been 80% African American previously were now roughly 50% African American (Foster 1997). Thus, there was much higher face-to-face daily contact among black and white speakers during the "busing era" as a result, which have led to this pattern of shift among realizations.

Although students may now have been attending more racially mixed schools during the day, after school, in their home community, many working class students returned to areas that were majority African American. This would continue to facilitate strong daily face-to-face interaction among African Americans, which might also lead to an increase in usage of more variables that may be somehow more ethnically marked. Hence, we see a simultaneous increase in the use of variables marked by divergence, such as raised articulations of KIT, DRESS, and BAT, as well as fronting of LOT and THOUGHT among our working class younger speakers. Considering that both African American class groups show strong patterns of convergence for the back vowel diphthongs, this suggests these variables may not be ethnically marked, perhaps due to their having less perceptual saliency as markers of ethnic identity among community members. Such a contrast would explain why working class speakers show contrasting patterns of convergence and divergence, dependent on the vowel subsystem under discussion.

The general pattern of convergence for both the front and low back vowels, as well as the back vowel diphthongs, among middle class speakers, are more straightforward to explain. The areas in which middle class African Americans live are more strongly integrated than the areas in which most working class African Americans reside. It is plausible that the frequency of daily face-to-face interactions between ethnic groups would be increased in this setting. In addition, among our speakers included in this study, the social networks of middle

257

class speakers are often more diverse and expansive than those of their work-ing class colleagues. These expanded networks include regular interactions with speakers of different ethnic groups – in particular, European Americans – a fact discussed by all of the middle class African Americans surveyed for this study during their sociolinguistic interviews. As a result, this stronger integra-tion among speakers, including extended interaction with European American speakers, seems to be encouraging stronger patterns of convergence, a fact re-flected by the patterns of vowel system convergence shown by the speakers in-cluding here in our analysis.

Clearly, given the complexities of the social situation in Columbus, these are issues that require a more detailed study for confirmation. For now, we find the results of our pilot study have provided us with some possible explanations for these patterns. These issues, as well as the more robust documentation of the comparative patterns of vowel variation noted, are matters we hope to explore in a future study.

Acknowledgments

We wish to thank Yolanda Holt and Tinisha Tolbert for conducting interviews with middle class African American informants, as well as Rick Jones and Tammy Snow for conducting the fieldwork with working class African American infor-mants. We also thank Don Winford for providing us with access to this data.

Abbreviations

AAE   African American English
EAE   European American English

References

Anderson, Bridget L. 2002. Dialect leveling and /ai/monophthongization among African American Detroiters. *Journal of Sociolinguistics* 6(1). 86–98.

Andres, Claire & Rachel Votta. 2010. African American vernacular English: Vowel phonology in a Georgia community. *Publication of the American Dialect Society* 93(1). 75–98.

Atwood, E Bagby. 1951. Some Eastern Virginia pronunciation features. In Fredson Bowers (ed.), *English studies in honor of James Southall Wilson*, 111–24.

Bigham, Douglas S. 2010. Correlation of the low-back vowel merger and TRAP-retraction. *University of Pennsylvania Working Papers in Linguistics* 15(2). 21–31.

Boberg, Charles. 2005. The Canadian shift in Montreal. *Language variation and change* 17(2). 133–154.

Boersma, Paul & David Weenink. 2020. *PRAAT: Doing phonetics by computer. [computer program].* (Version 6.1.35). Available online. http://www.praat.org/.

Britt, Erica & Tracey L. Weldon. 2015. African American English in the middle class. In Sonja Lanehart (ed.), *The Oxford handbook of African American language*, 800–816. Oxford: Oxford University Press.

Bryant, Vinnie V. 1983. *Columbus, OH and the Great Migration.* Columbus, OH. (MA thesis).

Burgess, Patricia. 1994. *Planning for the private interest: Land use controls and residential patterns in Columbus, Ohio, 1900-1970.* Columbus, OH: Ohio State University Press.

Carver, Craig. 1987. The midlands: The upper South and lower North dialects. In *American regional dialects: a word geography*, 161–204. Ann Arbor: University of Michigan Press.

Childs, Becky, Christine Mallinson & Jeannine Carpenter. 2010. Vowel phonology and ethnicity in North Carolina. *Publication of the American Dialect Society* 94(1). 23–47.

Clarke, Sandra, Ford Elms & Amani Youssef. 1995. The third dialect of English: Some Canadian evidence. *Language Variation and Change* 7. 209–228.

Collins, William J. 2020. *The great migration of Black Americans from the US South: A guide and interpretation.* Tech. rep. National Bureau of Economic Research. http://www.nber.org/papers/w27268.

Durian, David. 2012. *A new perspective on vowel variation across the 19th and 20th centuries in Columbus, OH.* The Ohio State University. (Doctoral dissertation). http://rave.ohiolink.edu/etdc/view?acc_num=osu1356279130.

Durian, David, Robin Dodsworth & Jennifer Schumacher. 2010. Convergence in urban working class Columbus, OH AAVE and EAE vowel systems. In Erik R. Thomas & Malcah Yeager-Dror (eds.), *Vowel phonology and ethnicity* (Publication of the American Dialect Society 93), 161–190. Durham, NC: Duke University Press.

Fogle, Deena. 2008. Indianapolis, Indiana: A prototype of Midland convergence. *University of Pennsylvania Working Papers in Linguistics* 14(1). 134–148.

Foster, Paul Nathan. 1997. *Which September?: Segregation, busing and resegregation in the Columbus public schools, 1944-1996.* Harvard University. (BA Honors thesis).

Fridland, Valerie. 2003. Network strength and the realization of the Southern vowel shift among African Americans in Memphis, Tennessee. *American Speech* 78(1). 3–30.

Fridland, Valerie & Kathy Bartlett. 2006. The social and linguistic conditioning of back vowel fronting across ethnic groups in Memphis, Tennessee. *English Language and Linguistics* 1(10). 1–22.

Gordon, Matthew. 2000. Phonological correlates of ethnic identity: Evidence of divergence? *American Speech* 755(1). 115–136.

Jacobs, Gregory Scott. 1994. *Getting around Brown: Desegregation, development, and the Columbus public schools, 1954-1994.* The Ohio State University. (Doctoral dissertation).

James, Felix. 1972. *The American addition: The history of the African American community.* The Ohio State University. (Doctoral dissertation).

Kennedy, Robert & James Grama. 2012. Chain shifting and centralization in California vowels: An acoustic analysis. *American Speech* 87(1). 39–56.

Kurath, Hans, Marcus Hansen, Julia Bloch & Bernard Bloch (eds.). 1939. *Handbook of the linguistic geography of New England.* Providence, RI: Brown University.

Kurath, Hans & Raven Ioor McDavid. 1961. *The pronunciation of English in the Atlantic states: Based upon the collections of the linguistic atlas of the Eastern United States*, vol. 3 (Studies in American English). Ann Arbor: University of Michigan Press.

Labov, William. 1991. The three dialects of English. In Penelope Eckert (ed.), *New ways of analyzing sound change*, 1–44. New York: Academic Press.

Labov, William, Sharon Ash & Charles Boberg. 2006. *The Atlas of North American English: Phonetics, phonology, and sound change: A multimedia reference tool*, vol. 1. Berlin: Walter de Gruyter.

Labov, William & Wendell A. Harris. 1986. De facto segregation of Black and White vernaculars. In David Sankoff (ed.), *Diversity and diachrony*, 1–24. Amsterdam: John Benjamins.

Labov, William, Malcah Yaeger & Richard Steiner. 1972. *A quantitative study of sound change in progress*, vol. 1. Philadelphia: US Regional Survey.

Lemann, Nicholas. 1991. *The promised land: The great black migration and how it changed America.* New York: Vintage Press.

Lentz, Ed. 2003. *Columbus: The story of a city.* Charleston, SC: Arcadia Publishing.

Lobanov, Boris M. 1971. Classification of Russian vowels spoken by different speakers. *The Journal of the Acoustical Society of America* 49(2B). 606–608.

Luthin, Herbert W. 1987. The story of California (ow): The coming-of-age of English in California. In Keith Denning, Sharon Inkelas, Faye McNair-Knox &

John R. Rickford (eds.), *Variation in language: NWAV-XV at Stanford*, 312–24. Stanford, California: Department of Linguistics, Stanford University.

Murphy, Melvin L. 1970. *The Columbus urban league: A history, 1917-1967.* The Ohio State University, Columbus, OH. (Doctoral dissertation).

Oriedo, Evelyn. 1982. *African American business development: Its impact on the economic status of the African American community in Columbus, OH.* Columbus, OH: The Ohio State University, (MA thesis).

Pederson, Lee A. 1965. *The pronunciation of English in metropolitan Chicago* (Publication of the American Dialect Society 44). Alabama: University of Alabama Press.

Podesva, Robert J, Annette D'Onofrio, Janneke Van Hofwegen & Seung Kyung Kim. 2015. Country ideology and the California vowel shift. *Language Variation and Change* 27(2). 157.

R Core Team. 2020. *R: A Language and Environment for Statistical Computing.[Computer program]. (Version 4.0.3).* R Foundation for Statistical Computing. Vienna, Austria. https://www.R-project.org/.

Reece, Jason, Christy Rogers, Matt Martin, Liz Colombo, Dwight Holley & Melisa Lindsjo. 2012. *Neighborhoods and community development in Franklin County: Understanding our past and preparing for our future.* Tech. rep. Columbus, OH: The Kirwin Institute for the Study of Race & Ethnicity. The Ohio State University.

Roeder, Rebecca & Lidia-Gabriela Jarmasz. 2010. The Canadian shift in Toronto. *The Canadian Journal of Linguistics/La revue Canadienne de linguistique* 55(3). 387–404.

Thomas, Erik R. 1989. Vowel changes in Columbus, Ohio. *Journal of English linguistics* 22(2). 205–215.

Thomas, Erik R. 1996. A comparison of variation patterns of variables among sixth graders in an Ohio community. In Edgar W. Schneider (ed.), *Focus on the USA: Varieties of English around the world (general series)*, vol. 16, 309–332. Amsterdam: John Benjamins.

Thomas, Erik R. 2001. *An acoustic analysis of vowel variation in New World English* (Publication of the American Dialect Society 85). Durham, NC: Duke University Press.

Thomas, Erik R. 2007. Phonological and phonetic characteristics of African American vernacular English. *Language and Linguistics Compass* 1(5). 450–475.

Thomas, Erik R. & Malcah Yeager-Dror (eds.). 2010. *Vowel phonology and ethnicity. Publication of the American Dialect Society 93.* Durham, NC: Duke University Press.

U. S. Census Bureau. 2010. *United States census 2010.* Tech. rep. http://www. census.gov.

Wells, John Christopher. 1982. *Accents of English: Volume 1: An introduction.* Cambridge: Cambridge University Press.

Wetmore, Thomas Hall. 1959. *The low-central and low-back vowels in the English of the Eastern United States* (Publication of the American Dialect Society 32). Tuscaloosa, AL: University of Alabama Press.

Wolfram, Walt & Erik Thomas. 2002. *The development of African American English.* Oxford: Blackwell.

Wolfram, Walter A. 1969. *A sociolinguistic study of Detroit negro speech.* Arlington, VA: Center for Applied Linguistics.

Chapter 10

Talking about Creole: Language attitudes and public discourse in the Caribbean

Susannne Mühleisen

Universität Bayreuth

Language attitude studies form an important indicator for the acceptability of a variety in general or in particular domains like education or the media. Caribbean Creole languages have traditionally been stigmatised due to the fact that they arose in contact situations during plantation slavery. Especially when they are in continued contact with their lexifier, the Creole is often not seen as a legitimate variety of its own. Language attitudes studies in Trinidad by Winford (1976) and Mühleisen (2001) show, however, how the acceptance of Creole versus English has changed within two generations of Trinidadian schoolteachers. Ever since the publication of these quantitative survey-based studies, public opinion on language has been overwhelmingly expressed in traditional and digital media. A qualitative and quantitative analysis of language attitudes expressed in a corpus of just over 100 letters to the editor and in online forums as part of a public language debate in Jamaica will therefore update and complement the research findings in earlier studies.

1 Introduction: language attitudes and Caribbean Creoles

Language attitude studies have a long tradition in Creole studies, starting with Haynes' (1973) PhD research on contrastive language attitudes in Barbados and Guyana, followed by investigations on teacher attitudes towards Creole versus English in Trinidad (Winford 1976), Rickford's 1983 exploration of prestige and solidarity values of Guyanese Creole in a rural community in Guyana, a follow-up study on the Winford publication (Mühleisen 1993, 2001) which focuses on po-

Susannne Mühleisen. 2022. Talking about Creole: Language attitudes and public discourse in the Caribbean. In Bettina Migge & Shelome Gooden (eds.), *Social and structural aspects of language contact and change*, 263–285. Berlin: Language Science Press. DOI: 10.5281/zenodo.6979335

tential change of language attitudes in the Caribbean, as well as Beckford Wass-ink's (1999) investigation in a semi-rural community in Jamaica. Post-millenium research moved on to explore more the acceptability of accents of standard English rather than attitudes towards Creole versus English in Barbados (Belgrave 2008), in Trinidad (Deuber 2013, Deuber & Leung 2013, Meer et al. 2019), in the Bahamas (Oenbring & Fielding 2014) and in Jamaica (Westphal 2015). With this almost exclusive focus on accents of English in media and educational contexts in the last two decades, one might ask: is there still any more need for talking about Creole?[1]

In this article, I would like to revisit some of the early studies, notably Winford (1976), on how Creoles were perceived by their speakers in the post-independence period in the Caribbean, to then contrast the results with later research (e.g. Müh-leisen 1993, 2001, Beckford Wassink 1999) to show how some of the linguistic research on Creoles starting in the 1960/70s has also triggered a change in beliefs about these languages. The question of whether or not this conceptual conversion has also changed the affective stance and the readiness to act, e.g. to accept changes in language politics, will be posed. For an inclusion of the "public voice" on language political proposals in Jamaica, an analysis of a corpus of ca. 100 letters to the editor of the *Jamaican Gleaner*, collected between 1999 and 2020, will shed light on potential changes in the acceptance of Jamaican Patwa in language domains previously reserved for Standard English. This focus on self-selected public opinions will be complemented with an inclusion of comments and posts on social media platforms on the language petition posed in 2019.

Language attitudes are important in sociolinguistic research in that they reveal social evaluations in connection with a particular group of speakers. Firstly, they are important in exposing associations between speech patterns and a speaker's membership in a particular social or ethnic group or community of practice. Secondly, they also show perceived correlations between speech patterns and personal qualities of an individual speaker (e.g. friendliness, intelligence, reliability, etc.). As mental variables, attitudes are not per se observable but they help to explain, predict or are related to patterns of behaviour. For language attitude

---

[1]The term Creole will be used in this paper as a general term for the type of contact language found in the Caribbean (and elsewhere). It is always capitalized to make clear its status as a language on par with English, French, etc. It can be modified (e.g. Trinidadian English Creole, Jamaican Creole) to denote the specific national Creole. Patois is the Jamaican name for their Creole, hence, the terms (Jamaican Patois, Jamaican Creole) will alternate without any meaning change. Patwa is a spelling variant of Patois which is often employed by the users themselves. This will be used especially in quotations and in the specific Jamaican language debate which is discussed in this paper.

studies, this means that this "learned predisposition to respond in a consistently favourable or unfavourable manner" (Fishbein & Ajzen 1975: 6) with regard to a particular language code has to be elicited indirectly: beliefs about the variety/speech pattern in question (cognitive component), feelings and emotions towards the variety/speech pattern (affective component) and disposition to act (behavioural component).

The practice of evaluating other people's speech positively or negatively has probably existed as long as there has been some kind of social differentiation between speakers in a community. In English language contexts, public debates about linguistic correctness and arguments about authority in the English language go back to at least the 18th century, when much of what is still seen as the standard conventions in English were established through works like Dr Johnson's *Dictionary* (1755) or the grammar books by Robert Lowth (1762) and Lindley Murray (1795). As Burridge (2010: 5) writes, they are often "complaints about the language of others; i.e. observations on what is viewed as bad grammar, sloppy pronunciations, new-fangled words, vulgar colloquialisms, unwanted jargon and, of course, foreign items." It is notable that, for the diglossic situation in the anglophone Caribbean (Winford 1985), the question of attitudes toward Creole, however, takes on a different dimension from the issues pointed out above: it is the evaluation of the two linguistic codes which have been used in functional distribution since the time of their presence in the Caribbean, one historically laden with the colonial baggage and association with slavery, the other not only the traditional "high" language in the diglossic situation but also a language with ever-increasing global significance (cf. also Mühleisen 2002). There are not only functional divides but also symbolic ones: as Reisman (1970) pointed out so succinctly, both Creole and English are implicitly not only linguistic but also cultural codes connected to values of British/European versus African/Jamaican heritage. It is therefore no surprise that in most Creole attitude studies (e.g. Rickford 1983, Beckford Wassink 1999) this linguistic and cultural ambiguity is also reflected in an ambivalent stance toward Creole by its speakers in that it achieves positive evaluations on a solidarity and friendship scale but low ratings on the level of power and authority.

2 50 years on: Language attitude studies as barometer of change in educational contexts

It is now five decades since Reisman's (1970) anthropological observation of the connection between situational language choice and alignment with cultural values in the Caribbean and since the research was conducted by Winford in 1970 for the first Caribbean language attitude publication (Winford 1976). The agenda pointed out in his article is first of all one of improving language teaching techniques for in the complex Caribbean language situation. Language attitudes by teachers, as Winford notes, might be a factor in determining progress in language acquisition:

> [Another] problem which must be stressed is the likelihood that the child's progress in the acquisition of new language skills is determined to a large extent by the attitudes to language varieties which prevail in the community. Again, relatively little research has been done in this area, and the present article attempts to remedy this situation to some extent by reporting on the attitudes of teachers themselves to the linguistic situation in their community. (Winford 1976: 48)

Winford's choice of educators as informants, then, was not random but well chosen: the position of the teacher is that of an influential multiplier of beliefs about language and other subjects and can help to shape future dispositions to act. On the other hand, teachers are also prone to follow idealized models of correctness. One of the most striking results of his questionnaire survey with 112 respondents (68 of Indian, 44 of African descent) from two different teacher training colleges in Trinidad was their evaluation of characteristics of Trinidadian Creole as "bad", "broken" or/and "incorrect":

> ...most of the respondents had a very clear picture of the characteristics of Trinidadian English that could be labelled "bad", "broken", "incorrect", etc., by comparison with whatever model of correctness each had in mind. At the same time, it seems clear that most respondents were not at all conscious of the fact that the Creole variety of Trinidadian English has its own grammatical system which operates according to different rules from those of Standard English. Informants generally show a great willingness to interpret what are essentially grammatically correct Creole structures as "corruptions" of "good English". (Winford 1976: 51)

One of the achievements of linguistics research and resolution is a greater consciousness of the nature and value of Creole languages. As a follow up study (Mühleisen 1993, 2001) to Winford (1976) shows, two decades after the initial research, the distinction between Standard English and Trinidadian English Creole (TEC) is more clear to the respondents in the 1990s. For the 90 primary and secondary school teachers in Mühleisen (1993, 2001) Creole is not seen any more as "bad English". As one respondents writes in an open question section:

It is an integral part of our society and is rich in our linguistic tradition. It has a vibrant role to play and should not be described as 'Bad English' since it is a language in its own rights. I think people have to be better educated about the richness and evolution of Trinidadian Creole and its importance in their everyday lives. The media especially has an important role to play. (Resp. 029: F/Age 1/Pr/TC/Semi-urban/Ind.) (Mühleisen 2001: 74)

However, along with the heightened awareness of the separateness of the codes, an attentiveness to their functional distribution in interpersonal and situational contexts has also increased (see Table 1 from Mühleisen 2001: 66)

Table 1: Language choice on an interpersonal level

	Creole	Standard	Both[a]
a. With Parents	76.1%	17.0%	6.8%
b. With Spouse	72.2%	22.8%	5.1%
c. With Children	28.2%	61.2%	10.6%
d. With Friends	65.5%	19.5%	14.9%
e. At Work, With Colleagues	22.7%	59.1%	18.2%
f. At Work, in Classroom	3.4%	91.0%	5.6%
g. In Church	9.5%	79.8%	10.7%
h. When "Liming"	84.9%	9.3%	5.8%
i. When Quarrelling	79.5%	12.0%	8.4%
j. Telling Jokes	92.1%	5.6%	2.2%
k. New Acquaintance	10.2%	84.1%	5.7%
l. When Introduced to a Trinidadian Abroad	30.6%	62.4%	7.1%

[a]This choice was not explicitly given in the questionnaire but some respondents ticked both Creole and Standard (English) in this section.

Creole as a language choice was clearly limited in classic (high) "H" domains classroom, church and work (e, f, g) and was also made less frequently in interpersonal contacts where awareness about one's self-presentation (k, l) is requested, or with children (c) where considerations of educational success and a desire for upward social mobility might be at stake. In contrast to the findings in Winford (1976), the limitation of Trinidadian English Creole is not seen in the code itself but rather in its restricted usefulness in particular language domains or as a language of international communication.

Susannne Mühleisen

The dynamic perspective in this diachronic-comparative study on language attitudes and factors of change shows that language evaluation patterns within the anglophone Caribbean are not unalterable. The conceptual level, beliefs and knowledge about an object, are usually seen as vital for attitude formation. Ajzen goes as far as postulating that "attitudes are not merely related to beliefs, they are actually a function of beliefs, i.e, beliefs are assumed to have a causal effect on attitudes" (1989: 247, italics in the original, S.M.). To put it differently, the concept of the nature of a Creole, what speakers know or think they know about Creole, may also influence their overall language attitudes. However, in surveys and interviews as well as in experimental research, respondents also often comply with what they think is expected by the researchers, especially in the educational context. While the cognitive part of their attitudes towards Creole may have been influenced by the learned knowledge that Creole is a legitimate language, the affective and behavioral part may not always follow in the same way. In a classroom report by Youssef & Deuber (2012) this becomes evident when linguistics students had access to schools and classroom and teacher discourse and were able to observe language attitudes in a variety of classes including some where the Caribbean Advanced Proficiency Examinations (CAPE) syllabus in Communication Studies which explicates and educates on the local language situation was conveyed. As they report,

> Only two days ago a student, now working part-time on the larger project, recounted to us an interaction within which a student had declared 'But the Creole sounds so 'retarded'!' and the teacher had replied 'Yes, but we have to accept it anyway!' Clearly, despite the syllabus' best efforts, negative attitudes to the Creole still loom large! (Youssef & Deuber 2012: 5)

In a different regional Caribbean context, the hierarchy of attitude components can also be seen in Beckford Wassink's study "Historic low prestige and seeds of change: Attitudes toward Jamaican Creole" (1999) on speaker attitudes in Gordon Town, Jamaica. Her structured interview questions are sub-grouped into three different categories – "feel", "use" and "hear" questions – in her investigation of patterns in respondents' attitudes towards Jamaican Creole. Questions designed to reflect the respondents' reported willingness to use Jamaican Patois in a number of contexts ("use"-questions such as "Would use JC to answer the telephone" or "Would address their employer/supervisor in JC") clearly scored lowest among speakers of all age and both gender groups while questions about knowledge and feelings (such as "Feel knowledge of JC is an asset" or "Believe JC can be used to say anything one could say in English") scored highest (1999: 72).

3   The linguist and the public voice: language ideology and politics in interaction

Linguistics research in the area of language attitudes towards Creoles and prestige change has not only sought to inform and increase the knowledge about the nature and value of the varieties but also to change people's disposition to act. The anglophone Caribbean country where linguistic debates and language politics have been led most publicly and fervently in the last three decades is, arguably, Jamaica. In 1986, Devonish states that "even when the language question is not raised in any explicit manner, social and political conflict in the area of language is nevertheless present." And he adds, "in fact, the absence of any open debate on the language question is itself and expression of the complete control which those who benefit from the linguistic status quo have over the minds of the population at large." But diglossic situations are not easily resolved, and especially when the H and the L (low) language are lexically related and the H language is one of not only local but also of global significance. Thus, some of the "popular struggles" Devonish describes in his *Language and Liberation* (1986: 87ff) are still being fought for the legal status and a function elevation of Creole in Jamaica and elsewhere, despite a number of macro-functional changes, for example in the inclusion of Creole in primary and, to some extent, secondary education (cf. Morren & Morren 2007).

The Jamaican Language Unit (JLU) of the University of the West Indies, with Devonish in charge as coordinator for much of its existence, has been influential in bringing language issues to the public. The adaptation of a consistent phonemic orthography (known as Cassidy orthography) to Jamaican Patwa did not remain in the university classrooms but were brought to the public by publications and user-friendly materials (Jamaican Language Unit 2009a,b), collaborations with translations of the New Testament (2012) and popular books like Alice in Wonderland (2016) into Jamaican Patwa in the Cassidy spelling and, last but not least, by the publication of a regular column in the *Jamaican Gleaner* by cultural studies professor Carolyn Cooper from the 1990s on (cf. also Mühleisen 1999).

There have been also a number of language political proposals to the Jamaican government, Ministry of Education, and the public spearheaded by the JLU. In 2001, a presentation was made to the House of Parliament of Jamaica on the issue of language rights in the Jamaican constitution. The Ministry of Education began the Bilingual Education Program (BEP) which included assigning equal status to Jamaican Creole in three pilot schools and supporting teachers in both languages (Morren & Morren 2007). In 2005, the Jamaican Language Unit conducted an island-wide Language Attitude Survey with 1,000 Jamaicans of various regional affiliations, age groups and social and occupational groups in order to generally assess the views of Jamaicans towards Jamaican Creole. Since one of the agendas of the survey was also to elicit whether or not the public would accept a proposal for making Patwa a co-official language in Jamaica, some selected results will be briefly discussed here.

There was large agreement (almost 79.5%) that Patwa is a language and that it should be made an official language alongside English (68.4%). There was an almost equal score on questions where the use of Creole in public written space (road signs, school books, medicine bottles, etc.) was concerned and a high number of respondents supported the use of both Patwa and English in school. But the results also showed a surprising number of persistent stereotypes in the affective section of the evaluations: the results for questions of what sounded more intelligent (Patwa: 7.3%, English: 55.0% and both: 32.9%) or educated (Patwa: 5.9%, English: 59.1% and both: 30.8%) seem to go along with the classic power associations from earlier studies like Rickford (1983). However, on the solidarity level Patwa also did not reach an unchallenged position: on the level of honesty (Patwa: 28.3%, English: 27.8%, both: 35.3%) and helpfulness (Patwa: 30.0%, English: 24.2%, both: 34.8%) Patwa and English were rated almost equally, but Patwa was scoring slightly better on the friendliness ratings (37.9%, 24.0%, 33.3%).

While the overall results of the survey remained ambiguous, the large agreement of the respondents would welcome Patwa as a co-official language in Jamaica paved the way to further proposals in that direction up to, finally, the submission of a petition in October 2019 to the Office of the Prime Minister demanding the government to take the necessary steps towards recognizing Jamaican Creole/Patwa as an official language alongside English (see analysis of comments in social media in section 4.2). For this step, the Jamaican public was not unprepared: ever since the early 2000s, Hubert Devonish and other members of the JLU regularly commented in the Jamaican newspaper *The Gleaner* (among others) on "language rights, justice and the constitution" (Devonish 2002), demanding to "stop demonizing Patois" (Devonish 2012), "end prejudice against Patois" (Devonish 2016) or "end Jamaican language apartheid" (Devonish 2018). The catchy titles of the linguist's opinion articles and comments, no doubt chosen by the editor of the newspaper, relate some of the heatedness of the debate which was not only taken up by linguists and politicians but also by members of the wider public, newspaper readers, in Letters to the Editor (LTEs) such as the following example from my corpus:

(1) **The patois debate continues,**

Published: 29 September 2001

THE EDITOR, Sir:

ONCE AGAIN the question of patois in schools is being debated. The statement by Minister Whiteman carried in the **'Gleaner'** of September 20 is very clear Jamaican Patois will not be taught in schools, and will not be elevated through the creolisation of the education system. This pronouncement should put to rest the fears (or hopes) of us all. As we all realise, English is the language of international diplomacy, trade and science. It is interesting to hear Macedonian townspeople speaking English to reporters, and even the Taliban leadership has at least one English-speaker. But we seem to have a problem here at home. As evidence, Minister Philip Paulwell told us on 'Nationwide' that a large tele-sales company in Montego Bay could not find enough speakers of standard English to fill the available jobs. This, in an English-speaking country, is beyond a joke.

Patois is a legitimate part of our identity and culture; we need not banish it from our lives. However, proficiency in English is almost mandatory today.

Incompetence can be a serious handicap; and the world is in no hurry to learn Jamaican Creole. My suggestion is that we treble or at least double current time and effort put into the teaching of English. Minister Whiteman used the word 'immersion'; which may be needed to make up for the lack of standard English in the daily lives of so many, especially our children.

(...)

So let us enjoy our patois; it is ours, it is astonishingly expressive and important to our identity. And what is to stop us earning the respect and admiration of the world for having made ourselves into the finest speakers of the English language on the planet.

I am, etc.,

D. B.

I will take these letters as expressions of language attitudes – this time not elicited from selected groups of respondents as in questionnaire surveys and experiments but self-selected by readers with a strong opinion on language matters. In the following section (§4.1), some examples of my corpus of just over 100 such letters on the Patwa language debate, collected in the Jamaican Gleaner between 1999 and 2020, will be given and analyzed with regard to the language attitudes expressed in them.

4 Letters to the editor and public language debates in Jamaica

Letters to the editor have existed as a genre at least since the late 18th century (cf. Sturiale 2016). As text type, the Letter to the Editor is typically argumentative, with the main communicative purpose of defending, analyzing or refuting an issue. While some letter writers might initiate a topic, the main body of LTEs are intertextual in that they are a reaction to a previously published article or letter by another reader. The example (1) above is therefore typical in its intertextual reference to another newspaper article, the statement by Minister Whiteman some days previous to the publication of the letter. LTEs are overtly addressed to the newspaper editor ("dear Editor, Sir", "dear Editor, Madam") but the covert addressee is the wider public and, specifically, the readership of the newspaper to which it is addressed. Expressing an opinion or making a complaint about something are primary functions of the genre LTE, others have been found to be "resolving a conflict, or to convincing readership and arousing reactions (cf. also Morrison & Love's reference as "problem-solution discourse", 1996: 50).

The proponents of the debate, Hubert Devonish or Carolyn Cooper as prominent UWI activists, are often subject of agreement or disagreement themselves, as some examples of titles from my corpus suggest, e.g. *"'God' to Cooper:* Tap di foolinish!" (03/05/2011), *Opposed to views of Boyne, Cooper* (28/12/2011), *The irony that is Carolyn Cooper* (08/08/2012), *The miseducation of Carolyn Cooper* (24/12/2014), or *Devonish's Patwa economics nonsensical* (04/02/2017). In contrast to the conventions to the genre, there is also one example in my corpus where the letter is directly addressed to Carolyn Cooper (as opposed to the editor):

(2)   **Patois is geographically limited**
      Published: Tuesday | August 10, 2010 | 12:00 AM
      THE EDITOR, Sir:
      PLEASE PUBLISH as a letter to Carolyn Cooper.
      Dear Carolyn: Re your August 8, 2010, article 'Reading and writhing':
      Most Jamaicans are not as concerned with the legitimacy of Jamaican as
      they are with its viability in the "flat world" in which we live. Can our
      present students become the assertive, effective arbitrators and wielders
      of power as they represent our country among the other world leaders
      with whom they must interact?
      It is interesting how vehemently you speak for the rights of the Jamaican
      student to speak his or her language even as you wield with great facility

and ease the words of the English language to cut down contemptuously those who would challenge you. Do you not recognise that that facility is exactly what the defenders of English crave for their children?

...

In this heated language debate, many people feel challenged in their notion of what is correct or what standards should be upheld. Any attempt to challenge the belief in such notions of unique and eternal standards of correctness will inevitably attract criticism, scorn, as some traitors to the creed – usually linguists – had to experience (cf. Burridge 2010: 6). She writes about the conflicting roles of language professionals versus users in language debates in Australia, "linguists are clearly also in a tricky position. In the eyes of the wider speech community, they are seen as supporters of a permissive ethos encouraging the supposed decline and continued abuse of Standard English (Burridge 2010: 8).

4.1 Data collection and analysis

My corpus consists of just over 100 LTEs to the *Jamaican Gleaner* in two time periods: 40 samples of LTEs on the Patois language debate were collected between 1999 and 2002 and another 62 cases between 2010 and early 2020. Therefore, the collection makes no claim to completeness but intends to provide a relatively good overview of the state of the debate in a large time frame. The examples were coded for a number of characteristics (sex of author, intertextual reference, potential claim of authority of author, overall communicative function of the letter and attitude towards elevating the status of Patwa and using it in public functions, i.e. in education, as co-official language or as language of writing. Table 2 gives that information together with title and date for the year 2011 as an example.

For the purpose of the reflection on the usefulness of including LTEs as material for language attitude studies, the results of the positive, negative or ambiguous evaluation of Patwa in public space will be given according to year of collection (for a more detailed analysis of other aspects of the data, cf. Mühleisen forthcoming).

Table 2: Dates, title and features of LTEs in 2011

2011	Title	Sex	Intertext	Authority	Function	Attitude
08/01	*Closing gaps in education*	M	+ article	-	inform	+/−
19/01	*Nationalising Creole? You've got to be kidding!*	M	+ article	-	disagree	−
12/04	*Defending Patois*	M	+ article	linguist	disagree	+
14/04	Fait a Yaad, Daans Abraad	F	-	-	disagree	+/−
17/04	*Teach English as foreign language*	M	-	teacher	disagree	−
19/04	*Argue logically for Patois*	M	+ article	-	inform	+/−
20/04	*Patois is best route to English*	M	-	-	agree	+
24/04	*Jamaica must stick to the rules of English*	M	-	-	disagree	−
27/04	*Blinded by self-importance*	M	+ letter	-	disagree	−
03/05	*'God' to Cooper:* Tap di foolinish!	?	-	-	disagree	−
07/05	*Ignorant stance on language*	F	+ letter	-	disagree	+
24/05	*Patois lessons quite realistic*	?	-	-	inform	+
03/10	*Dick's stance on Patois absurd*	M	+ article	-	disagree	−
18/10	*Patois as a first language: nonsense*	M	-	-	disagree	−
28/12	*Opposed to views of Boyne, Cooper*	M	+ article	-	disagree	−

The results show no coherent picture with regard to percentage of positive or negative language attitudes expressed in the letters, nor does there seem to be a linear development. Rather, there appear to be recurring swings in the one or the other direction. The overall number of positive (47) versus negative (45) language attitudes is almost perfectly balanced, with ambiguous attitudes expressed in 10 letters altogether. However, what is significant is the peak of letters in some

Table 3: Language attitudes in LTEs per year

Year	Total #	Pos. #	Pos. %	Neg. #	Neg. %	Ambig. #	Ambig. %
1999	11	5	45.45	5	45.45	1	9.00
2000	2	1	50.00	0	0.00	1	50.00
2001	15	8	53.33	6	40.00	1	6.66
2002	12	7	58.33	5	41.66	0	0.00
2010	4	1	25.00	3	75.00	0	0.00
2011	15	4	26.66	8	53.33	3	20.00
2012	7	5	71.43	2	28.57	0	0.00
2013	1	0	0.00	1	10.00	0	0.00
2014	2	1	50.00	1	50.00	0	0.00
2015	2	0	0.00	0	0.00	2	10.00
2016	5	3	60.00	2	40.00	0	0.00
2017	5	1	20.00	3	60.00	1	20.00
2018	3	2	66.66	1	33.33	0	0.00
2019	13	7	53.38	5	38.46	1	7.70
2020	5	2	40.00	3	60.00	0	0.00

periods of time, i.e. in 1999, 2001, 2002, 2011 and 2019. In the last case, the rise in participation in the language debate is clearly related to the petition submitted in October 2019 to recognize Jamaican Creole/Patwa as co-official language.

4.2 Langwij Pitishan: Comments in social media

The petition/pitishan was submitted in both English and Patwa to "make Jamaican an official language alongside English/Mek Jamiekan wahn ofishal langwij saida Ingglish."[2] Timed to celebrate the 100th anniversary of Jamaican poet Louise Bennett, "one of the biggest champions of the Jamaican language", the petition called "on the Government and Parliament of Jamaica to take all the steps necessary to grant official status to Jamaican, alongside English." The petition was also published in the Jamaican newspaper *Observer* on December 4th, 2019 with signatures from Jamaican and international supporters.

The appeal received a lot of attention but did not achieve the necessary number of votes – despite the overt agreement of respondents of the survey in 2005

[2]https://opm.gov.jm/participate/jamaica-house-petition/sign-petition/?pet=100

cited in section 3 of this article to make Jamaican Patwa a co-official language. Reactions to the petition can be seen in yet another public medium, the social media platform Facebook page of JLU member and proponent of the petition, Joseph Farquharson. The comments and contributions on this site on the issue of Patwa as official language, once again, may not be representative in that they do not include the voices of those who were not interested enough to sign the petition or reject it but, rather, is restricted to those who are happy to give their opinion about the issue in public.

As of January 24th 2020, there were 97 entries altogether which can be grouped into 40 comments with multiple interactive threads. The gender distribution of the contributors – deduced from profile name and/or picture of the person[3] – was clearly male-dominated, with 28 male contributors, 17 female writers plus the (male) author/moderator of the website.

Comment 1 (with three contributors and the author interacting) takes issue with the perceived difficulty to read and write Patwa (and practical reasons to not use it):

Comment 1

M1[4] This might become a reality but not in this life time, cause it's too difficult to read, spell and write, it would have to be a broad base approach where everyone wishes just write and spell the words his/her way, then everyone would go back to basic of spelling and pronouncing, honestly, I was reading a chapter of this language recently and it took me about an hour to do so, which then reminded me of my days at BASIC School learning to read.

4 likes, 1 love

F1 to M1 I love our native and first language, but if English so hard for some; how easy will it be for them to read and understand this our native language.

1 like, 1 love

M1 to F1 My conclusion is that the only aspect of this native language that most of us will ever understand is to speak it,but as it relates to the spelling and writing aspects it's a nono.

---

[3] This could be staged, of course, so there is no absolute certainty on the gender identity of the participants.

[4] The profile names of the Facebook users were anonymized and coded as Male 1 (M1), Female 1 (F1) in order of appearance. Author is abbreviated as A.

1 like

F2 to M1 learned it in a day, reading fluently from the patwa bible. (includes video)

A to M1 writing always has to be taught, no matter what language it is. People in England are not born writing in English. They have to be taught it in school.

The advantage of the contributions in the social media platform over the expression of opinions in the Letters to the Editor becomes immediately clear: the interactive format allows for immediate reactions to a post. Additional feedback (approval, humour) may also be seen in the distribution of a "like," "love," or "laugh" button by other participants. The author, in this and other comments, acts as a moderator to the discussion/debate. In comment 1, it becomes clear that the alleged necessity to write Patwa in a certain way forms an obstacle to M1 – a worry which is refuted by the other interactants in the thread. Other comments concern the affective stance of contributors and the belief that Patois is a hindrance to development (emotional and practical reasons), as can be seen in the following one:

Comment 17:

F8 English, English must be spoken and taught. Why are they encouraging people to be backward? This so called patio [sic] is just a massive hindrance to development.

1 laugh

A to F8 nowhere in the petition does it say English will not be spoken and taught. It says ALONGSIDE English.

1 like

F8 Patio should never be taught in schools at all it sounds ugly and vulgar it's total waste of time instead beautiful languages like Spanish French German should be that would be beneficial for job.opportunities and self improvement

1 laugh

A to F8 my mother language is not ugly and vulgar. I once saw a quote that said what we say about a language is a reflection of how we view the people who speak it.

M3 to F8 as much as I am against teaching patois in schools as standard your comments reeks of ignorance

1 like

The contribution by F8 shows a negative evaluation of Patwa on the level of emotive and behavioral stance. Again, we can see in the post of M3 to F8 how the interaction possibilities of the medium have an immediate counteractive effect. Not all comments are interactive, i.e. evoke a reaction by another participant. In the following, we have a number of relatively short and rather isolated comments, displaying both positive (comment 28, 31) and negative (29, 30) attitudes towards the petition. The rejection of the idea rests on practical reasons rather than aesthetic or emotive ones. Apart from the issue of the perceived difficulty of reading and writing the code, the matter of costs of the language political measure is addressed in comment 32:

Comment 28:

F15 A waa u sah man mi love strate patwa mi seh

Comment 29:

M19 lol cant even read it

A You can learn. You are one of our brightest minds. This can't be too hard for you.

Comment 30:

M20 It is, already

Comment 31:

F16 Same like how we learned to do everything else....

Comment 32:

M21 The money for changing all government forms and other documents is waiting already!

Comment 33:

M22 No way that is a dumb idea English or Spanish

A English is already official, and the proposal does not rule out other languages being taught/learned.

Finally, the significance of English as a global language was also stressed as a reason for rejecting the petition:

Comment 34:

M23 Patwa can't be used as our official language because the rest of the world barely understand our dialect. That's 17ridiculous. If you can't communicate the English language fluently or at a satisfactory level then that will cause major problems for our society in terms of business and communications to the world market.
We are quite fine as an English speaking country and proud of it.
Dialect is a part of our language as well for our unique culture and heritage as Jamaicans and we will never refute that. But knowing proper English is what will make many young youths more marketable and for worldwide social interaction in every industry as well as world power foreign relations

A to M23 the petition says alongside English not replacing English.

As with the Letter to the Editor data, the reactions to proposing Patwa to step out of its L language status and become an official language were consistently mixed. Out of the 28 male contributors of the discussion, 17 rejected the petition implicitly or explicitly, 9 supported it and the stance of 2 participants remained unclear. The opinion of the female contributors was more balanced: 7 of the female participants were in favour of Patwa and the petition while another 7 rejected it. 3 of the female contributors could not be placed in terms of their attitude towards the subject.

5 Conclusion

It seems that, 50 years after the first language attitude studies toward Creole in the anglophone Caribbean, talking about Creole has not become obsolete. Rather, Creole discourse in public outlets like newspapers and social media platforms appears to be as alive, fiery and divided as ever. Some of the issues that were prevalent in the early studies have almost disappeared: beliefs that Creole is not a language or merely a corruption of the lexifier English are hardly found or expressed in systematic attitude studies or in the public sphere. Most writers in Letters to the Editor or in the Facebook comments in the Jamaican context appear to value Patwa as their language but are hesitant to invest time or effort when it comes to elevating it to the status of official language. As one participant in the Facebook discussion writes in his post:

Comment 26:

M18 Y'all want too much. No one can even spell the words …isn't it enough that we all know and love it

In our more globalized world the importance of having a national language as expression of national identity seems to have decreased in comparison to the more immediate post-independence period. One of the great achievements of linguists in the standardization of Creoles, the creation of a consistent orthography which highlights the autonomy of the language and makes the language more visible, is seen as an obstacle by quite a few respondents. This is unfortunate for linguists but could also be seen as an unconscious resistance to authority on the part of the language user who might want to keep (and use) the language the way they want it. Writing practices have also changed and the use of Creole in the digital space is highly prevalent but, at the same time, the spelling remains anarchically creative and expressive (cf. Moll 2017) and continues to contribute to shape and transform the public discourse about Creole.

Abbreviations

LTE   Letters to the Editor
BEP   Bilingual Education Program
JLU   Jamaican Language Unit

References

Ajzen, Icek. 1989. Attitude structure and behavior. In A. R. Pratkanis, S. J. Breckler & Greenwald A. G (eds.), *Attitude structure and Function*, 241–274. Lawrence Erlbaum.

Beckford Wassink, Alicia. 1999. Historic low prestige and seeds of change: Attitudes toward Jamaican Creole. *Language in Society* 28(1). 57–92.

Belgrave, Korah. 2008. Attitudes of Barbadians to British, American and Barbadian accents. *La Torre: Revista de la Universidad de Puerto Rico* 13(49–50). 429–444.

Bible Society of the West Indies. 2012. *Di Jamiekan Nyuu Testiment/The Jamaican New Testament*. Kingston: Bible Society of the West Indies.

Burridge, Kate. 2010. Linguistic cleanliness is next to godliness: Taboo and purism. *English Today* 26(2). 3–13.

Carroll, Lewis. 2016. *Alis Advencha ina Wandalan: Alice's Adventures in Wonderland in Jamaican Creole*. Translated by Tamirand De Lisser. Portlaoise, Ireland: Evertype.

Deuber, Dagmar. 2013. Towards endonormative standards of English in the Caribbean: A study of students' beliefs and school curricula. *Language, Culture and Curriculum* 26(2). 109–127.

Deuber, Dagmar & Glenda Leung. 2013. Investigating attitudes towards an emerging standard of English: Evaluations of newscasters' accents in Trinidad. *Multilingua* 32(2). 109–127.

Devonish, Hubert. 1986. *Language and Liberation. Creole Language Politics in the Caribbean.* London: Karia Press.

Devonish, Hubert. 2002. *Language rights, justice and the constitution.* January 13 and January 27, 2002.

Devonish, Hubert. 2012. *Stop demonizing Patois - from a semi-lingual to a bilingual Jamaica.*

Devonish, Hubert. 2016. *End prejudice against Patois.*

Devonish, Hubert. 2018. *End Jamaican language apartheid.*

Fishbein, Martin & Icek Ajzen. 1975. *Belief, Attitude, Intention and Behaviour: An introduction to theory and research.* Reading, MA: Addison-Wesley.

Haynes, Lilith A. 1973. *Language in Barbados and Guyana: Attitudes, behaviors and comparison.* Stanford University. (Doctoral dissertation).

Jamaican Language Unit. 2005. *The Language Attitude Survey of Jamaica.* https: / / www . mona . uwi . edu / dllp / jlu / projects / Report % 20for % 20Language % 20Attitude%20Survey%20of%20Jamaica.pdf.

Jamaican Language Unit. 2009a. *Writing Jamaican the Jamaican Way/Ou fi Rait Jamiekan.* Kingston: Arawak.

Jamaican Language Unit. 2009b. *Writing Jamaican the Jamaican Way/Ou fi Rait Jamiekan.* https://www.youtube.com/watch?v=2rx4FAIxaTE (6 March, 2020).

Meer, Philipp, Michael Westphal, Eva C. Hänsel & Dagmar Deuber. 2019. Trinidadian secondary school students' attitudes toward accents of Standard English. *Journal of Pidgin and Creole Languages* 34(1). 83–125.

Moll, Andrea. 2017. Diasporic Cyber-Jamaican. Stylized dialect of an imagined community. In Susanne Mühleisen (ed.), *Contested Communities. Communication, Narration, Imagination,* 69–93. Leiden: Brill.

Morren, Ronald C. & Diane M. Morren. 2007. Are the goals and objectives of Jamaica's Bilingual Education Project being met? *SIL Working papers.*

Morrison, Andrew & Alison Love. 1996. A discourse of disillusionment: Letters to the editor in two Zimbabwean magazines 10 years after independence. *Discourse and Society* 7(1). 39–75.

Mühleisen, Susanne. 1999. Konkurrierende Orthographien. Kodifizierte Sichtweisen auf ‚Abstand' und ‚Ausbau' von English-orientierten Kreolsprachen. *Philologie im Netz* 10. 16–26.

Mühleisen, Susanne. 2001. Is 'bad English' dying out? A diachronic comparative study of attitudes towards Creole versus Standard English in Trinidad. *Philologie im Netz* 15. 43–78.

Mühleisen, Susanne. 2002. *Creole Discourse. Exploring Prestige Formation and Change across Caribbean English-lexicon Creoles*. Amsterdam: Benjamins.

Mühleisen, Susanne. 1993. *Attitudes towards Language Varieties in Trinidad*. Freie Universität Berlin. (MA thesis).

Mühleisen, Susanne. Forthcoming. Metathesiophobia, nutty professors and Patois: Language debates in Letters to the Editor (LTE) in a Jamaican newspaper. In Susanne Mühleisen (ed.), *Text Type and Genre in World Englishes: Case studies from the Caribbean*.

Oenbring, Raymond & William Fielding. 2014. Young adults' attitudes to standard and nonstandard English in an English-Creole speaking country: The case of the Bahamas. *Language, Discourse & Society* 3(1). 28–51.

Reisman, Karl. 1970. Cultural and linguistic ambiguity in a West Indian village. In N. E. Witten & J. F. Szwed (eds.), *Afro-American Anthropology*, 290–144. New York: The Free Press.

Rickford, John. 1983. Standard and nonstandard attitudes in a Creole community. In *Society for caribbean linguistics occasional paper*, 145–160. Mona, Jamaica: UWI.

Sturiale, Massimo. 2016. '[Sir,] Who is the English Authority on Pronunciation?': Accent and Normative Attitude in The Times (1785-1922). *Language and History* 59(1). 37–47.

Westphal, Michael. 2015. Attitudes toward accents of standard English in Jamaican radio newscasting. *Journal of English Linguistics* 43(4). 311–333.

Winford, Donald. 1976. Teacher attitudes toward language varieties in a Creole community. *International Journal of the Sociology of Language* 8. 45–75.

Winford, Donald. 1985. The syntax of *fi* complements in Caribbean English Creole. *Language* 61(3). 588–624.

Youssef, Valerie & Dagmar Deuber. 2012. *ICE Trinidad and Tobago: Teacher language investigation in a university research class*. Tech. rep.

Appendix: Facebook comments on the *Pitishan*

No.	Attitudes to:			Reason/Commentary
	spoken P	written P	Petition	
M1	positive	negative	reject	too difficult to read and write
M2	positive	positive	support	*unique language/love my language*
M3	positive	unclear	reject	which version of Patwa will be used
M4	positive	positive	support	*Mek patwa reconize as wi original langwij*
M5	unclear	unclear	reject	*if you cannot spell a word in English how can you spell one in patois*
M6	negative	negative	reject	*Patois cannot be a language :D we speak broken engllish/standard english*
M7	positive	positive	support	*...this generation writes and reads it well.*
M8	positive	negative	reject	*di xtraness nah go work*
M9	positive	positive	support	*how many Jamaicans read and speak English well*
M10	positive	positive	support	*If u can't read something as simple as patwah which we speak how are we to learn Spanish or French which we don't speak*
M11	unclear	unclear	unclear	*The statement extra n nobody nuh txt so*
M12	positive	negative	reject	*petition waste of time, too hard to read*
M13	unclear	unclear	unclear	Language examples instead of positioning
M14	unclear	negative	reject	*One more aim to keep the poor , poor and ignorant*
M15	unclear	negative	reject	*Nah for me, don't need to be taking English language exams when I wanna go college abroad*
M16	unclear	unclear	support?	*Ones have to be foolfool to think this a laafing mata!*
M17	positive	positive	support	*Our first language*
M18	positive	negative	reject	*Y'all want too much. No one can even spell the words... isn't it enough that we all know and love it*
M19	unclear	negative	reject	*lol cant even read it*
M20	unclear	negative	reject	*It is, already (i.e. too hard to learn)*
M21	unclear	negative	reject	*The money for changing all government forms and other documents is waiting already!*
M22	unclear	unclear	reject	*No way that is a dumb idea English or Spanish*

M23	positive	negative	reject	*Patwa can't be used as our official language because the rest of the world barely understand our dialect.*
M24	positive	positive	support	*The aim is to simply add structure and form to what is already there*
M25	negative	negative	reject	*How can you preach what you dont teach. i cant even speak that language*
M26	positive?	positive?	support	*Praktis mek Perfek*
M27	unclear	unclear	reject	*Find something better to do...smdh*
M28	unclear	unclear	reject	*pussy go look a real work*
F1	positive	positive	support	*how easy will it be for them to read and understand this our native language*
F2	positive	positive	support	*learned it in a day, reading fluently from the patwa bible*
F3	positive	positive	support	*are there hard copy petitions over the island?*
F4	positive	positive	support	*Its a damn shame n pity ow some ppl a react to this*
F5	positive	positive	reject	*trus mi mi write an read patoi and me is a proud Jamaican but mi seh NO*
F6	??	negative	reject	*Not interested, let's push English more.*
F7	positive	positive	reject	*How many Jamaicans can read Patois? Most of us can only "talk" it*
F8	negative	negative	reject	*Patio should never be taught in schools at all it sounds ugly and vulgar it's total waste of time*
F9	unclear	negative	reject	*This so called patio is just a massive hindrance to development*
F10	unclear	unclear	unclear	*yu miin 'ku'? As in 'Ku yu tu?!'*
F11	unclear	unclear	unclear	*It took me a while to read thr above*
F12	positive	positive	support	*Anyone who is proposing this is a nincompoop*
F13	unclear	unclear	unclear	*I can talk it but can hardly read or write it*
F14	unclear	unclear	reject	*Will never happen .too hard to read and write it*
F15	positive	positive	support	*A waa u sah man mi love strate patwa mi seh*
F16	positive	positive	support	*Same like how we learned to do everything else....*
F17	unclear	unclear	reject	*yes – in response to "find something else to do"*

Chapter 11

Jamaican Creole tense and aspect in contact: Insights from acquisition and loss

Trecel Messam

University of the West Indies, Mona

Michele Kennedy

University of the West Indies, Mona

This paper presents an account of the use of the progressive aspect and the simple past tense in the speech of three-year-olds from Jamaican Creole (JC) speaking communities, as well as in the speech of JC-speaking migrants to Curaçao, who now function in a second language (L2) dominant environment. We compare the two data sets, and find that parallels may be drawn between the interlanguages of these speakers; there are patterns of the mixing of the L1 with the languages in contact in the progressive construction, but little mixing in the past tense, where Creole forms persist in the speech of both sets of speakers. Such parallels may be unsurprising, given Winford's (2003: 256) assertion that "the phenomena involved in language attrition ... are similar to those found in many other cases of contact ...". We conclude that there are fundamental differences between the expression of pastness in JC and in the target languages, and suggest that this lack of congruence may cause difficulty in learning the L2 (Winford 2003: 252). We suggest further, that the promotion of language awareness in language arts classrooms will go a long way to overcoming this difficulty.

1 Introduction

A normally developing child is expected by age 5 to have acquired all the basic constructions that allow for native speaker functionality in the target language.

Trecel Messam & Michele Kennedy. 2022. Jamaican Creole tense and aspect in contact: Insights from acquisition and loss. In Bettina Migge & Shelome Gooden (eds.), *Social and structural aspects of language contact and change*, 287–324. Berlin: Language Science Press. DOI: 10.5281/zenodo.6979325

Chomsky, in Cockburn (1994), speaks of this process of language development as involving inherent cognitive mechanisms that allow us to naturally develop language in much the same way as we grow arms and legs. Yet, the mother tongue has proven not to be impervious to language change and loss. Research in the 1980s saw the advent of language attrition as a new subfield, with one of the first impactful collections of papers being Lambert & Freed (1982).

A reduction in input from the L1, a reduction in the use of that L1 as well as influence from an L2 may result in language attrition, which de Bot & Schrauf (2009: 11) define as "...the loss in language proficiency in an individual over time." The susceptibility of the L1 to deterioration is further compounded by the presence of two languages in the mind of the L2 user. These languages share a relationship that may be either total separation, interconnection or total integration that Cook (2002, 2003, 2016) has described as an integration continuum, reflective of a multi-competence model. In this model, Cook postulates that neither total integration nor total separation is possible as, in the case of total integration, the user has the ability to "keep one language at a time", whilst for total separation, the user is "belied by the use of the same mouth and ears for both languages" (2002: 12); in other words, their existence in the same mind renders autonomy impossible (2003: 7).

The Regression Hypothesis (RH), a framework introduced by Jakobson (1941), is a seminal theoretical model of first language attrition. It posits that the order of this process is the inverse of language acquisition (Schmitt 2019). A perspective of this hypothesis also incorporates the notion of complexity and frequency of use being a determining factor in language loss. The idea here is that features of the language which are learnt best and are frequently used are least susceptible to loss.

With the RH, we can look for parallels that presumably exist between first language attrition and language acquisition. Keijzer (2009) in a study of English (L2) and Dutch (L1) contact reports that the RH holds ground in accounting for loss in the morphological domain, but less so in the syntax. Keijzer makes a distinction between loss and L2 influence, and reports changes in the syntax being marked by L2 influence rather than loss. Parallels in L2 attrition studies have provided strong evidence in favour of the RH (Hansen 1999: 150). Further investigation in this area is required for L1 studies as the evidence is either sparse or conflicting. However, Keijzer (2010) found that of 15 features investigated in the case of Dutch L2 speakers of English, 9 parallels were found, leading to the conclusion that "regression only on the basis of L1 remodeling does not occur" (Keijzer 2010: 223–224). Further support of the credibility of the RH is found in the work of Slobin (1977), whose findings were later substantiated in Yağmur's (1997) investigation of L1 attrition in Turkish.

This paper brings together the findings of two studies within a creole environment: one on language acquisition and the other on language attrition. With a focus on the past tense and the progressive aspect, insights are sought on the parallels that may exist in the acquisition and attrition of these areas by L1 speakers of Jamaican Creole (JC). It presents an account of the acquisition of the simple past tense and the progressive aspect in the speech of three-year-olds from JC speaking communities as presented in Kennedy (2017), primarily. These data are presented alongside attrition data based on Messam-Johnson (2017) as attested in the speech of JC migrants to Curaçao, after residence for between 1 and 21 years in the Papiamentu (Pp)-dominant environment.

We compare the two data sets and find that parallels may be drawn between the interlanguages of these speakers: there are patterns of the mixing of the L1 with the languages in contact in the progressive construction, but little mixing in the past tense, where Creole forms persist in the speech of both sets of speakers.

§2 of the paper provides a brief background to the language situations in the relevant communities. §3 presents the methodologies of the two research projects. §4 provides the theoretical background on tense as well as its occurrence in the acquisition and attrition data. Findings are discussed in terms of whether the outcomes in attrition are in line with the predictions in the literature in terms of L1 acquisition. In cases where there is divergence from these expectations, possible explanations from L2 acquisition are sought. A similar approach is taken with regard to aspect in §5, then §6 concludes with the implications of findings for the language arts classroom.

2 The language situations in Jamaica and Curaçao

The assumptions here are that JC is the native language of the majority of Jamaicans, and that therefore, the official language English, or more accurately an indigenized variety commonly known as Jamaican English (JE), is spoken as an L2 by that majority. Implicit in this is the further assumption that JC and JE are two different languages (see Kennedy 2017: 10–13). They do not exist, however, as discrete languages. Instead, there are several overlapping varieties or codes, so finely articulated that they cannot be identified as discrete codes but have been characterized as a continuous spectrum of speech varieties (DeCamp 1971: 350). The spectrum comprises JC and JE at the extremes, with individuals occupying different spans of the spectrum. Indeed, at best JC and JE themselves are idealizations, since it is unlikely that any one speaker would use only forms belonging exclusively to one code or the other. The main sources of knowledge of the idealized JE for most speakers in Jamaica are formal education and writing (Devonish & Harry 2008: 256), to which they are exposed to varying degrees.

Such a spectrum is possible since the vocabulary of JC is largely derived from English – it is "English lexified", with words having originated on the slave plantation as English, the language of the colonizers, and incorporated into the JC phonological system. The result is that items of English origin make up the vast majority of the lexicon of JC (Devonish & Harry 2008: 256). Consequently, JC words can readily be seen to be related to their JE counterparts. In many cases, however, given the spectrum, there exist a variety of combinations of JC and JE forms. An example is the JC *yeside* 'yesterday', pronounced variously as *yestide, yestude, yestade, yestudie, yestadie, yestudee, yesterdie* and *yesterdee*, the JE pronunciation (Kennedy 2017: 60).

Similarities between JC and JE exist, then, at the lexical and phonological levels. These are considered to be superficial (Craig 1980; Kennedy 2017). A consequence of the superficial similarity between JC and JE, is that speakers often believe that they are using JE when in fact they are not. Speakers believe this, because noting the many similarities in vocabulary, they assume that the languages are similar at the deeper syntactic level as well (Craig 1980). This is not the case, however. We see in §4, for instance, that the way tense operates in JC is fundamentally different from how it operates in JE.

The language situation in Jamaica as outlined above, exists also to varying degrees in other Creole communities, inspiring the term (post-)Creole continuum. In continuum theory, the forms of speech that closely resemble the language considered to be the official language is termed the *acrolect*. The speech forms that maximally diverge from the former are referred to as the *basilect*. It has traditionally been assumed that communities in rural areas would be more likely to have speakers of more basilectal forms, since such areas are isolated in both geographic and socio-economic terms, remaining therefore relatively immune to more mainstream developments, including, it is assumed, linguistic behaviour.[1] As we would expect given the variation which exists, however, speakers do not fit neatly into these two categories: instead of consistently using only forms which are considered to be either basilectal or acrolectal, forms reflecting more or less "Creole-ness" are regularly used as well. People using such "midway" forms have been termed mesolectal speakers. Winford (1997: 236) indicates that the *mesolect*

---

[1]See, for example Patrick (1999: 49) who speaks of isolated rural areas as being culturally and linguistically conservative, and who quotes Rickford (1987: 23) as suggesting that rural variants are "characteristically Creole".

is used to refer to an area of interaction between a relatively basilectal Creole and the local standard, an area which appears to have no distinct status as a system, whose "existence has been and continues to be, dependent on the cross influences from the two extremes" (Craig 1971: 372).

The assumption of this chapter is that the input which children hear as they acquire language is characterized by variation, and will therefore form part of their own speech. However, yet another aspect of language use in the Jamaican society exists. This is also attributable to its emergence on the plantation. The colonizers spoke varieties of English, the language associated therefore with power and wealth, but the Creole which the enslaved developed was generally perceived to be a malformed version of English. Over the centuries, English has maintained its unique position since it remains the only official language of Jamaica, and since it continues to be the expected language for the conduct of government business, in the law courts, in schools as the language of instruction, in the mass media, in religious worship and in all other contexts where written language is required. In contrast, JC, the vernacular, is the expected language for use in private and informal interactions involving family and friends. For these reasons, the language situation has been characterized by some linguists as being *diglossic* (see Winford 1985 among others) where the language of high prestige used in the formal domain is known as the H(igh) variety, and where the L(ow) variety, the vernacular, is not generally used in that domain.

We do note, however, that as underlined by Devonish & Walters (2015: 231), in recent years, and particularly since Jamaica's independence in 1962, JC has become a symbol of national identity across all social groups, resulting in a growing acceptance of its use in the public arena in domains where in colonial Jamaica it would have been frowned on. The language situation in Jamaica, therefore, is very complex both in the forms and in the use of the languages.

Similar to many creole languages of the Caribbean, including JC, Pp is the product of European colonization. In Curaçao, this began in the 1500s. The Spanish occupied the island for over a century until Dutch colonisation in 1634–1654. Portuguese-speaking Jews then arrived on the island, resulting in the formation of Pp, a language with Spanish, but predominantly Dutch and Portuguese influence, and the creation of the multilingual situation that exists today.

The study of JC attrition was conducted in this situation (see Messam-Johnson 2017), a multilingual country with immigrants from diverse backgrounds. The informants on whose speech the study is based were speakers, who in light of their lower socio-economic status and level of education, among other social factors, were assumed to represent speakers of a variety closer to basilectal JC.

They were exposed to different degrees to multiple languages including English, Dutch, Spanish, and Pp the dominant language, the vernacular of Curaçao.

Kouwenberg & Murray (1994) indicate that most of the Curaçaon population consider themselves to be polygots, having varied competencies in Pp, Dutch, Spanish and English. If one were to encounter a monolingual resident of this country, however, the expectation would be that that individual is a Pp speaker. Though Dutch is the official language of the island, its use is restricted to higher education and government domains, where Pp is also present (Kouwenberg & Murray 1994). Pp, having an official status in Curaçao, is used in the education system and in the print and electronic media as well. Knowledge of this language was a job requirement for some informants, but all had to interact in Pp with employers, fellow employees, and members of the public whom they served at varying levels. Those who were currently in the education system would also have had sufficient exposure to Pp as it is a language of instruction as well as the main means of interaction with fellow classmates.

It is noteworthy, however, that upon arriving in Curaçao, to get around, the Jamaican immigrants would have initially tried to communicate using any proficiency in English they had attained whilst living in Jamaica, as some residents did speak English as an L2, and others as an L3 or even an L4. Upon arrival, then, in a country where speakers of JC do not form a community, the assumption is that the main mode of communication for the immigrants was a variety that assimilated features of the acrolect or the upper mesolect. It is not surprising then that these features, which would normally have been characteristic of the formal domain in the L1 country, would over time form part of the informal speech of the immigrants, often resulting in a replacement of the more basilectal features of the L1.

Though L2 speakers of English exist within the country, the immigrants would not have been able to rely on the use of English to live well within the country. A 2001 census showed that a vast majority of the Curaçaon population are primarily Pp speakers and a minority speak English (see Table 1).

With this shift in language dominance, given the Jamaican migrants' new language situation, Pp was expected to have an influence on the L1 forms that they would produce. It was however anticipated that with a need to communicate with persons in the L2 environment, these respondents, at least initially, would have had to utilize any knowledge of English they had prior to immigration. With an increased use of this English, however, further influence on the L1 would be expected. It was therefore critical that informants who were included in the study spoke a variety of JC that was closest to the basilect prior to migration. This had

Table 1: Census of 1981 and 2001 depicting percentage of language use in Curaçao (adapted from Maurer 1998: 143 and Kester & Fun 2012: 238 in Jacobs 2013).

	Curaçao, 1981	Curaçao, 2001
Papiamento	86.9	80.3
Dutch	6.8	9.3
English	3.3	3.5
Spanish	?	4.6

to be controlled for by selecting informants at the lower strata of the Jamaican society with whom varieties closest to the basilect are said to be associated.

3   Methodologies

3.1   The acquisition data

The acquisition data are drawn from the Child Language Acquisition Research (CLAR) project.[2] The aim of the project was to determine what language variety children speak as they enter the public school system.

A total of 80 children in their first month of Basic School participated in the study. We note that the Basic School system is said to have been created to cater mainly to the lower socioeconomic groups (Miller 2015).[3] In addition, though the language situation outlined above would suggest far more complexity than this, the assumption of the Ministry of Education is that the communities feeding such schools are mainly JC-speaking, and that the children are monolingual speakers of JC.[4] Thirteen Basic Schools were chosen from eight areas across the island, with care taken to have representation from schools in rural areas (six schools), cities (three schools) as well as towns (four schools). Though consideration of possible gender effects on the speech of children was not an aim of the study, an attempt was made to have equal numbers of boys and girls from each school,

---

[2]The project was fully funded by a UWI Mona New Initiatives grant, as well as the award of a year's sabbatical leave.

[3]In 2012 74.2% of children ages three–five years attending early childhood education institutions in the country were enrolled in Basic Schools (SABER Country Report 2013: 15, table 12).

[4]The 2001 Language Education Policy, for instance, states explicitly that JC is the language most widely used in Jamaica (p. 23).

totalling 43 and 37 respectively. Children were not assessed or screened for participation. Instead, they were chosen from among classmates on the basis of age and gender as outlined above, as well as using guidance from their teachers as to suitability in terms of expected levels of participation in interviews.

At the start of data collection half of the children were age 3;0± and the other half 3;6±.[5] Each set of children was interviewed once a month for six months, resulting in the collection of a virtual year of the speech of children falling within the age range of 2;9 to 4;2. This method was patterned after Meade (2001).

A total of 214 half-hour video-recorded interview sessions were conducted between September 2009 and April 2010 in the school setting (but not in the classroom), by JC native speaking graduate students at the University of the West Indies, Mona campus. In approximately half of the sessions (108/214), only one child was interviewed. For the remainder, interviews were of two children. The rationale for choosing to interview two children at a time was to allow us to analyse the children in interaction, and for linguistic as well as non-linguistic reasons such as assessing attitudes, fair-play and dominance.

The store of materials used for elicitation included laminated flash cards, story books, toys, colouring books, crayons, scrap books and markers. To allow for role-playing, there was a range of cooking utensils including a wooden stove, pots and food items, as well as telephones. The aim was for the children to interact naturally, and data were elicited primarily via conversation during play. Sessions were loosely structured, beginning with general discussion, encouraged as necessary, using books or pictures. This was intended to set the tone for the session and to put the children at ease; it was followed by guided conversations using the flash cards or objects chosen especially for the elicitation of a range of structures including tense and aspect constructions. The final segment involved the children in various activities such as free play, role-playing or colouring, intended to foster discussion and interaction guided by the interviewer. All told, 51,650 utterances were collected from the children.

Interviews were transcribed from the videos for manipulation in CHILDES, the Child Language Data Exchange System, which provides online tools for transcription and data analysis (MacWhinney 2000a,b). Transcriptions were orthographic, using the Cassidy-JLU writing system, modified to include JE vowels used by the children. Lexicon files were created for the purpose of tagging transcriptions, with coding for tagging adapted to suit the purposes of the analysis, and tagging then achieved using facilities provided by the CHILDES software.

---

[5] The age of children is recorded here in the format years;months. A more fine-grained representation includes the number of days as follows: years;months.days. This is in line with the convention in the field of first language acquisition, and will be used throughout.

The basis of the analyses is just over one hundred hours of data collected (107). This corpus linguistics approach greatly improved the empirical power of claims made here. As will become apparent, frequency of occurrence and the range and frequency of possible combinations of JE and JC forms play an important role in the interpretation of the data. This has allowed for trends to be detected, and for patterns which may not be immediately obvious to be easily confirmed by the flexible interrogation of the speech of children by gender, age, major region and parish, and by the rural/urban status of their communities.

3.2 The attrition data

The data on the attrition of the constructions presented in this paper are drawn from a broader study, which investigated the susceptibility of JC to attrition in an L2 dominant environment where there is a reduction in the use of the L1 and a reduction in input from that L1.

Data were elicited from 20 Jamaican immigrants to Curaçao, who had been residing in the L2 country for a period of between 1 and 21 years. Respondents had to have resided in Jamaica until they were at least five years old to ensure that the L1 had been acquired, and that any changes evident in the L1 post migration were not simply a result of imperfect acquisition. Informants were then categorised according to their years of exposure to the L2. This was determined by their length of residence in the L2 country: 1–5 yrs, 6–10 yrs and >10 yrs. This categorisation would allow for tracing of the stages of attrition in JC, from the point of initial contact with the L2 (1–5 ys) when mild effects would have been anticipated, to the point at which stability in the attrition process would be likely to be realised (>10 yrs). Having a representation of immigrants with varied lengths of residence in the L2 country would then have provided evidence of the points at which unconventional L1 features would be likely to appear in the repertoire of JC immigrants in an L2 contact situation; the time at which features would become susceptible to change would be revealed. With the inclusion of immigrants whose length of residence exceeded ten years, an overview of an attrited JC grammar would also be possible, as at ten years attrition is expected to be relatively stable (cf. De Bot & Clyne 1994; Waas 1993).

The investigation further included a verification group against whose linguistic competence the structures produced by the immigration group were measured. Members of the verification group had to have been native to the L1 country and had to have resided there from birth. These participants had never visited another country and had no immigrants from other countries in their circle. It was expected then that they could provide evidence of structures which would

reveal the norms of the L1. They were further selected with an intention of matching the socio-economic profile of the immigration group.

Following Ellis (1994), five data elicitation methods were used: natural use,[6]
clinical elicitation, experimental elicitation, metalinguistic judgements and self-
report. These data were collected from the 21 immigrants over a three-month
period, totalling 128 recorded sessions over 60 hours. Informants were given the
option to meet at a location of their choosing to ensure comfort and relaxation
throughout the process. This would have assisted in encouraging the natural
production of informal speech for which the use of JC is considered the norm.
Interaction with the participants was done individually to avoid external influence from other L2 users.

In eliciting spontaneous speech (natural use data), attempts were made to ensure participants spoke as naturally as possible. Participants spoke of their personal lives and on topics which were of interest to them. Utterances produced
through natural use are considered to be authentic (Ellis 1994: 671) and were thus
expected to reveal reliable evidence of L1 change. This task provided an opportunity to gather data which was a true representation of the participants' speech.
Unconventional L1 forms identified here, which suggested a change in the participants' L1 repertoire, would be targeted in following elicitation tasks to test if
they would be reproduced. This became the pattern with each task administered.

Clinical elicitation further provided informants with the opportunity to be creative in their output, thereby providing more spontaneous speech. This type of
data allows for elicitation through mostly unguided language use. Methods used
usually include film recalls, written composition, information gap tasks, oral interviews and role plays (cf. Ellis 1994: 672). Instruments such as picture sequenc-
ing and picture description tasks allowed for the production of targeted structures through unguided language use. Participants were allowed to create their
own stories and provide intuitive descriptions of images with which they were
presented. With the selected clinical elicitation tasks, it was possible to maintain some amount of control over the types of structures produced as the images
presented to the participants targeted particular constructions, including activities, for example, that would likely be described using progressive and past tense
forms, among others.

The experimental elicitation method, through the use of a scenario consideration and a translation task, directly targeted structures that were suspected to
be prone to attrition on the basis that they were either areas in which unconventional L1 forms were exhibited in the previous data collection tasks, or they were

---

[6]Natural use data represent the spontaneous speech of research participants.

areas of morpho-syntactic or syntactic differences that were identified as existing between the two primary languages in contact – Papiamentu and JC. Prior to entering the field, items included in instruments for testing were selected for inclusion by contrastive analysis on the premise that changes are likely to be evidenced in the areas in which the languages in contact differ.

Unlike the clinical elicitation method, there was greater control over the structures that informants produced. In the scenario consideration task, participants were presented with scenarios that were structured so as to prompt the use of the targeted structures. The translation task presented participants with Pp sentences that contained these targeted structures for which they were required to orally provide the JC equivalents. In doing so, participants would be less likely to use avoidance strategies in the production of structures that they may deem more difficult to produce. Participants also had to rely solely on their own knowledge of the L1 to produce the required translations.

In metalinguistic judgements, informants are asked to judge the grammaticality of sentences. Through the use of this task, the participants were able to evaluate structures, some of which had been their own productions in earlier tasks. This allowed for an indication of structures which were impermissible in JC and provided alternative structures that were acceptable in their variety. It further provided evidence of what the immigrants knew as opposed to what their speech reflected. This task was later administered to the verification group in a bid to determine the acceptability of the utterances the immigrants produced and accepted in the data collection sessions.

The final method elicited Self-report data which usually involved introspection, retrospection and think aloud tasks. These sessions allowed informants of the substantive group to provide, among other details, personal input on their experience in using the language and how it might have changed.

The analysis section of this paper includes examples from the data collected (Natural Use Data, Metalinguistics Judgements, Picture Sequence, Translation Task), which are relevant to the past and the progressive markers and it further specifies the elicitation task in square brackets.[7]

Transcription began after the completion of each recording session. This allowed for initial analyses to be carried out while data collection was still in progress. With this approach, forms in the natural use data that seemed to deviate from the L1 norms – based on the literature and the researchers' own native speaker knowledge of the L1 – were included in instruments used for the data

---

[7]For clarity, tasks from which the attrition data are extracted are denoted as Natural Use Data (NUD), Metalinguistics judgements (MJ), Picture Sequence (PS) and Translation Task (TT).

collection methods that followed. This was the pattern followed for other tasks, wherein findings from previous tasks would inform subsequent tasks, which were then amended to test for the reproduction of these questionable structures.

Transcription conventions followed the Cassidy-JLU orthographic system for JC utterances, whereas English and Papiamentu orthographies were used for those languages. Errors in the data and the frequency of their occurrence were identified in the transcriptions manually. Forms were determined to be erroneous or unconventional if they were primarily rejected by the verification group and if those forms could not be accounted for in the available literature on the JC grammar, including Bailey (1966), Patrick (2004), Patrick (2007) and Winford (2003).

4 The past tense

4.1 The past tense in JC and Pp

Tense comprises categories where time reference is the primary dimension. We may say that it locates an eventuality in time. An eventuality is taken to refer not only to events but also to situations and states. In the following, we will see that JC and JE contrast with regard to Tense, both in the form of tense marking and in the ways the temporal systems operate. We then apply these concepts to the acquisition and attrition data with a view to finding parallels and contrasts between trends in the two phenomena.

The grammatical expression of Tense is different in JE and JC. Indeed, the TMA (Tense, Mood and Apect) category is said by Hackert (2004: 12) to be one of the areas which sets creoles off most visibly from their lexifiers. Basilectal JC uses independent pre-verbal tense markers *e(h)n* and its geographically determined variants *me(h)n, we(h)n, mi(h)n* and *be(h)n*. The variants *dii* and *did* have traditionally been considered to be mesolectal, used particularly in urban areas, and presumed to have arisen from JE. Note, however, that, like so many other forms, although JC *did* and its variants are similar in form to JE 'did', they function differently in the two languages. In JC, this is an independent past tense marker (*im did nuo* 'he knew' vs. *im did bai* 'he had bought'), functioning like other pre-verbal markers in the language. Such functions are discussed below. This contrasts with JE 'did' which serves as an emphatic marker in a declarative sentence ('he did go' meaning "he definitely went"). Differences in stress accompany these functions: in JC it is unstressed, whereas as a marker of emphasis in JE, it is necessarily stressed.

In JE, every finite verb which represents an eventuality taking place prior to the moment of speaking must be marked for the past tense. Such a language is considered to be tense prominent. JC, like other Creole languages is not tense prominent, since temporal fixing may but need not be determined in the syntax by grammatical marking – it may be set by other means such as by the inherent meaning of a verb, by the discourse or by adverbs. In his seminal 1947 work, Reichenbach constructed a theory of tense structure which has informed the linguistic study of Tense. The components of the theory are the time of utterance or speech (S), the time of the event (E) and the Reference Point (R). Tense is explained in terms of how these time points are related. This model has been applied to the study of temporal interpretation in Creole languages by Winford (2001), Lefebvre (1996), Muysken (1981) and others.

In the Reichenbach model, absolute tense such as exists in English, locates E in the past with respect to S. In contrast, tense in Creole languages is said to be Relative, that is, E is relative to R, not to S; the typical use of the tense marker is to locate some situation as occurring prior to the point under focus in the discourse (Winford 2001: 162). A determinant of the location of R in Creole languages is the (semantic) class of the verb. This makes it possible for the time of action to be implied merely by the aspects of verbal forms (Bhat 1999: 123). This is the domain of lexical or inherent aspectual properties, *aktionsarten*, which results in default tense interpretations for different lexical classes of verb in the absence of any overt tense marking, and also contributes to the determination of when such marking is present, as we now see.

Stativity and nonstativity are the major classes of verb relevant to the discussion of lexical aspect.[8] As will become apparent, the two aspectual classes of verbs have different temporal interpretations when modified by the past tense marker; in effect, aspect overrides tense. Stative verbs constitute a relatively small class, including verbs such as *nuo* 'know', *lov* 'love', *waahn* 'want', *a(v)* 'have'[9], all of which convey (typically continuous) physical or internal states. Following Vendler (1967), and using semantic criteria, Andersen (1990: 63) characterizes such verbs quite unsurprisingly as requiring no energy for them to continue once the state has been entered, although the point of entering or leaving the state may be conceived as nonstative, depending on the particular circumstances.

---

[8]We acknowledge that the stative/non-stative distinction is very broad, and is not adequate to provide a full account of the effects of lexical aspect in creole languages. More fine-grained sub-divisions such as telic/non-telic for non-statives, for instance, are explored and applied to creole data by Gooden (2008), McPhee (2003) and Hackert (2004). For the purposes of this article, however, we restrict our discussion to the major stativity divisions and their interactions with past time reference, since that will suffice for laying the foundations for what follows.

[9]We note that three of these, *waahn* 'want', *nuo* 'know' and *av* 'have', are among the top eight JC stative verbs most used by the children.

The default tense reading for bare or zero-marked (Ø) statives (that is, stative verbs not accompanied by a tense marker) is the present (Winford 1993: 33).[10]

(1) bare stative: present
     im   Ø   nuo.
     3S.SUBJ TENSE know
     'He (or she) knows.'

Nonstative verbs such as JC *ron* 'run', *push* 'push', *jrap* 'drop', or *jomp* 'jump' require energy for the action or event to take place and to continue (cf. Andersen 1990: 63 for reference to their English counterparts). For this reason, such verbs have also been termed *dynamic*. The default tense interpretation for bare nonstatives is said to be the past.

(2) bare nonstative: past
     di man Ø   tiif i.
     DEF man TENSE steal 3s
     'The man stole it.'

The interpretational consequences of the use of the tense marker in interaction with stativity are illustrated in (3–5). What happens here is that R, the time of Reference, is established by the verb. It is established as present (S) by statives (*si* 'see' in (3)), and as past – prior to S – by nonstatives (*bait* 'bite' and *ron* 'run' in (4) as well as *kik* 'kick' in (5)). The anterior tense marker serves to shift the event (E) to a point prior to R in each case, resulting in a past interpretation for statives (*dii si* 'saw' in (4)) and past before past for nonstatives (*wehn bait* 'had bitten' in (5)).

(3) DAN: mi si wahn kloud ina dis.
          1s see INDEF cloud in   this
          'I see a cloud in this.' [V6-MOB-N:426-3;4.6]

---

[10]The characterization of a non-overtly marked verb as bearing null tense is controversial. Here, without entering the controversy, we follow the generative approach, where every finite verb bears tense, but a tensed verb need not be overtly marked for tense. Even when not overtly marked for tense, tense must still be accounted for in the syntax, and is represented by a null marker (Ø), to indicate that it is expressed, though not phonologically. We say that the verb is zero-marked or that it is bare.

(4)   ROD: Tishien dii   si   wahn ... daag ... de   pan i   varanda   an   ...
           Tishien PAST see INDEF   dog   COP on   DEF verandah and
iihn bait Tishien ahn Tishien ron im.
3s   bite Tishien and Tishien run 3s
      'Tishien saw a dog on the verandah and he bit Tishien and Tishien
chased him away' [V1-BAL:342-3;3.25]

(5)   ANG: yie, im wen bait mi an   mi kik af a   mi han.
          yes 3s PAST bite 1s and 1s kick 3s off 1s hand
      'Yes, it had bitten me and I kicked it off my hand.'
[V3-MOB:676-3;4.22]

Other than the inherent aspectual properties of the predicate, R can take its
reference from the discourse, so that once the discourse context establishes R
to be past, unmarked statives can have past time reference (Winford 2000: 396).
In story-telling, for instance, once past time reference has been set, that can be
assumed to persist until the speaker notifies otherwise (Winford 2001: 159), and
the events that make up the main narrative are conveyed by unmarked verbs
(Winford 2000: 404).

Following Chung & Timberlake (1985), Gooden (2008) uses the term tense locus (TL) to refer to the point in time in relation to which an event or state is
perceived as past. TL may or may not be the time of speech (S), but it is located
relative to S. Gooden (2008: 322ff.) provides Belizean Creole data which show
that in discourse, once the reference point is set in the present, the past tense
marker can be used to distance the situation described by both states and events
from speech time, resulting in an absolute past reference.

The marking of tense in Pp follows a pattern similar to that of JC, insofar as
an independent pre-verbal marker indicates the simple past. Much like JC also,
the choice of preverbal marker in Pp is dependent on the stativity of the verb.
However, unlike JC, a past marker is obligatorily present for past reference: the
regular past is marked by perfective *a* and is restricted to non-stative verbs (6),
whilst *tabata* marks past reference for the stative verb (7). A reduced form of
tabata is used with the Pp verb *tin* 'have', resulting in the form *tabatin*, exemplified in (8):

(6)   Ayera   mi a   come pan
      Yesterday 1s PAST eat   bread
      'Yesterday, I ate bread.' [Adapted from Goilo 2000: 54]

(7) Mi tabata ke   kuminda
     1s PAST   want food
     'I wanted food.' [Kouwenberg & Ramos-Michel 2007:309]

(8) Mi tabatin   cincu buki riba mi   mesa
     1s have.PAST five   book on   POSS table
     'I had five books on my table.' [Adapted from Goilo 2000: 59]

The marker *tabata* may also occur with non-stative verbs, but only allows for a past imperfective interpretation, as will be shown in section §5, where the progressive aspect is of focus.

4.2 L1 acquisition of the JC past tense

All subjects in the attrition study were presumed to be native speakers of JC, the youngest having migrated to Curaçao at age five. In this section, we look to data from the CLAR children regarding trends in the first language acquisition of the past tense in JC and to provide a basis therefore for investigating similarities and contrasts with the attrition process.

De Lisser (2015: 95ff) studied the early acquisition of JC by six children in the age range 1;6–3;4 from Creole-speaking communities in Western Jamaica. She makes the point (p. 96) that because the unmarked verb is used to express both a past and a present reading, it is not possible to determine the exact point at which children acquire the concept of tense. She reports that of 5,836 utterances with a past time interpretation, only 33 (or 0.6%) were used with an overt tense marker to express the simple past tense.

The CLAR children were older (2;9–4;2) than those in the De Lisser study, but there is nonetheless a reported sparse use of the markers: pre-verbal *wehn* (seventeen (17) instances) and *did* (124) with its phonologically reduced variant *dii* (31), totalling 172. There is variation in the use of these forms. All but one of the occurrences of *wehn* were by CLAR children in the West, as might be expected, but these children were also responsible for 25.8% of the uses of *did* and 41.9% of *dii*. There are cases of the use of *did* and its variant *dii* with non-stative verbs conveying a past-before-past reading; (9) is an example.

(9) ROD: Kim dii   bai wahn chriichip fi   mi   aahn rat bait i.
         Kim PAST buy INDEF CheezTrix for 1s.OBJ and   rat bite 3s.OBJ
         'Kim had bought a pack of CheezTrix for me and a rat chewed it.'
      [V1-SER:l 145-3;3.25]

The stative verb did appear without the marker to convey a past meaning, as in (10) below. In adult JC, the marker would need to accompany *av* for a past interpretation:

(10)   ASH: mi   mada   Ø   av   wan a dem kyaar ya   we   Ø   mash
             POSS mother PAST have one of DEM cars   there which PAST mash

op.
up

       'My mother had one of those cars which mashed up.' [V3-KN2:l
63-3;9.2]

Later in the same interview (l. 1033), ASH uses the past marker with the same stative *av* 'have', as would be required in adult JC, and a non-stative *mash op* 'destroyed' with no marker, both indicating the absolute past as in (11) below:

(11)   ASH: mi dii   av   wan a dem biebi   ... it Ø   mash op.
            1s PAST have one of DEM baby-PLU   3s PAST mash up
       'I did have one of those babies ... it got destroyed.'

Variation is evidenced throughout. An example is (12) below, where SHA, in explaining what took place on a TV show, first uses the tense marker as would be required, then corrected himself, and produced an unacceptable sentence with the marker omitted:

(12)   SHA: <den im did> [/-] im Ø   av   aan dis pan i   an   dehn dis
            <then 3s PAST >   he PAST have on this on POSS hand then this
       Ø   krash dong dis pahn ort.
       PAST crash down this on   earth
       'He had this on his hand, then this crashed down on the earth.' [V6-KN1:l
390-3;10.0]

In the dialogue in (13) below, the interviewer believes that GAB is speaking about a man currently in her life, until she reveals that he had been killed. The interviewer's question *so wier im liv?* is very clearly present tense, following another question also in the present tense. Nonetheless, the child begins a story about the man, using the same form of the verb (stative *liv* with no marker) to express the past tense. Interestingly, GAB's sentence would be acceptable in (adult) JC with the interpretation she intended. It may be that the past interpretation of stative *liv* is coerced by the necessary interpretation of *kil* as past, and allowed by the possibilities available in the discourse.

(13) INV: so im liv wid yu?
              so 3s live with 2s
              'So, does he live with you?'
     GAB: *uhnuhn.*
     'No.'
     INV: so wier   im liv?
              so where 3s live
              'So, where does he live?'
     GAB: im Ø   liv de a im yaad an poliis kil im.
              3s PAST liv LOC at 3S yard and police kill 3s
              'He lived at his home, and the police killed him.' [V6-SER:1
     283-4;0.0]

This may now shed some light on the interpretation of (10) and (12) above, pointing once more to the possibility of TL being set by the discourse. The sparsity of use, and the variation in both the form and the usage of the past tense by these L1 acquirers of JC may suggest more reliance on strategies used in the discourse than that used by adult speakers and pointing therefore to late acquisition of how the temporal system works in JC. Because aspects of L2 acquisition are relevant to discussions of attrition (see §4.4), and because Jamaican migrants would have been exposed to English before as well as after migrating to Curaçao, we now look at features of the L2 acquisition of the English past tense by the CLAR children with a view to investigating whether trends found in these data might shed some light on the attrition phenomena.

4.3 L2 acquisition of the English past tense

As indicated in §4.1 above, for the past tense to be expressed in JE there must be tense marking on the verb regardless of contextual grounding. Marking of the regular past is by way of an inflectional suffix ('-ed') which is attached to the verb stem, and realized differently across words (e.g. /kuk/+/t/ but /beg/+/d/). Irregular past tense forms are created in an unpredictable fashion (e.g. 'know' → 'knew'). As we have also seen, marking apart, Tense operates very differently in JE and in JC, and it is not the case that the child learning JE must learn simply that there are inflectional endings on the verb in that language. Instead, the child must learn that the temporal systems differ in important ways. This will impact the JC native speaker's production and understanding of JE. This becomes relevant as the findings from language attrition are explored below, and as we consider the implications which language acquisition and language attrition have for the language arts classroom (see §6).

L2 acquisition of the regular English past tense is a late acquisition and is in fact among the last morphemes to be acquired. Much like in the L1 acquisition of English, the irregular forms are predictably acquired earlier than the regular forms.[11] From a processing point of view this has been accounted for by calling on a dual-system mechanism, which posits that regular past tenses involve the acquisition of rule-based mechanisms whereas irregular past tenses are directly retrieved from memory since they exist separately from their stems in the lexicon (Pliatsikas & Marinis 2013: 4). This is supported by studies finding that frequency effects apply to irregular verbs, in that more frequent forms are understood and produced faster than less frequent ones, but are not common in regular verbs (ibid, 5).

In line with such findings, the CLAR children, the oldest of whom was 4;2, displayed sparse use of the English past tense, and particularly of the inflected forms. We might also look to the L1 itself to explain this late acquisition: Paradis et al. (2008: 698) speak to differing acquisition by children whose initial state grammar might be close to the target than those whose initial state grammar is not. Since JC does not have inflectional morphology for tense, this would presumably put L1 JC speakers at a greater disadvantage than speakers of other L1s with the morpheme.[12]

The findings were as follows. Only two verbs inflected with the regular JE past inflectional ending '–d' were attested in the CLAR data. In (14), NAT is speaking about going to the beach. He uses the stem *waant* 'want', which must be considered a JE form since the JC counterpart *waahn* has a final nasalized vowel, not a consonant cluster.

(14) NAT: an a   waant-ed to kach shel.
       and 1s.SUBJ want-PAST INF catch shell
       'And I wanted to get shells.' [V4-STJ:1 443-3;8.23]

The second instance of JE past inflection is an instance of over-generalization, shown in (15). Over-generalization of the English past tense marker is well-

---

[11]For a discussion of L1 and L2 morpheme order studies, see Meisel (2011: 67ff).

[12]Interestingly, for the L2 learning of English by child and adult speakers of Cantonese, a language where, much like JC, tense is not represented by an affix attached to the verb, Yang & Huang (2004) report that as proficiency increased, learners did switch gradually to marking verbs for tense using inflections, relying less on pragmatic and lexical devices for expressing tense, and more on grammatical devices.

attested universally in L1 acquisition, and reported to be "perhaps the most noto-rious error" in language development among English-speaking children (Marcus 1996: 81).

(15) DAN: di boi mada   kom-d.
          DEF boy mother come-PAST
          'The boy's mother came.' [V6-MOB:l 627-3;4.16]

In this case, the past inflection is attached to a shared form *kom* 'come', a verb with irregular past tense formation in JE. Presumably the ending was considered by the child to be usable in JC and JE alike. (14) and (15) were the only occur-rences of a regular past tense form. The CLAR children used irregular JE past forms, but rarely so: eight different verbs a total of twelve times: *bawt* 'bought' (one instance), *brawt* 'brought' (one), *brook* 'broke' (two) , *got* (three), *had* (one), *jangk* 'drank' (one), *keem* 'came' (one) and *sed* 'said' (two), all used in past tense contexts.[13]

4.4 The past tense in attrition

Given the late acquisition of tense in the CLAR children's L1, we would expect that for attrition, tense would be highly susceptible to change in the early stages of the onset of this process, if we were to adopt the postulation made by the RH that that which is acquired earlier is lost last, and vice versa (see Köpke & Schmid 2004: 16). Further discussion on this hypothesis and the implication it has for acquisition and attrition ensues as the attrition of the past marker is examined. Contrary to expectations, the attrition data reveal that past marking is hardly likely to be subject to language attrition in the presence of influence from an L2 and in the face of reduction in both input and use of the L1. Tense remained intact, showing minimal evidence of attrition.

In the attrition data, deviation from the pattern of tense marking by JC native speakers was exhibited predominantly through the absence of a tense marker where one was required, and further through the rejection of the overt mark-ing of tense in metalinguistic judgements. The first evidence of deviation was the production of a structure indicating past reference of a stative verb, without

---

[13]Grabowski & Dieter (1995) provide a corpus-based list of the most frequently used irregular verbs in two major corpora of the English of adult speakers. The list includes all of these irregular past tense forms with the following rankings: 'bought' #48, 'brought' #18, 'broke' #43, 'got' #8, 'drank' #70, 'came' #5 and 'said' #1; 'had' was not included in this ranking, since it had a far higher absolute frequency count (4.5 times higher) than 'said', the highest to be ranked. There are no similar studies for frequency of use in Jamaica.

the inclusion of a pre-verbal tense marker. In these cases, the absence of overt tense marking rendered the past interpretation recoverable through an adjoining clause or the context of the discourse (illustrated in (16) and (17) below). Though evidenced in the speech of five informants, the structure was only used more than once by an informant with 16 years exposure to the L2. This is reminiscent of the early stages of L1 acquisition, where, as discussed in §4.2, there was a sparse use of the tense marker by the CLAR children, resulting in the interpretation of past reference for some of their utterances being understood through context.

(16) If yu ∅   waahn   nuo, yu   wuda kom.
      if 2P PAST PERF/PAST want know 2P   COND PERF come
      'If you had wanted to know, you would have come/If you wanted to know, you would have come. [9yrs- Informant, SCT]

(17) Im ∅   jronk?
      3P PAST drunk
      'Was he drunk?' [13yrs- Informant M, NUD]

In (16), for a past perfect or past interpretation to be allowed in the subordinate clause, a variant of the past marker is required. In the absence of the pre-verbal marker with stative *waahn* 'want', a construction that conveys reference to a present state is produced for that clause. In considering the complete utterance as intended by the speaker, a past interpretation is recovered through the main clause. Despite the absence of a tense marker preceding non-stative *kom* 'come', the conditional perfective *wuda* 'would have', enables the listener to place the preceding subordinate clause *If yu waahn nuo...* 'If you want to know...' within the past for an '*If you wanted to know/If you had wanted to know*' interpretation. In JC, a variant of the past marker such as *wehn* would have preceded the verb, resulting in the construction *wehn waant* 'wanted/had wanted'.

A similar construction is realized in (17) with the adjectival predicate *jronk* 'drunk'. Here, the speaker is enquiring about the mental state of the driver of a car who had been involved in an accident that had occurred 18 years earlier. However, without the context of the discourse, the past interpretation intended by the speaker is irrecoverable. Though context assists in this interpretation, the JC conventions in such instances are reliant on structure, not context.

Further evidence that this is a case of attrition in the use of the past tense marker is provided by the informants' rejection of the tense marker in constructions that participants of the verification group deemed acceptable. Sentence (18), for example, is an item included in the metalinguistic task that was administered to both the immigrants and the verification group. Sentence (19) represents a 'correction' of this acceptable task item. The informant does not reject the presence of a tense marker, when presented with the task sentence but rather rejects the particular variant included in the task item, with a request that *wehn* be substituted for *did*. The informant further modifies the placement of the marker relative to the copula *a*. The rejection of acceptable JC variants was not evidenced in the verification group, regardless of the variant that existed in their variety of JC.

(18) Maas Juo a   wen wahn gud man.
      Mister Joe COP PAST INDEF good man
      'Mr. Joe was a good man.' [MJ, 135]

(19) Maas Juo did a   wahn gud man.
      Mister Joe PAST COP INDEF good man
      'Mr. Joe was a good man.' [1yr 6mths, MJ]

The informant in (20), however, in tandem with the covert tense marking previously discussed, rejects the presence of the tense marker, and in correcting the perceived erroneous construction, suggests a structure which would normally be interpreted as present.[14]

(20) Maas Juo Ø   a   gud man.
      Mister Joe PAST COP good man
      'Mr. Joe was a good man.' [9yrs- Informant K, MJ]

A loss of variation may be acknowledged as a feature of reduced proficiency or loss in one's L1. Instances of this are paradigm levelling and a loss of stylistic options. With the informants here, unlike those who formed the verification group, there is seemingly a rejection of variation in the past tense.

The RH postulates that the processes of language acquisition and language attrition are parallel, in that attrition mirrors acquisition. This hypothesis, being one of the earliest hypotheses accounting for attrition processes was later modified, theorizing that that which is learnt first is lost last and that which is learned best, used often and thus reinforced, is lost last (cf. Köpke & Schmid 2004: 16). By this logic, it would have been expected that the past tense form would have fallen susceptible to attrition in the early-mid stages of L1 attrition given its late acquisition by the CLAR children.

The attrition of the tense maker in JC cannot be claimed to be representative of attrition that is to be expected at any stage of attrition between 1–21 years,

---

[14]Notable as well, but not relevant to this discussion, is the deletion of the indefinite article.

however, as the attrition of this feature is not convincingly characteristic of any of the established groups in the JC L1 attrition study. For a feature to have been labelled as being characteristic of a group or stage, prevalence of that unconventional feature in the speech of three or more informants within any one category needed to be evidenced. No three participants of either category had recurring instances of the effects discussed here.

The resistance of the past tense marker to L1 attrition may not be surprising given the revelation made by Keijzer (2010) in her study of the attrition of L1 Dutch. Though Keijzer's study found 9 parallels in language acquisition and language attrition of 15 features investigated in her study of Dutch-English contact, the author states that regression solely on the basis of L1 remodeling does not occur in the simple past. She suggests that other variables must be considered including, notably, L2 influence.

It would stand to reason that if this feature is acquired late in the L2 (Pp), then its influence on the attriter's L1 would be delayed or less likely to occur. The data available on the CLAR children have revealed that the past construction is also acquired late in L2 acquisition, with only two instances of an inflected verb indicating past reference occurring in the data. If applicable to adult second language acquisition, successful maintenance in this area by the attrition group may be explained. Dulay & Burt's (1973) Accuracy Order of Grammatical Morphemes in L2 acquisition, places proficiency in tense at a late stage of the process, being ranked number 6 of 8 stages. The stability of the JC past tense form may then be a result of a number of considerations, including first, the imperfect acquisition or a lack thereof of the English tense marker. This is worthy of consideration, as attrited data covering other areas, such as the progressive below, reveal that in the case of JC attrition, effects of L2 influence may take the form of English markers being adopted.

As explained earlier in §2, the language situation within the Jamaican community is one where JC exists alongside English on a creole continuum. Jamaicans acquire JC as their native language and learn English as an L2; however, the marking of tense is a problematic area in adult L2 speech, especially for those whose language would span the range of the continuum that the informants' speech represents. Though formal study on the L2 adult acquisition of JE past tense is lacking, as shown with the CLAR children as well as other research on the L2 acquisition of the English past, it is acquired late (cf. Dulay & Burt 1973). Upon arriving in Curaçao, the JC immigrants would have opted to use whatever English proficiency they possess to get around the island. If they had not acquired the English rule, however, an English form could not have been adopted. There were no instances of the inflected verb in the attrition group's representation of JC. There were however instances of the irregular past included in the attrition data. This bears similarity to the acquisition process, which revealed more instances of the irregular past than the regular past. It is acquired earlier in L2 acquisition, thus may be more likely to make an impact in L1 attrition.

It is noteworthy, however, that as discussed in §4.1, the past tense marker in Pp is realised as an obligatory independent morpheme, not an inflection. This brings us to the second more plausible reason for the retention of the past tense marker, which may be a confounding factor to consider when investigating the parallels between language acquisition and language attrition. If tense is mandatorily marked in Pp, influence from this L2 would facilitate the retention of the marker, rather than its loss. It stands to reason, however, that for some attriters, whose number would be fewer than those who retain the marker, there would be a tendency to unconventionally omit it. A plausible alternative interpretation is that it could be due to the fact that they are unsure about the use of the marker and thus overgeneralise omission as a strategy.

This may be representative of attrition through omission that may be independent of L2 influence. Seliger & Vago (1991) refer to changes such as these as internally induced language change, which may take the form of simplification, regularization, naturalness, intra-linguistic effects or conceptual/cognitive/innate strategies, for instance. These changes are stated to be motivated by universal principles or are 'related to some fact in the particular grammar of the L1'. This may be the seemingly optional nature of the occurrence of the tense marker in JC.

In consideration of the role of Pp in the attrition of the simple past in JC then, it may be that the obligatory nature of pre-verbal tense marking in Pp may have impacted the retention of the JC tense marker. Instances of loss without replacement may have been a result of internal language change, where in attrition, there is a tendency of simplification of the grammar, which may be exhibited as loss without compensation.

5 The progressive aspect

5.1 The progressive aspect in JC and Pp

Aspect concerns the temporal structure of the situation, its internal make-up, or as Comrie (1976: 3) puts it, it refers to the different ways of viewing the internal temporal constituency of a situation. Unlike tense, aspect does not locate situations in time. It is not unconnected with time, but it does not relate the time of a situation to any other time-point. In this section, the discussions of aspect in acquisition and attrition centre around the progressive aspect. Progressive aspect expresses duration over some period of time, however short. "John was reading" is an example in English provided by Comrie, where "reference is made to an internal portion of John's reading, while there is no explicit reference to the beginning or to the end of this reading" (1976: 4).

Progressive aspect may be expressed syntactically in JC using the pre-verbal marker *a* or its (rural) variants *de* or *da* followed by the invariant verb, so that in (21) below, the event (the twisting of the doll's hair) is presented as one taking place (at the present time), an eventuality which would take the form 'You are twisting ...' in JE.

(21) TAS: yu   a   twis i   dali ier.
      2S.SUBJ PROG twist DEF dolly hair
      'You are twisting the dolly's hair.' [V1-SMR:l.704-3;3.11]

The English progressive is expressed with a form of the auxiliary 'to be' agreeing with the subject in number and person, followed by the lexical verb inflected with the invariant participle '-in(g)' as in 'He is playing'. This contrasts with the JC form where, as we have seen, both the progressive marker and the lexical verb are invariant.

The marking of the progressive in Pp bears similarity to English whereby, in contrast to JC, non-past *ta* and past *tabata* may combine with suffixal *-ndo* in progressive constructions as exemplified in (22) and (23) below (Kouwenberg & Ramos-Michel 2007: 310). The English equivalent would have been 'is' and 'was' in conjunction with suffixal '-ing'

(22) E   kos   ta   bay-endo hopi leu.
      DEF thing PRES go-PROG very far
      'The problem is becoming insurmountable.' [Kouwenberg &
      Ramos-Michel (2007: 310)]

(23) ... den ora nan di marduga ora   nos tabata patruyando kaya.
          in hour PL of dawn   hour 1PL PAST patrol-PROG street
      '... in the early hours when we were patrolling the streets.' [Maurer (1988:
      406) in Kouwenberg & Ramos-Michel (2007: 311)]

Unlike English, however, an inflected verb in such a construction is not obligatory:

(24) Mi tabata kana.
     1SG PAST walk
     'I was walking/I have walked.' [Kouwenberg & Lefebvre 2007: 61]

5.2 Aspect in acquisition

The progressive construction was used by children of all ages from all regions, over 3,000 times. Early acquisition of the JC progressive aspectual marker by Jamaican children is also reported by De Lisser (2015): children produce the construction as early as 1;9.5 (p. 106), and use it with five different predicates, indicating consistent use, as early as 1;11.12 (p. 115).

In addition to the regular JC progressive construction, the bare verb (the verb without the JC progressive marker) is used throughout by the CLAR children in subjectless answers to questions using the progressive, as illustrated in the responses below by the youngest, and the oldest children in (25) and (26), respectively.

(25) INV: wa   im   a   du?
          what 3s.SUBJ PROG do
          'What's he doing.'
     ARI: iit xxx.
         eat xxx
         'Eating xxx.' [V1-STT:l 141-2;9.0]

(26) INV: So what is this boy doing now?
     DEV: brosh ihn   tiit.
         brush 3s.POSS teeth
         'Brushing his teeth.' [V6-SMR;l 435-4;3.1]

The absence of the aspectual marker cannot be said, however, to reflect necessarily either a lack of aspect marking as such or incomplete acquisition, since alongside the use of the bare verb, the youngest child in the CLAR study aged 2;9.0 made use of the (adult) JC form *a* + verb. Its absence may simply illustrate a common conversational strategy used in both adult JC and JE, particularly where it is given as an answer to a question about what someone is doing, as in (24) and (25) above.

The progressive construction may be expressed in the past by combining the progressive marker with the past tense marker *dii*, *did*, (*b*)*ehn* or *wehn* (27), but the tense marker need not be used if contextual grounding in the past is clear, as seen in (28).

(27) OSS: ... mi   mada   wehn de   krai.
          3S.POSS mother PAST PROG cry

     'My mother was crying.' [V5-STJ:l.327-3;7.14]

(28) DON: ye kaa   mi   si im   wen taim im   a   sliip lef
          yes because 1S.SUBJ see 3S.OBJ when time 3S.SUBJ PROG sleep leave
    di   biebi.
    DEF baby

     'Yes, because I saw him the time that he was sleeping, leaving the
baby.' [V6-KN1-J:l.493-3;11.12]

A past tense marker was used in only 7 cases, or 1.1% of all progressive *a* constructions, and its use must therefore be considered to be rare overall; in all of these instances, the marker used was *did* or *dii*.

We now look at the acquisition of the JE progressive. With regard to the use of this form, Stewart (2010) shows that the children began using structures with the morpheme '-*ing*' at age 2;5. Certainly, as we have seen, the youngest children in the substantive CLAR study were already using the construction regularly.[15]

The CLAR children use the JE auxiliary *iz* 'is' followed by an uninflected (bare) verb thirty-six times, with just under a half of these (41.7%) by children from rural areas. This use of *iz* + bare V is not associated necessarily with the age of the children. There is one child at age 3;5.22 who used JE *iz* + bare V in a progressive construction for the first time in his last recording, but all others who use the construction make use also of *iz* + V-in(g).[16] The youngest child to do so was 3;1.29 and the oldest, 4;2.1. In fact, instances of V-in(g) without the auxiliary are used alongside, and twice as often as JE PROG + V-in(g), even by the oldest children. The variation appears, then, to be characteristic of the speech of the children, as indeed it is in the input.

5.3 Aspect in language attrition

In the case of JC attrition, stages are noticed in the changes that occur in the progressive construction. The JC progressive aspect construction stands in contrast to the simple past with attrition effects being evidenced in three ways. The most

---

[15]Stewart (2010) served as a pilot for the CLAR study, hence the use of 'substantive'; Stewart began publishing as Kennedy in 2013.

[16]The choice of –*in* or –*ing* is not considered to characterize a speaker as being a JC or a JE speaker, and so is not factored in here. Both variants exist in both languages. Indeed –*in(g)* does not appear as one of the ten load-bearing oppositions proposed by Irvine (2005) as signaling an (in)ability to speak JE. As might be expected, 75.7% of the inflections used were –*in*.

pervasive effect is the marking of the present progressive through an inflected verb, in the absence of an independent progressive marker. In (29–31), *waakin* 'walking', *livin* 'living' and *avin* 'having' are examples, where the English suffixal -*in* marks the progressive. This contrasts with the JC use of the progressive aspectual *a* and the bare verb.

(29)   Mi no   waahn waak-in   roun ...
      1SG NEG want   walk-PROG round
      'I do not want to be walking around ...' [8 yrs, NUD]
      [JC: Mi no waahn fi a waak roun]

(30)   Di pikni   dem a   mek siks yier liv-in   ina Kyuuraso.
      DEF children PL   PROG make six year liv-PROG in Curaçao
      'It will be six years since the children have been living in Curaçao.' [16 yrs, MJ]
      [JC: A go siks yier nou sins di pikni dem a liv ina Kyuuraso]

(31)   Dem fren   dem av-in   wahn hapi die.
      POSS friend PL   have-PROG INDEF happy day
      'Their friends are having a happy day.' [19 yrs, PS]
      [JC: Den fren dem a av wahn gud die]

Within the Jamaican situation, the use of -*in* to mark the progressive is English-influenced and is therefore typical of mesolectal varieties closer to the acrolectal end of the continuum. The use of these varieties in everyday informal speech does not correlate with the linguistic profiles of the participants as also evidenced through the rejection of this form by the verification group, whose grammar is taken to span a similar range of the language continuum. In the formal domains of the Jamaican society, Jamaica's diglossic situation would have rendered the prevalent use of English-influenced forms such as those exhibited with the progressive construction an expectation or norm. It is therefore no surprise that these forms exist in the linguistic repertoire of the immigrants, and that the CLAR children would have produced them, since these forms are indeed in the input. In the informal domains, however, where JC is used, forms that range closer to the basilect are typical in the speech of the representative group of speakers. In instances where English-influenced forms are prevalent and even dominated the more Creole-like forms (as with the past progressive below), the question of a change in L1 use becomes evident.

A second way in which the present progressive was expressed, was with the omission of the marker and the use of the uninflected verb. In (25) and (26) above,

we saw such a construction being used by the CLAR children in subjectless answers to questions. In the attrition data, however, this was problematic, since
it resulted in a construction that is typical of the simple past in JC. A progressive interpretation therefore only becomes recoverable through the discourse
or through the presence of another verb in the utterance that has been overtly
marked for this feature.

In (32), the speaker refers to the action of 'drying' (represented as *jrai* 'dry')
that a boy continues to do, describing an action that was taking place in a picture she was shown. The omission of aspectual *a* results in a construction that
is erroneous in JC; the correct interpretation could only be retrieved through
context.

(32) Di bwai av   di   towil Ø   jrai out iihn ed.
      DEF boy have DEF towel PROG dry out 3s   hair
      'The boy is drying his hair with the towel' [16 yrs, PS]

In attrition, a progressive aspectual interpretation in other contexts is dependent on structure. In (33), one is able to derive a progressive meaning for the
bare verb *se* 'say' since the previous non-stative verb *taak* 'talk' accompanied
by aspectual *a*, conveys the progressive aspect. *Waahn* 'want' would have been
unmarked, as stative verbs are not overtly marked for progressive aspect in JC.
The speaker is *talking* and the bystander would wish to hear what he or she is
saying.

(33) If yu a   taak pan i fuon an ... dem waahn ier wa yu Ø   se.
      if 2s PROG talk on DEF phone and   3PL want hear what 2s PROG say
      'If you're on the phone and ... they want to hear what 'you are saying.'
      [13 yrs- Informant B, NUD]

The omission of the progressive aspectual marker in the ASP+ bare verb structure is revealed in the attrition data to be a feature that is likely to be evidenced
in late attrition, that is, attrition occurring post the ten-year period, since it was
uncharacteristic of productions made by JC immigrants who had been residing
in the L2 country for a period under ten years. Such a conclusion has been made
on the basis that of the seven informants each in the 1–5Y and 6–10Y category,
only one informant from each category had this feature present in their speech.
This is contrary to the >10Y category, where this feature was evidenced in the
speech of four of the six informants.

The third deviation in the construction was with the past progressive form,
where constructions consisted of an independent past progressive marker accompanied by the inflected verb. If we consider that the past marker was used

only seven times in the L1 acquisition of the progressive, the implication for the attrition of progressive constructions would be that the past progressive is affected early, since it is acquired late in the L1. It is however acquired late in the L2 as well, which may delay cross-linguistic influence at an early stage.

Deviation in the past progressive construction, illustrated in (34) and (35), is in the attrition of JC presented in the form of past *woz* co-occurring with the verb bearing suffixal -*in*. This stands in contrast to the PAST+ASP+VERB structure conventionally used in varieties of JC that are closest to the basilect.

(34) Dem woz mek-in a mes.
     3PL PAST make-PROG INDEF mess
     'They were making a mess.' [6yrs- Informant L, PS]

(35) Mi tel ar di chiljren dem woz fait-in in di klaas.
     1s tell her DEF children PL PAST fight-PROG in DEF class
     'I told her that the children were fighting in the class.' [13 yrs- Informant M, SCT]

This feature is characteristic of attrition six years and beyond, and is therefore not a feature that is expected of the earliest stages of attrition.

Of note in attrition data is the correction of the conventional JC *a liv* to the inflected verb by an informant who had been residing in the L2 country for 16 years at the time of data elicitation. This structure is evidenced in early attrition and is maintained throughout, even as stability is achieved.[17]

If one were to consider the attrition facts related to the progressive aspect, the conclusion may be made that it is one of the earliest features to fall susceptible to language change in JC. Changes in this area do not take place at once but do so gradually. In the initial stages, the aspectual marker is likely to be omitted and the verb inflected. In the 6–10 year stage, it is likely for there to be an omission of the inflection as well as the independent marker, with the bare verb standing alone. This construction becomes a variant. At the final stage of the attrition of the JC progressive construction, the past progressive becomes susceptible to change with past 'woz' being combined with an inflected verb. This is evidence of the past progressive being fully formed. Its occurrence in the final stage of the attrition of the progressive is plausible given the evidence from the L2 acquisition data, which shows that the past auxiliary is acquired late, with its use lacking among the CLAR children.

---

[17]A feature is considered to be stable if it was found to be characteristic of the three established year groups in the attrition data.

It stands to reason, then, that in the attrition of the first language under influence from an L2, the progressive aspectual construction typical of the L2 would be among the first features transferred into the L1.

6 Conclusion and implications for the language education classroom

The findings from acquisition show a likelihood for the marking of the past tense to be acquired late by JC speakers, but that the progressive will be acquired early. As for attrition, it has been revealed that the past tense shows some resilience, whilst the progressive (past and present) is prone to attrition in stages. Divergent forms occurring in the data were not expected in the variety investigated, especially in the informal speech contexts in which they were used. Use in the ways identified is more prevalent in the upper mesolectal varieties. If it were then to be argued that these changes reflect a minor strategy of the language, change within these areas can still not be denied. As discussed and illustrated by the data, the use of the V+ing form for the past progressive out-numbered that of the bare verb, a major strategy. In the CLAR acquisition data, there is sparse use of past tense forms, taken to suggest late acquisition. One would then expect that the attrition data would reveal early effects in this construction. The attrition data however reveals that the JC past tense form is resistant to attrition, having remained stable in the speech of the attriters.

We have claimed that this may not be surprising in light of the fact that Pp obligatorily marks the past tense. This would have aided the retention of the past marker, both in obligatory and non-obligatory contexts. Possible Pp influence could become apparent if data from the attrited group were to be compared with equivalent data from a control group to determine frequency of overt tense marking by the groups. A more prevalent use of tense by the attriters could be a sign of possible influence, whereby Pp, unlike JC, requires that a tense marker precede both stative and non-stative verbs

The resilience of the past tense marker to change may also not be surprising as research on the accuracy order of grammatical morphemes has shown that the past tense is also acquired late in L2 acquisition, as discussed in §4.4. In light of the similarity in marking the past tense in JC and Pp, this argument primarily becomes relevant to this situation where the influence of English as an L2 is considered. In instances where some attriters omitted the past tense marker from obligatory contexts, an early acquisition of the English past tense could have

enabled attrition by replacement with an L2 form. As discussed, it has been pos-
tulated that in other areas of attrition data, there has been a transfer of English
forms, which are usually used in the attriters' attempt to apply a Pp rule. English
effects in the creole grammar without Pp influence was however also evinced
in this contact situation (Messam-Johnson 2017). This is not attested in the attrition of past tense forms, with the data being void of the English past marker.
The absence of English forms in this area may be indicative of a difficulty in
the mastery of English tense marking, which, from a pedagogical perspective,
may require that primary focus be given to this feature in the development of a
curriculum geared toward the learning of English as a second language.

For this, given the acquisition and attrition trends found, a strategic approach
will be possible. Whilst for Pp, there is some similarity with JC in the marking of
tense, in that both systems utilise an independent past marker, this may be perceived as a shared fundamental difference between these systems and English,
for which the marking of tense is inflectional. This supports the possible difficulty L2 learners of English might be having with mastering tense, as such a
lack of congruence between language systems has been said to cause difficulty
in learning the L2 (Winford 2003: 252). Learning English for these speakers will
also need to involve more than an indication that the past is marked by an inflectional ending, rather than with an independent tense marker. Learners ought
to be encouraged to notice that not all verbs in the L1 require a marker, but that
once the past tense is expressed in English, it must be marked.

An analysis of the findings for the progressive constructions reveals that the
present progressive aspect is acquired early, with an expectation of attrition effects being shown at a later stage. The past progressive construction on the other
hand is acquired late, thereby resulting in an anticipation of early attrition. It has
however been shown that cross-linguistic effects in the present progressive are
evident from the early years, whilst in contrast to the expectation for the past
progressive, deviations in structure were characteristic of the later stages of the
attrition process, the point at which stability in the attrited grammar is expected.
Similar to the past tense construction, it is clear that the attrition effects represented for the progressive do not support the RH in terms of the order of attrition
being the inverse of acquisition. The findings, however, have implications for the
Jamaican language arts classroom.

Progressive constructions for both the CLAR children and the attriters reflect
features of their JE counterparts to varying degrees: the auxiliary may or may not
have been omitted, and the lexical verb may or may not have been inflected, but
acquisition was attested early, and the attrition of the JC form also had an early
start. This may be explained by the fact that the progressive constructions in the

three languages (JC, JE and Pp) comprise an auxiliary followed by a lexical verb; in JE and Pp the verb also bears an inflectional ending, but the interpretations in all languages are parallel – they express a continuous reading. Possible issues with concord apart, this construction may then prove to be less challenging to the L2 learner, and unlike the past tense, may be less of a priority in teaching English as an L2.

Abbreviations

JC	Jamaican Creoles		RH	Regression Hypothesis
JE	Jamaican English		DEF	definite
ASP	aspect		POSS	possessive
INDEF	indefinite		NEG	negative
PROG	progressive		PL	plural
CLAR	Child Language Acquisition Research			

References

Andersen, Roger W. 1990. Papiamentu tense-aspect, with special attention to discourse. In John Victor Singler (ed.), *Pidgin and Creole tense-mood-aspect systems*, 59–96. Amsterdam/Philadelphia: John Benjamins.

Bailey, Beryl. 1966. *Jamaican Creole syntax*. Cambridge: Cambridge University Press.

Bhat, D. N. Shankara. 1999. *The Prominence of tense, aspect and mood*. Amsterdam/Philadelphia: John Benjamins.

Chung, Sandra & Alan Timberlake. 1985. Tense, mood and aspect. In Timothy Shopen (ed.), *Language Typology and Syntactic Description. Vol. 3: Grammatical Categories and the lexicon*, 202–58. Cambridge: Cambridge University Press.

Cockburn, Alexander. 1994. *The golden age is in us: Noam Chomsky interviewed by Alexander Cockburn*. Grand Street. http://chomsky.info/19940622/.

Comrie, Bernard. 1976. *Aspect: An introduction to the study of verbal aspect and related problems*. Cambridge: Cambridge University Press.

Cook, Vivian. 2002. Background to the L2 user. In Vivian Cook (ed.), *Portraits of the L2 user*, 1–28. Clevedon: Multilingual Matters.

Cook, Vivian. 2003. *Effects of the second language on the first*. Clevedon: Multilingual Matters.

Cook, Vivian. 2016. *Second language learning and language teaching*. 5th ed. London/New York: Routledge.

Craig, Dennis. 1971. Education and Creole English in the West Indies. In Dell Hymes (ed.), *Pidginization and Creolization of Languages*, 371–91. Cambridge: Cambridge University Press.

Craig, Dennis. 1980. Language, society and education in the West Indies. *Caribbean Journal of Education* 7(1). 1–17.

De Bot, Kees & Michael G. Clyne. 1994. A 16-year longitudinal study of language attrition in Dutch immigrants in Australia. *Journal of Multilingual and Multicultural Development* 15. 17–28.

De Lisser, Tamirand N. 2015. *The acquisition of Jamaican Creole: The emergence and transformation of early syntactic systems.* (Doctoral dissertation).

de Bot, Kees & Robert Schrauf. 2009. *Language Development over the Lifespan.* New York: Routledge.

DeCamp, David. 1971. Toward a generative analysis of a post-Creole speech continuum. In Dell Hymes (ed.), *Pidginization and creolization of languages*, 349–370. Cambridge: Cambridge University Press.

Devonish, Hubert & Otelemate G. Harry. 2008. Jamaican Creole and Jamaican English: Phonology. In Edgar W. Schneider (ed.), *Varieties of English 2. The Americas and the Caribbean*, 256–289. Berlin/New York: Mouton de Gruyter.

Devonish, Hubert & Kadian Walters. 2015. The Jamaican Language Situation: A Process, not a Type. In Dick Smakman & Patrick Heinrich (eds.), *Globalising Sociolinguistics. Challenging and Expanding Theory*, 223–232. New York/London: Routledge.

Dulay, Heidi & Marina Burt. 1973. Should we teach children syntax? *Language learning* 23(2). 245–258.

Ellis, Rod. 1994. *The study of second language acquisition.* Oxford: Oxford University Press.

Goilo, Enrique R. 2000. *Papiamentu textbook.* Oranjestad, Aruba: De Wit Stores N. V.

Gooden, Shelome. 2008. Discourse aspects of tense marking in Belizean Creole. *English World-Wide* 29(3). 306–346.

Grabowski, Eva & Mindt Dieter. 1995. A corpus-based learning list of irregular verbs in English. *ICAME Journal* 19. 5–22.

Hackert, Stephanie. 2004. *Urban Bahamian Creole: System and variation.* Amsterdam/Philadelphia: John Benjamins.

Hansen, Lynne. 1999. Not a total loss: The attrition of Japanese negation over three decades. In Lynne Hansen (ed.), *Second language attrition in Japanese contexts*, 142–153. Oxford: Oxford University Press.

Irvine, Alison G. 2005. *Defining good English in Jamaica: Language variation and language ideology in an agency of the Jamaican state.* Kingston: University of the West Indies. (Doctoral dissertation).

Jacobs, Bart. 2013. Thoughts on the linguistic history of Curaçao: How Papiamentu got the better of Dutch. *Revue Belge de Philologie et d'Historie* 91(3). 787–806.

Jakobson, Roman. 1941. *Child language, aphasia and phonological universals.* The Hague: Mouton.

Keijzer, Merel. 2009. The regression hypothesis as a framework for first language attrition. *Bilingualism: Language and Cognition* 13(1). 9–18. DOI: 10.1017/S9990356.

Keijzer, Merel. 2010. *First language acquisition and first language attrition: Parallels and divergences.* Germany: LAP Lambert Academic.

Kennedy, Michele M. 2017. *What do Jamaican children speak? A language resource.* Jamaica/Barbados/Trinidad & Tobago: UWI Press.

Kester, Ellen-Petra & Jennifer Fun. 2012. Language Use, language attitudes and identity among Aruban students in the Netherlands. In Christa Weijer Nicholas Faraclas Ronald Severing & Elisabeth Echteld (eds.), *Multiplex Cultures and Citizenships*, 231–248. Curaçao: University of Curaçao/ Fundashon pa Planifikashon di Idoma.

Köpke, Barbara & Monika Schmid. 2004. First language attrition: The next phase. In Merel Keijzer Monika Schmid Barbara Kšpke & Lina Weilemar (eds.), *First language attrition: Interdisciplinary perspectives on methodological issues*, 1–43. Amsterdam/Philadelphia: John Benjamins.

Kouwenberg, Silvia & Claire Lefebvre. 2007. A new analysis of the Papiamentu clause structure. *Probus* (19). 37–73.

Kouwenberg, Silvia & Eric Murray. 1994. *Papiamentu.* München: Lincom Europa.

Kouwenberg, Silvia & Abigail Ramos-Michel. 2007. *Papiamentu (Creole Spanish/-Portuguese).* John Holm & Peter L. Patrick (eds.) (Westminster Creolistics Series 7). London: Battlebridge. 307–332.

Lambert, Richard & Barbara Freed (eds.). 1982. *The Loss of language skills.* Rowley: Newbury House.

Lefebvre, Claire. 1996. The TMA system of Haitian Creole and the Problem of Transmission of Grammar in Creole Genesis. *Journal of Pidgin and Creole Languages* 11(2). 231–311.

MacWhinney, Brian. 2000a. *The CHILDES project: The database.* 3rd ed. Hillsdale, NJ: Lawrence Erlbaum Associates.

MacWhinney, Brian. 2000b. *The CHILDES project: Tools for analyzing talk.* 3rd ed. Hillsdale, NJ: Lawrence Erlbaum Associates.

Marcus, Gary F. 1996. Why do children say 'breaked'? *Current Directions in Psychological Science* 5(3). 81–85.

Maurer, Philippe. 1988. *Les modifications temporelles et modales du verbe dans le papiamento de Curaćao (Antilles Néerlandaises)*. Hamburg: Buske.

Maurer, Philippe. 1998. El papiamentu de Curazao. In Matthias Perl & Armin Schwegler (eds.), *América negra: Panorámica actual de los estudios lingüísticos sobre variedades hispanas, portuguesas y criollas*, 139–217. Frankfurt & Madrid: Vervuert.

McPhee, Helen. 2003. The grammatical features of TMA auxiliaries in Bahamian Creole. In Michael Aceto & Jeffrey Williams (eds.), *Contact Englishes of the eastern Caribbean*, 29–49. Amsterdam/Philadelphia: John Benjamins.

Meade, Rocky. 2001. *Acquisition of Jamaica phonology*. Amsterdam: Holland Institute of Generative Linguistics/Netherlands Graduate School of Linguistics.

Meisel, Jürgen M. 2011. *First and Second Language Acquisition. Parallels and Differences*. Cambridge: Cambridge University Press.

Messam-Johnson, Trecel. 2017. *Attrition of a Creole: The syntactic effects of the L2 acquisition of Papiamentu on Jamaican Creole*. Kingston: University of the West Indies. (Doctoral dissertation).

Miller, Errol. 2015. *Educational Reform in Independent Jamaica*. http : / / www . educoas . org / portal / bdigital / contenido / interamer / bkiacd / interamer / Interamerhtml/Millerhtml/mil_mil.htm.

Ministry of Education, Youth and Culture, Jamaica. 2001. *Language Education Policy*. Kingston.

Muysken, Pieter. 1981. Creole TMA systems: The unmarked case? In Pieter Muysken (ed.), *Generative studies on Creole languages*, 181–99. Dordrecht: Foris.

Paradis, Johanne, Mabel Rice, Martha Crago & Janet Marquis. 2008. The acquisition of tense in English: Distinguishing child second language from first language and specific language impairment. *Applied Psycholinguistics* 29. 689–722.

Patrick, Peter. 2007. Jamaican Creole (Patwa English). In John Holm & Peter L. Patrick (eds.), *Comparative Creole syntax*, 127–152. London: Battlebridge Publications.

Patrick, Peter L. 1999. *Urban Jamaican creole: Variation in the mesolect*. Amsterdam: John Benjamins.

Patrick, Peter L. 2004. Jamaican Creole: Morphology and syntax. In Bernd Kortmann (ed.), *A handbook of varieties of English*, vol. 2, 407–438. Berlin & New York: Mouton de Gruyter.

Pliatsikas, Christos. & Theodoros Marinis. 2013. Processing of regular and irregular past tense morphology in highly proficient second language learners of English: A self-paced reading study. *Applied Psycholinguistics* 34(5). 943–970. DOI: doi:https://doi.org/10.1017/S0142716412000082.

Reichenbach, Hans. 1947. *Elements of symbolic logic.* New York: Macmillan.

Rickford, John. 1987. *Dimensions of a creole continuum.* Stanford: Stanford University Press.

SABER Country Report. 2013. *Jamaica. Early Childhood Development.* http:// wbgfiles . worldbank . org / documents / hdn / ed / saber / supporting _ doc / CountryReports/ECD/SABER_ECD_Jamaica_CR_Final_2013.pdf (28 April, 2015).

Schmitt, Elena. 2019. Morphological Attrition. In Monika S. Schmid & Barbara Köpke (eds.), *The Oxford Handbook of Language Attrition,* 228–240. Oxford: Oxford University Press.

Seliger, Herbert W. & Robert Vago. 1991. The study of first language attrition: An overview. In Herbert W. Seliger & Robert M. Vago (eds.), *First language attrition,* 3–15. Cambridge: Cambridge University Press.

Slobin, Dan. 1977. Language change in childhood and in history. In John Macnamara (ed.), *Language learning and thought,* 185–214. New York: Academic Press.

Stewart, Michele. 2010. Jamaican Creole alongside Standard Jamaican English in the speech of two-year-olds from urban Kingston. *Caribbean Journal of Education* 32(2). 177–201.

Vendler, Zeno. 1967. *Linguistics in philosophy.* Ithaca, NY: Cornell University Press.

Waas, Margit. 1993. *Language attrition among German speakers in Australia: A sociolinguistic inquiry.* Sydney: Macquarie University. (Doctoral dissertation).

Winford, Donald. 1985. The syntax of *fi* complements in Caribbean English Creole. *Language* 61(3). 588–624.

Winford, Donald. 1993. *Predication in Caribbean English Creoles.* Amsterdam: John Benjamins.

Winford, Donald. 1997. Re-examining Caribbean English Creole Continua. *World Englishes* 16(2). 233–79.

Winford, Donald. 2000. Tense and aspect in Sranan and the Creole prototype. In John McWhorter (ed.), *Language change and language contact in pidgins and Creoles,* 383–442. Amsterdam: John Benjamins.

Winford, Donald. 2001. A comparison of tense/ aspect systems in Caribbean English Creoles. In Pauline Christie (ed.), *Due respect: Papers on English and*

English-related Creoles in the Caribbean in honour of Professor Robert LePage, 155–83. Kingston, Jamaica: UWI Press.

Winford, Donald. 2003. *An introduction to contact linguistics.* London: Wiley-Blackwell.

Yağmur, Kutlay. 1997. *First language attrition among Turkish speakers in Sydney.* Tilburg: Tilburg University Press.

Yang, Suying & Yue Yuan Huang. 2004. The impact of the absence of grammatical tense in L1 on the acquisition of the tense-aspect system in L2. *International Review of Applied Linguistics in Language Teaching* 42. 49–70.

Name index

CPSIA information can be obtained
at www.ICGtesting.com
Printed in the USA
LVHW020745131022
730612LV00005B/214

9 783985 540440